Barack Obama and the Politics of Redemption

Every new president raises many questions in the public mind. Because Barack Obama was a relative newcomer to the national political scene, he raised more questions than most. Would he prove to be a pragmatic centrist or would his politics of hope ultimately flounder on the rocky shoals of America's deep political divisions? What of his leadership style? How would the uncommonly calm character he demonstrated on the campaign trail shape Obama's political style as commander-in-chief?

Based on extensive biographical, psychological, and political research and analysis, noted political psychologist Stanley Renshon follows Obama's presidency through the first two years. He digs into the question of who is the real Obama and assesses the advantages and limitations that he brings to the presidency. These questions cannot be answered without recourse to psychological analysis. And they cannot be answered without psychological knowledge of presidential leadership and the presidency itself. Renshon explains that Obama's ambition has been fueled by a desire for redemption—his own, that of his parents, and ultimately for the country he now leads, which has enormous consequences for his choices as president of a politically divided America.

Stanley Renshon is a Professor of Political Science at the City University of New York, Herbert Lehman College and The Graduate School and University Center. He is the author of over 100 articles and sixteen books and is a certified psychoanalyst.

Barack Obama and the Politics of Redemption

Stanley A. Renshon

Routledge
Taylor & Francis Group

NEW YORK AND LONDON

First published 2012
by Routledge
711 Third Avenue, New York, NY 10017

Simultaneously published in the UK
by Routledge
2 Park Square, Milton Park, Abingdon, Oxon OX14 4RN

Routledge is an imprint of the Taylor & Francis Group, an informa business

Library of Congress Cataloging in Publication Data
A catalog record has been requested for this book

ISBN13: 978-0-415-87394-9 (hbk)
ISBN13: 978-0-415-87395-6 (pbk)
ISBN13: 978-0-203-86413-5 (ebk)

Typeset in Bembo
by Taylor & Francis books

Printed and bound in the United States of America on acid-free paper by Walsworth Publishing Company, Marceline, MO.

"Redemption" definition: Copyright © by Houghton Mifflin Harcourt Publishing Company.
Reproduced by permission from The American Heritage Dictionary of the English Language, fourth edition.

Transformation definition from Collins English Dictionary – 30th Anniversary Edition 10th Edition 2009
© William Collins Sons & Co. Ltd 1979, 1986
© HarperCollins Publishers 1991, 1994, 1998, 2000, 2003, 2005, 2006, 2007, 2009

973.932
R29B
2012

For my wife Judith …

        A warm woman
        A loving mother
        A true partner
        And the love of my life.

For my children David and Jonathan …

        Principled
        Smart
        Thoughtful
        Accomplished
        And above all, nice people.

Every man is either trying to live up to his father's expectations or making up for his mistakes.

Barack Obama, NPR Interview, July 27, 2004[1]

I want to transform this country.

Barack Obama, Cedar Rapids, Iowa, February 2007[2]

"He is still a mystery to a lot of people. Actually, what is confounding is that he seems more a mystery to people now than he did when they elected him president."

Peggy Noonan,[3] August 27, 2010

redemption

Pronunciation: \ri-'dem(p)-shən\

noun

1. an act of redeeming or the state of being redeemed.
2. deliverance; rescue.
3. Theology. deliverance from sin; salvation.
4. atonement for guilt.

transformation

(trænsfə'meiʃən)*n*

1. a change or alteration, esp a radical one.

Contents

Preface

This analysis of Barack Obama is the third in a series of psychologically framed analyses of a sitting president, each of which began with both a psychological and political question. The first, *High Hopes: The Clinton Presidency and the Politics of Ambition*,[4] took as a fact that this president had almost always been able to rescue himself from the brink of disaster, but asked why he so frequently found himself in that position. The political question was how this very smart and loquacious president would be able to bridge the gap between his own liberal instincts and a public that had grown increasingly skeptical of large-scale government solutions to pressing social problems.

The second book, *In His Father's Shadow: The Transformations of George W. Bush*,[5] began with the question of how this man, who woke up with a hangover on his fortieth birthday and had a history of more effort than success found a way to become both a successful adult and a president in a relatively short period of time. The political question that originally animated that analysis—how would a right-center president try to bridge the same governing divide that Bill Clinton faced, soon gave way to the question of how he would respond to the unprecedented national security implications of the 9/11 attacks.

Barack Obama and his presidency present their own unique questions. The political question that frames this analysis is whether Mr. Obama can succeed in his quest to be a transforming president, one whose accomplishments reframe, redirect and then consolidate major policy departures, as he did in passing historic health care legislation and hopes to do with energy production and consumption, economic distributions, and foreign policy without further damaging the increasingly frayed fabric of American social capital and political community.

David Broder may well have been almost right on target when he wrote more than a year into the Obama Presidency that,

Halfway through the 2010 primary season, the fundamental tension in the American political system is becoming more clear: A liberal government is struggling to impose its agenda on an electorate increasingly responsive to an activist conservative movement operating inside the Republican Party.[6]

Or, to put the matter more generally, the president and his administration are "doing a lot of big things, but a lot of people do not like what they are doing. Others do not know what they are doing. And hardly anyone likes the way they are doing it."[7]

The 2010 midterm election would seem to have entered at least a temporary verdict on Obama's ambitions and efforts. But this president is very smart and has throughout his life been extraordinarily adaptive. A major question before him now in the aftermath of that election is whether his much-touted pragmatism will trump his enormous and deeply rooted ambitions to transform and redeem.

Barack Obama's personal story is by now familiar. Michiko Kakutani, reviewing a new Obama biography in the *New York Times*, wrote,

> By now, Mr. Obama's story has been told many times—by journalists and the authors of several biographies and campaign books, and most memorably by the president himself, who in the days before he became a politician wrote a remarkably eloquent and searching memoir (*Dreams from My Father*) about his youth, his struggle to come to terms with his absent father, and his groping efforts to forge an identity of his own.[8]

Another review of the same well received book says of it that, "If 'The Bridge' fails in any regard, it's in recycling a lot of shopworn stories—but this, of course, can't be helped."[9] Michiko Kakutani's review of another Obama study of his first year in office says, "The overall portrait of Mr. Obama that emerges from these pages is one that will be familiar to readers of earlier books like Richard Wolffe's 'Renegade,' and 'The Audacity to Win' by the former campaign manager David Plouffe. ... "[10]

The question then legitimately arises: Why another look back at the by now well known Obama story? One answer is that as the quotes gathered in Appendix B indicate, President Obama is truly a puzzling person and president as well to Americans from all points on the political spectrum. They simply aren't sure of who he really is, where he really stands, what he really stands for, and above all what really motivates and animates him.

Peggy Noonan captures the puzzle well;

> When the American people have looked at the presidents of the past few decades they could always sort of say, "I know that guy." Bill Clinton: Southern governor. Good ol' boy, drawlin', flirtin', got himself a Rhodes Scholarship. "I know that guy." George W. Bush: Texan, little rough around

the edges, good family, youthful high jinks, stopped drinking, got serious. "I know that guy." Ronald Reagan was harder to peg, but you still knew him: small-town Midwesterner, moved on and up, serious about politics, humorous, patriotic. "I know that guy." Barack Obama? Sleek, cerebral, detached, an academic from Chicago by way of Hawaii and Indonesia. "You know what? I don't know that guy!"[11]

As is the case with many presidents and especially one whose story has been told so often, a great deal of conventional wisdom has accumulated. The *New York Times* review of the Remnick book sums this up quite well:

> Like many reporters, Mr. Remnick describes Mr. Obama in these pages as cool, charismatic, slightly detached: an autodidact with a lawyer's analytical intelligence and a novelist's empathetic temperament; an idealist who is also a pragmatist; a politician inclined to be methodical and cautious in his decision making.[12]

Like much conventional wisdom, however, these characterizations of President Obama obscure more than they reveal and leave important questions unanswered. Yes, the president is "cool" and somewhat "detached," but how can such a person at the same time have an "empathetic temperament" and what of the range of feelings that normal people experience? Or consider the conventional wisdom that the president is a "pragmatist." As a new intellectual biography of the president says, "It has become a cliché to characterize Obama as a pragmatist."[13] But of course just because such thinking has become a cliché, doesn't mean its right. How is it possible for Obama to aspire to be a transformational change president and still be a pragmatist? Is fundamental transformation by whatever means it takes to bring it about still pragmatic?

Narratives rooted in conventional wisdom owe a great deal to Obama's characterization of his own life and miss some key elements that help to make sense of it. How can one explain the numerous questions quoted in Appendix B of this book, gathered from the left, right, and center of the political spectrum that directly ask a very basic question: "Who is Barack Obama?"[14] For all the conventional wisdom, Obama remains in many important respects a mystery which political psychology can help to solve.

In this book I offer what I hope and believe to be a useful answer to that question. Understanding the personal forces that fueled the meteoric political rise of Barack Obama, and that now animate his presidency, involves an analysis focused on four substantive narratives of *redemption*. The first concerns Barack Obama himself and his struggle to come to grips with his own family, race, and identity. It is a story of temptations considered, but ultimately put aside in the service of finding and acting on the purpose of his life. It is a story, as well, of his father's complicated legacy, first as an absent but iconic ideal and then as a fallen idol whose place in Obama's life needed to be redeemed. It is also a story of his complicated relationship with his mother, who both loved him, yet left him on his own. Her unexpected and premature death at the time that Obama was almost wholly focused on his father led him to reconsider her and elevate her, and her advocacy of "fairness," posthumously to iconic status, thus redeeming her and their relationship. And it is now, with Obama as president, the larger issue of America's ideals and its failure to live up to them at home and abroad, and the president's efforts to reclaim, through example, policy and the force of his moral vision—viewed through the organizing lens of "fairness"—that is a legacy of his idealization of his mother, its legitimacy in the world.

Ironically, in the aftermath of the recent midterm election, it is Obama's presidency and his political future that is most in need of redemption. And the question is: can he give up transformation for redemption?

Obama is an unusual president in the limited experience of my three in-depth presidential studies because the psychological and political questions that frame this analysis are more closely connected with him than they were with the others. President Clinton's personal proclivity for risk did not carry over very substantially to his policy leadership. Indeed, his key policy approach, triangulation, was an attempt to hedge his bets and his political prospects. George W. Bush's quest to find a path to a successful adulthood had little to do with the crucial national security issues that shaped his presidency.

In Obama, the connections between his psychology, personal development, and presidency are quite pronounced. He is, in the most important of ways in his presidential policy ambitions, his father's son. Yet in his ambitions' nature and reach, he also reflects the legacy of his mother's ideals. Both are complicated by a racial identity constructed out of fragments, real and imagined, of a difficult and complex mix of national and personal experience.

Unraveling those complex knots of experience, the psychology they helped to consolidate, and their implications for some of the most basic elements of President Obama's leadership and policy choices is the purpose of this analysis.

A Framework for Analysis

This analysis starts from a theoretical model of presidential performance developed and applied over a decade of work.[15] That psychological theory focuses on three core elements—found in every person including presidents—ambition, character integrity (ideals and values), and relations with others (relatedness) and their relationship to political leadership and decision-making, the twin cores of presidential responsibilities.

Of Obama's ambition, we ask about its nature, purpose and the skills that sustain it. Of its nature we can say it's vast, and of its purpose—transformational. Of his skills we can confidently say that they include a substantial and fluid intelligence, resilience and determination in the service of his own success, an attention to preparation, an ability to convey a calm poised temperament even though he is no

Spock, an ability to get along well with others as needed and to convey the impression that he is open to other viewpoints, a level of self confidence that can sometimes veer off into overconfidence and overreaching, and the ability to sometimes inspire with his oratory and ideals.

Of his values and ideals, we ask what they are, whether he has the courage of them, how they shape or are shaped by his ambition, and how in turn they affect his leadership choices and judgments. One inescapable conclusion is that the president is a stanch liberal, or progressive if you prefer, but his policy premises and views are shaped by something far more basic and profound to him than orthodox liberal ideology—the moral imperative of fairness.

And of his connections to others (relatedness), we trace his relationships to/with other people—his supporters, opponents, and enemies. Here we encounter the paradox, and perhaps the irony, of his reserved, self-contained demeanor and the outpouring of enthusiastic, even euphoric feelings for him among many of his supporters. This ardor, on the part of many, has cooled considerably in the first two years of his presidency leading directly to the question: Just what was at the basis of the euphoria that greeted Obama's candidacy and why, exactly, did it sour?

Obama's ambitions, ideals, and his relational style did not spring up spontaneously upon being elected to the presidency. They begin, as they do for everyone, with his parents' psychologies and the options those legacies presented to him. In Obama's case, this includes the consequences of a union between an enormously talented but emotionally flawed Kenyan man and a free-spirited woman with a somewhat romantic view of the world, whose openness to different cultures and ideas was certainly ahead of its time, but which could also shade over into reckless choices that had consequences not only for herself but also for her son.

Following the rapid failure of their bi-racial union, Obama was left with an absent father and an uncertain personal and racial identity. That story is told by Obama in his well received, but for purposes of accuracy somewhat elusive, autobiography, *Dreams from My Father*. That book is of course a narrative of a boy's search for a lost father and a personal identity. Among the most possibly prophetic things Obama has said of his father is that he "had returned to his native Kenya bursting with intellect and ambition, only to devolve into an embittered bureaucrat because he couldn't find a way to reconcile his ideals with political realities."[16] His father's failure weighed heavily on his son and is doubtlessly the source of a quote that Obama has brought up more than once: "Every man is either trying to live up to his father's expectations or making up for his mistakes."[17]

Obama's mother presented an idealized version of his absent father to Obama. Yet, there is little evidence in Obama's early ambition or performance of his trying to measure up to it. Once the difficult truth of his father's failed aspirations and life became clear though, they proved to be a very heavy weight on Obama and his father's life became a cautionary tale. However, in following in his father's chosen path, as a transformer of his country, there lay the possibility of redemption of his father's legacy and a continuation of his own.

If Obama's ambition carries the weight of his father's personal and political failures, the nature of his values and ideals reflect the legacy of his mother's ideals, encapsulated in the cardinal virtue of "fairness" to overcome social injustice. The power of that legacy was enhanced by Obama's idealization of her after his father's iconic image suffered at the hands of reality. In Obama's view, the United States has much ground to cover economically and politically before it can redeem and live up to its true promise. *Redemption* therefore is a key to both Obama's personal, policy, and larger political ambitions.

Obama emerged into his adulthood a deeply ambivalent man. He had mixed feelings about his father, whom he idealized, but who had gotten knocked off the pedestal that his mother had constructed for him. He was angry about his mother's long absences, but came to idealize her during precisely the same time period when he needed an iconic replacement for his father. He struggled with his racial identity and has not yet fully resolved the gap between the grievance and post-racial elements of his identity. The same is true of his views and feelings about the United States. He has expressed his love for the country almost as often as he fully details its failings, past and present, for which he aspires to be the instrument of its redemption and ours.

Obama was, as a child, both loved and lonely. He had no father and his mother left him for long periods with devoted grandparents who were however not really in a position to help him with the identity problems with which he struggled. There is, then, some truth to Obama's observation that at some level he raised himself. The result of those efforts was to make a man who was used to being on his own.

Obama grew to maturity negotiating two racial worlds, but he learned to keep his conflicts hidden and developed a number of strategies that kept people in the dark about where he really stood, what he stood for, and what he really thought. That is the basis of Obama's Rorschach strategy and he has carried it into his presidency.

Obama has centralized power in the executive branch to an unprecedented degree. The presidency, as an institution, amplifies its occupant's psychology. And this is especially true, for a president like Obama, who prides himself on his mastery of policy and above all on the quality of his judgments.

Yet, the very centrality of this president in the key decisions of his administration raises important questions. Was it wise to take on so many major issues so early in his presidency, and what, if anything, will the president draw from this experience?

The ironic question that Obama faces as he runs for reelection is not whether he can rescue his father's failed legacy, or successfully insist that the country accept his mother's (and his) idealized view of fairness. It is certainly not whether he can really transform the country that he sees as so often having failed to live up to its ideals. That is highly unlikely.

It is at this point, whether he can redeem his own presidency.

Acknowledgements

Every book is, in reality, a collective effort. The author develops and stands behind his analysis, but many others help shape and support those efforts.

A number of people read, commented, or discussed with me various aspects of the analysis presented in this book, and that effort has been much improved by their questions, comments, and criticisms. Thanks to my wife Judith Beldner and my son Jonathan Renshon, and to my colleagues Michael Doran, Rick Friedman, Fred Greenstein, Erwin Hargrove, Barbara Kellerman, Peter Loewenberg, Harry Paul, Jerrold Post, Mac Runyan, and Stephen Wayne. Bob Baden undertook a full reading of the manuscript in the midst of his own academic work that is much appreciated.

I've had the benefit of presenting the ideas that underlie this analysis in several venues, among them The International Society of Political Psychology Meetings in Dublin, Ireland in the Summer of 2009 and the Center for Public Leadership at Harvard University in the Spring of 2010.

I want to thank Michael Kerns at Routledge, who was the acquisition editor for this book, and my agent Linda Langton, for their strong and continuing support of this project. Thanks also to Siân Findlay and Alf Symons for overseeing the production process in their customarily effective and responsive way and to Jacqueline Dias, who had their work cut out for her copyediting my manuscript but who handled the assignment with a keen eye and deft touch. I would also like to express my sincere appreciation to my research assistant, Mr. Nicholas Petaludis, with whom I've worked, always fruitfully, on several books. Every writer should be so fortunate as to have someone of his caliber to depend upon.

Part I
FOUNDATIONS

1

THE EARLY OBAMA PRESIDENCY: FROM CAMPAIGNING TO GOVERNING

Every new president steps into the Oval Office facing a large in-box of public expectations. These are the result of issues that were on the public's mind during the presidential campaign and the campaign's response to them, the issues that the candidates stressed and their promised solutions, and the public's mood—an emotional barometer of their experience during the years of the president in office at the time of the campaign. Elections are generally prospective in that they are focused on the future, but that prospective stance contains a retrospective element. People are either satisfied with the past and want more of it, or they want a break with the past and vote for "change," however the winning candidate defines that. Either way, it is the past that helps define the future.

The same is true of the president himself. The Obama narratives are by now an often-told story. As a result, there is now widespread acceptance of a great deal of conventional wisdom about this president. He is cool, charismatic, slightly detached, deliberative, highly intelligent, verbally fluent, and a pragmatist more interested in policies that work than in scoring ideological points. All true, but only to a point. Obama is emotionally cool and detached. He is more likely to know your position than feel your pain. But he is also a president who has proved to be quite at home with harsh personal and political characterizations of those who hold different policy views. The president may be cool, but he is often not temperate.

The president presents himself as deliberate and methodical in his decision-making and judgments. And he definitely can be, but there is much more there than conventional wisdom allows. The president can also be impatient and ambitious; two core characteristics that sometimes trump his deliberativeness. Moreover, the president is an enormous risk taker, a quality that few have mentioned or analyzed.

Yes, the president is very intelligent and fluent in policy nuance, but he has also adopted a personal and political Rorschach approach of strategic ambiguity. This has left allies and opponents alike wondering just who is the real Barack Obama? That question is not likely to be answered without understanding what really motivates this unusual and in many ways unique president.

Yes, the president did search for his racial identity. But where between an early history of racial grievance and post-racial identity did Obama finally wind up? And yes, Obama's book *Dreams from My Father* is the story of his coming to grips with his absent father. But those factors don't begin to do justice to the real motives underlying Obama's quest to become a transformational president. Those motivations, in a word, revolve around the core motivating dynamic of *redemption*—Obama's, his father's, his mother's, and ours.

Yet, there is more to Obama's presidency than his organizing motivations. He is a president faced with real policy problems, and he has adopted a leadership style that carries with it many consequences that have yet to be discussed, much less analyzed. Is Obama just preternaturally self-confident or arrogant? And where, exactly, did that self-confidence come from and what does it mean for how he approaches his leadership and judgment responsibilities?

These, and others, are the questions that frame the analysis that follows.

A President in Office

The nature of the presidential campaigns and a president's initial period in office are of interest for many reasons. They give a preview of a president's approach and success in assembling winning collations that have implications for governance. They provide information about the president's psychology and skills in a publicly visible set of high stakes circumstances. And once a president is in office, his choices provide a set of public responses to an enormous range of policy and leadership questions that serve to validate, refine, or negate initial impressions gathered during the course of the campaign.

The 2008 presidential campaign did provide a great deal of useful information about Mr. Obama. We learned about his intelligence, temperament, rhetorical fluency, organizational talents, and ability to inspire large numbers of his supporters. What the campaign did not reveal was how Mr. Obama understood his mission of change and what that might actually mean in concrete terms once he was elected. That understanding has become clearer as the president assumed the actual responsibilities of his office.

Presidential campaigns are also important because they reveal a great deal about the public—its hopes, fears and expectations. They are a substantial part of the governing context within which the new president will operate. Mr. Obama read the success of his campaign as providing vindication for the view that the public wanted a clean break with the Bush Administration and *all* that it represented and endorsed. That conclusion may have been the first substantial misjudgment of the Obama Presidency, but it wasn't the most important one.

At the outset of his presidency, Obama faced daunting domestic problems. The country was descending into a substantial recession, unemployment was high and rising, revenue collection was down, resulting in large and growing state and federal deficits, the housing market was deteriorating and major financial institutions and manufacturing industries were hemorrhaging money and in danger of insolvency. President Obama, like President Bush before him, understood the stakes and acted forcefully. In the words of one news analysis he "largely hewed to the emergency policies of former President George W. Bush in trying to resuscitate the economy with stimulus measures, tax cuts and bailouts."[1]

Each of these measures was controversial at the time that President Bush initiated them and became more so as President Obama invested his political capital in a second and third attempt to stimulate the economy by massive government spending. Critics argued that tax cuts were more stimulating than large-scale government spending. The public didn't support Wall Street "bailouts" especially when they learned that high risk trading with complex and unregulated financial instruments had caused great economic damage. There were worries that in gaining a controlling interest in banks, financial institutions and automobile companies (GM and Chrysler), the Obama Administration was involving itself in a way and to a degree in the private sector that was unprecedented. The president's plans to rescue homebuyers who couldn't pay their mortgages also spurred fears that those who had taken on mortgages they couldn't afford, or who had speculated on the basis of a government supported housing boom, threw into doubt the prudent assumption of risk that characterized the majority of Americans who did repay their debts. And on top of that the president insisted on passing a huge and complex reorganization of the American health care system that would touch, in ways both foreseen and unanticipated, the health care of every American.

Still the president pressed on. Advised to reign in his ambitious agenda after Congress passed his health care legislation the president said, "what I'm not going to be dissuaded from is going ahead and taking on these big challenges that are critical in terms of America's long-term economic health."[2] The president then specifically mentioned energy and immigration policy as well as financial regulatory reform. Whether the public was ready for further large-scale presidential initiatives is the defining question to date of the president's first term in office.

Why Obama Won

It was the central insight of the Obama campaign that the election would turn on "change" and that this term needed to be defined as a clean break with what were widely considered the controversial stances and emotionally draining arguments that characterized the Bush Administration.[3] Not all of President Bush's policies, especially in national security, were necessarily wrong, as evidenced by the fact that the Obama Administration adopted many of them. However, the shrill debates surrounding almost every one of them fueled the perception that the Bush Administration was unnecessarily confrontational, too willing to follow its own views without listening to allies, and engaged in policies like invading Iraq that had high and brutal costs associated with them, in part because of early missteps. Although Mr. Bush was not running for reelection, having served two terms, he was front and center as a campaign subtext for Mr. Obama from the start. In an interview, David Axelrod, Obama's chief strategist, said

> So we had a very simple premise about the general election, which is that these Bush policies had failed, that McCain was essentially carrying the tattered banner of a failed Administration, and that we represented a change from all that. There have been zigs and zags in the road, but that's essentially the strategy that we have executed from the start.[4]

A Gloomy Public Mood

President Obama gained office in November 2008 with a public mood that was deeply dour. As of May 2008 an astounding 82 percent of a national sample of respondents had said the country was going in the wrong direction.[5] Why the doom and gloom? In truth, there are so many plausible reasons that one is hard pressed to winnow a long list that includes: unusually high gas prices, the threat of renewed inflation, a surge in unemployment to 5.5 percent, the housing market meltdown, continuing public regret about having invaded Iraq and continuing uncertainty about the sustainability of progress there, the abysmal standing of America in the world, and the continuing poisonous atmosphere of Washington national politics. To those "atmospherics," one could easily add concerns in the policy areas of immigration, health care, and energy.

As befits a country that increasingly looks to the president to shape and beneficially order the political universe,[6] Mr. Bush was held largely responsible for all these maladies. Indeed, on issue after issue—the situation in Iraq, the economy, energy policy, health care, and immigration—the president's net approval ratings were negative.[7] Mr. Bush's popularity, having reached stratospheric levels after 9/11 (90 percent), descended slowly and steadily until it had reached almost subterranean levels (28 percent).[8] Not surprisingly, 74 percent of respondents in one national survey said that the next president "should take a different approach than George Bush has."[9] Mr. Obama's repeated claim to be the candidate of "hope" and "change" therefore took root in fertile ground and helped propel him to victory.

Catharsis and Change

Americans wanted "change" but it was not clear they all wanted the same kind of change. Nor was it clear that they all wanted the kind of change reflected in President Obama's first two years in office. Americans were also conflicted about the qualities they wanted in the next president. In one national survey, the quality most picked by respondents was "strong leadership."[10] On the other hand, the same polling organization reported in a survey taken the preceding month that respondents chose "working well with leaders of other countries" as the most important characteristic (32 percent), while "bringing unity to the country" was a close third (25 percent) after "having strong moral and family values."[11] In that context Obama's campaign narrative and reputation as a bridge-builder and pragmatist was a central element in his political attractiveness.

Given the public mood, it was not surprising that Obama's election would be viewed through the prism of repudiation of his predecessor. Adam Nagourney wrote in the *New York Times* that

> The election of Mr. Obama amounted to a national catharsis—a repudiation of a historically unpopular Republican president and his economic and foreign policies, and an embrace of Mr. Obama's call for a change in the direction and the tone of the country.[12]

This was true, to a point; but it missed certain limits and their implications.

Certainly, the economic downturn was not a result of Bush economic policies. And "tax cuts for the rich" was a partisan talking point, not a fair or accurate description of them. The wars in Iraq and Afghanistan were genuinely disturbing to Americans across the political spectrum but there were legitimate, if contested, rationales for them. As to the perception that American standing abroad had declined, that was true, but the reasons for it were complex and not all reducible to the decision to invade Iraq. And many Americans decried the decline of civility and bipartisanship of American political life, but this too was hardly the sole fault of the Bush Administration.

Still, complex or unfair as the case may be, the controversies took their political and emotional toll on the American public. Catharsis is both a feeling of relief and an expectation that the tensions that made catharsis necessary would not return because President Obama would behave differently. So, the "national catharsis," to the extent that it existed, was in fact a sense of relief whose origins were not uniform. Some wanted to renew America's image abroad; some wanted to leave Iraq while others wanted to do so after completing the war's mission, and others wanted more political comity. As a result, the expectations that arose from these varied views led to different expectations about what policies the new administration ought to pursue. These different meanings and understandings provided the seeds for the president's deteriorating public support over his first two years in office.

There were Democratic partisans who were ecstatic that the Bush Presidency was over. Liberals or progressives might disagree with some Obama Administration policies, but their catharsis was based on the fact that ideologically Obama was no George W. Bush. They had high expectations for the enactment of a range of liberal or progressive policies

There were other Americans who worried about the economic downturn, the country's standing in the world, and the failure to find common ground on either domestic or foreign policies. They were looking for policies that would help the country through its economic difficulties, a less overtly combative foreign policy stance while still backing strong national security measures to protect the country, and answers to long term policy issues, like energy or health care that were moderate, effective and increased individual options rather than government control.

Independents and moderates were not looking for liberal or progressive policies to replace the conservative policy perspective of the Bush Administration. Indeed, many moderates and independents seemed genuinely taken aback by the seeming return of the era of big government that President Clinton had said was over in the first year of the Obama Administration.

Viewed from this perspective, "change" was a powerful emotional lever for all groups, but one that was likely to result in a "catharsis gap" once the expectations generated by campaign slogans were forced into concrete policy form when Obama took office. And it did. Liberals and progressives were generally in support of the president, although they might prefer even more progressive or liberal policies. Moderates and independents were put off the policy alliance between a self-described progressive president and a clearly liberal Democratic Congress.

The catharsis gap was clearly evident in national polls. Andrew Kohut, President of the Pew Research Center, said

> *A desire for smaller government is particularly evident since Barack Obama took office.* In four surveys over the past year, about half have consistently said they would rather have a smaller government with fewer services, while about 40% have consistently preferred a bigger government providing more services.

In October 2008, shortly before the presidential election, the public was evenly split on this question.

The public is now divided over whether it is a good idea for the government to exert more control over the economy than it has in recent years. Just 40 percent say this is a good idea, while a 51 percent majority says it is not. Last March [2009], by 54 percent to 37 percent, more people said it was a good idea for the government to exert more control over the economy. The exception here is the undiminished support for the government to more strictly regulate the way major financial companies do business. This is favored by a 61 percent to 31 percent margin."[13]

In promising change, premised on hope, Obama engaged the idealism and hopefulness of his followers, but he also laid down a vague metric in which almost any departure from the Bush Administration could be touted as a successful early accomplishment of a key campaign promise. So, for example, foreign policies that focused on engagement certainly seemed to make good on one of Obama's key campaign promises, though their efficacy in producing concrete results was not clear even as the second year of Obama's presidency came to an end.

Mystery Man?

Obama emerged from his presidential campaign as a man of some mystery. Before he was elected one very sympathetic commentator wrote, "Sixteen months after announcing his candidacy, and after twenty-six presidential debates, and thousands of public speaking engagements, Obama remains a puzzle to many voters."[14] On the most important and basic questions regarding this president that is still the case. A *New York Times* analysis concluded,

> On this much, President Obama's friends and foes could agree: He eludes simple labels. Yes, he's a liberal, except when he's not. He's antiwar, except for the one he's escalating. He's for bailouts, but wants to rein in the banks. He's concentrating ever-more power in the West Wing, except when he's being overly deferential to Congress. He's cool, except when he's fighting-hot.[15]

The analysis concludes, "As he tries to absorb the lessons of his first 12 months in office and push ahead with his agenda in an election year that holds great peril for his party, Mr. Obama faces a narrative vacuum." A narrative, of course, is a story constructed with facts selected for a purpose, in the president's case to establish his virtuous qualities, his leadership, and the policy need for him to pursue his ambitions.

Like Bill Clinton before him, Obama says he eschews the old categories of left and right. He presents himself as the consummate pragmatist, interested in solving problems by taking the best ideas, be they liberal or conservative. Yet, his stimulus package, his health care plans and his energy bill all stress traditional Democratic liberal policy options and premises. Obviously there is a question here. Can President Obama be both a strong liberal (or progressive) and a pragmatist? The editor of the *Washington Post*'s editorial page thinks that question unlikely to be answered anytime soon. He has written, "President Obama's true nature—radical or pragmatist, partisan or conciliator—is a subject of endless debate. No doubt it will be still a century from now."[16]

It is true that the debate may well continue but there is an accumulating body of evidence that allows us to resolve this question well before a century passes. One can discern in this president, as in others, twists and turns of policy and leadership. Modern presidents gain office because they have substantial political skills. Among these are political tacking and packaging.

President Obama is certainly no exception and may even be its exemplar. At any rate, the question is whether through close inspection one can discern clear patterns in which the exceptions do not negate the rule. I think the answer to that question is yes. It is not so much the president's somewhat opaque leadership style and psychology that are really as puzzling as they seem to some observers, but that their meaning and implications are elusive.

Obama's substantial level of personal ambition does not make him different in kind than other modern presidents, but the *scope* of his policy ambitions does set him apart. In his first year, he proposed and began to act on a wide range of large policy initiatives including those in foreign policy, energy policy, and health care policy. When his major health care ran into major difficulties in Congress, and when Democrats lost a U.S. Senate election in Massachusetts, many urged him to scale back his proposals. He didn't. On, the contrary, he put forward an even larger plan. As one news story reported, "Obama plunged in ahead of Thursday's bipartisan health care summit with a sweeping plan that laid to rest any question about whether he would scale down his ambitions."[17] He didn't, and he eventually prevailed, but at what cost to public support for the plan or his own leadership legitimacy remains to be seen.

Moreover, after his health care legislation was passed and public opposition to it and the rest of his agenda began to rise, the president did not step back from further pushing his transformational agenda. "President urges expansion of agenda" ran the headline, the first line of which read: "President Obama called Tuesday for sticking with his domestic agenda even if it's not always popular."[18] It was not. A June 2010 NBC News/*Wall Street Journal* poll found that, "Americans are more pessimistic about the state of the country and less confident in President Barack Obama's leadership than at any point since Mr. Obama entered the White House."[19]

These polls reflect an important clarifying fact. For all the mysteries that surround a candidate before entering office, the presidency itself is a clarifying institution. The reason is rather simple. The presidency requires its occupants to make decisions and in so doing to choose. A president's past may be shrouded by the passage of time, selective or protective memories, or difficulties in appreciating why a president's personal history matters for his political present. Campaigns are, in many important respects, not very revealing. They consist of having candidates answer general questions about their philosophy, or about hypothetical choices. Answers to these kinds of questions may provide a general map, but not a reliable guide. A presidential candidate's campaign involves choices of course, but these are all geared to winning not governing. They are therefore primarily strategic.

Presidential decisions are clearly not devoid of strategic political concerns, but in the arena of policy they basically reflect a president's efforts to accomplish his purposes. Presidents try to do so within their own political calculus, but what they choose and their calculations in doing so, are themselves revealing of the psychology behind their leadership choices. Only in the thousands of choices that a president must make, many of them part of the public record, do the president's premises, worldview, ambitions and governing psychology come into clearer view.

The meanings of a president's choices do not always follow easily or directly from a president's behavior since a president's choices rarely reflect one motivation or a single calculus. But they do clarify, when carefully examined over time and circumstances, the president's psychology, ambitions, and judgment. Barack Obama is certainly no exception to this general rule.

What the 2008 Campaign and Obama's First Two Years in Office Revealed

Obama's performance in the 2008 presidential election, and in the initial part of his first term as president, showcased an exceptional set of personal and organizational skills. Among them were: the successful development of a vast grassroots campaign that brought hundreds of thousands of new voters into his column; a long and ultimately successful primary campaign against an extremely formidable rival (Hillary Clinton); and a successful presidential campaign that made clear his exceptional rhetorical skills, subtle intelligence, and very attractive political persona as a post-partisan and post-racial candidate.

To have started where Obama did, with no vast organizational network or political experience, little money, and to have prevailed against a well connected, well funded and well organized opponent in the primaries and a bone fide war-hero in the national election was a remarkable accomplishment. And indeed Obama argued that this accomplishment was directly relevant to his ability to successfully carry out the responsibilities of presidential leadership. He said,

> where I went from zero, starting from scratch, to compete with a legendary political organization 20 years in the making, built by a former president … is not an accident. It shows my capacity to put together a team and point it in a direction that I think is important, and that success illustrated the skill sets that are required to move the country.[20]

Doing all this while negotiating the tricky currents of race and partisan divides only underscores the magnitude of what Obama accomplished. The presidential campaign made clear that Obama is a very talented man whose skills promised the possibility of a successful and consequential presidency. The question that arises though for any successful presidential candidate is: will the skills that brought electoral success in fact translate into leadership and governing success in the presidency? And that question leads directly to the nature of presidential leadership.

The Tasks of Presidential Leadership

The essential tasks of political leadership are mobilization, orchestration and consolidation.[21] The first reflects the ability to arouse and engage your supporters and those who might become supporters. The second requires the skill to organize them for common purpose, and the third requires the ability to actually achieve and consolidate it. Obama clearly was successful in these essential tasks during his presidential campaign, but the nature of these tasks changes once you assume office.

In presidential campaigns, the target audience for mobilizing supporters is much narrower, both politically and emotionally. Obama's task in the primaries was to mobilize Democrats and some left leaning independents, not the general public. His target audience was therefore predisposed to his general political stance in a way that the general public did not prove to be as his first two years in office unfolded.

Orchestration changes too from the context of campaigning to governing. In campaigns, orchestration entails organizing supporters for a clear and finite goal, an election vote that will put the candidate on top. All of the organization and financial efforts are geared toward the voting booth and the electoral benefits that winning contests confers. Consolidation in a campaign context means leveraging the results of electoral success to gain more of the same. The transition from primary to general election campaigns widens the frame of electoral efforts, and adds policy legacy considerations to it. A president not only wants to solve problems but to leave in place political architecture that reflects his unique and hopefully effective solutions.

Presidential Leadership: Campaigning vs. Governing

The transition to governing requires substantial changes in the understanding and successful enactment of these three leadership tasks. Obviously, the president can no longer be solely focused on his narrow party constituency. Moreover, his frame of reference for the success of his domestic and foreign policies must not only be the American public but leaders and publics abroad as well. This is the key insight of Rose's view of the "post-modern presidency."[22] Presidential success at home and abroad requires the ability to engage the world, including its leaders, whose interests rarely completely coincide with his as well as American public opinion. The degree to which domestic and foreign policies are now related for these three presidential leadership tasks has only increased in the economically globalized post-9/11 national security world.

There are other differences as well. As noted, campaigns deal with conjecture while presidents are faced with the consequences of real choice. In campaign debates and in countless Q&A interviews, candidates state their views and their preferences. They can, if they are as smart and well informed as Obama is, give nuanced and knowledgeable answers to a range of policy and political questions. But these are not the same as the real world choices the president will face and the need to balance real world considerations and consequences. So, to give one concrete illustration of this difference, in a Q&A a presidential candidate might list five factors that would influence his decision to either commit more troops to Afghanistan or not. Yet that answer, however nuanced and complex, gives no clue as to how the president will weight the risks of the various factors in arriving at his actual decision.

Measuring Presidential Success

Whereas winning votes is the holy grail of electoral campaigns, the metrics of presidential success are far wider, ambiguous, and in a highly partisan political environment, contentious. They consist of two essential keys: policy success and public support. Policy success does not only mean passing legislation, although it is often confounded with that narrower slice of presidential performance. It means enacting policies, whether by legislation or by presidential decision, that effectively address the problem at hand, without themselves creating circumstances that undermine their effectiveness.

This requirement is easier to state than to measure. It requires analysts of presidential success to take on the arguments that frame a policy's justifications. If there is a moral argument to be made in favor of insuring more people, the question of whether the same goal of more coverage could not have been accomplished with less dislocation to everyone's medical care by simply opening up Medicaid to poorer persons of whatever age needs to be fairly addressed. If there is an economic argument to be made regarding the president's goal of lower medical costs, it ought to address and fairly assess the various independent analyses which cast severe doubts on the legislation's ability to accomplish this purpose.[23] And regarding the question of ameliorating insurance abuses, a fair analysis must ask whether covering preexisting conditions won't result in some people delaying the purchase of insurance until *after* they need it. Such an analysis might also ask whether it isn't possible to ensure that insurance can be portable across jobs and geographical boundaries without the necessity of a large scale government program.

Perhaps most difficultly, it is crucial to go beyond noting that legislation passed, to consider the many unintended consequences that often flow from major legislation, even if it is desirable. For example, the 1965 Voting Rights Act, a very important and desirable anti-discrimination law, has had an enormous range of effects over the years, some of which, like the drawing up of districts with the intent to increase minority representation, have been paradoxical. The massive health care legislation signed into law in Obama's first year as president will doubtlessly have many unanticipated effects when it becomes fully operational in 2016, well after Obama runs for a second term. Any fair assessment would try to distinguish between the president's success in enacting legislation and the actual success of the legislation itself in addressing the problems it was designed to cure.

So while the president should get "credit" for the passage of "historic" health care legislation, its effectiveness remains to be demonstrated. And there are signs of trouble ahead. Critics have called attention to the Massachusetts health care system in which non-profit health care providers went to court to overturn a denial of rate increases that they said would force them into insolvency.[24] A *New York Times* article pointed out that New York's insurance system

> has been a working laboratory for the core provision of the new federal health care law—insurance even for those who are already sick and facing huge medical bills—and an expensive lesson in unplanned consequences. Premiums for individual and small group policies have risen so high that state officials and patients' advocates say that New York's extensive insurance safety net … is falling apart.[25]

It is difficult to assess these elements given that they involve future events and complex counterfactuals, and political analysts want some measure of success *now*. The easier and more available default metric is: did the legislation pass? If it did, presidents and their supporters will claim victory, and observers will count it towards the president having gained one of his objectives. Whether the policy works as hoped for or as intended is often left for the historians and partisans.[26]

Perhaps it would be possible to separate out political from policy success. In the first, the president gets credit for having been able to shepherd though his legislation or policy. In the second, some assessment of the likely unfolding consequences is attempted. In any event, simply counting legislation passed or policies developed as indicators of presidential success seems somewhat superficial, premature, and imprudent.

The other key measure of presidential success is public support. There has been over the past decade a great debate about whether the American public and their leaders have become more polarized.[27] That term is generally thought of as involving two groups of opinions at opposite ends of a political spectrum, with few persons occupying a center position.[28] Viewed that way it is clear the word is being defined somewhat loosely. Careful studies show that there is no general polarization of the country either on ideology or issue areas in that sense. What there does seem to be are increasing partisan differences on a variety of issues and specific policies in which the public and those in leadership positions are increasingly differentiating themselves from those who don't share their policy views. So, while these increasingly important partisan gaps on a variety of issues are consequential, they are not synonymous with general society-wide polarization.

The question that arises here is how has Obama tried to position himself to handle these divisions? He has done so by forging an unusual and until recently successful highly personalized political identity. He has also done so while eschewing the emotional tone of "heroic leadership," while nonetheless aspiring to its results. And he has developed, as befits a careful, well-organized planner, a flexible political style.

A Flexible Political Style?

During the Democratic nomination campaign Obama ran as a pragmatic realist with populist overtones. He presented himself as a moderate centrist willing to take strong international stands when necessary but not before exhausting the virtues of international cooperation and engagement.

After winning the Democratic nomination Barack Obama moved decisively to the political center.[29] Among the many positions he modified were those dealing with his support for restrictive gun laws,[30] national security related wiretapping laws (FISA),[31] NAFTA,[32] debating his opponent in a series of town hall meetings,[33] his policy on Iraq[34] and on Iran,[35] his policy about talking to dictators without preconditions,[36] Social Security tax hikes,[37] and refusing public financing for his campaign when he vowed to use it.[38] The number and importance of these shifts led to charges of "flip-flopping,"[39] but movements to the center from either the left or right, depending on the candidate, are politically *de rigueur*.

After he won the election, but before he entered office, Obama said of himself that he was a "progressive pragmatist." Introducing Governor Tim Kaine as his choice to head the Democratic National Committee, Obama said, "Tim and I share a philosophy. It's a pragmatic progressive philosophy that was at the heart of my campaign and will be at the heart of this administration."[40] What is a progressive pragmatist? According to the news report,

> The alliterative phrase … is a catchy shorthand for two themes he has long emphasized. It encapsulates both the way in which Obama has presented himself as someone who can "disagree without being disagreeable" while, at the same time, reminding voters that there is an underlying progressive content to his politics that was most clearly on display when he opposed the Iraq War before it began.

Upon entering office, Obama tacked left. His major health care legislation and the major spending initiatives that have been used to fund major Obama policy goals are all in the service of the president's progressive agenda. And his foreign policy of engagement reflects a policy perspective of "liberal internationalism"[41] and "progressive realism"[42] with an emphasis on multilateral organizations, binding treaties, and international collaboration.

Populist moderate, pragmatic centrist and progressive pragmatist are words and phrases that cover a lot of a wide swatch of political terrain, without necessarily providing the policy benchmarks that would allow Obama to be placed in conventionally understood ideological space. Indeed, Gallup found that "large segments of all three ideological groups are unsure what 'progressive' means," which may be precisely its virtue and therefore its point.[43] The mystery of Obama's real political views owes much to Obama's own efforts.

Ambiguity and opaqueness may be elements of a winning strategy during the nomination process. However, they raise a difficult public leadership question for a president that makes use of them. That question is: just what, if anything, does Obama truly believe in outside of adapting the best strategy to gain office? Republicans raised that question,[44] but it didn't keep Obama from winning a commanding election victory. However, once in office Obama began to define himself more clearly with his policies and as a result his level of support substantially eroded. In some ways this was not surprising. Running for and gaining office as moderate, whether pragmatic or progressive, and then supporting policies that many in the public didn't like and which they see as decidedly liberal, is a recipe for disenchantment and even anger at being misled.

By November 4, 2009 a majority of Americans thought that Obama's policies were "mostly liberal."[45] Polls taken a year apart showed a similar trajectory. In late

November 2008, 24 percent of the public saw Obama as "very liberal" and 19 percent as "liberal." One year later, those figures were 34 percent and 20 percent respectively.[46] By June of 2010, "More Americans continue to say that Obama is listening more to liberals in his party than to moderates (46% vs. 34%)."[47] By whatever terms Obama and his supporters might choose to call his philosophy and worldview, the public increasingly seems to be settling on its own characterizations of his politics and policies.

The Public's Response to Obama: Admiration, Hope, Support and Disappointment

Obama is, of course, a major historical figure by virtue of being the first American of African descent to win the presidency. His election unleashed an unprecedented level of expectation both in the United States and abroad. A November 2008 post-election poll found that nearly seven in 10 adults, or 68 percent, said they had a favorable opinion of president-elect Obama. Almost that many—65 percent—said they thought the country would be better off four years from now.[48] National polls, however, fail to capture the emotional intensity of many of Obama's supporters and followers.

For a substantial number of people, Obama assumed iconic status, a status that is infused with powerful feelings of affection and even adulation. These are powerful emotional forces, but they are difficult to maintain when policy choices must be made, legislation must be negotiated, other domestic and international power blocs flex their muscles in pursuit of their own goals, and unexpected events like a major oil spill intrude on supporters' idealization. Disappointment is the price that idealization pays for wishful thinking.

Obama, as he does with his identifications with Lincoln and his attempts to harness and make use of his celebrity status, encouraged the idealization of his followers. *The Economist*,[49] a moderate somewhat staid journal of political analysis, presciently pointed out the downside of trying to both stimulate and harness the passions surrounding him,

> Perhaps Mr. Obama inwardly cringes at the personality cult that surrounds him. But he has hardly discouraged it. As a campaigner, he promised to "change the world", to "transform this country" and even (in front of a church full of evangelicals) to "create a Kingdom right here on earth". As president, he keeps adding details to this ambitious wish-list. He vows to create millions of jobs, to cure cancer and to seek a world without nuclear weapons. On July 20th he promised something big (a complete overhaul of the health-care system), something improbable (to make America's college-graduation rate the highest in the world by 2020) and something no politician could plausibly accomplish (to make math and science "cool again").

The Economist continues, "All presidential candidates promise more than they can possibly deliver. This sets them up for failure. But because the Obama cult has stoked expectations among its devotees to such unprecedented heights, he is especially likely to disappoint." And he apparently has.

That disappointment has taken the form of a substantial slide in the popularity of both the president and his policies. The Pew Research Center polls are emblematic. They found that,

> In April, 62% of the public approved of Barack Obama's performance as president and 26% disapproved. In August, just four months later, 52% approved of Obama's job performance while 37% disapproved. Obama's approval rating has declined across nearly all major demographic and political groups: It has fallen 11 points among women and nine points among men; by 12 points among Republicans, 10 points among Democrats and nine points among independents.

By June of 2010, "Sixty-two percent of adults in the survey feel the country is on the wrong track, the highest level since before the 2008 election."[50] And, "For the first time, more people disapprove of Mr. Obama's job performance than approve."[51]

Why that happened has been subject to various interpretations.[52] Among them: a continued deterioration of the labor market along with a slow, partial, and halting economic recovery; the passage of a major stimulus program that became controversial with regard to the measurement of its claims and impact; administration commitments for over 9 trillion dollars in new spending coupled with a substantial increase in government indebtedness; a major and controversial initiative to deepen government involvement in the American health care system which will also involve major new government spending and debt; a major and controversial bill to have the government regulate the energy sector through cap and trade legislation; the lack of any bipartisan support for these initiatives; and the public perception that all these domestic initiatives represent the return to a new and unprecedented level of "big government."

There are many surveys covering these issues, but two stand out for their startling findings. A poll reported by Public Policy Polling[53] found that,

> Perhaps the greatest measure of Obama's declining support is that just 50% of voters now say they prefer having him as President to George W. Bush, with 44% saying they'd rather have his predecessor. Given the horrendous approval ratings Bush showed during his final term that's somewhat of a surprise and an indication that voters are increasingly placing the blame on Obama for the country's difficulties instead of giving him space because of the tough situation he inherited.

The other startling poll was conducted by CNN and Opinion Research[54] and asked, "Do you think Barack Obama deserves to be reelected, or not?" Identical percentages of "All Americans" and "Registered Voters" said that he should (44 percent) and should not (52 percent). Of course, Obama does not stand for reelection until 2012, and that is more than several lifetimes in political life. Nor do these numbers reflect any possible turnaround brought about by a number of initiatives that a president might propose and carry out to recover his standing.

Still, the two sets of findings, coupled with the more detailed polls available suggest that the general public's hopeful anticipation, and for some idealization, has begun to recede, pushed in part by economic anxieties and growing reluctance to support the president's large-scale solutions to the problems he has chosen to address. The Obama Presidency, although it has a long way to go, has reached something of a political fork in the road.

Obama's Leadership Style and Public Discontent

It is revealing to more closely examine the sources of public discontent with President Obama. These can be reduced to the view that he tried to do too much,[55] not enough,[56] concentrated on the wrong policies to push,[57] or hasn't clearly defined his message or persona.[58] To some extent, of course, these different views of where the administration went off track reflect the normal selective perceptions of those with different partisan and ideological views.

Those on the left argue that Obama should have insisted on a much larger stimulus, pushed a single-payer health care reform bill, been much harder on Wall Street speculators, and committed fewer troops to Afghanistan, among other things. Those on the right argued that the president's large policy ambitions outstripped his support, that he had failed to really look for, much less try, to find common ground with those who disagreed with him, and that he had failed to approach policy issues from the pragmatic, incremental stance he had promised and on which his candidacy had been based. These profound disagreements were accompanied by a vast partisan gap in approval and support. A Pew Research Center poll[59] found Obama's approval rating among Democrats was an astronomical 88 percent and among Republicans a dismal 27 percent, for a gap of 61 percent. Pew characterized this gap as "the most polarized early job approval ratings for a new president in 40 years." Another Gallup poll found that the president's approval ratings were even more polarized in his second year in office than they were in his first.[60]

The wildcard in this rather conventional set of responses was Obama's political persona. Like many other modern presidential candidates, Barack Obama has had to address the issue of reconciling his own political views with an electorate that was increasingly divided along partisan and ideological lines. Bill Clinton tried to square that circle by proclaiming himself a "New Democrat," implicitly distancing himself from the old ones. George W. Bush, before 9/11, presented himself as a "compassionate conservative," implying that perceptions of the GOP were not sufficiently sympathetic.

Obama's approach to this dilemma was to declare himself a "pragmatist." Obama's candidacy was premised in part on his promise to bridge political divides and pragmatism was his means of doing so. He was a leader who was interested in what worked, not in hewing to any particular ideological line.[61] Evidence to be presented later in this analysis suggests this isn't an accurate description.

The Dilemmas of an Obama Presidency

Naturally, a new president and administration raises many questions. What will the successful candidate really be like as president? What qualities of character, identity, temperament, and leadership will shape the new presidency? How will the new president's worldview shape his domestic and foreign policy choices and his chances for successfully achieving them? And finally, how will these elements play out in the context of the public's psychology—its framing of the issues, views, hopes, and expectations?

The Question of Leadership Style: No Hidden-Hand Presidency

Some years ago, Fred Greenstein pointed to Dwight Eisenhower as an example of a "hidden-hand presidency."[62] As his correspondence and memo notations made clear, Eisenhower was comfortable, indeed preferred, to operate behind the scenes, presenting a public persona of a kindly grandfather figure who occasionally came up rhetorically short. In fact, he was smart, strategically sophisticated, and possessed generally good policy judgment.

Even if that notion of behind the scenes leadership appealed to Obama, and it doesn't appear to, that stance would be politically difficult to sustain. Obama is *the* unique and sole embodiment of the movement that has coalesced around him. He has therefore needed to play a very public role of reassurance given the hope, idealization, and transformational policy initiatives that followers expect as part of his presidency.

We can see some foreshadowing of this in Obama's decision to give his acceptance speech to a crowd of 75,000 at the Denver football stadium rather than the more limited seating venue of the Pepsi Center.[63] Some left center commentators worried about the large-scale adulation that was on display there and Obama's apparent comfort with being its object.[64] It also seems clear that Obama and his advisors are sensitive to the importance of spectacle, perhaps more so than any president since Ronald Reagan. Reagan, however, combined a strong sense of theatrics with an equally strong reputation for conviction. Obama may well appreciate and even have mastered the first, but the second remains to date elusive.

Clearly Obama has tried to set the terms of debate, but has run into several difficulties. His frame and narratives must compete with other narratives and be consistent with his actual policies. And, while his followers may accept and try to amplify his narratives and framing, there is no guarantee that the general public will accept and act upon that framing, assuming that they hear it.[65] This is a particular problem for the Obama Presidency because of his singular identity as the unique embodiment of his leadership.

There is no other member of Obama's administration that even remotely rivals him for national presence, celebrity standing and, in certain quarters, iconic status. That means that there is no one who can be in any competition with the president. But it also means that no presidential surrogates have the stature to take some of the criticism that inevitably flows to a president, especially one with transformational ambitions. One result of this is that, "Obama remains the colossus of his administration—to a point where trouble anywhere in the world is often his to solve," and he has become a "Velcro president," rather than a "Teflon president" like Reagan.[66]

Decoding Obama's Identity: Words

For Obama, "words have power,"[67] and he uses many of them. In less than six months following his inauguration, Obama had uttered more than half a million words.[68] At the end of his first year in office the president had made/given 411 speeches, comments and remarks, 42 news conferences, and 158 interviews.[69] Obama is not only verbally prolific, but prolix. He once gave a 304-word, single-sentence answer to a question.[70] Even that presidential record was eclipsed by his 17-minute, 2,500-word response to a woman's claim of being "over-taxed."[71] Meaning is easy to lose track of in 304-word sentences and 17-minute, 2,500-word responses to questions.

The president's ubiquitous political presence has also been duly noted.[72] Overall, it is an impressive verbal start and is consistent with Obama's stated views on "the power of the Presidency that I don't see used enough. The capacity to explain to the American people in very prosaic, straightforward terms; here are the choices we have."[73]

But words don't speak for themselves, especially with someone so fluent, nuanced and knowledgeable as President Obama. Words can certainly inform, but they can also mislead. There are many ways in which this can happen. Words may not be consistent with deeds. Words can convey intentions that may not come to pass, beliefs that may not be accurate, or convey facts that on closer inspection are more variable than the impression given. To anticipate a theme that will be taken up in more detail, intelligent, rhetorically fluent, and very informed presidents like Mr. Obama present special difficulties for any student of his presidency.

A New Progressive Majority?

The question that Obama faces is whether it is possible to deliver on his transformational promises given that the country remains quite politically divided. Here Obama will come face to face with the dilemma that has faced America's last two presidents.

President Clinton fit comfortably within the Democratic Party's left center views on domestic and foreign policy issues, but had to govern a country in which many had grown skeptical of some of those policies. His answer to this leadership dilemma was triangulation—modest reform of limited aspects of various core Democratic Party policies while preserving and adhering to the central premises of those paradigms. That was the essential nature of being a "New Democrat."

George W. Bush governed openly from the right center although he tried to leaven his basic approach early in his administration with claims to be a "compassionate conservative." 9/11 ended his attempts to develop and consolidate that leadership persona. Thereafter he governed directly and forcefully as a wartime president. The question then arises: How does Obama view the difference between his clearly liberal worldview and policies and the more moderate inclinations of the American public?

Some Obama supporters said that the country has shifted to the left in recent years as a result of public disenchantment with the war in Iraq and the Bush administration more generally.[74] They bet that the country will be open to the development of a new "progressive majority" that will allow Obama's liberalism to become the new political center.

Obama seems to hold this view, as well, having commented, "I think there's the possibility of a significant realignment politically in this election."[75] In another interview he said, "I think what people are looking for right now is somebody who can bring the country together and maybe *shape the kind of majority that will actually deliver on health care, that will actually deliver on a bold energy strategy, that can actually do something about serious education reform.*"[76]

It hasn't worked out that way. In a July 2010 *Washington Post*-ABC poll on the president's performance it was found that, "nearly six in 10 voters say they lack faith in the president to make the right decisions for the country, and a clear majority once again disapproves of how he is dealing with the economy."[77] That same poll showed that, "most Americans would now like to see a Republican Congress as a check on the chief exec from Illinois."[78] In November, 2010 they got their wish.

Prematurely enthusiastic news reporters/pundits heralded Obama's election as something that transcended just race, "maybe, just maybe, something new has arrived: a post-partisan approach to governing, founded on the Obama Coalition, fueled by young and minority voters, powered by the 21st century technologies that helped turn a first-term senator from Illinois into a historic lodestone."[79] The problem with that kind of analysis is that it neglects the fact that one election is unlikely to constitute realignment and it is perhaps better viewed as an audition for one.

That audition seems to have failed. Before Obama took office and had completed the first substantial portion of his first term there was some reason for his advisors' optimism. A 2007 Pew survey found that there had been a decided shift toward the Democratic Party.[80] However, by April of 2010, more than a year into Obama's term of office, the Gallup poll found that, "The advantage in public support the

Democratic Party built up during the latter part of the Bush administration and the early part of the Obama administration has all but disappeared."[81] Almost all the gains of the Republican Party were, "due entirely to a growing proportion of independents who lean to the Republican Party, rather than an increase in the percentage of Americans who identify as Republicans outright."[82]Outside of a core group, party identification seems to be a variable rather than a constant. That is, people identify more or less strongly with each political party, and this seems to be especially true of "independents."

It is important however to keep in mind the distinction between party identification and political ideology. The Democratic Party, as a whole, is more liberal than the Republican Party, and the latter are in turn more conservative than the Democrats. This is because while each party has an ideological center of gravity, there is some dispersal around the mean. Thus there are liberal Republicans and conservative Democrats, and core issues that can expand or contract a person's ideological position. So, for example, the 2007 Pew poll noted above which found a shift toward the Democratic Party, did not report a shift toward liberalism.

That survey did find an increase in the number of people who agree "today it is really true that the rich get richer while the poor get poorer." This would seem to be fertile ground for left center populist appeals. The only problem is that populist "us vs. them" rhetoric is that it is inconsistent with a central element of Obama's political persona as a pragmatist and "uniter."

Perhaps more promising was the finding in that survey that 54 percent believed that "government has a responsibility to take care of people who cannot take care of themselves even if it means adding to the deficit." However, 69 percent of the same survey also agreed that, "poor people have become too dependent on government programs." So there is serious public ambivalence about what constitutes fairness and support for government interventions as the Obama presidency heads into the second part of its first term.

The Era of Big Government Again?

In 1996, Bill Clinton in his State of the Union Address famously announced that "the era of big government is over" while listing many new government initiatives.[83] Reconciling an activist government with a smaller limited government has been a difficult conceptual and practical task for Democrats, progressives and liberals, and even conservatives. And President Obama is no exception.

In an interview given after he became president-elect, Obama was asked about the public's suspicion of big government,[84]

> What Reagan ushered in was a skepticism toward government solutions to every problem, a suspicion of command-and-control, top-down social engineering. I don't think that has changed. I think that's a lasting legacy of the Reagan era and the conservative movement, starting with Goldwater. But I do think

[what we're seeing] is an end to the knee-jerk reaction toward the New Deal and big government.

He then added:

> What we don't know yet is whether my administration and this next generation of leadership is going to be able to hew to a new, more pragmatic approach that is less interested in whether we have big government or small government, [but is] more interested in whether we have a smart, effective government.

Obama's attempt to bypass the big vs. smaller size government debate is consistent with his attempts to finesse the left vs. right debate via the frame of pragmatism. However, his framing of the issues does not appear to be gaining traction with the public. A comprehensive survey of public views of the government found that "74% think that the federal government does only a fair or poor job of running its programs."[85] A majority (52 percent) think the federal government is too powerful, 62 percent say government policies unfairly benefit some groups while 56 percent say it doesn't do enough to help average Americans.[86] And in spite of the fact that Americans now have a very negative view of banks and financial institutions (65 percent negative) and large corporations (64 percent negative), "The public is now evenly divided over whether federal government programs should be maintained to deal with important problems (50%) or cut back greatly to reduce the power of government (47%)."[87] In 1997 a clear majority (57 percent) said government programs should be maintained.

There are of course partisan differences in these findings, with Democrats much less likely (27 percent) to want to reduce the power of government. Yet, in a line worth repeating, the Pew study says rather directly that, "*A desire for smaller government is particularly evident since Barack Obama took office.*"[88]

These data suggest that on a core ideologically defining issue separating liberals, conservatives and independents, the actual behavior and policies of the president have a decided impact. That effect seems to parallel to some degree party identification. It also appears to reinforce the need for a close fit between real facts and presidential narratives. The narrative of President Obama as a moderate pragmatist cannot rest on rhetoric alone. Not surprisingly, the public pays attention to the president's actual behavior and policies in assessing how well the narrative fits.

At this point, the evidence for a new progressive majority is thin and the question then arises regarding Obama's leadership premises: What then? Obama himself has provided another answer. Asked about his liberal record in the Senate and how that record can be the basis of bringing Americans together, he argued that Senate voting is polarized because "The only votes that come up are votes that are purposely designed to divide people." However, he continued, "as president, I would be setting the terms of debate."[89] Here Obama expressed his optimism and confidence in his ability to frame the discussion and control the narrative, but these accomplishments have eluded him.

If America Remains Divided: What Then?

So, if Obama cannot count on either the American public coalescing around a new progressive majority or controlling the framing of the public discussion, what are his leadership options? The most likely, is a strong emphasis on rhetorical pronouncements and attempts to shape legislative support by the use of bridging euphemisms like "fair," "reasonable," "common sense solutions," and "balanced." Also likely to be pressed into service are comparative statements that provide no metrics for really assessing the progress claimed. Typical are Obama's claims during a recent immigration speech that,[90]

> Today, we have more boots on the ground near the Southwest border than at any time in our history. Let me repeat that: We have more boots on the ground on the Southwest border than at any time in our history. We doubled the personnel assigned to Border Enforcement Security Task Forces. We tripled the number of intelligence analysts along the border. For the first time, we've begun screening 100 percent of southbound rail shipments. And as a result, we're seizing more illegal guns, cash and drugs than in years past. Contrary to some of the reports that you see, crime along the border is down. And statistics collected by Customs and Border Protection reflect a significant reduction in the number of people trying to cross the border illegally.

Briefly, the "more boots" than "at any other time" doesn't speak to the question of whether that number is adequate. Doubling and tripling various units doesn't answer that question either, or say what the base number was so that the claim can be assessed. Seizing "more illegal guns, cash and drugs" may be true but irrelevant if the numbers of such items have simply risen. Indeed, one could seize "more" and still be falling behind. And finally, the reduction in the number of illegal immigrants that cross the border *may* have to do with increased personnel, but may also be more of a function of the economic slowdown in the United States, the lack of jobs and thus the lack of economic incentive to make the trip.

A large part of Obama's post 2010 strategy will be to figure out just how to make use of his diminished Democratic majority in the Senate and the loss of his majority in the House. This will entail figuring out to what degree he will need to cede or compromise his policy preferences to get the minimum number of votes to pass his legislation. This is *not*, it should be noted, a true "centrist" strategy. It might be called a minimalist or strategic centrist strategy. Its purpose is not to forge legislation that truly finds large swaths of common ground, but to do just enough to gain the votes necessary to get most of what you want.

It is at this point that several elements of Obama's leadership strategy are likely to come into conflict, and the true contours of his presidency will emerge. Obama has staked his political persona as a conciliator and bridge builder although there is not much evidence that he has attempted to perform this role in his time as a Senator and the evidence is decidedly equivocal in the initial period of his presidency. Obama is quoted as saying, "we need a leader who can finally move beyond the divisive politics of Washington and bring Democrats, independents and Republicans together to get things done."[91] Yet it is very unlikely that Republicans in general, or conservatives in particular, will be won over to supporting a liberal or progressive Obama agenda. What then?

At this point there are several possible ways for Obama to proceed. He could move to harshly criticize those who he might say, "stand in the way of progress that a majority of Americans voted for." However, the problem is that this kind of rhetoric is inconsistent with "bringing Americans together." There is evidence that Obama can be very tough-minded with those who stand in the way of his personal and political ambitions, but whether he would be equally tough-minded in pursuit of maximizing progressive policies is a wholly separate question.

With a Congress that is majority Democratic, he has been able to push through a host of "progressive" legislation. However, this has been hard to square with the moderation and pragmatism that Obama has adopted as his leadership narrative, or with his migration to the political center after he had won the nomination.[92] The real test of the Obama presidency and his transformational aspirations is clearly going to be found in his response to the results of the November 2010 elections.

Mapping the Psychological Contours of the Obama Presidency

The first two years plus of the Obama Presidency have been characterized by his decision to simultaneously pursue a number of large complex domestic and foreign policy initiatives. Domestically, those areas include the economy, health care, and energy policy. In foreign policy, the president is seeking to resolve the Arab-Israeli conflict, reset relationships with allies and enemies alike, move toward a nuclear-free world, and resolve the tendentious issues of Iran, Iraq, and North Korea. The decision to set all these large policy initiatives in motion not only reflects the size and range of Obama's policy ambitions, but also represents a clear test of his political judgment, and is as well an enormous test of his leadership skills. What distinguishes Obama here is not that he feels he must do *something* about all these matters, but rather that they *are* all high-priority items.

While the president is a smooth, knowledgeable, and articulate champion of his preferred policies, his initiatives such as health care are large, complex, and consequential in ways that no one in his administration has tried to, or perhaps is capable of predicting. This has created a substantial degree of public ambivalence and anxiety. This set of circumstances provides a test not only of President Obama's leadership skills but also of our theories of what it takes to succeed given Obama's ambitions and the response of the public to them.

2

THE PUZZLE OF OBAMA'S POLITICAL IDENTITY

Obama's search for his personal identity shaped his adolescence and early adulthood. It also helped to define important elements of his psychology. And ultimately, it provided the foundation for his political identity.

As is well known, Obama had an African father and a Caucasian mother, and came of age raised in large part by his mother's parents. Coming to grips with the real nature of his father's decision to abandon his mother and him, and understanding his own identity as an American of African descent, have been central to Obama and to his psychological and political development. Not having his real father at home to guide him, Obama was forced to construct his racial identity out of fragments—some real, some heard or read about and identified with, and some imagined.[1] His mother, a 1960s liberal, made an effort to connect him with the black experience as she understood it. Although Obama personally missed the civil rights movement of the sixties, he clearly identified with it—its leaders, its goals, and even at times its understandable stridency.

That fact is reflected in his poignant and beautifully portrayed search for his father and his identity in his first book, *Dreams from My Father*. Michiko Kakutani, writing in the *New York Times*, said the book provided, "a revealing, introspective account of his efforts to trace his family's tangled roots," and that,

> the book gave the reader a heartfelt sense of what it was like to grow up in the 1960's and 70's, straddling America's color lines: the sense of knowing two worlds and belonging to neither, the sense of having to forge an identity of his own.[2]

In some important respects Obama's racial and political identity remain incomplete. Ordinarily, a strong political identity is built on a well-developed personal identity.

What happens though when one central element of that personal identity, in this case Obama's racial identity, contains conflicts that appear to be unresolved? To this we might well add the question in Obama's case: What happens to a president's political identity when he comes into office with one that either has not been consolidated or, for strategic reasons, is not made clear?

In his first press conference as president-elect, Obama was asked a question about what kind of dog he was going to get for his daughters and he replied,[3]

> We have two criteria that have to be reconciled. One is that Malia is allergic, so it has to be hypoallergenic. ... On the other hand, our preference would be to get a shelter dog. But obviously, a lot of *shelter dogs are mutts, like me.*

At first glance his remarks seem self-disparaging or perhaps a self deprecating signaling that he sees himself as being of no particular distinction (which is paradoxical given his Ivy League pedigree and his investment and confidence in his own ideas). This of course is untrue. Unlike the shelter mutt to whom he refers, Obama knew both his parents and both were high-achievers—his father in economics and his mother in anthropology. Unlike the typical mutt, Obama obviously knows where he came from even if it has been difficult for him to sort through the meaning of it.

Somewhat oddly, the president repeated a similar sentiment in an appearance on a daytime variety show. Asked about his background of having a black father and a white mother he replied speaking of African-Americans: "We are sort of a mongrel people."[4] Realizing that didn't sound quite right, he quickly added, "I mean we're all kind of mixed up. That's actually true of white people as well, but we just know more about it."

And at an August 2010, Labor Day rally he had this to say about his political difficulties:

> Some powerful interests who [sic] had been dominating the agenda in Washington for a very long time and they're not always happy with me. *They talk about me like a dog.* That's not in my prepared remarks, but it's true.[5]

I don't want to make too much of this. On the other hand, given Obama's obvious and troubled search for an identity that reconciles the disparate racial elements that are part of his growing up experience, and their relationship to his transformational political identity, it would be remiss not to consider it. In some respect Obama's mutt comment reflects an unfinished identity, or at least one in which some ambivalent elements have yet to be resolved. Both the words "mutt" and "mongrel" convey an unknown lineage and certainly one of no distinction. The two spontaneous comments made years apart suggest that Obama has still not wholly reconciled himself to his mixed race and cultural background in spite of all the political mileage he has garnered from it.

There are basic questions as well about Obama's political identity that began with his search for community and a role to play in it. That search first took him to New York after two years at a suburban California college, and then on to Chicago and an initial career as a community organizer in a historically black South Side community. It also led to his joining the Reverend Wright's Afro-centric South Side church, and ultimately to his marriage with Michelle Robinson, an American of African descent with generational ties to Chicago's African-American community. It was there that his search for identity and his desire to make a difference coalesced into a political career and the beginnings of a political identity.

That identity has raised numerous questions. Is Obama a liberal? A socialist? A pragmatist? A moderate? All of these terms have been applied to Obama at one time or another and they are a testament to the difficulties of gaining a firm fix on where, exactly, to place Obama. This difficulty owes much to Obama himself, who has adapted political ambiguity, a Rorschach strategy, to give his ambitions maximum flexibility and opportunity.

The Nature of Political Identity

Political identity has become a legitimate shorthand for an important element of a president's essential leadership style and basic worldview. Political identity and its related but not synonymous term, *persona*, provides accessible and possibly accurate answers to questions of a candidate's values, virtues and the prospects for a successful presidency. That is why the public puts so much stock in these conceptual shortcuts and campaigns spend so much time trying to ensure that their versions are seen as the correct ones.

Political identity is one part character, one part convictions, and one part image. The first reflects the candidate's basic stance and worldview toward life and experience. The second reflects the candidate's distinguishing principles and policy views. And both of these are filtered in presidential campaigns through the prisms of public perceptions of political campaigns and later White House attempts to frame it. These perceptual prisms, both those generally used by the public and those used by campaigns and White House advisors to influence the public, are the basis of candidate personas, defined as carefully constructed images that reflect both fact and artifice.

A presidential candidate's persona is one essential element of a three-pronged effort to influence public perceptions and votes. The others are framing and the construction of pro-candidate story lines otherwise known as narratives.

Framing an Electable Identity

Framing is a term that has become familiar to political scientists because of the Nobel Prize winning work of Daniel Kahneman and Amos Tversky.[6] Their basic experimental insight was that how researchers framed a problem dramatically influenced how people understood it and how they made their choices. Individuals who approached a set of alternatives that had the exact same outcome probabilities behaved very differently when they were presented as more likely to lead to losses rather than to gains, even small ones.

Consider the authors' famous "Asian disease problem" in which subjects are given a scenario of choices concerned with the outbreak of a disease.[7] When the problem was framed in terms of lives *saved*, the majority choice was risk-averse; however, when the same problem (identical in likelihood of outcomes in all aspects) was framed in terms of lives *lost*, the majority choice was risk seeking. When the framing of the problem is changed, people's preferences shift accordingly.

Political operatives in presidential campaigns were relatively quick to pick up the implications of prospect theory for defeating their candidates' opponents. In 1996, the GOP presidential candidate, Bob Dole, said in his acceptance speech that he would build a bridge to an earlier time of tranquility. The Clinton campaign then accused the Senator of wanting to build bridges to the past, while he, Bill Clinton, would be busy building "bridges to the future." As one study put it, Dole "struggled against, but was unable to break out of, Clinton's frame."[8] In the 2000 election campaign the GOP effectively framed Al Gore as a serial exaggerator and in 2004 framed John Kerry has an aloof flip-flopper. In both cases, the frame gained traction and caused political damage.

Some have treated the power of framing as irresistible and unstoppable,[9] but it is neither. Framing in political life and psychological experiments differ in important ways. In the prospect theory experiments conducted to investigate framing, the frames themselves are always given by the experimenter and accepted as authoritative by participants.

In political life, frames are not given; they must compete with other frames, and at least in presidential campaigns are often strongly contested by those who are the object of them.

Frames gain political traction from their consistency with other information. Bob Dole's bridge comment about a more tranquil past gained traction for the Clinton campaign's framing of it because of Dole's age, the correct sense that he had been a political player for some time, belonged to a different generation, and was generally reticent to engage in the campaign of emotional intimacy pioneered by his opponent. All these elements were consistent with his characterization as a candidate who looked to the past, when voters wanted to know about their future.

Campaign and Presidential Narratives

The use of framing in presidential races is a powerful but inadequate tool for accomplishing a campaign's purposes. Framing an issue or a candidate in a way that advantages a campaign is a benefit if the public accepts it. Yet, there are many issues over the life of a campaign or a presidency, and trying to frame them all, one at a time, stands the risk of having voters fail "to connect the dots." Moreover, framing a particular candidate trait, as Obama did with the issue of bringing people together, is not enough to answer more basic and profound questions about a presidential candidate, namely: who is he or she?

Campaigns and administrations need a vehicle with which to distill an "essence" of their candidate or president, in a way that conveys their virtues. At the same time, citizens need some reliable information-reduction metric by which to judge candidates and presidents—their personal strengths and weaknesses, the nature and quality of their leadership, and their proposals to solve policy problems. In the past, both campaigns and citizens counted on party identification to help manage the wide range of information about candidates and their policies that became available during a presidential campaign. This metric faltered because of two developments.

First, presidential candidates, beginning with Richard Nixon, began to blur ideological policy lines as a means of appealing to a wider group of potential voters.[10] The net result of candidates' attempts to square the ideological circle, bypass it, transcend it, or encompass it has resulted in a situation where, with certain exceptions like Ronald Reagan and George McGovern, a candidate's party identification no longer serves as a highly reliable guide to his views, or at least that is what candidates now routinely say.

Second, a series of presidential legal transgressions, lapses of personal judgment, and questionable policy decisions, also beginning with the presidency of Richard Nixon, led many to conclude that the psychology of presidential candidates required more careful scrutiny. Voters want to know about the character and background of their presidential choices. They want to know not only whether candidates are smart, but also whether they are principled. They also want some sense that presidential candidates can stand up to the demands of the office and to America's enemies abroad. And increasingly, they also want presidents who can find common ground given the acerbic political debates that began in the 1960s and have yet to show signs of abatement.

The information that citizens need to make such assessments is complex and requires some psychological sophistication. Lacking both the necessary information and the theoretical grounding necessary to make use of it, an opening was created that campaign operators quickly exploited. The rise of narratives was the result.

Narratives are every campaign's answer to the questions that voters ask. They are first and foremost stories about a candidate constructed for a purpose. That purpose is to elect the candidate or buttress support for one's president. They are not representative of the full range of a candidate or president's psychology, positions, experience, or leadership and are not designed to be so. They are constructed to convey a more circumscribed "truth," at least as seen by those in the candidate's campaign or the president's advisors.

Authenticity and Identity Narratives

Trust is central to a candidate or president in two critical ways. The first lies in the importance of a candidate or president actually being the person he or she represents himself to be. This is not only a question of the integrity and authenticity to which a candidate's identity and persona lay claim; it is also the only reliable basis on which citizens can make an informed judgment about a candidate's capacity to successfully address unanticipated circumstances. The question of authenticity speaks to the legitimacy of the leadership a candidate claims he will provide, and also to his capacity to effectively carry out his presidential responsibilities.

The question of authenticity is closely connected to the ability to lead and govern effectively in a society divided along partisan lines as this one is. Authenticity is also central to the question of *leadership integrity,* which we take up in more detail in Chapter 6. Leadership integrity is one possible by-product of a president having the courage of his convictions (character integrity). However, a president must not only be who he claims to be, but actually must govern in a way that is consistent with those claims. His leadership, however authentic, must also be within a governing range that the public does or can be educated to accept.

Most candidates for president put themselves forward on the basis of their successful political experience. They point to their success and tout the skills that led to their accomplishments. Their implication is that past success will be the basis of future success, a formula that is premised on the assumption that a successful presidency rests directly on the skills and experience that the candidate has already demonstrated. This was difficult for Barack Obama since his record of accomplishment in the Senate was rather thin, reflecting the fact that he had only been there two years before he began his quest for the presidency. He could point with some truth to his ability to inspire hope in his eloquent speeches and he did argue that this would be a decided advantage should he gain the presidency, which it was. Yet this decided advantage proved to have definite limits in Obama's first two years in office.

The narratives that accompany meticulously constructed personas are fertile ground for counter narratives rooted in assessment of other less winsome leadership traits. And this has happened to Obama. Being relentlessly low key can raise questions of passion and commitment. Quiet determination can spill over into insistent obstinacy. And of course inspiring hope can raise questions about whether that has led to results.

The Question of Obama's Political Identity

Personal identity is the answer to a very basic question: Who am I? And political identity is the answer to the public question: Who is he or she? The building blocks of a possible identity in the United States are varied and variable, up to a point. However, ordinarily in early adulthood, a core set of elements comes into view and begins to form the consolidated basis of an established identity. That process consists of selecting the identity elements that most closely feel like a good fit psychologically, while at the same time providing an accepted way to make one's way in the world.

It is generally not a problem to figure out a presidential candidate's basic political identity because most seek the presidency well into middle or later adulthood after long-established political careers. Barack Obama is an anomaly in this respect. His lack of a long political history, especially at the national level, allowed him to define the elements of a developing political identity he preferred to emphasize, for example his identity as bridge-builder and change maker. The danger of an opaque or amorphous political identity that is not firmly and publicly established is that it lends itself to counter narratives, for example the charge of opportunism or a lack of authenticity—both of which were leveled at then Senator Obama's decision to opt out of public financing[11] and other matters.[12]

It is also unclear how Obama's experiences growing up in bi-racial, multi-cultural and cross-cultural family settings directly resulted in the psychological traits that are related to being able to bridge political, racial or other divides. His political successes, outstanding in many respects, have not been directly attributable to, or necessarily reflective of, the leadership promises that were the basis of his campaign's primary narrative.

Framing Obama's Persona

The attempt to frame an attractive persona was instrumental to Obama's success, and it worked because other elements of his persona tended to reinforce, not contradict the frame. He presented himself as someone who could, "move beyond the divisive politics of Washington and bring Democrats, independents and Republicans together to get things done."[13] He presented himself not as a liberal, a term that is consistent with his Senate voting record both in Washington[14] and Springfield (see p. 45), but as a "pragmatist" who looks for practical not ideological solutions. His attempt to escape the liberal label was aided by a persona that comes across as radiating reasonableness and fair-mindedness, traits that are viewed as being inconsistent with ideological zealotry.[15]

Senator Obama also stood out for his calm equanimity, even in the midst of a long tough campaign that took many twists and turns[16] He has been cool, analytical, and ironic, often to the point of seeming detachment. This too reinforced his reframing claim.

The Obama Narrative

Narratives ordinarily consolidate a "story line" that links biography, outlook, and leadership in a way that is responsive to the campaign or administration's estimation of the underlying psychology of the public mood. So, for Barack Obama, the biographical fact of his African American and Caucasian background coupled with his exotic geographical upbringing in Indonesia and Hawaii emphasizes his stature as both familiar and different, someone whose atypical background gave him standing as an agent of change. Reduced to its essence the Obama campaign narrative equated his atypical experience with fostering the development of a psychological perspective and style that bridges differences.

Obama's campaign narrative promised that if elected, the search for bi-partisan common ground would be successful. Obviously it has not been. And here, the downside of successful but not necessarily accurate narratives comes into sharper view. Successful campaign narratives, like Obama's, become the benchmark against which actual leadership performance is judged once in office. This gap is at the core of steady deterioration of the president's support.

Supporters of the president were soon saying that the president needed to develop a new narrative. Frank Rich said that, "The problem is not necessarily that Obama is trying to do too much, but that there is no consistent, clear message to unite all that he is trying to do."[17] Others chimed in with suggestions.[18]

The problem here for the administration now into its second year is twofold. First, the president's "bully pulpit" is not as powerful as it is reputed to be.[19] And second, any new narrative would have to compete with other, perhaps equally compelling, counter-narratives and also with the defining power of the president's own choices and policies.

The narrative of Obama's early years as planting the seeds of openness to other viewpoints and perspectives and thus a more moderate outlook gained traction for several reasons. It provided a storyline that plausibly dealt with his novel circumstances. There had been many rags to riches stories in the American presidency, but no presidential candidate with the racial and geographical background of Barack Obama. Moreover, that narrative had no legitimate competitors. Insinuations that Obama was not really an American citizen or that he was a Muslim never gained traction for the obvious reason that there was little or no evidence to support these views.

Once Obama became president, his policies and his governing choices presented a difficult to avoid touchstone for the supportive narratives his advisor attempted. The president's health care initiative in particular stimulated substantial concerns in the American public regarding its effects on their medical care, costs, and choices. As Frank Rich notes, the president's message has been somewhat muddled; he "has variously argued that health care reform is a moral imperative to protect the uninsured, a long-term fiscal fix for the American economy and an attempt to curb insurers' abuses." As a result,

> between the multitude of motives and the blurriness (until now) of Obama's own specific must-have provisions, the bill became a mash-up that baffled or defeated those Americans on his side and was easily caricatured as a big-government catastrophe by his adversaries.[20]

Multiple messages are inconsistent with the clean, clear singular lens of presidential framing or narratives.

Moreover, facts and analyses that are inconsistent with an administration's preferred narratives can be the foundation of powerful counter-narratives and arguments. Narratives, like framing, must be in accord with other facts to be successful. Paradoxically, allies of the president like Rich quoted above, downplay the important narrative information contained in the president's actual policies and leadership choices. Actions may not speak louder than words in the presidency, but they do have a certain defining power when they are clearly visible and clearly controversial, which many of Obama's policies are.

Words have an important meaning to President Obama. He has risen politically on their wings. And it is tempting to a very smart, verbally fluent president like Obama to depend on his power as an aid to his leadership and governing style. Yet, a president can only gain so much traction in the face of contradictory evidence from his own choices.

The disconnection between the president's transformative ambitions and counter-narratives that reflect the concerns of the ordinary public were, as noted, well captured by numerous public opinion surveys. This then is the great domestic divide of the Obama Presidency: a president who wants to transform America and a public that is increasingly resistant and worried about his plans.

Understanding President Obama: Conventional Wisdom

One of the many paradoxes of this president is that his ubiquitous public presence and consistent public demeanor helps convey the impression that we already know a great deal about him or that what we see is all there is. As a result, conventional wisdom is already firmly established. Much of it needs to be rethought.

Barack Obama is the most visible of modern presidents. The first two years of his presidency, as noted, have been characterized by unprecedented exposure and availability,[21] whether in the form of press conferences, media interviews, high-focus travel abroad, major policy initiatives, or numerous mass-culture venues like providing sports commentary or appearing on late-night entertainment shows, resulting in a virtual torrent of words.[22] Obama is clearly the most public face of his administration, yet all that exposure is both informative and misleading.

Extensive public exposure in so many diverse circumstances informs because it provides analysts with a wealth of information to sort though and compare. Yet, all the copious data of this president's public performances is not synonymous with having understood him. On the contrary, Obama is on record as having expressed himself on so many sides of the critical issues he faces that it is not wholly clear just where he stands.

Obama is touted as a president whose unique bi-racial background makes him the ideal leader to help America overcome its racial divisions. He is lauded as a leader who is much more pragmatic than ideological and thus uniquely situated to help transcend the ideological divisions that have permeated American politics for more than fifty years. And he is thought of as having a temperament uniquely suited to making thoughtful, balanced decisions—avoiding the errors often imposed by ideology and emotion.

These, and other premises of an Obama Presidency, stem from narratives that have gained the imprint of conventional wisdom, but they are very far from the whole story, and in some cases are incorrect. Whether the subject is Obama's background and its real meaning for the transformational ambitions that animate his presidency, the nature of his political views, or the ways in which his psychology both confirm and contradict the emotionless Spock-like view of his decisions, Barack Obama is a more complicated man than his admirers know, his opponents give him credit for, or Obama allows to be seen.

Conventional wisdom has come to the conclusion that this president is unusual in being so well versed on the issues that he is at ease not only with his own arguments, but those of his opponents. And that is true. Yet, being able to give public voice to more than one side of a policy debate is not the same as being clear about how you assess their relative weight and legitimacy in actually making a decision. Moreover, understanding your opponents' policy positions is not the same as thinking that they have valid points. Nor is it the same as actually taking them into account.

Consider the paradox, and perhaps the irony, of Obama's reserved, self-contained demeanor and the outpouring of enthusiastic, even euphoric feelings for him among many of his supporters. Many of them have crossed over from admiration to adulation. However, the strong emotions of his admirers are unrequited. There is an emotional asymmetry of substantial proportions between Obama and his followers and the emotional outpourings flow in only one direction.

Commentators have endlessly noted the president's Spock-like character, but have failed to see that the president's sometimes harsh rhetoric is the opposite side of the same coin. It is as if his sometimes harsh rhetoric against opponents is a displacement and a method of diffusing the tensions of always having to appear reasonable. Moreover, they have failed to appreciate that being able to keep your emotional distance has both advantages and disadvantages when it comes to presidential leadership and decision-making. They certainly have not asked what the relationship is between keeping your emotional distance and the impact of world-view or ideological beliefs. To anticipate a line of argument, keeping your emotional distance from a set of policy decisions does not mean that ideology or belief play no role. Indeed, in such circumstances they may have more of an impact.

Or consider the conventional wisdom about Obama's intelligence. It is certainly real, but it has been touted without benefit of either context or theory. Conventional wisdom does not consider how Obama's intelligence is related to other important elements of his psychological makeup or the range of its implications for his leadership style and judgment. It is a point worth repeating that skills and intelligence, however great, are encased in and are part of a person's psychology. President Obama is no exception. Being smart is a very useful and important attribute for any president. However, it is not synonymous with having good judgment.

Obama, for example, has often expressed what he sees as his prescience in opposing the Iraq War in 2002. However, a closer look at his early stance suggests his cautions were generalities, and the foundation on which they were built, the capacity to restrain Saddam Hussein through sanctions was, and still is, hotly debated. On the other side of the Iraq judgment ledger is Obama's unequivocally stated opposition to the so-called "surge" because, among other reasons, it would make matters worse. It didn't.

These examples, to be taken up in more detail later, provide a cautionary correction to all the attention that has been paid to the clearly deliberative processes that have become the hallmark of this administration's approach to addressing the issues it faces. Intelligence and deliberation are a hedge against errors of bias and judgment, but no cure for them.

Obama as an Emotional Magnet

Obama successfully established himself politically in a somewhat unusual, but very powerful, way. He did not present himself as the head of a restoration movement as Ronald Reagan had done for conservative Republicans, or Bill Clinton had done for "New Democrats." Nor did he campaign as the political heir of any of his Democratic predecessors, as George H.W. Bush did following Reagan.

Rather, he campaigned as the singular embodiment of a leadership style, personal temperament, and political persona premised on a unique ability to bridge disagreements, recoup what some felt was America's lost respect and legitimacy in the world, and resolve difficult domestic and international issues by applying his sophisticated, reasoned, and reasonable understanding to them. A *Washington Post* editorial, ordinarily not given to rhetorical hyperbole, said this in its endorsement,

> Mr. Obama is a man of supple intelligence, with a nuanced grasp of complex issues and evident skill at conciliation and consensus-building. ... Some have disparaged Mr. Obama as too cool, but his unflappability over the past few weeks [when the extent of the economic crisis became clear] during the—indeed, over two years of campaigning—strikes us as exactly what Americans might want in their president at a time of great uncertainty. ... Mr. Obama's temperament is unlike anything we've seen on the national stage in many years. He is deliberate but not indecisive; eloquent but a master of substance and detail; preternaturally confident but eager to hear opposing points of view. *He has inspired millions of voters of diverse ages and races, no small thing in our often divided and cynical country.*[23]

Inspiration, Adulation, and the Escalation of Expectations

I have emphasized the last sentence in the *Washington Post* endorsement because it captures another major element of this president's appeal. He is a candidate and president who has inspired unprecedented and almost rapturous responses from a number of his supporters. Yet, that same set of almost rapturous feelings among many of his supporters has made it more difficult to bring this president into clearer and sharper focus.

During the campaign, his aides were taken aback by the "blind faith in and passion for Obama … ," though they appeared to share it. These same aides referred to Obama as the "Black Jesus."[24] And David Axelrod, Obama's chief political advisor, said, "it's like you are carrying this priceless porcelain vase through a crowd of people and you don't want to be the guy who drops it and breaks it."[25] Of course having your most intimate advisors think of you in terms that parallel God's Son, or as something rare and priceless, has its problems. After all, who would dare to tell an even symbolic reincarnation of Jesus that he shouldn't do something?

That kind of fawning outlook has consequences. Eleanor Cliff, a long time liberal reporter and columnist writing of the post 2010 midterm election results said,

> Soul-searching is under way at the White House, but so far it looks pretty sterile … Part of Obama's problem is that there's too much hero worship around him, and that translates into a reluctance to fault him for anything, except maybe that he didn't make a good enough case for all the wonderful things he's done.[26]

The Economist, not given to rhetorical excess, wrote,[27] "Mr. Obama has inspired more passionate devotion than any modern American politician. People scream and faint at his rallies. Some wear T-shirts proclaiming him 'The One.'" This title was bestowed on him by Oprah Winfrey on national television,[28] and others, perhaps mimicking the views of Obama's aides, wore T-shirts noting that "Jesus was a community organizer." *New York Times* columnist Judith Warner wrote a column about her dreams of Obama, including the fantasy of having him with her in the shower. After launching a set of email inquiries she found that, "Many women—not too surprisingly—were dreaming about sex with the president."[29] An editor at *Newsweek* described him as "above the country, above the world; he's sort of God."[30]

Obama became not only an icon, but also a celebrity. Paparazzi "snapped pictures of a buff and shirtless Barack Obama."[31] He was proposed for a place on Mt. Rushmore before he took the oath of office.[32] And planning was already underway for a national holiday honoring the new president immediately after his election."[33] Mr. Obama appeared on so many magazine covers, that the American Society of Magazine Editors created a special cover award for those covers that depicted him.[34]

A Celebrity President Who Enjoys Being One

To an unusual and unprecedented degree Obama has made numerous forays into the cultural and entertainment world. He has become "celebrity-in-chief"[35] as well as president. From encouraging the mystique of the presidency, "He has opined on virtually everything in the hundreds of public statements he has made on culture: basketball star LeBron James' career plans,[36] baseball rules,[37] and Chelsea Clinton's wedding."[38]

He taped a plug for and has appeared on George Lopez's late night show,[39] did the same for Conan O'Brien,[40] appeared on the David Letterman Show,[41] and the Jay Leno Show.[42] Some of these appearances clearly had the strategic intent of reaching a large public audience with the president's view of his policies,[43] an example of the president trying to harness his celebrity status to buttress his policy leadership. Yet some of them were clearly because Obama seems to enjoy these venues, and he has done others like them. For example, he called the play by play in a NCAA Georgetown-Duke basketball game,[44] and agreed to an interview with John Walsh for the 1,000th episode of his show America's Most Wanted.[45] He filled out his bracket predictions for the 2010 NCAA Men's and Women's Basketball Tournaments with ESPN sports.[46] He was the first American president ever to appear on Comedy Central's Daily Show.[47] And he was the first sitting president ever to appear on a daytime major network talk show.[48] Ironically, the day after this appearance an article on Obama appeared with the subtitle "Aides are seeking to downsize his exposure."[49]

As is the case with the parallels that the president has often drawn between himself and Lincoln, the White House thinks these appearances are politically useful and they have been adopted as an element of its governing strategy. As a result,

> The White House, eager to cultivate an image-making media machinery that thrives on personality, has invited coverage from such outlets as television's "Access Hollywood" and "Extra." These glimpses into the Obama household are far from spontaneous. Instead, they are part of a careful strategy that has helped bolster the new president's popularity and political clout—even as he promotes some economic policies, such as bailouts for banks and automakers, that lack broad appeal.[50]

In the mix of the president's enjoyment of these cultural venues, the strategic intent of appearing in some of them, and presidential leadership lie the dangers of over exposure and the slow decline for Obama of the real sources of presidential prestige. Especially in a milieu in which the amplification powers of the bully pulpit are in decline because of alternative megaphones, information saturation, and now very low levels of trust and confidence in government, Mies van der Rohe's insight that "less is more" appears to apply as well to politics as to architecture. Peggy Noonan[51] captured the dilemma well:

> In the time since his inauguration, Mr. Obama has been on every screen in the country, TV and computer, every day. He is never not on the screen. I know what his people are thinking: Put his image on the age. Imprint the era with his face. But it's already reaching saturation point. When the office is

omnipresent, it is demystified. *Constant exposure deflates the presidency, subtly robbing it of power and making it more common.*

Yet, there is another element to all of this celebrity exposure that goes beyond strategy and is perhaps as or more important. It is clear from the number and variety of these cultural outings, that Obama enjoys his celebrity status and sees nothing wrong with frequently indulging in it.

A Great President Already?

The emotional response to Obama fueled an early, and premature, inclination to compare him to our greatest presidents or those associated with iconic policy accomplishments. Usually sober-minded scholars have compared his first year efforts to the great legislative accomplishments of LBJ and FDR.[52] Niall Ferguson, the Harvard historian, was asked in a *Der Spiegel* interview whether Obama will truly change the world and world politics, and answered, "Yes, by virtue of his very existence."[53] Michael Beschloss and Alan Brinkley discussed the new president on the Charlie Rose Show and agreed he had the skills to be a "great" president and would likely be a "transforming one."[54]

Journalists were less restrained. One saw him as FDR.[55] Others noted all of the Lincoln-Obama parallels,[56] including what seemed to be the parallels to Lincoln's "Team of Rivals"[57] to which Obama himself called attention.[58] Some likened him to JFK.[59] And a surprising number of others have compared him to Ronald Reagan because of his low-key temperament and rhetorical abilities.[60]

More recent comparisons have been less flattering, with some comparing him to Richard Nixon[61] and many more comparing him to Jimmy Carter.[62] Perhaps more indicative of political trouble ahead for President Obama have been the commentaries suggesting the president might usefully learn to improve his leadership and prospects from other presidents and political leaders, among them Abraham Lincoln,[63] Ronald Reagan,[64] FDR,[65] Bill Clinton,[66] and New Jersey Governor Chris Christie.[67]

A Siena College Research Institute (SRI) Survey of U.S. Presidents, undertaken after Obama had been in office just a year, reported that Obama had already been ranked fifteenth of America's forty-four presidents.[68] The survey apparently takes seriously all the respondents' abilities to assess presidents separated by vast historical, cultural and political differences on such undefined characteristics as "imagination," "ability," and "intelligence." Adding to the lack of seriousness of this premature assessment, the survey's methodological note states that, "Respondents ranked each of 43 presidents on a scale of 1 (poor) to 5 (excellent) on each of twenty presidential attributes, abilities and accomplishments." Of course President Obama is America's forty-fourth president.

Obama was already highly rated by these respondents on imagination (6th) (beating out such presidents as Jimmy Carter—ranked 7th and James Madison—ranked 8th), communication ability (7th) and intelligence (8th), but he scored poorly on "background" (family, education [sic!] and experience). Even before Obama and Congress had passed Obama's historic but controversial health care legislation, these "238 presidential scholars, historians and political scientists" were catapulting President Obama to the top tier of all American presidents.[69] One skeptic titled his analysis: "Obama the Great?"[70]

The desire to find parallels with past presidents is a natural one for pundits and news commentators seeking to understand and find a frame within which to analyze a new administration. It is also natural for presidents to try and help journalists select a frame and a narrative of the president's preferred choosing. Yet this strategy runs the obvious risk of premature or erroneous labeling without benefit of much data. This is a clear danger given that Obama is a president that many agree "remains hard to read or label—centrist in his appointments and bipartisan in his style, yet also pushing the broadest expansion of government in generations."[71]

Early Coverage of Obama: Accentuate the Positive?

The search for parallels with iconic or "great" presidents is but one aspect of the general substantial "positivity bias"[72] that was detected early on, but has started to shift because of the president's declining public support.[73] One reporter, surveying the unprecedented response of newspaper reporters to Obama's candidacy noted that, "we [who report the news] seem to have crossed a cultural line into mythmaking."[74] Another noted that, "Obama infatuation is a great unreported story of our time," and asked, "Has any recent president basked in so much favorable media coverage?"[75]

Empirical data bear out these points. The Pew Research Center's Project for Excellence in Journalism surveyed the coverage of the new president over his first hundred days in office and covering a wide range of news outlets found, "President Barack Obama has enjoyed substantially more positive media coverage than either Bill Clinton or George W. Bush during their first months in the White House." More specifically, "positive stories about Obama outweighed negative by two-to-one (42% vs. 20%) while 38% of stories have been neutral or mixed."[76] Another study of first year news coverage found that Obama drew 46 percent positive evaluations on the NBC, ABC, and CBS evening newscasts. By comparison, those networks were harder on George W. Bush (23 percent positive), Bill Clinton (28 percent) and Ronald Reagan (26 percent) in the first year of their terms.[77]

Even those studies that chart the decline of positivity in reporting on the administration over its first year plus in office note that it is the president's policies that have come in for some degree of criticism, and not the president himself. Stories about the administration's policies were 43 percent positive and 57 percent negative, while all the other evaluations of the president were 68 percent positive and 32 percent negative.[78] As a result of the positivity skew in the president's first-year news coverage, clear, focused, and independent minded coverage and analysis of the president and his leadership were relatively rare.

Obama's Opaque Political Identity

Obama is a president who has said of himself more than once, "I am like a Rorschach test."[79] Elsewhere he said more specifically that he was, "a blank screen on which *people of vastly different political stripes* project their own views."[80] However, Obama did not become a blank screen accidentally.

Ambiguity in a president's political identity can be a function of strategic choice or personal style. Its advantages are obvious in the political circumstances in which Obama finds himself. Not to be typecast on one side or the other of the political spectrum, or at least resisting being put in to a hard and fast ideological category increases presidential choice. There is also the possibility that in blending different policy arguments a president can seem to, or actually reflect the effort to find some common ground

Yet, it can also lead to the very blunt question: Where, really, does he stand? This has been and is a continuing issue for President Obama. He views his pragmatism as being beyond ideology, as do his supporters.[81] That is increasingly, however, not how the public sees him.[82] And this mismatch between Obama's perception of himself and the public's view of his policies presents a major problem for his presidency.

Obama's Elusive Political Identity: Bipartisanship?

Like any president facing a large philosophical, political and partisan divide on issues of major importance to him, Obama has emphasized his bipartisan policy outreach efforts.[83] Before a bipartisan meeting he had called, he came down squarely on the side seeking common ground,[84]

> As I said in my State of the Union, part of what we'd like to see is the ability of Congress to move forward in a more bipartisan fashion on some of the key challenges that the country is facing right now.

It is, as we shall see easier to see where on the political spectrum Obama really stands than to discern much consistency in how he describes himself. He has, as noted, described himself as someone not very interested in the traditional left–right arguments, and as a pragmatist. Yet he has also given himself diverse conventional political labels. "Privately, Mr. Obama has described himself, at times, as essentially a Blue Dog Democrat, referring to the shrinking caucus of fiscally conservative members of the party."[85] He told one member of a group of progressive bloggers that met with him at the White House that he was a "progressive."[86] When he met with a group of moderate Democrats, he told them "I am a New Democrat."[87] Perhaps the president believes that he embodies all of these quite different political perspectives in his political identity.

An emphasis on bipartisanship is a smart political tactic.[88] However, one of the debates that has broken out during the president's first term is exactly how serious the president has been in including ideas drawn from those who oppose his policies. This is not an easy question to answer. Peter Baker of the *New York Times* wrote,

> While Republican leaders resolved to stand against Obama, his early efforts to woo the opposition also struck many as halfhearted. "If anybody thought the Republicans were just going to roll over, we were just terribly mistaken," former Senator Tom Daschle, a mentor and an outside adviser to Obama, told me. "I'm not sure anybody really thought that, but I think we kind of hoped the Republicans would go away. And obviously they didn't do that."[89]

Three days after Obama assumed office, he met congressional leaders including Republican Eric Cantor on ways to address the country's economic downturn. Cantor,

> handed President Barack Obama a list of ideas to fix the economy. Pointing to a small business tax-cut item, Obama said: "We disagree on tax policy." When Cantor tried to justify his own position, Obama responded: "Elections have consequences, and at the end of the day, I won."[90]

Indeed according to another *New York Times* news report, "It took president Obama 18 months to invite the Senate Republican leader, Mitch McConnell, to the White House for a one-on-one chat."[91] And that came about inadvertently. Not long before the meeting took place, Trent Lott, the former Republican Senate leader, lamented to his onetime Democratic counterpart, Tom Daschle, that Mr. Obama would never get an important nuclear arms treaty with Russia ratified until he consulted top Republicans. Mr. Lott, who recounted the exchange in an interview, was counting on Mr. Daschle, a close Obama ally, to convey the message; lo and behold, Mr. McConnell soon had an audience with the president. The reporter then makes the fair point that, "*the fact that a former Senate leader found it necessary to work back channels to put Mr. Obama and Mr. McConnell in touch* suggests the difficult road the president will face if Republicans win control of one or both houses of Congress on Election Day." It also casts some light on the seriousness of the president's bipartisan efforts.

It is sometimes difficult to discern the difference between a token nod in your opponent's direction and finding real common ground. Does including several small state demonstration projects for tort reform in the major health care initiative qualify? Does including GOP ideas about preventing fraud change the fundamental thrust and nature of the president's health care legislation? Clarifying the extent to which a bill really does reflect common ground requires some assessment of the various elements involved, their weight into the overall legislative package, and whether they reflect or avoid the core concerns of the "other side."

As noted, the president is firmly on record as being in favor of bipartisanship. Yet, he also had this to say about it in an early 2008 interview,[92]

> You can have the best agenda in the world, *but if you don't control the gavel you cannot move an agenda forward.* And, when you do control the gavel, not only can you move an agenda forward but you can actually [move them]. I constantly see opportunities for collaboration across ideological lines to get stuff done. *But you have to be the one who's dictating how the compromises work.* If it's somebody who's not interested in compromising who's in charge, you can come up with all sorts of good ideas, and they'll stiff you. *If you're the person who somebody else has to come to, you can actually engage,* and that's how, for example, we got the death-penalty reform.

I read this to mean that bipartisanship, from the president's point of view and experience, is best served when it is the president's priorities and legislative policy assumptions that are given the primary role in any search for common ground. There is nothing unusual about this view among presidents, but it does suggest prudence in assessing just how "bipartisan" a particular effort truly is.

And finally there is the issue of the president's goal of transformation. Obama has said,

> I think that there are certain moments in history when big change is possible ... certain inflection points. And I think that those changes can be for the good or they can be for the ill. And leadership at those moments can help determine which direction that wave of change goes.

Asked whether this is one of those moments, he replied, "Yes, I firmly believe that."[93] He has also said quite clearly, "I want to transform this country. ... "[94] So, in Obama's view, we are at a pivotal point in our history and he wants to determine the direction of that wave of change by transformation. Whether "transformation" is consistent with pragmatism is a critical question.

Obama's Pragmatism: An Inkblot Phenomenon?

The puzzled "Who is he?" quotes noted in Appendix B make it quite clear that the questions "Where does he stand?" and "What does he stand for?" are matters of strenuous debate regarding President Obama, even now. Obama's relatively brief political résumé explains only part of that debate. The more important factors are a direct result of the president's leadership claims and strategies themselves.

Of the claims, none is more important than the mantle of pragmatism. Of his stylistic strategies, none is more important than striking a listening stance and conveying the impression of sharing common ground. Let us examine each in turn.

Obama claims that he is a pragmatist. In Obama's view getting things done trumps any political ideology. In an interview he described it this way:[95]

SCULLY: Your Senior Advisor David Axelrod describes you as a pragmatist, what does that mean?

OBAMA: Well, I think what it means is that I don't approach problems by asking myself, is this a conservative—is there a conservative approach to this or a liberal approach to this, is there a Democratic or Republican approach to this. I come at it and say, what's the way to solve the problem, what's the way to achieve an outcome where the American people have jobs or their health care quality has improved and our schools are producing well-educated workforce of the 21st century. And I am willing to tinker and borrow and steal ideas from just about anybody if I think they might work.

Elsewhere, in an interview he said,

The average baby boomer, I think, has long gotten past some of these abstract arguments about Are you left? Are you right? Are you big government, small government? You know, people are very practical. What they are interested in is, Can you deliver schools that work?[96]

In short, deliverable results trump ideological labels.

Others have seconded that characterization. Ruth Marcus calls him a "progressive pragmatist."[97] David Brooks calls him a "center-left pragmatic reformer."[98] Brooks based this conclusion on the observation that Obama "always uses the same on-the-one-hand-on-the-other sentence structure."[99] Yet a little biographical research would have alerted Brooks to the fact that this president is so well versed on the issues that he is at ease not only with his own arguments, but those of his opponents. Indeed, Obama has publicly taken pride in that skill[100] and has, for a long time, made good political use of it.[101]

He is already an insider at the highest level of government power, buttressed by a working majority of the legislative machinery of the national government. Brownstein, who interviewed the president on exactly this subject, says of him: "Obama was flexible about tactics and *unwavering in his goals*. He signaled that he's open to consultation, compromise and readjusting his course to build inclusive coalitions, *but fixed on the results he intends to produce*."[102]

Analyzing the goals of presidential ambition, especially in a mature democracy like the United States, requires a rethinking of the relationship between revolutionary tactics and transformational outcomes. Like FDR and Lyndon Johnson before him, President Obama has leveraged legislative majorities to produce enormous, and perhaps even transformational change (in health care), one part of his larger agenda of "transforming America."

The answer to the question of whether pragmatism is possible in the service of transformation would seem to be yes. At the same time, it is as well not to give too much weight to pragmatic tactics in the service of transformational change. In mature democracies, transformation is largely a result of pragmatic considerations, do what's necessary within the system's boundaries to accomplish your purposes. Yet tactical pragmatism in the service of historic political transformations does not translate to policy moderation.

Political Ideology: Obama's Liberal Policy Premises

During the presidential campaign

> there were questions about where Obama really stood ideologically. He talked like a centrist, a pragmatist, someone who would work actively with Republicans. But his agenda—a big health care package, higher taxes on the rich, an aggressive alternative energy plan—sounded conventionally liberal.[103]

The focus on the president's calm, cool demeanor also helped push questions about his actually political philosophy to the sidelines. Remnick notes that while Obama's "views, foreign and domestic, were generally progressive ... their expression was more analytic and deliberative than passionate."[104] The president has insisted, and there is evidence to support the view, that he worked with Republicans while a state legislator in Illinois.

Still, a *Washington Post* reporter covering Obama's years in Springfield as a state senator wrote that he arrived there as, "a committed liberal."[105] Another *Washington Post* reporter covering his tenure there wrote that, "Obama and three other members ... made up a faction known in Springfield as "liberal row,"" that "his record leaned more liberal than other senators," and that he "stayed true to his liberal principles."[106] One of Obama's biographers, who covered him for the *Chicago Tribune,* called him "aggressively liberal."[107]

So, anyone who looked at his state legislative career would not be surprised that the nonpartisan *National Journal* rated Obama as the most liberal member of the Senate in 2007,[108] or that he voted with his party 97 percent of the time in 2007.[109] Remnick concluded in his Obama biography that his votes in the Senate were more predictably liberal than he advertised."[110]

But there's no need to rely solely on what others say. Here is what Obama says of himself: "everything I absorbed from the sixties was filtered through my mother, who to the end of her life would proudly proclaim herself an unreconstructed liberal."[111] Moreover, "I am a Democrat ... my views on most topics correspond more closely to the editorial pages of the *New York Times* than those of the *Wall Street Journal.*"[112] Or elsewhere in that same book, "I won't deny my preference for the story the Democrats tell, nor my belief that *the arguments of liberals* are more often grounded in reason and fact."[113]

This last quote conveys either obvious wisdom or partisan hyperbole depending on your political point of view, but from an analytic perspective it establishes a point on the political continuum in which it is legitimate to place this president. And that is important because it helps to provide a base line with which to dispel the confusion regarding the president's political views, temperament, and rhetorical style that led David Brooks to confound Obama's rhetorical style with his ideological position.

It is also an important and telling revelation because it underscores the fact that however pragmatic Obama may be with regard to particular policy debates, his assumptions, those beliefs that frame his analysis, are clearly and decidedly liberal. Indeed, at a Democratic fundraising event in August 2010, Obama boasted, "We have been able to deliver the *most progressive legislative agenda*—one that helps working families—not just in one generation, maybe two, maybe three."[114] And in a *Rolling Stone* interview published shortly before the 2010 midterm elections, and commenting on this he said, "It is very important for progressives to understand that just on the domestic side, we've accomplished a huge amount."[115] The merger of his views and the aspirations of "progressives" who occupy the left wing of the Democratic Party is quite clear and unequivocal.

Where Does He Stand?

Among the most basic questions that arise in relation to Obama's political identity is the question of *where* does he really stand. This is related to but separate from the more leadership oriented question of what does he really stand for, a question that we shall take up shortly. One reason that both questions have arisen is because Obama has developed a style that conveys the impression of openness to others' viewpoints, but how much actual openness exists is not easy to discern. Gerald Kelman, an early Chicago mentor from Obama's community organizing days, says of him, "One of the remarkable things is how well he listens to people who are opposed to him."[116]

One reporter noted that President Obama, "has the unique ability to offer doctrinaire liberal positions in a way that avoids the stridency of many recent Democratic candidates."[117] However, his true leadership skill is the ability to convey the impression of sharing common ground. How does he accomplish this? His preferred rhetorical device, one evident earlier in his career, is that

> When he addresses a contentious issue, Mr. Obama almost always begins his answer with a respectful nod in the direction of the view he is rejecting—a line or two that suggests he understands or perhaps even sympathizes with the concerns of a conservative.[118]

Obama, channeling what he sees as Abraham Lincoln's skill,[119] has said of himself on this matter that,

I've always been struck by the fact that, if you can get me in a room with a group of people, even who disagree with me violently on an issue, they'll still take the time to listen. They might not, at the end of it, agree with me, but having seen how I'm thinking about a problem, having a sense of how I'm making decisions, that I understand their point of view, *that I can actually make their argument for them* ... it gives them a sense, at least, that they've been heard. ... [120]

Yet, being able to give public voice to more than one side of a policy debate is not the same as being clear about how you weigh their relative importance and legitimacy. And understanding your opponents' policy positions is not the same as thinking that they have valid points. Nor is it the same as seriously taking them into account. And being able to see each side of an argument is not the same as letting people know where you stand.

Obama may well be a good listener, but a key question is: How much does he modify his views in response to what he's heard?[121] There is very little public evidence to date of Obama having actually changed or substantially modified his views in response to information developed in either public or more private debate. It may well be that someone as self confident and invested in his own ideas as the president is would have trouble doing so.

That question comes up as well in another way. It is clear that Obama's racial identity plays a central role for him, a fact reflected in his poignant and beautifully portrayed search for his father in his first book. It also seems clear that President Obama's racial identity contains a duality whose resolution is not yet clear.

On one hand, there is Obama's white mother and his own development of an outwardly conciliating stance towards others, an element that can be found in his political style as well.[122] Yet, there is also the fact that as Obama passed from adolescence to young adulthood he experimented with a more racially charged persona.[123] He wrote in his first book that even while doing that he wondered whether it was just a pose,[124] but there is evidence that it has persisted (in Chapter 4) even if not always fully in the public's view. In any event there is evidence that Obama has yet to fully resolve that question.

After college, Obama moved to Chicago and began his three-year period as a community organizer. There, he looked for and found his religious home with the pastor who served as his spiritual mentor, advisor, and obvious surrogate father figure. That choice clearly reflects the powerful emotional magnet of racial grievance. Mendell, Obama's *Chicago Tribune* biographer, wrote of Wright that, "His intellectual sermons sometimes more resemble left-wing political rants than religious teaching."[125] Obama writes in his first book of the first Reverend Wright sermon he heard that it contained a ringing denunciation of poverty caused by "white greed."[126] In an early interview Obama said that he had joined Trinity because it wasn't one of the churches he was trying to organize, "And part of it was there was an explicitly political aspect to the mission *and message of Trinity at that time that*

I found appealing."[127] Obama later disowned agreeing with that message, but it was consistently present during the time that Obama and his family attended the church.

Wright's views are now widely known, and it is difficult to believe that they weren't a recurring staple of the services that Obama attended for twenty years.[128] Indeed, when Obama read the first description of Wright's views in a mass circulation magazine in early in 2007, his response was not one of shocked surprise at something he didn't know, but rather the more politically realistic one: "This doesn't sound real good."[129]

It is easy to criticize Obama for joining and remaining in that church, but a more important question is: Why did he simply not leave? Part of the answer is that Wright's views resonated with some part of him. Perhaps it was his missing out on the radical sixties and hearing about them only through the second hand stories that his mother told him. Perhaps it stemmed from personal experience or identification with the anger he thought he was supposed to, or wanted to feel as an "authentic black." Whatever its source, it seems that the conflict between the racial reconciler and the identification with racial grievance was never fully resolved. In that sense Obama himself is not fully "post-racial" and it is unrealistic to expect him to lead the United States to that Promised Land.

One reason he can't is because the United States can't embrace its post-racial future, whatever that term might mean, before addressing, and resolving, its past racial history. And that requires, in Obama's view, a politics of redemption. In order to be free of its past the United States must truly atone for it. From the standpoint of racial reconciliation Obama is a transition figure.

One indication of this was Obama's decision to check the category "black" on his 2010 census form. He could have checked both black and white, or written in "multi-racial" but did not.[130] Yet, having spent so much time searching for and developing his own black racial identity, and the early questions of whether Obama was "black enough," it would have been surprising had he done otherwise.[131] Still, it would have been an enormous and startling statement in favor of a post-racial American identity had he written in "multi-racial," or even more radically "American."

What Does He Stand For?

The question of what Obama actually thinks regarding the various issues that have arisen when he was a state legislator and U.S. Senator is directly related to another very critical question: What does he stand for? The first question, where does he stand, asks where to locate Obama's views on a political continuum. The second asks what he is really willing to stand up for.

The second question contains both a character and an authenticity question. Are his stated principles and ideals the anchor of his ambitions or are they in the service of them? Or, to put the issue in a slightly different way: Is Obama's "post-partisan" building bridges persona more of a strategic political construction than a true core of his political identity?

As a result of Obama's cool, analytical, and often ironic stance, the public gained few clues during the presidential campaign of his passions, the convictions that fire him. What policy or leadership issues really move him? What does he feel passionately about? Which, if any, is he willing to go to the mat for?

Although delivered in Obama's typical cool and reserved way the answers to these questions have come into clearer view in his presidency. Coolness and passion do apparently coexist in Obama. That passion takes the form of a determination to push through, regardless of the odds, risks, or public receptivity, a transformation agenda in the service of redemption.

3

THE ARC OF AMBITION AND THE DEVELOPMENT OF A STYLE

The presidency is an office in which the occupant's psychology matters a great deal. The reasons are not hard to discern. The president is the United States' only elected official charged with the overall responsibility of the country's domestic and foreign policies. He has ultimate responsibility for the vast federal bureaucracies that deal with all these myriad issues in both areas. His position in the political hierarchy ensures that he has a great deal of policy leverage. His substantial constitutional power, historical precedent, and public expectation amplify that leverage. And lastly, and very importantly, his decisions about whether or not to act and how to do so involve a large element of discretion.

This degree of discretionary power and policy latitude intrinsic to the office means that the president's views of the circumstances that he faces, his views of the tools available to him and their use, and his views of the right course of action are central to understanding the choices and decisions made by his administration. Given the singularity of his position and the discretion of his ultimate decision-making power in so many areas of domestic and foreign policy, examining a president's psychology as it relates to his leadership and the judgments he makes is a necessity, not a luxury. The question is how best to do so.

It is useful to distinguish between a president's character and other elements of his psychology. Character stands at the core of a person's psychology and is the basic foundation upon which personality structures develop and operate.[1] Character shapes beliefs, information processing, and ultimately styles of behavior. It is, therefore, deeply embedded in the most basic and important foundations of psychological functioning and as such it is no surprise that it is deeply embedded in Obama's approach to his presidency.

Character is, basically, a person's psychological stance as he or she confronts the three core domains of experience; finding one's place in the world, developing values and rules by which to navigate life's currents, and developing an understanding of how to deal with the variety of relations that populate every person's life. These three core dimensions of life have corresponding character elements that develop in response to them. They are *ambition*—the development of life's purposes and the honing of the skills to realize them. Developing a viable set of ideals and values to live by and having the courage to follow through on them is the area of *character integrity*. And finally, dealing with the many varieties of interpersonal relationships that characterize life is analyzed under the rubric of *relatedness*.

Obama's Ambition: A Developmental Perspective

Ambition and its realization are central to a well-realized life. Purpose gives life direction. It not only crystallizes goals, but also helps give life meaning.

Ambitions, and the attempt to achieve them, also help focus and channel motivational energies. They can lead people away from dead ends or errors and toward the realization of their aspirations. Working towards ambition's goals is also instrumental in developing habits consistent with their realization. The ability to work hard, to choose responsibility over pleasurable distractions, and to practice the skills necessary to become proficient at your chosen work are all part of the process by which ambition shapes a person's psychology. All of these are evident in Obama's developmental history.

Calling Barack Obama's political rise meteoric may be the true definition of understatement. The basic outlines of the Obama story are well known. He was born into a racially mixed family in 1961 and abandoned by his father at the age of two. His mother remarried an Indonesian man she met at the University of Hawaii and Obama spent his early life in Indonesia and Hawaii. He was a modestly successful high school student, spent his first two college years at a small liberal arts College in California where he was an adequate but not an outstanding student, and then transferred to Columbia where he graduated in 1983. He then worked in New York, first for a business-consulting firm, and then for a public interest research group before moving to Chicago to work as a community organizer for three years before entering Harvard Law School in 1988. While there he was selected as an editor of the *Harvard Law Review* in his first year, and elected as its president in his second year at the age of twenty-eight. He graduated in 1991 and then returned to Chicago where, in 1993, he joined the firm of Davis, Miner, Barnhill & Galland at the age of thirty-two. In 1995 at the age of thirty-four his book *Dreams from My Father* was published. In 1996 he won election to the Illinois state senate and served there from 1996 to 2004, ran for a seat in the House of Representatives in 2002 and lost, then ran successfully for a U.S. Senate seat in 2004.

Two years later on November 8, 2006 Obama and his advisors met to plan a possible presidential campaign.[2] On November 16th, his advisors prepared a detailed memo outlining a strategy,[3] and he announced his candidacy for the presidency in February 2007 at the age of forty-one and was elected president in

November 2008. The president was an archetypical late bloomer, but once his ambition and skills developed and consolidated, he has been on a very fast track indeed.

Family Themes

Looking at the arc of Obama's ambition and his values and ideals, reveals a clear but complicated history. That history includes his mother Stanley Ann Dunham,[4] a strong-willed, unconventional, and politically liberal Caucasian woman who grew up in Iowa, spent her adolescence in Washington State and, when her family moved to Hawaii, enrolled at the university to study Anthropology. There, she met and married Barack's father, an intellectually gifted student from Kenya who, unbeknownst to her, already had a wife and child back home. Barack Obama Sr. left his new American wife and child to attend Harvard where he earned an M.A. in Economics. He never returned.

Instead, he went back to Africa in 1965 with a woman who would become his third wife. He also returned there with large ambitions for an important government position. That dream never materialized either because of policy disagreements with then President Jomo Kenyatta, or perhaps the way in which Obama Sr. expressed them. Like his son, he was a man of strong views and high self-confidence.

Before his father died in 1982, Obama saw him only once more, an awkward, painful, and brief reunion when Obama was ten. Obama's book *Dreams from My Father* is a beautifully written and poignant meditation on his search for an emotional, racial, and communal connection with the father who had abandoned him. His mother would also leave him too, but in a different way. Two years after her divorce, she remarried an Indonesian student, Lolo Soetoro, that she had also met at the University of Hawaii, and the family moved back to his country in 1967, when Obama was six years old. The family lived in Jakarta for four years. Concerned about her son's education, she made arrangements with her parents for Barry (as he was known then) to move back to Hawaii and live with them while finishing school.

It is also possible that the move had something to do with his mother's deteriorating relationship with her second husband. Why that happened has never been discussed, but Judith Kampfner, who is producing a documentary of Ann Dunham's life, wrote in a news account of Obama's mother that, "In Indonesia, she supported radical groups opposed to the military dictatorship."[5] Whether, and to what extent, this is true remains unclear.[6] However, what is clear is that her husband's job and advancement in it were tied to acceptance of the government, not opposition to it.

Obama writes that his mother and stepfather argued about her attending the social gatherings with oilmen from Texas and Louisiana. Attendance was part of his job with the government relations department of an American oil company. Obama quotes Lolo as asking his mother during one fight how it would look for him to attend alone, and reminded her that these were her people, to which she replied "These are *not* my people."[7]

So it is not clear whether Obama's mother was put off by the social requirements of her husband's job, or whether the clash stemmed from her disapproval of her husband working for the government, or both. In any event, by the time Obama's mother moved back to Hawaii with her then young daughter Maya Soetoro, she and her husband had separated.

Obama has made clear that his high school years in Hawaii were a time of questioning, ambivalence, and anger as he tried to navigate his diverse identity elements, both Caucasian and black. In spite of his mother's efforts, much of what he learned about his black identity was self-taught. Her experience with race was viewed through her very optimistic outlook, liberal views, and the events of the 1960s. By the time Obama began his adolescent search for identity over a decade later, the racial calculus of the country had begun a dramatic shift, and of course Hawaii never resembled Mississippi or Chicago for that matter.

All of Obama's identity turmoil took place mostly out of sight of his mother, grandparents, and friends. His mother's research in Indonesia took her away from a primary on-the-spot-mothering role for years at a time and those included his identity forming years as an adolescent. In Remnick's poignant words, "Barry was growing up on the margins of her vision." Obama's grandparents loved him, but their life dreams and experiences had little to offer his quest to forge a racial identity. As to his friends, Obama said little to them about the inner turmoil he later wrote about, keeping his personal struggles to himself even then. In fact, a number of Obama's high school friends were surprised by the force and turmoil of his high school search for racial identity when they read about it in his book *Dreams from My Father*.[8]

Obama considered staying in Hawaii and attending a junior college, but his mother pushed him to reach higher and he attended Occidental College, a small liberal arts college in Southern California. Here again, he was an adequate but not an outstanding student. Yet, it was here that Obama got the first sense of his future political skills, as a speaker in an anti-apartheid rally.

It was at Occidental that Barry became Barack, and he seemed to seriously confront for the first time what he wanted to make of himself and do with his life. He transferred to Columbia University, where he lived a much more monastic life than he had either as an adolescent in Hawaii or as a barely post-adolescent at Occidental. His New York and Columbia years seem to have been the start of Obama taking his life seriously, perhaps stimulated by the death of his father whom he had not seen since the age of ten and with whom now there was no chance of other than a one-sided reconciliation on Obama's part.

From there, the trajectory of Obama's ambition picked up speed and purpose. He experimented, briefly, with the wealth and status temptations that were part of working in the financial services industry, but left to find his calling in community organizing and service. That quest led him eventually to Chicago and the realization that the kind of change he envisioned himself making was better accomplished from the top down than the bottom up.

The conventional wisdom regarding Obama's move to Chicago from New York is that, "Fired with political idealism, he decided to become a community organizer."[9] However, as is often the case with Obama, the truth is more complicated. One of the less widely appreciated aspects of Obama's decision to become a community organizer was that it had as much to do with his own ambitions as a writer as it did with his desire to "leave the world a better place," as he told his grandmother.[10] Remnick, after interviewing Obama's Chicago community organizing mentor, writes,

> Obama admitted to Kellman that he had another motivation for wanting to be an organizer on the South Side. He was thinking about being a novelist. "He told me he had trouble writing, he had to force himself to write. ... He was looking not only for experience, an identity, and a community; he was also in search of material."[11]

Obama's detailed written reports of his fieldwork therefore served another purpose for him as well. "I want to be a writer," Obama told a friend one day referring to those reports. "These are for a book I plan to write."[12] At night, Obama would craft short stories, basing his characters on people and situations he encountered in Roseland, though none of them was ever published. He also apparently kept a daily dairy while living in California, New York, and Chicago, which has not to date been made public.[13]

After several years of hard and frustrating work as a community organizer, Obama realized that any change he might hope to accomplish was better organized from the top down rather than the bottom up. It was then that he applied to and was accepted by Harvard Law School. While there, he achieved his first real independent political success, by being chosen to head the *Harvard Law Review*, the first African American to have achieved that honor. He did so on the basis of the skills that would become so familiar in his later political career, a mix of intelligence, seemingly dispassionate analysis, and an ability to convey the impression to all political sides that he understood and respected their positions.

It was at Harvard as well that he became the beneficiary of an unusual number of professors, who saw these traits and their political potential, and became the first in a long list of mentors in every one of his subsequent legal and political roles that helped him learn the ropes and advanced his career. The nature of those relationships is worth further examination, but here it is enough to note that Harvard seems to be the place where Obama's intelligence, interpersonal skills and the response he evoked solidified his sense of confidence. It also ratified his life's purpose, which was to be in a political position that allowed him the opportunity to make good on his father's failed ambition. Later, that purpose would be fused and viewed through the cardinal virtue of fairness, an important part of his mother's legacy. That legacy was made more powerful by ·her early death just as Obama had started to cease idealizing his father and come to terms with his life long search to understand and accept the father who had abandoned him.

Family Ambitions

In Obama's family and developmental history, we can discern the origins of both his ambition and some of its complications. His father was a person of substantial intellectual abilities who had dreams of great and ultimately unrealized accomplishments. He went back to Africa in 1965 with large ambitions for an important government position. That dream never materialized, as noted, because of his policy disagreements with then President Jomo Kenyatta, or perhaps the way in which Obama Sr. expressed his views.

He was, like his son came to be, a man of strong opinions and high self-confidence. Obama Sr. was the first person in his African district to study abroad and he was the first from his area to travel in an airplane.[14] He was, in terms of intelligence, and in this time period in Africa someone very different from the average and he knew it. Neil Abercrombie, who eventually became a Democratic Congressman, knew Obama Sr. when he first arrived in Hawaii. He and his friends were impressed with "the way he held forth hour after hour,"[15] and he was "the dominant voice in every conversation."[16] Abercrombie said of him though that, "He couldn't bring himself to finesse people. He had to tell them exactly what he thought and what he thought of them. He had to offend them."[17] Obama himself spoke of "my father's imperious manner."[18]

There are several first hand accounts from this period that give a flavor of Obama Sr.'s psychology. In one, Obama Sr. asks his new girlfriend, Ann Dunham, to meet him at the library at one o'clock. She did, and waited, and when he didn't show up at the appointed time, she lay on the grass and fell asleep. She told her son that an hour later,

> He shows up with a couple of his friends. I wake up and the three of them were standing over me, and I heard your father saying, serious as can be, "You see gentlemen, I told you that she was a fine girl and that she would wait for me."[19]

It's a compliment of sorts, delivered in the context of demonstrated and perhaps deliberate rudeness leavened by self-importance.

The other story concerns a trip that Obama Sr. took up to the Lookout, a high spot on Oahu. Obama Sr. drove all the way up the mountain on the wrong side of the road, and as Obama's mother told him, "if you said something, he'd just huff about silly American rules."[20] Rules were for others.

On this particular trip they were accompanied by a newly arrived African student who, taken with Obama senior's pipe, asked if he could try it. He did and started coughing so hard he dropped the pipe and it fell ninety feet down the lookout point. Obama Sr. insisted that the student climb down after it, and the student offered instead to buy a replacement. At that point "your dad picked him clear up off the ground and starting dangling him over the railing." This went on for several moments as people began to stare and finally Obama Sr. put the man down and acted for the rest for the day as if nothing had happened. Obama's mother was very upset, but her future husband told her, "Relax, Anna, I only wanted to teach the chap a lesson about the proper care of other people's property!"[21] There is in this story more than an undertone of arrogance and even sadism. The picture that emerges of Obama's father is that of a very smart man, confident of his talents, and a man who strongly felt that his view of things was the norm against which he should be judged.

Obama's mother, too, was a person of substantial intellectual abilities, with less grandiose ambitions than her husband, but her dreams too led to a separation from her son while she pursued fieldwork, and their fulfillment was cut short by a terminal illness three years after she received her Ph.D.

Thwarted ambitions are also to be found elsewhere in Obama's early experience. The soft-spoken Indonesian Lolo Soetoro, the second husband of Obama's mother, became "a detached heavy drinker and womanizer," family members in Indonesia say.[22] His grandfather Stanley Dunham (whom Obama called "Gramps") with whom he lived while his mother was away doing fieldwork, worked in a series of furniture stores and moved to Hawaii to find better opportunities. His wife, Obama's grandmother, found hers with the Bank of Hawaii where she was eventually promoted to vice president. Her husband faired less well and Obama describes in his book the evenings of quiet desperation as he tried and failed to sell insurance by phone.[23] Obama, then, has had three experiences with close male family figures who wound up failing in their life's ambitions.

The specter of failure must weigh very heavily. And it would not be surprising if Obama avoided risk. Yet he has done precisely the opposite in the first two years of his presidency.

The Arc of Obama's Ambition

The outward manifestations of Obama's ambitions are easily marked. They reflect an early and ambivalent stance toward achievement, and a later transition to its full embrace. One can chart an arc of his ambitions, and the energy and seriousness with which he pursued them, starting with inauspicious beginnings in Indonesia and then Hawaii, and beginning to pick up speed and seriousness sometime at the end of his first year of college. For Obama, as for other Americans, education proved to be both the key and the reflection of that arc.

Indonesia

When Obama's mother married Lolo Soetoro and moved to Indonesia with Barack, he was six. His parents enrolled him in a new neighborhood Catholic school. As the new kid and one who had different features from the other kids, he was teased. He would yell back "Curang, curang!" which translates to "cheater" or "unfair."[24]

Obama writes that he became fluent in Indonesian within six months, but his teachers and classmates remember it differently: "Teachers, former playmates and friends recall a boy who never fully grasped their language and who was very quiet as a result." Israella Pareira Darmawanreira, Obama's 1st-grade teacher, said she attempted to help him learn the Indonesian language by going over pronunciation and vowel sounds. He struggled greatly with the foreign language, she said, and with his studies as a result.[25]

In the 2008 presidential campaign an essay that Obama wrote in the third grade about wanting to be president when he grew up became a small issue. Political opponents tried to suggest that this showed Obama's early and overweening ambition; but this is hardly likely. Indonesia had an office of the president as well, and it is much more likely that the essay represents a child's wish to be or do something important. In the third and fourth grades, "Obama sat in a back corner. He sketched decidedly American cartoon characters during class." Drawing Spider-Man and Batman seem to be about the same level of childhood fantasy as writing you would like "to be president" when you are eight years old. That is to say, it is a child's magic-laden fantasy of having outsized capacities and impact, while being too young to understand how adults have really acquired their capacity to accomplish their life's purposes.

Whether it was because of the difficulty of mastering a new language, his mother's ambitions or worries, or the state of education in the schools that he attended, she signed up for a correspondence course to supplement Obama's education. He writes that his mother used to wake him up at 4 a.m. to study his correspondence course materials, and that he balked at doing so as any child that age would.

Hawaii—The Punahou School

His mother became increasingly dissatisfied with the educational opportunities available to her son in Indonesia and after discussing the situation with her mother and father in Hawaii, she decided to send Obama there for the next stage of his education. With the help of his grandparents, Obama gained a place in the exclusive Punahou School and began his schooling there in the fifth grade.

At Punahou, Barry, as he was called and called himself then, "was never the top student in his class or the hardest worker—a pattern that persisted from the fifth grade to the end of high school."[26] Remnick writes, and it seems clear now that he does so accurately, "Obama had the capacity to be an A student, but his overall aimlessness, the partying, his lack of direction, held him back."[27] Eric Kusunoki, Obama's homeroom teacher, said of him, "All of the teachers acknowledged that he was a sharp kid. Sometimes he didn't challenge himself enough or he could have done better."[28] Obama says of himself during this period, "In Hawaii, I was sort of a goof-off."[29]

Mendell reports that Obama "was always a solid B student, but by his senior year, he was slacking off on his school work in favor of basketball, beach time and parties ... drugs and alcohol."[30] It is clear that whatever academic potential Obama had at this point was undercut by a lack of serious or focused purpose. He was not the all around scholar-athlete, as at home in academic life as on the playing court. And, at that point, he had clearly not absorbed the serious ambitions of his father's legacy or even his mother's more available example.

Obama's mother too noticed that Obama's grades were slipping during his senior year and noticed that he hadn't yet started any college applications. She said to him at one point, "Don't you think you're being a little casual about your future?"[31] At this point, Obama writes that, "I started to tell her how I'd been thinking about maybe not going away for college, how I could stay in Hawaii and take some classes and work part time."[32] She cut him off by telling him he could get into any college in the country if he just put in a little effort—"remember what that's like? Effort?"[33]

She then warned him against becoming a "good-time Charlie." Obama wrote that he replied, "a good-time Charlie, huh? Well, why not? Maybe that's what I want out of life. Look at Gramps. He didn't even go to college." When his mother looked shocked Obama realized he had stumbled onto a mother's fear: "Is that what you're worried about? That I'll end up like Gramps?"[34] His life ambitions had ended with his unsuccessful phone efforts to sell insurance late in the evening.

Later, of course, the worry in Obama's life was he would fail as his father had. When he talks about his father now, "Obama frequently summons a quotation that he believes explains how it directed him. Every man is either trying to *make up for his father's mistakes* or live up to his expectations."[35] Former federal judge Abner Mikva, a longtime Obama mentor, said of Obama, "I think he sees this as a challenge every day, that I want to do better than my father."[36]

Yet, at that point Obama had not learned the difficult truth of his father's life. In his first days in New York he wrote, "I imagined my father sitting at his desk in Nairobi, a big man in government, with clerks and secretaries bringing him papers to sign, a minister calling him for advice, a loving wife and children waiting at home. ..."[37] The reality, Obama would soon learn, was quite different. However, it is interesting that Obama did wind up living out his fantasy of his father's life.

Occidental College

Obama writes that he was accepted into "several respectable schools" and chose Occidental College mainly because of a girl from LA that he had met while she was vacationing in Hawaii. He writes of "just going through the motions" and being as "indifferent towards college as towards most everything else."[38] At Occidental, as had been the case at Punahou, Obama was smart, but still a classic underachiever. One of his professors at Occidental, Roger Boesche, recalled that he had urged Obama to apply himself more vigorously. At the time Obama said he was still "partying pretty hard."[39]

Mendell reports that Obama attended Occidental on a full scholarship.[40] Even so, his time at Occidental was an uneven mixture of studying, partying, identity search, leftist politics, and general college hanging out—a typical amalgam of the proto-typical undergraduate experience in the aftermath of the sixties. It is clear though that race and identity were growing in importance for him.

Obama writes that at Occidental, "to avoid being mistaken for a sellout, *I chose my friends carefully.*"[41] His carefully chosen friends included "the more politically active black students. The foreign students. The Chicanos. The Marxists professors and structural feminists and punk-rock performance poets." As befits those with liberal views, Obama and his friends discussed "neocolonialism, Franz Fanon, Eurocentrism, and patriarchy"[42] in late night college bull sessions.

What stands out here is Obama's studied calculation and its focus. Remember Obama is an adult writing of himself as an eighteen year old, that he carefully selected his friends to solidify both a part of his developing identity and to cultivate an image that is consistent with it. This is the first public mention of this trait, one of Obama's critical talents, but it is certainly not the last. It turns up in his studiously developed persona as a leader able to hear all sides of an argument and respond. And it turns up as well in his moderate persona—although politically he has a strongly liberal, or progressive, outlook. Ultimately, it raises questions of who, exactly, is the "real" Obama, and whether that word has much meaning in such a carefully constructed persona.

This quote also reveals that beneath Obama's calm, placid exterior beats a normal person's efforts to get their way and accomplish their purposes. This helps to explain how the mild mannered Obama ruthlessly and effectively challenged his competitors' nomination petition signatures, including those of his mentor Alice Palmer, to run unopposed for the Democratic Party nomination to the Illinois state senate, which he won.[43] It also helps to explain how Obama managed to win passage of his health care legislation, pragmatically using every procedural maneuver and doing everything it took to gain the necessary votes. And it helps to make clear that the president's attempt to clear the Democratic field of potential rivals to candidates preferred by the president and the party organization for Senate races in Pennsylvania[44] and Colorado[45] is no anomaly.

Obama may be an "idealist" as the conventional wisdom argues, but he is clearly capable of the most hard-headed, even ruthless determination to accomplish his purposes, be they for himself or his presidency. Somewhat bemused, reporter Gwen Ifill, reviewing David Remnick's Obama book, says that in it the president "is also revealed to be, of all things, a politician."[46] Or as another headline put it, "Obama not above political manipulation after all."[47] The surprise that Obama is capable of and often engages in cool, psychologically interior and entirely politically self-interested calculation can be a surprise only to people who have confused dis-passion with lack of self interest, or who have not paid close attention to Obama's political career or behavior in office, or are inhibited by support or idealization from seeing him clearly.

Ambition Ascendant

We can see the arc of Obama's ambition begin to rise and his ambivalence toward achievement begin to get resolved in the change from being a student attending Occidental College in Los Angeles to finishing out his college years at Columbia University. Four more years in New York including a year at Business International and another at the Public Interest Research Group led to an eventual career in politics.[48]

From there, Obama went to Chicago to work as a community organizer as director of the Developing Communities Project. At a Harvard conference he attended two years after moving to Chicago, he raised the question with his first Chicago mentor of whether, "he should go to law school at Harvard and prepare for a life in politics."[49] This is, of course, precisely what he did. To another colleague during the same period he confided an even more ambitious goal—"someday following Harold Washington as mayor of Chicago."[50] By the time Obama got to law school, a classmate remembers him saying "that governor of Illinois would be his dream job."[51] And when he first started to date his future wife Michelle in 1989, her brother Craig Robinson asked him about his plans, and quotes Obama as saying: "I think I'd like to teach at some point in time, and maybe run for public office." Robinson assumed Obama meant he'd like to run for city alderman, but "He said no—at some point he'd like to run for the U.S. Senate. Possibly even run for president at some point."[52]

At Harvard Law School, "he was also among the most driven in his class. In his first year, he entered the competition for the law review."[53] His second year he entered into the stiff competition to become president of *Hardward Law Review* and won, the first American of African descent to reach that position.

Thereafter his skills deepened and his successes multiplied. He emerged from Harvard with a book contract from a major publishing firm and a fair amount of public recognition for a recent law school graduate,[54] even one from Harvard.[55] The law firm that Obama chose, from among the many prestigious offers he received, was one whose principal, Judson Miner, was Chicago's corporation counsel under Harold Washington, the city's first black mayor and he introduced the young attorney to a large number of people involved in Chicago politics.[56]

From there the arc of Obama's ambition and its fulfillment rises in a steep trajectory, though in many instances not fast enough for Obama. There was an appointment to teach at the University of Chicago Law School, board of directors positions, election to the Illinois state senate in 1996, reelected in 1998 and again in 2002, keynote speaker at the Democratic Convention in 2000, election to the U.S. Senate in 2004, Democratic presidential nominee in 2008 and then president.

Once Obama's ambition took hold, he was in a great hurry to realize it. Obama arrived in Springfield Illinois in January 1997, and less than two years later described himself as suffering "chronic restlessness."[57] It was at that point he began his only unsuccessful political campaign, a run for a Congressional seat held by a very popular Democrat Bobby Rush.

Obama's ambitions for higher office were "an open secret in Springfield."[58] Steven J. Rauschenberger, a longtime Republican Illinois State Senator, said of Obama, "He is a very bright but very ambitious person who has always had his eyes on the prize, and it wasn't Springfield. If he deserves to be president, it is not because he was a great legislator."[59]

Obama in the White House: Hard Working, but Not a Workaholic

Obama's work patterns are puzzling. Obama has said of the presidency,

> that the hardest part of the job is staying focused. Because there are so many demands and decisions pressed on you. And you've gotta be able to sort through what are the things that you can delegate, what are the things that deserve just a little bit of your attention, what are the things where you've gotta sit down and really think through—what the options are[60]

Asked by Steve Kroft during a *60 Minutes* interview how many decisions he made each day, Obama replied, "Can't count them." Asked if he was briefed before each meeting he said,

> I am. I spend a lot of time reading. People keep on asking me, "Well, what are you reading these days?" Well, mostly briefing books. You know, you get a little time to read—history or—you know, policy books that are of interest. But there's a huge amount of information that has to be digested, especially right now. Because the complexities of Afghanistan—are matched, maybe even dwarfed, by the complexities of the economic situation. And there are a lot of moving parts to all of that. And although you can't be an expert in all these areas, in order to make good decisions, you've got to have enough depth—that you understand what the core question is—what the main issue is. And—and that requires a lot of—a lot of work.

This seems like a fair description of presidential decision-making and the enormous amount of time it consumes. Obama, as noted, is a person who likes to be prepared, and has substantial confidence in himself—his knowledge, analytical skills and ability to ask the right questions and get to the heart of matters. Given the workload, and the 24/7 pace of events that have to be monitored, addressed, and responded to, Obama's response to the question, "Do you take a day off?" was somewhat unexpected; "I do. It's never a full day. But—*typically Saturdays and Sundays.*"

Obama says his schedule starts about 7 a.m. with a workout, then breakfast, then reading the morning intelligence digest, and then a meeting with the national security staff. And then,

> From 10:00–10:00 on, we're gonna be doing anything from traveling to California, to meeting with governors here, to—you know, sitting down with—my secretary of state, to calling foreign leaders. There's a whole range of things that we might be doing.[61]

This accords with information gathered by other reporters who add to the picture that Obama, "eats dinner with his family, then often returns to work; aides have seen him in the Oval Office as late as 10 p.m., reading briefing papers for the next day."[62] A president's schedule can obviously vary by the day with planned and unannounced trips. And it would probably be too strong to say that presidents are the prisoners of their schedule. They do after all ultimately choose what they do with their time.

The presidency is by no means all work. Play enters in as well. Aside from his daily workout, there are White House dinners and musical evenings,[63] weekend vacations, trips to New York to see Broadway plays,[64] thirty-nine games of golf on presidential road trips as of June 2010,[65] and many other perks that go with being president. I mention these not to criticize Obama's ratio of relaxation to work, but simply to note that while Obama works hard when he works, he is by no means always working.

Obama seems to enjoy glamorous events in contrast to, for example, past presidents like Jimmy Carter or George W. Bush. And, as noted, he also seems to relish the ceremonial aspects of his role like throwing out the first ball at the All-Star Game, making the first pitch on opening day,[66] or ceremonial lunches at the White House for visiting dignitaries.[67] Obama also seems to enjoy his role as a celebrity who is also president. He is not the first president to appear on a late night television show, but he has done more of them and more other kinds of mass entertainment shows (see pp. 37–38) than any other president. This is a president who likes to relax, enjoys his public status as the president and has mixed his celebrity and presidential status to a degree never seen before. This is in large part because no other president has blended the stature of the presidency with such high levels of public acclaim, a mixture of iconic and celebrity status.

Ambition's Skills

Successful ambition requires skills to realize it. Obama's primary skills are clearly his substantial intelligence, his attention to preparation, his ability to convey a calm poised temperament, his ability to get along well with others and to convey the impression that he is open to their viewpoints and perhaps as well their actual positions, and the ability of his oratory to inspire.

It is well to remember that all a candidate's traits and skills are embedded in a psychology and don't necessarily "speak for themselves." Intelligence, for example, is a desirable trait in a president, but there are different kinds of intelligence. Moreover intelligence and good judgment are not necessarily synonymous. And we must also ask of any characteristic to what purposes it is applied. And that is an issue of character.

Intellect

Like much else about Obama, his intelligence has inspired a great deal of hyperbole. Describing Obama as "brilliant" is the most often repeated example of that. The questions that arise here are: what's the difference between being smart and brilliant, and what difference does it make in the presidency?

It is very clear that Obama is, obviously, a very smart man. He is a frequent reader of policy papers and his ability to discuss issues in some depth suggests that he is fully able to absorb the information that he is presented with.[68] He is also a master in the give and take of debate, press Q&As, and in a variety of public settings. As one analysis concluded, "President Obama demonstrated pretty clearly at the Republican retreat that he's quite good off the cuff, nimble and familiar with the details of policy. It pretty much rebutted the charge that he relies on a teleprompter because he needs it."[69] He is, in many ways, an impressive person with the intelligence and rhetorical skills to be an unusually effective leader and possibly among the best of our presidents.

Obama's level of intellectual capacity certainly seems sufficient to have done very well at a top-tier competitive law school. Lawrence Tribe, a Harvard Law School professor who supported his candidacy, remembers the young Obama as "obviously a serious intellectual as well as a fantastic campaigner who can reach across boundaries."[70] Testimonials from such partisan supporters make it difficult to separate out the first characterization from the second. More convincing is a testimony from Republican Steven Rauschenberger, who served with Mr. Obama in the state senate. He says of him, "Barack was one of the smartest people I ever worked with. ... "[71]

It does seem fair therefore to say that Obama has given ample evidence of his intelligence and a supple mind, honed by lawyers' skills in parsing and presenting his preferred positions to the best advantage. There is, however, little evidence that Obama is brilliant. That term ordinarily describes an outstanding talent, evidence of which is significant long lasting accomplishment. We have no difficulty suggesting that Mozart was a brilliant composer, or Thomas Jefferson an accomplished master of many fields. Yet, brilliance does not depend on genius. A new biography of Albert Einstein, thought of as a genius by many because of his quantum theory breakthrough, makes the case that he arrived at this cosmic rearranging of our understanding, not by brilliance, but because of innovative thinking that refused to think inside the conventions of the day.[72]

At any rate, it is hard to find any concrete reflections of brilliance in Obama to date. He was a fair, but not outstanding, student in high school and college. His essay on the nuclear freeze movement, published while he was at Columbia, reflects his political views, but is fairly predictable in its conventional liberal perspective. At

Harvard, he did get good grades and graduated at the top but not the very top of his class. He was selected as a member and then president of the *Harvard Law Review*, but he published no signed articles or opinions, outstanding or otherwise.[73] His community service work in Chicago was intense and dedicated but did not achieve any particularly outstanding results; indeed Obama was very disappointed in what he had been able to achieve.[74] This is no reflection on his efforts. The South Side Chicago housing project where he worked was a very difficult place to make any progress.

One could make the argument that it is in politics that Obama's brilliance shines. Obama himself has pointed to his successful presidential campaign as a strong indicator of his readiness to be president, and to some extent that was true. His campaign was well thought out, well organized, effective and, of course, ultimately successful. It was an impressive performance, but it is not clear that it is any more "brilliant" than the, at the time, innovative 1992 presidential campaign of Bill Clinton. And it certainly didn't keep Obama from running into major difficulties in keeping public support for his agenda.

The Irony of Obama's Rhetorical Skills

If we look to Obama's oratorical skills there is no doubt that he can, as he said of himself, "give a good speech."[75] Fred Greenstein has observed,

> In the use of the bully pulpit, Obama is in a league with the most gifted modern presidential public communicators—Franklin D. Roosevelt, John F. Kennedy, and Ronald Reagan. This proficiency was manifested in the 2004 Democratic convention address that put him on the national political map and continues to be evident in his presidency.[76]

Rhetorical ability, however great, does not exist in a vacuum. Successful rhetoric is a byproduct of its fittingness to the circumstances and its ability to convey an understanding of those circumstances that resonates with the public's sense and responds fairly to its concerns. Obama has had issues in both areas over the years.

In Springfield Obama had to learn to adjust his rhetorical style;

> He had a mastery of constitutional law and a talent for elegant speaking, assets that served him well as a University of Chicago law professor, where students would listen to his lectures, rapt. But in Springfield, his speeches sometimes played out to a soundtrack of groans or the background chatter of indifference. Colleagues sometimes walked around the room while Obama spoke, and he often sat down discouraged.[77]

Moreover, Obama's speeches, as is the case with any candidate or president, have run the gamut. Some are soaring and inspiring to his supporters, others more pedestrian. A basic function of political rhetoric is not only inspiration, but also persuasion. Here Obama has been less successful than his level of skills would lead one to expect.

Two cases in point are the public's support for the president's stimulus and health care initiatives. The president has literally given hundreds of speeches, interviews, and remarks touting these programs but has yet to convince a majority of the public of their benefits. Rhetorical skills, however great and refined by practice as they have been in Obama's case, are most effective when they are used on behalf of policies that resonate with the American public. And in this respect, Obama has a decidedly mixed political record. How else can you explain a headline on the front page of a major American newspaper that reads: "White House searching for a way to reconnect with voters over economy."[78]

Connection is of course a psychological term of particular importance to presidential leadership. For a president, that connection allows him access to present and explain his policies and to ask for support. For the public, that connection is the conduit for their hopes, fears, and questions. They would like to be heard, understood, and listened to, and hear the president explain plainly, fairly, and logically why he has chosen a particular direction. And, if they demur, they want him to explain, plainly and fairly, why he has chosen not to heed them on a particular matter.

Obama has a reputation for a having a cool, steady temperament, and with some exceptions to be covered later that is true. As Obama says of himself, "my wife will tell you I'm not someone who gets too worked up about things."[79] That cool level-headedness helped him in a very rough and tumble presidential campaign,[80] but its impact on his performance in the presidency is more mixed.

Greenstein points out one potential liability of that cool demeanor which is that, "His temperament is *so* even that he risks failing to convey the passion needed to win support."[81] And indeed Obama has been criticized for not showing enough passion about matters like in the recent case of the Gulf oil spill.[82] This led to the spectacle of reporters demanding that the president's press secretary say whether the president was angry at the spill and how, specifically, he had expressed it.[83]

The problem with this is that it neglects the point that the public wants the president to be passionate about policies they think are correct or on which they are open to being convinced. They are not supportive of a president's passion on policies they feel are in error. Critics of Obama's passion level err in not understanding that determination is a very strong passion, though it can be expressed quietly. And that is where Obama's passion lies, in his determination to "power through" on behalf of his redemptive and transformative ambitions. The only problem with this is that the public is definitely not supportive of more passion, even of the determined type, by a president on behalf of policies they outright oppose.

This is the Achilles' heel of the Obama presidency. Obama is famous for being able to repeat, in detail, the arguments of his opponents, but what is less clear is how much he really listens to them with an open mind. The president's self-confidence in his own policy ambitions, reflected in his full steam ahead approach regardless of dropping levels of public support, means in effect he is either not listening to the public, or has heard and discounted them. Either conclusion is not a sanguine development for furthering connection.

In the end it may turn out that Obama is a very talented politician, skilled at negotiating the vicissitudes of his own personal and political ambitions, whose presidency runs into trouble not because his ambitions have kept him from knowing the public's concerns, but because they lead to him discounting or ignoring them.

Organization and Planning

Obama's lofty rhetoric might give the impression of someone who is a bit of a dreamer, and both his wife and his legislative chief of staff have called him one.[84] This is possibly one source of the view that Obama is an "idealist." He may be, but not at the expense of careful planning, and not when it comes to his own ambitions and policy agenda. Obama's domestic policy ambitions may be too much for many to support, and his foreign policy approaches may strike some as utopian, but they are both the result of strongly held views and an equally strong determination to put them into effect. There may well be then the paradox of a president who aspires to idealist policies that are embedded in the application of determined power politics.

As one longtime observer notes, too much focus on his high-minded mission statements, "obscures the real-world organizing skills that proved relevant to Obama's political skills."[85] Another reporter covering him noted, "he is no accidental political tourist. He studies his chosen world like a Talmudist, charting trends and noting which rivals are strong and which weak."[86]

His focus on observational learning started early. Mendell writes of him in his Chicago community organizing period that, "Obama was known for his detailed and calculating planning, a trait he would carry over into politics. He did not like to be surprised in a meeting and he especially loathed being unprepared."[87]

In his early days as a community organizer, Obama was responsible for outreach and writing reports on those that he talked with. As one observer noted, "He studied the characters he encountered so closely that Kruglik says Obama turned his field reports into short stories about the hopes and struggles of the local pastors and congregants with whom he was trying to commune."[88] Another reporter who looked into Obama's early experiences at the Developing Communities Project wrote that,

> Obama's hallmark at DCP was meticulous planning. Before encounters with public officials, Obama would have members rehearse possible scenarios over and over to minimize surprises. DCP board meetings dragged on for hours. There was a meeting before the meeting to map out what was to be

discussed. Then there was the meeting. Then there was the meeting after the meeting to critique how it all went.[89]

Obama used those skills to advantage when his early Chicago political mentor, Alice Palmer, decided to stand for reelection to her old Illinois house seat instead of running for Congress as she had originally planned. Obama, who was then preparing to run for her old seat, filed a series of technical challenges to her nomination petitions that knocked her (and every other potential candidate) out of the race.[90] His decisive and successful effort to terminate her candidacy divided Chicago Democrats for many years. Asked about his choice and tactics, he said, "If you can win, you should win, and get to work doing the people's business."[91] That's not exactly a means justify the ends statement, but it does seem to give his personal ambition wide scope.

His organizing skills have impressed those on both sides of the political isle. The *Wall Street Journal* observed that Obama,

> No doubt ... benefited from the desire of even many Democrats to impeach the polarizing Clinton era. But he also beat Hillary and Bill at their own game. He raised more money, and he outworked them in the small-state caucuses that provided him with his narrow delegate margin. Even now, he is far better organized in swing states than is John McCain's campaign. All of this speaks well of his preparation for November, and perhaps for his potential to govern.[92]

Obama prepares relentlessly for his big events. Remnick notes that it took "hundreds of speeches in black pulpits around the city [Chicago] before he acquired the sense of cadence, Biblical reference, and emotional connection that marked his performances later on."[93] Evans, who covered the Obama campaign, writes that, "Obama studied for the three official presidential debates ... as if he were taking the bar exam. He memorized details on new weapons systems so that he wouldn't look like a neophyte on national defense."[94] In the weeks and days leading up to his speech at the 2004 Democratic convention he worked very hard and deliberately, sometimes sneaking off from the floor budget debates in Springfield and working in a nearby men's room. He had sessions to master the teleprompter, which he had never used before and toured the hall to get a sense of its size and acoustics. He also watched a number of speech videotapes, and received detailed instruction in cadence and delivery.[95]

Obama is clearly a man who takes his performance responsibilities seriously, and has the focus and determination to see them through.

His Father's Voice: Words and the Development of a Style

It was at Occidental College that a seminal event occurred in Obama's life. Though its duration was only a few minutes it echoed down through his life and *was the spark that helped to ignite his meteoric political career. In his first year of school, Obama was asked to speak at a rally against apartheid in South Africa.

The plan among the activists was for Obama to speak for a few minutes and then be hauled off the stage to symbolize what was happening to the black majority there. At first, in Obama's telling, he barely spoke loudly enough to be heard, but then his voice picked up strength and, "the Frisbee players stopped. The crowd was quiet now watching me. Somebody started to clap. ... Then the others started in, clapping, cheering and I knew that I had them, that the connection had been made." His friends came up to remove him from the stage as they had planned,

> and I was supposed to act like I was trying to break free, except a part of me wasn't acting, I really wanted to stay up there, *to hear my voice bouncing off the crowd and returning back to me in applause.* I had so much left to say.[96]

It is clear from this passage that what is being validated or affirmed here is a skill related to accomplishment and self-esteem, but not in the sense of Obama as a good person, which is the basis of the latter. It is at this historical moment that Obama's public racial and political persona begins to come together. He is, after all, speaking out against injustice that is both racial and political. In so doing, he is affirming his identification both as a black and someone willing to take a public moral stance in defense of fairness.

But there is more to this moment than Obama's discovery of his skill at political public speaking and the beginning of the fusion of his racial and political identity under the banner of fighting injustice. It is a direct identification with his father, and his father's once commanding skills. In beginning to find his own voice, Obama rediscovered his father's.

His father's voice was a large part of a commanding presence. Obama's grandmother, with whom he lived during high school, said of his father that "he had a voice like black velvet ... with a British accent. And he used it effectively."[97] Pake Zane, a Chinese Hawaiian who knew Obama's father when he was a student in Hawaii, recalled that,

> the most impressive thing was his voice. His voice and his inflection—he had this Oxford accent. You heard a little Kenyan English, but more this British accent with this really deep, mellow voice that just resounded. If he said something in the room and the room was not real noisy, everybody stopped and turned around. I mean he just had this wonderful, wonderful voice. He was charismatic as a speaker.[98]

And for Obama too, his father's voice became part of an enduring image:

> whenever he spoke—his one leg draped over the other, his large hands out-stretched to direct or deflect attention, his voice deep and sure, cajoling and

laughing—I would see a sudden change take place in my family. ... It fascinated me, this strange power of his.[99]

At Occidental College, sitting down to prepare his two minute anti-apartheid speech, Obama writes of his memory of his father's visit to his class when he was ten, "I started to remember my father's visit to Miss Hefty's class ... *the power of my father's words to transform.*"[100] So here is a direct link between words, the moral framework of speaking out against racial and political injustice and a direct connection and identification with his father, his powerful speaking skills, and their power to transform.

Building on Rhetorical Success

James David Barber called our attention to the importance of a future president's "first independent political success." Barber defines this term somewhat broadly as the period when a future president "found himself" and

> moved beyond the detailed guidance of his family, then his self-esteem was dramatically boosted; then he came forth to be reckoned with by other people. The way he did that was profoundly important. Typically, he grasps that style and hangs on it. Much later, coming into the presidency, something in him remembers his earlier victory and re-emphasizes the style that made it happen.[101]

Barber's account represents a useful initial insight that can, however, be refined and strengthened. Indeed, Obama's developmental history both requires that we do so and suggests on what basis it should be done.

The first modification that might be useful is to focus on a skill rather than or perhaps in addition to the development of a full-fledged style. In this respect political style can be considered as part of the relations dimension of character and reflects how the president deals with his relationship with others, in which a future president's skills are encased. Second, political style can sometimes take a long time to develop and consolidate. This is in part a function of career choices. Obama did not run for and win political office until 1997 at which time he was thirty-four years old. Moreover, based on the evidence Obama's *political* style did not really develop and consolidate until he had served several terms as a state legislator.

It seems more accurate to say in Obama's case then that the interpersonal skills he developed and honed before he entered political office, for example in navigating the left-right debates at Harvard, preceded the opportunity and the fact of the development of his political style in Springfield. Rather than being something that happens "much later" once a president is in office then "remembers" his earlier victory and "re-emphasizes the style that made it happen," the interplay and consolidation of skills and style would seem to develop somewhat in tandem with the discovery of one's skills as the foundation for the development of one's style.

In Obama's case, his style was built on a foundation of intelligence and public fluency that started with that brief speech as a college sophomore, continued its development at Harvard Law School, continued with his now famous anti-war speech delivered in 2002,[102] reached its culmination in Obama's very well received Democratic Party keynote address, and now seems to have found final expression in a seventeen minute, 2,500 hundred word answer to a question about health care.[103] Yet, Obama's political style cannot be reduced to either his intelligence or his speaking skills. It has a great deal to do with the interpersonal aspect of political style, most importantly, his reputation as a conciliator and pragmatist.

Harvard Law School: The Beginnings of a Rorschach Style

Obama has said of himself more than once, "I am like a Rorschach test"[104] and that seems accurate on a personal and political level. Among the most basic questions that arise in relation to Obama's stylistic demeanor is the question of *where* does he really stand. One reason that this question has arisen is because Obama has developed a style that conveys the impression of openness to others' viewpoints, but how much actual openness exists is not easy to discern. Gerald Kellman, an early Chicago mentor from Obama's community organizing days, says of him, "One of the remarkable things is how well he listens to people who are opposed to him."[105]

Larry Walsh, a former Democratic Illinois state senator, said Obama, "was competitive yet careful—and always hard to read."[106] Friends of his from that time say that, "even those close to him did not always know exactly where he stood."[107] It seems fair to say that holding his cards close to his vest is a personal and political stance that allows Obama to put ambiguity to a strategic purpose. In that respect Obama is the creator of his own inkblots.

As one analysis of his style by a member of the law school review noted, "Surrounded by students who enjoyed the sound of their own voices, Mr. Obama cast himself as an eager listener, *sometimes giving warring classmates the impression that he agreed with all of them at once.*"[108] One of the most contentious issues at Harvard and especially at the *Law Review* during his term as editor was the legitimacy and appropriateness of affirmative action. Kantor reports that

> He won the presidency of the Harvard Law Review in part because, weeks before voting, he made a speech in favor of affirmative action that so eloquently summarized the objections to it that the Law Review's conservatives decided he felt their concerns deeply.[109]

Whether he shared them as well as felt them is unclear.

That article also reports,

> People had a way of hearing what they wanted in Mr. Obama's words. Earlier, after a long, tortured discussion about whether it was better to be called "black" or "African-American," Mr. Obama dismissed the question, saying semantics did not matter as much as real-life issues, recalled Cassandra Butts, still a close friend. According to Mr. Ogletree, [a Harvard law professor and a mentor of Mr. Obama] students on each side of the debate thought he was endorsing their side. "Everyone was nodding, Oh, he agrees with me," he said.[110]

Yet, in an interview with the *New York Times* just after being elected as editor, he said of his goals, "I personally am interested in pushing a strong minority perspective. I'm fairly opinionated about this."[111] So a puzzle arises here. Here is an issue on which Obama says he was fairly opinionated, yet he didn't state his view in this fierce debate. One possible answer to that puzzle is that Obama feels that even if he is "fairly opinionated" about an issue his role as leader is to encourage others to reach common ground. Yet, this does not seem to have happened with the affirmative action debates at the *Law Review*.

Obama's campaign theme of trying to bridge differences and find common ground could possibly be one reflection of a view that places guiding debates, but not committing oneself, at the center of the leadership stance he might assume as president. However, this is very inconsistent with public expectations for presidential "leadership," and also is inconsistent with the fact that Obama does have and has expressed specific policy views that he has not been shy about pushing as president.

There is, however, another possible answer to the puzzle and that is found in Obama's observation in that same interview that while he was "fairly opinionated" on this issue it was also true as Obama said that, "as president of the law review, I have a limited role as only first among equals."[112] That quote raises the issue of what he would do as president occupying a very powerful office equipped with many levers of power and authority to leverage his political ambitions.

Obama's first two years of office have offered us an answer. He is a strong and determined advocate for his policy views and ambitions, while maintaining a rhetorical style that emphasizes understanding and appreciating diverse points of view. Yet, in the end, Obama marches to the drumbeat of his own ambitions and worldview.

Obama's Oratory: Power and Puzzles

Among the most important and obvious skills that sustain Obama's success and ambition is his ability to deliver speeches that his adherents view as soaring and inspiring. His speech on race relations, for example, was hailed, even exalted. "One for the history books," "brilliant," and "unequivocal and healing" are some of the accolades heaped upon it. This praise reflects the extraordinary rhetorical skill and power that Obama can bring to bear.

There can be no doubt about the power of Obama's oratory to inspire his followers.[113] His rhetorical skills have been noted and praised by persons from both sides of the political aisle.[114] Yet, Obama's rhetorical skills have not won universal praise, either from the right (as expected), the left, or the center. Some have pointed out that his charisma has the trappings of a "cult of personality."[115] Others, both on the left and the right, have pointed to the gap between "inspiration and substance."[116] Some have wondered whether eloquence is "overrated."[117]

Obama has "the unique ability to offer doctrinaire liberal positions in a way that avoids the stridency of many past Democratic presidential candidates.[118] How does he do this? His preferred rhetorical device, one evident earlier in his career, is that

> When he addresses a contentious issue, Mr. Obama almost always begins his answer with a respectful nod in the direction of the view he is rejecting—a line or two that suggests he understands or perhaps even sympathizes with the concerns of a conservative."[119]

The question is how much of this is rhetorical cover and how much of it is genuine.

Obama is among the youngest presidents ever to serve in that office. His résumé is also among the thinnest of those who have served. This being the case it is not easy to reconcile the record that does exist, as the most liberal senator in that chamber in 2007, with the primary rhetorical emphasis of his campaign, which was pragmatic but also with his call for transformational change. Even those last two terms seem contradictory, but it is in the gap between Obama's sometimes messianic rhetoric and his moderate, pragmatic political persona that the real contradictions come plainly into view.

Obama has made wide use of soaring rhetoric often of apocryphal and biblical dimensions. Building to the rhetorical climax in the speech in which he claimed victory in his quest for the Democratic Party's nomination, he said,

> I am absolutely certain that generations from now, we will be able to look back and tell our children that this was the moment when we began to provide care for the sick and good jobs to the jobless; this was the moment when the rise of the oceans began to slow and our planet began to heal, and so on. ...[120]

Close your eyes and you can easily imagine Obama as a new world prophet forecasting a spiritual and political awakening. Indeed that is how many of his adherents viewed him and it became an enormous problem for him once he was elected and had to lead and govern rather than run for office.

Part II
UNDERSTANDING THE OBAMA PRESIDENCY

4

OBAMA'S PRESIDENTIAL LEADERSHIP: TRANSFORMATION AND REDEMPTION

Presidential leadership is one of the two key elements of presidential performance. Its centrality stems from the president's constitutional position as the fulcrum of policy execution. It is augmented by the increasing centralization of power into the executive branch. This happened as a result of public expectations that the president would assume responsibility for the economy which began with the onset of the Depression and then of national defense and security during the Cold War. Public expectations for an energetic and involved executive, and the enormous power that has been accumulated in the modern presidency, have also influenced the kind of candidates who vie for the office. They are men and women who share a high level of ambition, of course, but they also share a determination to do something with the time they have in office if elected. A core question then is not only what do they want to do but why do they want to do it? This question is a basic one and immediately relevant to Barack Obama and his presidency.

Of Barack Obama, we can legitimately say that he is a puzzling, controversial president whose true nature and political views are difficult to discern, much less categorize. As early as 2007, one commentator noted,[1]

> his entire political persona is an ingeniously crafted human cipher, a man without race, ideology, geographic allegiances or, indeed, sharp edges of any kind. You can't run against him on the issues because you can't even find him on the ideological spectrum.

Three years later, as president, the puzzlement and mystery have not subsided: "President Obama's true nature—radical or pragmatist, partisan or conciliator—is a subject of endless debate. No doubt it will be still a century from now."[2]

How to understand the Obama presidency? This analysis puts forward one linked key; the theme of redemption in the service of transformation viewed through the basic frame of fairness—of the country he leads, the tarnished legacy of his father, his relationship with his mother, and starting with his own self-rescue and redemption.

Understanding President Obama

Obama emerged from his presidential campaign as a man of some ambiguity and mystery. The most obvious reason is that he reached the presidency with a relatively brief political résumé. Obama had served in the Senate only two years (2005–7) before announcing his presidential candidacy in February 2007.[3] And he had served in the Illinois House of Representatives for four two-year terms (1997–2004) before running and winning office as a U.S. senator. However, much of that time, until 2003, was spent as a Democratic junior state senator in a legislature in which Republicans were in the majority. Certainly, his political rise from state senator to president in the space of eleven years can aptly be called meteoric. Moreover, he is, of course, a major historical figure by virtue of being the first American of African descent to run for and win the presidency.

Along the way, he has demonstrated himself to be smart, shrewd, thoughtful, knowledgeable, aloof, charismatic, determined, charming, ambitious, prickly, temperate, idealistic, pragmatic, bold, and visionary. He is clearly a complex president and, as this list of adjectives indicates, a man of many seeming contradictions. That is one reason why it is so easy to find quotes like the ones noted above and in Appendix B.

Obama is an unusual president because the psychological and political questions that frame this analysis are more closely connected for him than they were for the two presidents who preceded him. President Clinton's narcissistic proclivity for risk did not carry over very substantially to his policy leadership. Indeed, his key policy leadership approach, triangulation, was an attempt to hedge his bets and his political prospects. George W. Bush's quest to find a path to a successful adulthood had little to do with the crucial national security issues that shaped his presidency.

However, in Obama the connection is quite pronounced. He is, in his presidential ambitions, his father's son. His father also aimed to be a transformational leader, but failed, bequeathing to Obama a legacy summed up in a quote that Obama has repeatedly used and is clearly very important to him,[4] "Every man is either trying to live up to his father's expectations or making up for his mistakes."[5] This is not merely the ambivalence expressed in someone else's aphorism, but his own experience with his father. Obama has written, "whereas once I had felt the need to live up to his expectations, *I now felt as if I had to make up for all his mistakes.*"[6]

The theme of redemption emerges quite clearly here. It emerges repeatedly in Obama's now famous *Dreams* autobiography, the title of which is about his father, but the substance of which is really about Obama's own self redemption. And there is, finally, Obama's view of this country as one that has, in important ways, failed to measure up to its ideals or its promise. It too stands in need of redemption, and a major purpose of Obama's presidency is, through the force of example, policy and his moral convictions, to insure it.

The Politics of Redemption

Redemption is a term more frequently heard in theology than psychology or political science, but its basic dynamic would be familiar to any psychoanalyst. It begins with a transgression in which the person or object, in this case a country, or a parent, violates either a personal or community norm and feels guilt (or ought to), or does so in a public way, in which case the transgression leads to shame. Obama has said of his past that it, "left me feeling exposed, even slightly ashamed."[7] Redemption is the vehicle through which the person, a president's country, or a president's father, or mother, reacquires standing and legitimacy in the community and it begins with atonement.

The steps through which this can happen are fairly clear in both personal and political life. First, there must be a public acknowledgement of the error or transgression. That is ordinarily followed by a public commitment to change one's ways, and some evidence that you are doing so. And lastly, it involves some form of compensation for the transgression to make those who have been harmed whole.

Some commentators have claimed that, "*Obama's victory, no matter what one's politics is a redemptive moment in the life of a nation* for which race has been called, simply and starkly, 'the American dilemma.'"[8] And there is some truth in that assertion. However, the issue of redemption goes well beyond whatever racial reprieve Americans might have earned by voting an American of African descent into the White House for the first time.

My working theory is that the president entered office having struggled through his personal life and political career with four sets of redemption issues. The first concerns Barack Obama himself and his struggle to come to grips with his family, race, and identity. It is a story of temptations considered, but ultimately put aside in the service of finding and acting on the purpose of his life, pursuing the iconic ends of "fairness" and "social justice." This was a legacy of Obama's mother and his attempts to redeem their relationship. It is a story as well, of his father's complicated legacy, first as an absent but idealized figure and then as a fallen idol whose place in Obama's life needed somehow to be redeemed. And it is now, with Obama as president, the larger issue of America's ideals and its failure to live up to them at home and abroad, and the president's efforts to reclaim, through example, policy and the force of his moral vision, its legitimacy in the world. In the case of the United States, Obama's redemptive ambitions bear a strong resemblance to his presidential initiatives in both domestic and foreign policy.

Obama's Redemption

Remnick, one of Obama's biographers, writes of Obama's autobiography that it is a "mixture of verifiable fact, recollection, recreation, invention, and artful shaping."[9] It is, he suggests, a narrative of assent, which in African American autobiographies the author "begins in a state of incarceration or severe deprivation. He breaks those bonds so that he may go out, discover himself, and make his imprint on the world."[10]

Yet, beginning in a state of severe deprivation that the protagonist overcomes is a difficult barrier for Obama since he grew up middle class, had a loving mother, attentive and caring grandparents, went to elite schools, and was the racial beneficiary of growing up in the post civil rights movement when major laws had been passed and racial attitudes had begun to change for the better.[11] Obama "darkens his canvas as well as he can,"[12] but growing up without a father, because of death, divorce, or abandonment is more common than unique and Obama's middle class circumstances and elite school opportunities are more like life-fulfilling launching pads than barriers to be overcome.

Obama's story is clearly one of assent, but what has been missed so far is that it is at base also a narrative of redemption—Obama's. The redemption narrative requires both a temptation, turned aside or overcome, and a difficult quest, ultimately successfully accomplished after struggle. Obama's autobiography contains both.

A Narrative of Assent Built on Redemption

His remembered childhood begins with an absent, but iconic African father, and a Caucasian mother who takes him to Indonesia to live with her second husband. In one telling,[13] that of his sister Maya, and in Obama's, it is in Indonesia that Obama sees the extreme disparities of wealth and poverty that can be consequences of accidents of birth and that "taught him, at an early age, to empathize with those at the very bottom of the third world" or in Obama's words, "There was a sense, even as a child, that there was this *fundamental unfairness*. ... "[14] Here, at least in one version of Obama's telling, is the possible childhood origin of one part of his presidential quest to help his country live up to its ideals as a place of opportunity and fairness.

The theme of life's unfairness, Obama's notice of it, and his view of its effect on him arise in other contexts as well. In 1999, he wrote an article for his high school magazine, from the perspective of an accomplished graduate, and noted, "My budding awareness of life's unfairness made for a more turbulent adolescence than perhaps some of my classmates' experiences."[15] Obama is speaking here of course as a thirty-eight year old man who has already served four years as a state legislator and fervently aspires to higher office. And in that context, Obama's remembrance of his own moral development may well contain an element of political positioning as well as historical truth.

Searching Grievance for a Cause

Obama was sent back to Hawaii to live with his grandparents and struggled to develop his own character and figure out his racial identity. Living in relatively privileged circumstances, he nonetheless experimented with drugs, racial anger, lackadaisical ambition and sub-par performance. Obama, looking back, said of himself, "As a kid from a broken home and family of relatively modest means, I nursed more resentments than my circumstances justified."[16]

Herein lies the first temptation and challenge to be overcome. In Obama's words, "Junkie, Pothead. That's where I had been headed: the final fatal role of the young would be black man."[17] Friends from this period remember Obama as a rather straight drug dabbler, not someone teetering on the edge of a drug abyss.[18] But the dramatic license fits in well with Obama's redemption narrative. He was someone on the brink, who pulled himself back. This last point is of some importance. In many redemption narratives, the temptations are turned aside or overcome with the help of others. Not so in Obama's case. He was the author of his own redemption. And, having successfully redeemed himself, it follows that he will be able to do the same for this country.

In New York, Temptation

Arriving in New York as a Columbia University student, Obama entered what he called his "monastic period."[19] He wrote of this period, "I decided to buckle down and get serious. I spent a lot of time in the library. I didn't socialize that much. *I was like a monk.*"[20] The parallel is fitting. After all, monks withdraw from society for a time to hone their estheticism and become better able to resist society's temptations. And tempted was what Obama surely was. He wrote of that time,

> with the Wall Street boom, Manhattan was humming, new developments cropping up everywhere; men and women barely out of their twenties already enjoying ridiculous wealth, the fashion merchants fast on their heels. The beauty, the filth and the noise and the excess, all of it dazzled my eyes ...[21]

and clearly tempted him.

Obama wrote that, "There seemed no constraints on ... the manufacture of desire—a more expensive restaurant, a finer suit of clothes, a more expensive nightspot, a more beautiful woman, a more potent high" and there is little doubt that he felt himself in danger of succumbing. He said of himself at the time, "*Uncertain of my ability to steer a course of moderation, fearful of falling into old habits,* I took on the temperament if not the convictions of a street corner preacher, *prepared to see temptation everywhere*, ready to overcome a fragile will."[22] Obama writes that when he first arrived in New York, a friend asked him "what brings you to our fair city?" and Obama's reply obviously reflected his felt need for redemption, "*I want to make amends*, make myself of some use."[23]

At college, Obama began to discover his own voice, literally, and it is the commanding voice and presence of his father. He became politically interested, transferred to a more demanding College (Columbia) and environment (New York), educated himself politically, racially, and culturally, was briefly tempted by the business world, but turned to community organizing and then law school and politics to "make the world a better place." And he tried to do so, first as a community organizer, then as state and then U.S. senator, and now as president.

The Temptations of Capitalism

Herein lies Obama's second temptation, the allure of business, status, and money. After college Obama considered his options. He was drawn to political organizing and he daydreamed through, "romantic images of a past I had never known. They were of the civil rights movement. ... "[24] He saw "the African American community becoming more than just the place you were born, or the house where you had been raised. Through organizing, through shared sacrifice, membership had been earned."[25] And of course membership in the black community, earned membership because as the child of a mixed race family, his racial identity was not fully "given."

Obama then goes on: "That was my idea of organizing. *It was a promise of redemption.*"[26] But that promised redemption had to first survive Obama's flirtation with capitalism.

He wrote to many civil rights organizations for work, but got no replies and decided to take a job at a mid-Manhattan multinational corporation. As the months passed, Obama "felt the idea of becoming an organizer slipping away from me."[27] He got promoted, got his own office, secretary and had money in the bank. Worse,

> I would catch my reflection in the elevator doors—see myself in a suit and tie, a briefcase in my hand—and for a split second, I would imagine myself a captain of industry, barking out orders, closing the deal before I remembered who it was that I had told myself I wanted to be *and felt pangs of guilt for my lack of resolve.*[28]

During this period he wrote to his mother about his corporate job and referred to it as "working for the enemy."[29]

It was at that point that he received a reply to one of his inquiries from Marty Kaufman who was starting an organizing drive in Chicago, and the rest, as they say, is history. So, the second temptation, to which Obama almost, but doesn't, succumb leads him to Chicago, the start of his finding the community he had been searching for, the family that he had longed for, and the work that allowed him to feel that he had redeemed the promise of his ideals.

Abandonment and Redemption

A psychoanalyst would be remiss in not pointing out another deeper level of personal redemption that seems plausibly related to the motivations that fuel the ambitions of this president. And that has to do with the personal redemption made more necessary by having been left on his own, first by his father and then by his mother. It's not at all unusual for children that live though these kinds of circumstances to ask why they weren't enough in some way to keep their parent(s) from leaving. Such experiences can cause a feeling of having not been or done enough to forestall the abandonment, and lead to a sense that in accomplishment there is proof that one was worth staying for.

It is prudent not to place too much weight on this particular element of Obama's transformational ambitions. After all, this analyst has no particular access to that level of Obama's feelings. And this possibility must also contend with the fact that even if this element does hold some importance in Obama's quest for self-redemption, it was rather late in showing itself given Obama's status as a late bloomer. Though one might consider that Obama's lackadaisical approach to his academic achievements and his life more generally, before he started to turn the corner in his very early twenties, was in part a form of self-confirmation of not being good enough to keep his father and then his mother from leaving.

Still, it's worth considering that the *choice* that Obama's father and mother made left him with what would be considered a very normal question under those circumstances and the desire to prove in some way that he really was worth staying around for.

Obama's Redemption and America's

In a 2008 interview, Obama came full circle and linked his own redemption with that of the country. The interview was about his *Dreams* book and Obama was asked about racial progress in the country since Dr. King and the civil rights movement. Obama replied,

> Well, you know, it is frustrating, I think. I talk a lot in the book about my attempts to renew the dream that both of my parents had. I worked as a community organizer in Chicago, [and] was very active in low-income neighborhoods working on issues of crime and education and employment, and seeing that in some ways certain portions of the African-American community are doing as bad, if not worse, and recognizing that my fate remained tied up with their fates. *That my individual salvation is not going to come about without a collective salvation for the country.* Unfortunately, I think that recognition requires that we make sacrifices, and this country has not always been willing to make the sacrifices necessary to bring about a new day and a new age.[30]

In this quote we find two themes. The first is that Obama believes that his and all Americans' salvation is dependent on the collective salvation of the country. Embedded in that view is the assumption that the country and its citizens need salvation. Why? Because they failed to make the sacrifices that Obama views as necessary. And in that view lie the seeds of Obama's transformative ambitions.

Obama's Transformative Ambitions

It is instructive that Obama's autobiography is titled *Dreams from My Father*, rather than *Dreams of My Father*. Obama's *Dream* book is of course a narrative of a boy's search for a lost father and a personal identity. If it were only that, Obama could have easily spoken of the dreams he had of his father's life and identity, which he did to a great degree in his book. But there was more there than that. Obama's dreams *from* his father include transformative ambitions.

After marrying Obama's mother, Barack Obama Sr. was accepted into an economics doctoral program at Harvard and left his wife and new son to attend, but never returned. Instead, he went back to Africa in 1965 with another American woman who would become his third wife, an M.A. in economics and large ambitions for an important government position. Like his son, Obama Sr. had plans to be a transformational leader and "shape the destiny of Africa."[31] That dream soured as a result of a disagreement over national economic policy that led to a break with then President Jomo Kenyatta, a rupture that helped destroy his career. He began drinking more heavily and died a bitter and defeated man.

It is clear from other interviews that Obama has thought about his father's life a great deal.[32] At a conference he attended at Harvard while working as a social worker with Gerald Kellman, the man who had brought him to Chicago, he confided the lessons he had learned from his father's life: "the elder Obama had returned to his native Kenya bursting with intellect and ambition, only to devolve into an embittered bureaucrat because he couldn't find a way to reconcile his ideals with political realities."[33] That is part of the story and the narrative that helped Obama reach a posthumous reconciliation with his father and the idealized image his mother had given him.

Mendell, Obama's biographer, writes that, "Obama idealized his father, or at least the image of his father that was presented to him—brilliant, powerful, confident, successful, moral."[34] It wasn't until much later that Obama learned the truth.

Obama Learns the Truth about his Father

The apocryphal and climactic scene in Obama's *Dreams* book concerning his coming to terms with his father occurs when he visits his father's grave and has an emotional epiphany regarding the nature and meaning of his father's life.[35] That emotional catharsis at his father's gravesite is also a dramatically constructed story, one of the "novelistic contrivances"[36] that Obama uses. Remnick writes that the grave scene has its parallels and that

> At the end of each of the memoir's three long sections ("Origins", "Chicago" and "Kenya"), the narrator is in tears and experiences an epiphany: first, he weeps when he sees his father in a dream and resolves to search for him; then he cries in Jeremiah Wright's church when he sees that he has found both a community and a faith; and, finally, he collapses in tears at his father's grave, when he realizes that after discovering so much about his father—his intelligence, his failures, his tragic end—he is reconciled to his family and his past.[37]

Obama writes in *Dreams* that he learned about the reality of his father's life from his (Barack's) half sister Auma when she visited him in Chicago. She asks about his organizing, which dates the visit to a time when Obama first came to Chicago,[38] and Obama writes of it being fifteen years later than the date of his father's visit when he was ten, so that places the year at 1986 when Obama was twenty-five.

He writes that the iconic single image he had constructed of his father—"brilliant scholar, generous friend, upstanding leader," compliments of his mother's gauzy narratives, crumbled before the much harsher realities of his father's life as "a bitter drunk, an abusive husband, a defeated lonely bureaucrat."[39] And who, through his father, had Obama sought to indentify himself with? "*It was in my father's image ... that I had packed all the attributes that I sought in myself, the attributes of Martin (Luther King), and Malcolm (X), (W.E.B.) DuBois, and (Nelson) Mandela*"[40]—transformational leaders all.

And anticipating the book's narrative of redemption, his own as well as his father's, Obama ends with a series of questions rather than any conclusion; "What had happened to all his vigor, his promise? What shaped his ambitions?" That scene ends with Auma telling Obama that he must return "home" to Africa to "see his father there," a trip that Obama eventually takes, and ends with the cathartic scene at his father's grave.

That trip took place in the summer of 1988, when Obama was twenty-seven years old and just two years after his half-sister Auma visited him in Chicago and told him the real story of his father's life. Consider the periods of time involved in Obama's narrative. Starting from his earliest childhood, with the aid of his mother's unrealistically elevating stories about his father's nature and accomplishments, Obama took in these images and made them his own. They developed and con-solidated over at least two decades before they were roughly destroyed by truth. The truth hit Obama pretty hard. He writes that, "I felt as if my world had been turned on its head; as if I had woken up to find a blue sun in the yellow sky, or heard animals speaking like men."[41]

And yet, just two years later, during which he faced the difficult daily task of organizing on Chicago's South Side, Obama would have us believe that he resolved the disorienting truth of his father's real life, in the space of a climactic gravesite epiphany. Perhaps, but literary contrivances aside, it is far more likely that the complete and almost immediate reorientation of a core aspect of one's identity is unlikely to take place on such short notice. It's more likely that Obama did the best thing possible in those circumstances, which was to find a way to forgive his father, which he did by understanding more deeply his father's circumstances and the pressures on him. This is, of course, one way to redeem his father in his own identity, and there then remains only the task of redeeming his father's ambitions through his.

Freud thought fathers and sons were often in competition, and there is truth to that. Yet, it is also true that parents can often live out aspects of their own unfulfilled ambitions, even though they may be relatively successful, through the successful accomplishments of their children. That is, the key dynamic is not so much competition, but compensation. But of course, Obama's father was not alive to do that. And so, on Obama fell the double task of understanding and reclaiming the meaning of his father's real life as part of his own legacy, and redeeming his father's legacy through his own successful ambitions.

Redemption, Transformation, and Presidential Greatness

And that brings us directly to Obama's leadership ambitions and style. That subject begins with a question. How do you successfully redeem yourself, your relationship with your mother, your father and your country? The answer is by becoming a successful and "great" transformational leader whose ambition is in service of national redemption, framed through the iconic legacy of his mother's fairness. Obama's efforts to redeem his relationship with his mother is the other major redemption task that has motivated him and is so central to his presidency that it is taken up separately in Chapter 5 (see pp. 100–101).

Obama has been quite clear about both of these goals. Announcing his candidacy in Springfield, Illinois he said, "let us transform this nation."[42] Campaigning in Iowa he said directly "I want to transform this country … "[43] Campaigning in New Hampshire, he told those assembled, "we're going to change the country and change the world."[44] In his inaugural address, he called on his fellow citizens to help "remake America"—not change mind you, but remake.[45] On his hundredth day in office at a town meeting he said,

> So today, on my 100th day in office, I've come to report to you, the American people, that we have begun to pick ourselves up and dust ourselves off, and we've begun the work of remaking America. We're working to remake America.[46]

Asked in an interview about his personal list of heroes that include Lincoln, FDR, Gandhi, and Martin Luther King he replied, "When I think of what makes them together, I'm enamored of people who change the framework, who don't take something as a given, but scramble it."[47] Discussing Obama's role as commander in chief and having two wars to contend with, one report noted, "Mr. Obama sees them as 'problems that need managing,' as one adviser put it, while he pursues his mission of transforming America."[48]

Is this merely political rhetoric, just an administration meme? Perhaps, but Obama's large scale, transformative policy agenda would seem to indicate that he is serious. By succeeding in what he feels is the urgent task of transforming the country and redeeming its promises of justice and fairness, his mother's redemptive legacy, at home and abroad, Obama carries on his father's life work, but success-fully, thus vindicating his efforts and burnishing his tarnished legacy. At the same time, by so doing, he establishes himself as a "great president" and redeems his promise and own early lack of accomplishment. Obama has been quite clear about the link between both of these goals and that it is precisely what he said he aspires to. After Republican Scott Brown was elected senator in liberal Massachusetts and some in the administration suggested pulling back on health reform, Obama said to his advisors, "I'd rather be a one-term President *and do big things* than a two-term President and just do small things."[49]

Ryan Lizza, who covered Obama on the campaign trail wrote that he is,

> keenly aware that presidential politics is about timing, and that at this extre-mely low moment in American political life, there is a need for someone—*and he firmly believes that someone is him*—to lift up the nation in a way no politician has in nearly half a century.[50]

In an early interview, he himself said directly that he wished to be a "great president."[51] He was then asked about what he meant during a *Meet the Press* interview:[52]

MR. RUSSERT: You told *Men's Vogue Magazine*, that if you wanted to be president, you shouldn't just think about being president, that you should want to be a great president. So you've clearly given this some thought.

SEN. OBAMA: Yes.

MR. RUSSERT: And what would, in your mind, define a great president?

SEN. OBAMA: But I think, when I think about great presidents, I think about those *who transform how we think about ourselves as a country* in fundamental ways so that, that, at the end of their tenure, we have looked and said to ours—that's who we are. And, and our, our—and for me at least, that means that we have a more expansive view of our democracy, that we've included more people into the bounty of this country. ... *And they transformed the culture* and not simply promoted one or two particular issues.

The exchange makes Obama's view of transformation as involving remaking America's basic culture and identity in the service of his view of fairness quite clear.

These purposes are, in important respects, compensatory, but not directly for Obama himself. He had, after all, redeemed himself, as a careful analysis of his life's narrative makes clear.

There remains the question of how one becomes a great president. There is no doubt that "greatness" comes in successfully meeting a great national crisis, as Lincoln did with the Civil War or FDR did with Pearl Harbor and the Great Depression. Obama came to office with no comparable crisis. The solution to the liquidity crises, the enormous infusion of government funds (TARP), was put into effect by George W. Bush and Obama's role was to continue that policy and to help resolve the economic dislocations that resulted from the recession.

That is one of several reasons that Obama tried to leverage the economic situation he inherited in order to accomplish big things. In his speech to a joint session of Congress in February of 2009 he said, "History reminds us that at every moment of economic upheaval and transformation, this nation has responded with bold action and big ideas."[53] His use of the word "upheaval" rather than "crisis" was both honest and telling. Still, as we will discuss in a later chapter (p. 144), Obama has tried to use that upheaval to further a host of major policy initiatives that have very little direct relationship to it.

If you can't have a major war or a Great Depression to increase your presidential stature, the next best thing is to be on record as having passed major legislation. Alter writes of the decision regarding health care, "So Obama decided early to bet his domestic presidency on health care. It wasn't that he would face certain defeat in 2010 without it; *unemployment and Afghanistan were much bigger issues for voters. But for greatness he needed health care. ...* "[54]

As important as big, major, and historic legislation is to Obama's greatness ambitions, his claims, in his eyes, do not rest on the accomplishment of his policy objectives alone. There is no doubt that part of presidential greatness in Obama's eyes has to do with moral vision and urgency. Here Martin Luther King is one of Obama's great exemplars. But there is more to greatness than moral vision; there is the successfully accomplished transformation that comes from having confronted and resolved a problem of enormous public magnitude. King did it for American race relations, although his work remains to be finished. Yet, it is clear that this avenue of historic accomplishment is a dead-end for Obama. It is clear that Obama will not usher in a new golden post-racial age in America because his identity is still so closely tied to the old one.

Who else is there for Obama to aspire to? Franklin Delano Roosevelt? He addressed and is given historical credit for having laid the groundwork for victory in World War II and for recovery from the 1939 depression. But moral vision? Not really; FDR is legitimately remembered as having a political grasp on presidential necessity, not a moral one.

Woodrow Wilson? His moral vision for the world never passed the Senate. Lyndon Baines Johnson? His "Great Society" has to be measured on the scales that contain Vietnam and the souring of the public toward "big government." Ronald

Reagan? Obama credited him with having been a successful transformer,[55] but he has spent his life fighting the ideas that Reagan proposed and has frequently and harshly critiqued the lack of any ethical or moral concerns reflected in Reagan's policies toward the plight of the less fortunate.

The only American political leader with the moral vision and stature and transformational accomplishments to qualify as iconic in Obama's firmament of heroes is Abraham Lincoln.

Obama as Lincoln

The themes of redemption and transformation that underlie the Obama presidency also throw light on the meaning of Lincoln to the president. The president has encouraged comparisons to Lincoln,[56] so much so that one of his supporters has noted, "Barack Obama has never been shy about comparing himself to Abraham Lincoln."[57] Evidence to support this conclusion abounds.

Obama's announcement of his candidacy in Springfield, Illinois "was aimed at assimilating the greater imagery of Lincoln that looms over Springfield, of a man who sought to heal a nation at war with itself, its populace sharply divided."[58] He took his oath of office using Lincoln's Bible,[59] the luncheon afterwards served food enjoyed by Lincoln (seafood stew, wild game, root vegetables, and apple cake) on a replica of the china service selected by Lincoln's wife,[60] and a gala pre-inaugural party was staged at the Lincoln Memorial.[61] In a more political vein, Obama specifically encouraged the idea that he, like Lincoln, would appoint a "team of rivals" in his cabinet.[62] And he followed Lincoln's route to Washington by train for his inaugural.[63] All of these efforts led one *New York Times* reporter to write, "Mr. Obama has taken the identification with the 16th president to a new level."[64]

Obama sees himself as following in Lincoln's footsteps in more ways than one. He has written,

> In Lincoln's rise from poverty, his ultimate mastery of language and law, his capacity to overcome personal loss and remain determined in the face of repeated defeat—in all this, he reminded me not just of my own struggles. He also reminded me of a larger, fundamental element of American life—the enduring belief that we can constantly remake ourselves to fit our larger dreams.[65]

Obama has often named Lincoln as one of his political heroes. In doing so, there is the obvious political benefit of publicly identifying with a president that most Americans and scholars rate as a great one. Yet, there is more to it than that. Lincoln of course took office at the time of the greatest crisis in American national history, the potential break up of the union. He saw that crisis through to a successful conclusion and in the process of doing so removed an ugly stain on the country's character and history by signing the Emancipation Proclamation.

Lincoln is commonly called the "great emancipator," but he was as well a redeemer, redeeming the United States from the stain of slavery.[66] In an interview with the author of a book that used that phrase in its title, Allen C. Guelzo notes that, "The phrase is actually borrowed from an editorial Walt Whitman wrote for the Brooklyn Daily Eagle in 1856, when Whitman was bemoaning the disastrous lack of character in the presidential candidates of that year. He hoped for a 'redeemer President.'" But Guezlo also notes that beyond the association with Whitman, the phrase "Redeemer President" also underscores that "Lincoln turned out to be much more a redeemer than Whitman could have dreamt in 1856: Lincoln redeemed the republic from slavery and disunion, and allowed it once more to stand up as the champion of human freedom."[67] Of course a redeemer in this instance is one who undertakes, and in Lincoln's case succeeds, in a political act of national redemption.

And therein lies the basis, I think, of Obama's identification with Lincoln. In his view, like Lincoln, he too faced a large crisis, indeed more than one, on coming into office. And while Lincoln correctly saw slavery as the great moral stain on American democracy, Obama too sees other multiple stains on the United States' national identity that must be expiated, including but not limited to the continuing vestiges of racism, arrogance, and economic inequality.

And keep in mind that in Obama's view of Lincoln, "when the time came to confront the greatest moral challenge this nation has ever faced, this all too human man did not pass the challenge on to future generations."[68] We can hear echoes of Obama's view of why Lincoln is a great president, and his own aspirations to be like him in any number of his "why we can't wait" pronouncements:

> What I say is that the challenges we face are too large to ignore. The cost of our health care is too high to ignore. The dependence on oil is too dangerous to ignore. Our education deficit is growing too wide to ignore. To kick these problems down the road for another 4 years or another 8 years would be to continue the same irresponsibility that led us to this point. That's not why I ran for this office. I didn't come here to pass on our problems to the next President or the next generation; I came here to solve them.[69]

It is difficult not to notice that the president's pronouncements do not appear to apply to his large budgets or the enormous debt they generate.[70]

Speaking of the need for "comprehensive immigration reform," the president said, "And while this work isn't easy, and the changes we seek won't always happen overnight, what we've made clear is that this administration will not just kick the can down the road. Immigration reform is no exception."[71]

America's Foreign and Domestic Policy Failings

Redemption requires the acknowledgement of moral, ethical or behavioral failures. It is clear that the president sees America as not having lived up to its ideals and responsibilities in foreign policy as well. In a series of highly visible venues abroad, the president has called attention to the errors and arrogance of this country's foreign policy. His purpose in doing so is both strategic and redemptive.

The strategic aspect of these expressions of mistakes is clearly intended to reset America's relationships with the world and herald the arrival of Obama's new approach to American foreign policy. The assumption behind doing so is that if the country admits error and publicly promises to turn a new leaf, our allies and our competitors will take note and our enemies will feel that they may be able to reach accommodation with a new, less belligerent and more honest America. That remains to be seen.

Aside from whatever strategic calculations and hopes are involved in Obama's quotes that are reported and analyzed below, they mark an extraordinary public announcement of error and contrition on the part of an American president. In their number, range, and sharpness they are simply unprecedented. And they are all the more so because strategically, they represent a calculated risk with low probabilities of high pay-offs.

Some of the president's criticisms make fair points. Others make points that have been, are, and ought to be furiously debated. What unites both kinds, however, is that Obama clearly believes them to be true. Taken as a whole, his remarks definitely indicate that he believes that the country has made mistakes of style but also serious and harmful strategic and policy mistakes that ultimately are a reflection of moral and ethical failings, going back decades. The president not only means to name them but correct them, and in this ambition lies the administration's politics of redemption.

America's Faults: A Bill of Particulars

Obama implicitly chastised the United States in a 2009 Prague speech, "as having a moral responsibility to act to abolish nuclear arms because it was the only nuclear power to have used a nuclear weapon."[72] Clearly that decision was morally tainted in Obama's view and calls for reparative, which is to say redemptive, policies. His policies that aim for a world without nuclear weapons are a response to that view.

In a European town hall meeting, Obama said that the United States had "failed to appreciate Europe's leading role in the world" and that "there have been times when America has shown arrogance and been dismissive, even derisive."[73] Perhaps Mr. Obama was referring to his view that, "we dismissed European reservations about the wisdom and necessity of the Iraq war."[74] Obama had also written, "In Asia, we belittled South Korean efforts to improve relations with the North."[75]

In a speech to the Turkish parliament, Obama said,

> The United States is still working through some of our own darker periods in our history. Facing the Washington Monument that I spoke of is a memorial of Abraham Lincoln, the man who freed those who were enslaved even after

Washington led our Revolution. Our country still struggles with the legacies of slavery and segregation, the past treatment of Native Americans.

And he also noted in the same speech that, "in the United States, we recently ordered the prison at Guantanamo Bay closed. That's why we prohibited—without exception or equivocation—the use of torture."[76] More specifically and pointedly in a speech at the National Archives on the government's post 9/11 response, Obama said,

> faced with an uncertain threat, our government made a series of hasty decisions. I believe that many of these decisions were motivated by a sincere desire to protect the American people. But I also believe that all too often our government made decisions based on fear rather than foresight; that all too often *our government trimmed facts and evidence to fit ideological predispositions. Instead of strategically applying our power and our principles, too often we set those principles aside as luxuries that we could no longer afford* ... In other words, we went off course ... decisions that were made over the last eight years established an ad hoc legal approach for fighting terrorism that was neither effective nor sustainable—*a framework that failed to rely on our legal traditions and time-tested institutions, and that failed to use our values as a compass.*[77]

The implication of this statement is that the United States had, until he prohibited it, practiced and condoned torture and tried to obfuscate its role in doing so. Clearly the public statement of transgression, and the public acknowledgment are part of Obama's public process of atonement and redemption.

Along similar lines, at the Summit of the Americas Obama said, "we have at times been disengaged, and at times we sought to dictate our terms. But I pledge to you that we seek an equal partnership."[78] And in the president's first interview with an Arab newspaper he said of the United States, "all too often the United States starts by dictating ... "[79] He went on to say, "the same respect and partnership that America had with the Muslim world as recently as 20 or 30 years ago, there's no reason why we can't restore that."[80]

Obama made these statements officially, as president of the United States. In doing so he presumed to speak for the whole country, although many Americans would disagree with the specifics of his characterizations, and the legitimacy of his voicing these contested claims abroad as official statements of a U. S. president. As noted, a number of these criticisms are debatable. For example, regarding Iraq, it would be more accurate to say that the Bush administration did consider European objections, but decided it had to act in spite of them. Or with regard to the Bush administration's response to South Korea's Sunshine Policy, a more accurate statement would have acknowledged that the Bush administration worried that such overtures would reward provocative North Korean behavior and not result in any policy changes, a worry that seems prudent given North Korean military threats to attack South Korea,[81] its decision to go ahead with a second nuclear bomb test[82] and the testing of new missiles.[83]

Criticizing Arizona

It is possible to assert that the criticisms that Obama leveled during the campaign of American's past and present foreign policies were part of the expected behavior of a candidate trying to gain office. It is also possible to assert that the president's public criticisms abroad of American policies, however unusual, were offered in an attempt to "reset" what the president felt were hostile views of past policies and hence the United States (A less charitable view would assign some motivation for these public rebukes as an effort for the president to disparage his predecessors and at the same time raise his own moral or leadership stature.)

Both of these possible explanations for Obama's criticisms of American foreign policy however, are called into question by the president's critical comments on a bill passed by the Arizona State Legislature and signed into a law by its governor. His comments echoed the harsher characterization of the law by Mexico's president who was standing beside him at a joint news conference. The Arizona law made it a crime to be in the state illegally. It also allowed the asking of questions about a person's immigration status if police in the process of enforcing another law stopped them. The response to the law was shrill, with some comparing Arizona to Nazi Germany and South Africa. Accusations of "racial profiling" were also made.[84] Others expressed the view that enforcing the country's immigration laws was long overdue and a national Pew survey found broad support for allowing police to require documents verifying legal status (73 percent), detaining people who didn't have then (67 percent), and allowing police to question anyone they thought was in the country illegally (62 percent).[85]

Almost a month before the press conference with Mexican President Calderón, Obama said of the law that it threatens to, "undermine basic notions of fairness that we cherish as Americans ... "[86] A little later, in another speech, alluding to the failure to pass what proponents term a "comprehensive" immigration law, Obama said, "Our failure to act responsibly at the federal level will only open the door to irresponsibility by others. That includes, for example, the recent efforts in Arizona."[87] So, the Arizona law was irresponsible.

In his prepared remarks at a joint press event with the Mexican president, Obama called the law "misguided," and said "I want everyone, American and Mexican, to know my administration is taking a very close look at the Arizona law. We're examining any implications, especially for civil rights." In his prepared remarks President Calderón said of the bill,

> we will retain our firm rejection to criminalize migration so that people that work and provide things to this nation will be treated as criminals. And we

oppose firmly the S.B. 1070 Arizona law given in fair principles that are partial and discriminatory.

Lawrence Jacobs, a respected American politics professor, said it was "almost unheard of" for a foreign leader to criticize a state law while visiting the United States. He noted "The common practice and courtesy is not to interfere in another country's internal affairs."[88] President Obama was asked in the Q&A whether he agreed that the law was "discriminatory" and "destructive." He replied,

> I think the Arizona law has the potential of being applied in a discriminatory fashion ... I think a fair reading of the language of the statute indicates that it gives the possibility of individuals who are deemed suspicious of being illegal immigrants from [sic] being harassed or arrested.

He went on to say that, "In the United States of America, no law-abiding person— be they an American citizen, a legal immigrant, or a visitor or tourist from Mexico—should ever be subject to suspicion simply because of what they look like."[89] That same report noted that, "Obama didn't seem put off" by Calderón's remarks and indeed it seems highly unlikely that that would have been made public without President Obama's prior assent.

The next day, in a speech before a joint session of Congress, President Calderón said of the law that "it institutes a terrible idea making racial profiling as a basis for law enforcement."[90] Democrats and White House officials rose to their feet to cheer, including Attorney General Eric Holder and Homeland Security Secretary Janet Napolitano."[91]

The point here is not to take issue with the president's reservations about the Arizona immigration law. Though his stated worries are concerns not actual facts, he is certainly entitled to them. Nor is the point to debate the president's questionable assertions like his view that Americans are frustrated because Congress has not yet passed "comprehensive immigration reform," a term that has varied meanings and public responses which are complex, ambivalent, and strongly held.

The point here is that the president certainly agreed to allow a foreign leader to criticize an American law duly and legally passed that has the support of a majority of the American public. The president in no way disassociated himself from the Mexican president's harsh and in fairness inaccurate depiction of the law, and indeed joined him in criticizing the law, thus seeming to add legitimacy to the Mexican president's claims. Moreover, senior members of the administration then joined in this public criticism by giving it a standing ovation when it was repeated before Congress. This too reinforced the sense that it is not only the president's view, but also the view of his administration, that the United States, and especially Arizona and its duly elected political leaders, are ethically, politically, and legally on the wrong side of Obama's moral calculus and thus in need of redemption.

American Exceptionalism: The Moral Example Dimension

The idea of American exceptionalism is central to American identity, although scholars and pundits don't agree on exactly what it entails. For James Q. Wilson, Alexis de Tocqueville had it right in his 1835 analysis, *Democracy in America*,[92] by concentrating on the fact "That there was and continues to be now in this country a remarkable commitment to liberty, egalitarianism, individualism, and laissez-faire values."[93] For the seminal analysis of Seymour Martin Lipset, the core question was applied in the context of efforts to account for the weakness of working–class radicalism in the United States.[94] And for some, especially those on the left, American exceptionalism is a myth.[95]

At its core, the term reflects America's unique cultural amalgam of freedom and individualism coupled with egalitarian values including a commitment to opportunity and economic mobility. These are encased in a political culture that emphasizes that being an American is a matter of affirming and accepting the country's cultural, economic, and political premises rather than a matter of racial or ethnic lineage. And it reflects the belief that despite the errors this country has made at home and abroad, the United States has, overall, been a force for freedom and opportunity worldwide. It is a country in which more of its citizens express pride than any other country in the world, and in which it has become somewhat taken for granted that its president would have the same pride as well.

On this matter, as on others, it is difficult to pin the president down since he has repeatedly publicly praised the country's virtues and also criticized it for its strategic and moral failings. So, early in his presidency, asked about American exceptionalism, he had this to say:

Q: Thank you, Mr. President … could I ask you whether you subscribe, as many of your predecessors have, to the school of American exceptionalism that sees America as uniquely qualified to lead the world, or do you have a slightly different philosophy? And if so, would you be able to elaborate on it?

PRESIDENT OBAMA: I believe in American exceptionalism, just as I suspect that the Brits believe in British exceptionalism and the Greeks believe in Greek exceptionalism. … [96]

One might characterize this as the view that America is special, but every person believes their country is, and so in that respect Americans' view of their own country being special is in itself nothing special. However, Obama is also on record as supporting the unique nature of America and its role in underwriting "global security for over six decades—a time that, for all its problems, has seen walls come down, markets open, billions lifted from poverty, unparalleled scientific progress, and advancing frontiers of human liberty."[97]

So, which is it? As with many issues, Obama has spoken so often and approached the issue from so many sides that it is hard to pin down exactly what he thinks. But a possible resolution of the issue comes from Valerie Jarrett, one of the president's closest Chicago friends and now a senior White House advisor. In an interview conducted for David Remnick's Obama biography, she recalled her first meeting with Obama during which they had a long discussion of their childhood travels. Jarrett, daughter of a prominent Chicago African American family, had been born in Iran and was fluent in Farsi and French. She told Remnick, "He and I shared a view where the United States fits into the world, which is often different from the view people have who have not traveled outside of the United States as young children." Through her travels, she told Remnick, "she had come to see the United States with a greater objectivity, *as one country among many*, rather than as the center of all wisdom and experience."[98] This was, presumably, one of the views she shared with Obama.

Critics have read Obama's statement to mean that America itself is nothing special and that is a plausible inference, but there is more going on here than that. There is one understanding of the national uniqueness that Obama has expressed a number of times and that is consistent with Obama's general redemptive assumptions. It is that America has a unique responsibility of being a moral exemplar, and can fulfill this role according to Obama only by example of its behavior and living up to its responsibilities as Obama sees them.

America's Special Role: Leading by Example

Obama has made this argument: "I do believe that America has a special role to play in trying to lift up a set of ideas, a set of rules of conduct for countries that aren't imposed by force but by example."[99] Traveling in the Middle East he said, "I think the thing that we can do most importantly is serve as a good role model."[100] At his maiden speech at the United Nations, Obama said that, "Every nation must know: America will live its values, and we will lead by example."[101]

It is tempting to view the president's "leading by example" motif though the lens of inspirational rhetoric honored more in the abstract than in fact. And there is some truth to this view. Leading by example has not kept the president from increasing troop levels in Afghanistan, increasing the number of drone attacks against terrorists in Pakistan, or exploring whether to carve out an exception to Miranda warnings for captured terrorists. On the other hand, it would be premature to dismiss these statements for two reasons: they are central to the administration's approach to some basic national security issues, and second, they are consistent with Obama's redemption approach to American foreign policy even within the framework of American exceptionalism.

The leading by example motif in Obama's worldview shares the cognitive underpinnings of behavioral economics. This alternative to the traditional rational actor models sees individuals struggling to make rational choices but beset by myriad information processing errors and "biases." This is the view of the two key University of Chicago members of the Obama administration, Austan Goolsbee at the Council of Economic Advisers and Cass Sunstein, Director of the Office of Information and Regulatory Affairs in the Office of Management and Budget. Their initiatives have centered on rearranging the behavioral incentives that government provides in its policies so that people can make "healthier choices," as defined by those who lay them out.[102] This they term "libertarian paternalism" and view it as "neither right nor left neither Democratic or Republican."[103]

What its authors view as their non-ideological premises fit in rather well with Obama's views of himself as being pragmatic and non-ideological and with the idea that government should intervene in a number of areas in the lives of its citizens by shaping the choices that they have available. This is, of course, what government policy has always done, but Thayer and Sunstein see a difference this time because government is acting on the principles derived from a scientifically based paternalism. And as one report noted, "this Administration is using it to try to transform the country."[104]

What does this have to do with the United States leading by example in its foreign policy? Just this. Among the elements that comprise the field of behavioral economics is a focus on social norms, the ways in which the behavior of the group can influence the behavior of the individual. This is conventional wisdom in social psychology research and has been since Solomon Asch demonstrated that individuals would distort clearly obvious physical data to comply with the (rigged) views expressed by a group.[105]

What Thayer and Sunstein focus on though is the way in which government behavior can set the norm that others will presumably follow. One small illustration of this assumption in action is the president's executive order banning civilian employees in the federal government from texting while driving on the assumption that, "the Federal Government can and should demonstrate leadership in reducing the dangers of text messaging while driving."[106] The idea that the government has a moral and policy responsibility to set the tone and lead by example is consistent with Obama's moral framing of policy issues and the view that both he and his administration must be exemplars of the social norms he is trying to establish in domestic as well as foreign policy.

The leading by example of this premise was clearly evident in the president's decision that the United States would not develop new nuclear warheads, a step which supporters like the *New York Times* praised: "the administration has rightly decided to lead by example."[107] And the United States and Russia announced a joint agreement to decrease the numbers of nuclear weapons which an official administration news dissemination website characterized as follows:

> As owners of more than 95 percent of the world's nuclear weapons, Obama said, the United States and Russia will lead by example, taking concrete steps toward the long-term diplomatic goal of disarmament while sending a powerful message to countries such as Iran, whose controversial nuclear program is currently subject to three rounds of U.N. Security Council sanctions supported by the White House and the Kremlin.[108]

More specifically, after meeting with President Medvedev of Russia, Obama said, "And I had an excellent meeting … to get started that process of reducing our nuclear stockpiles, which will then give us greater moral authority … to say to North Korea, don't proliferate nuclear weapons."[109]

There is of course a legitimate question about whether taking useful, but not comprehensive steps beyond symbolic nuclear warhead reductions will really increase America's moral standing on these issues. And there is a question as well, as to whether any limited increase in America's standing here will have concrete strategic benefits on the calculation of national interest by America's competitors or enemies. It is wholly unclear that the limited reduction of America's nuclear arsenal will minimize the advantages to a country like Iran that would benefit by having a nuclear deterrence. And it is unclear how seizing the high moral ground in one area (reduction of nuclear weapons numbers) while relying on *real politik* in Afghanistan and Pakistan influences the overall moral calculation.

Yet, beyond the strategic assessments here lies the moral calculation contained in the lead by example motif. Implicit in Obama's formulation here is his view that in the past America has not lived up to either its ideals or its responsibilities. Therein lies the gap that must be narrowed. Redemption here consists of living up to American foreign policy ideals as Obama understands and interprets them. His moral calculus is the beginning point of that assessment and thus his view that America has failed to measure up leads to a strategy of acknowledgement of error, a public affirmation not to repeat them, and policies that affirm both the errors of the past and the intention to turn over a new policy leaf so to speak.

In Obama's view, "if we are practicing what we preach, if we occasionally confess to having strayed from our values and our ideals, that strengthens our hand; that allows us to speak with greater moral force and clarity around these issues."[110] Aside from distinguishing his administration from his predecessors', Obama views his criticisms of this country as having both a moral and strategic purpose, which are perhaps related. Moral standing confers legitimacy that gives the United States policy leverage. That moral standing is increased if the United States is "practicing what it preaches." The issue is that while other countries may respect moral consistency, they are not likely to sacrifice their core interests as a reward for American moral virtue.

There is another issue as well. Aspiring to moral leadership in a complicated world is difficult when you also pride yourself on embracing a policy of realism. So keeping supply lines open to Afghanistan is very important to the United States, as is reducing theft risk by securing highly enriched uranium, and as a result, countries such as Kazakhstan and its leader Nursultan Nazarbayev are wooed by the United States, in spite of repeated criticism of this regime by human rights groups. In a world where ideals and self-interest are not synonymous, moral leadership must sometimes share the stage with blunt necessity, as it did when Mr. Obama met with Nazarbayev and understandably stressed their mutual interests, not his human rights moral gap.[111] This kind of strategic necessity, like others, makes clear the difficulties and the costs of trying to pursue moralism and realism as equal foreign policies. The difficulty is that sometimes interests must trump moral standards, and this leads to the cost which is that moral standards will be seen to be, and will in fact sometimes be, a matter of expediency.

One gets a sense of the difficulties involved when Michael McFaul, the National Security Council's senior director for Russia and the Caucasus, reported that President Obama said to Mr. Nazarbayev, "we too are working on our democracy," a comment that seemed to place the dictatorship and democracy on an equal moral footing. Nor were matters improved when Mr. McFaul insisted, "There was no equivalence meant whatsoever, [Obama's] taken, I think, rather historic steps to improve our own democracy since coming to office here in the United States."[112] What those "historic steps" were and what they implied about the country's need for them were left unclear.

What does seem clear is that, in Obama's view, America's moral standing is directly related to the policies that he pursues and the mistakes those policies help make up for. This underscores an unacknowledged point regarding Obama's political leadership; it has a profoundly moral dimension. Being the only country to have used an atomic bomb was not only bad policy, but also a moral failing that must be atoned for with a policy that seeks to rid the world of nuclear weapons. Not having spent "enough time" thinking about the issues of poverty, racism, and sexism or doing something about them, as Obama believes is the case, is not only a matter of policy failure but of moral failure as well.

So, adding up the president's remarks about American responsibility for such events as the worldwide economic downturn and the melting of the polar icecaps,[113] his criticism of U.S. foreign policy beginning with Truman, his stated views on race and voting and other similar comments, it seems safe to say that the president thinks the United States has a lot to make up for, and that of course brings us squarely back to the issue of redemption.

Conclusion: A Moral and Transformative Leader Coming into Clearer View

The desire to quickly enact large policy initiatives while your party is still in control of both houses of Congress is understandable in one sense. The opportunity presented by this fact is likely to be fleeting. But it is also the case that the opportunity won't carry transformative policy very far without a president who is committed to making use of the opportunity, and Obama certainly is so committed.

Obama's decision to take that opportunity required him to argue, very debatably, that the issue with which most Americans were concerned, the economic downturn, was being addressed by passing major health care legislation, major energy legislation, and major immigration legislation. It's possible to argue, and the president did, that all of these issues had to be resolved for the long-term economic health of the country. Yet, that relationship was tenuous at best, and the particulars of the policies involved were fraught with more than economic implications; they were for Obama moral imperatives as well.

Obama's low-key style does not trump his ambition for transformative change framed through the lens of leveling the economic and foreign policy playing field. Nor, if you think about it, should there be any reason that it would. We are used to thinking of heroic presidents as mounting the barricades. But cool calculation can be just as ambitious as clarion calls. Whatever pragmatism is at the core of Obama's transformative ambitions, they are about means, not ends.

What we now have in plain view is a stanchly liberal and activist president of transformative and redemptive ambitions in the service of what he views as fairness and who has aspirations to anchor America's moral center around his view of where that is located. By succeeding in his ambitious task to transform the country and make it both more just and fair, his mother's redemptive legacy to him, Obama not only reaffirms their relationship but vindicates his father's life work, thus burnishing his tarnished legacy.

Obama has shown his willingness to bend, through legislative mandate, a demonstrably unsupportive public to his vision of fairness. In doing so, he has demonstrated that he has both the courage of his ambitions and his ideals with regard to truly remaking America. His health care legislation is just the first step.

A prudent president, having won such a victory, might well pivot to smaller less publicly divisive initiatives rather than energy policy or more stimulus spending and replenish political capital. He has not, as his third trillion dollar budget suggests.[114] Obama went all in for his health care legislation and won. For a president whose self-confidence is already unusually high, such a win is likely to stimulate an ambition surge and the temptation to bet his remaining political capital on the next big agenda items.

If he does pursue his cap and trade energy policy or a major overhaul of the immigration system, including the legalization of ten million undocumented persons living in the United States, the major question would be whether substantial segments of the public would continue to support a president who wishes to remake America to conform to his vision of fairness without seriously taking into account theirs.

5

THE MORAL THRUST OF OBAMA'S AMBITION: FAIRNESS

Although ambition has a mixed reputation in personal and political life, it is the lifeblood of a well-realized life. Without ambition there can be no accomplishment or the consolidation of self-respect and esteem that are its byproducts. Yet, presidents differ in their level of ambition, the quality of the skills they bring to bear on being able to realize it, and whether it is anchored by ideals and values.

The purpose of ambition is also important. Is it meant to "overcome low estimates of self" as Lasswell suggested?[1] Or, as was the case with Bill Clinton, was its purpose to buttress already high estimates of the self?[2] Is ambition in the service of a president's ideals and values, or are a president's professed ideals and values really in the service of his ambition? And if ideals and values do anchor a president's ambition, which particular ones are central?

If Obama's ambition carries the weight of his father's, step-father's, and grandfather's failed experience, the nature of his values and ideals reflects the legacy of his mother's ideals, encapsulated in the cardinal virtue of "fairness" to overcome social injustice. Of his commitment to this very large term, a useful rhetorical vehicle for the country's transformation that he seeks, there can be little doubt. Obama has written that among the values his mother stressed was "fairness."[3] One of his biographers adds, "Obama, without argument, is imbued with an abiding sense of social and economic justice."[4] To an unusual degree, Obama is a president who truly does seem to view policy through a moral lens, his.

Obama has often talked of the importance of trying "to find something much larger than myself. *In my case, it was trying to promote a fair and just society.*"[5] It is also the basis of Obama's egalitarian presumption that "when you spread the wealth around, it's good for everybody,"[6] as well as his lament in a 2001 radio interview that the Supreme Court, "never ventured into the issues of redistribution of wealth and sort of more basic issues of political and economic justice in this society."[7] In a campaign debate with Hillary Clinton he said that "economic fairness" was something he would continue to fight for and when asked why he said he would raise the capital gains tax when research said doing so actually brings in less money, he replied, "for purposes of fairness."[8]

Obama's health care legislation is specifically designed to redress economic and health access disparities and unfairness. One commentator noted that,

> The bill that President Obama signed on Tuesday is the federal government's biggest attack on economic inequality since inequality began rising more than three decades ago. ... This fact helps explain why Mr. Obama was willing to spend so much political capital on the issue, even though it did not appear to be his top priority as a presidential candidate. Beyond the health reform's effect on the medical system, it is the centerpiece of his deliberate effort to end what historians have called the age of Reagan.[9]

Given the centrality of fairness and justice to Obama it is not surprising that well before Obama became president, he "portrayed himself as a moral leader."[10] Remnick reports that Obama's favorite quotation was one from Martin Luther King, "the arc of the moral university is long, but it bends towards justice."[11] In a 2003 interview, Obama named Gandhi, Lincoln, and King as the men he most admired. Why? Because they were able "to bring about extraordinary changes and place themselves in a difficult historical moment *and be a moral center*."[12]

It seems clear that Obama intends this role for himself as well. And one of the ways in which such leaders help bend the arc of the moral universe toward justice and that they take the role of a country's moral center in difficult times is that they lead followers or fellow countrymen beyond the personal and moral lapses that accompany self-interest to redemption. And that redemption requires individuals to join the moral fight and bend the moral arc of the universe towards justice. At a little noticed Knox College commencement speech in 2005 Obama may as well have been speaking of himself as giving advice to his audience and had this to say: "[I]ndividual salvation has always depended on collective salvation."[13]

Fairness and Redemption: Idealization's Impact

Obama's mother spent her life in Indonesia and South East Asia working for change and fairness at the village level. Obama writes in the new preface to his autobiography that, "She travelled the world, working in the distant villages, helping women buy a sewing machine or a milk cow or an education that might give them a foothold in the world's economy."[14] She was also, "a generous benefactor whose gifts of money, food and schoolbooks helped numerous villagers."[15]Adi Sasono, chairman of the Co-operative Council of Indonesia, who watched Ann Dunham's micro-finance achievements said that, "In Obama's books and speeches, I see the same sensitivity, the same concern for common people and *for justice*."[16]

That was a bottom up strategy that Obama emulated in becoming a community organizer, before abandoning it to follow in his father's footsteps and aim for a political position where redistributive fairness could be brought about by the policy leverage that high level leaders are able to wield. Yet her influence on Obama's outlook goes beyond the example she set in her work or the injunction to make fairness a central value in his life.

The power for her legacy to her son was propelled in part by guilt, Obama's.

Ambivalence and Reconciliation

Remnick writes of their relationship that

> as a grown man, Obama … wrote skeptically not only about his father, but about his mother's youthful romanticism. He was not entirely easy on his teen-age mother, but ultimately reconciled to her innocence and good intentions—and her love for him.[17]

Remnick is right about the reconciliation, but he missed a key point about its origins and nature.

In the new preface to the 2004 edition of his autobiography, Obama laments the fact that he so neglected the large role that his mother, played in his life. There, he wrote,

> I think sometimes that had I known she would not survive her illness, I would have written a different book—less a meditation on the absent parent, more a celebration of the one who was the single constant in my life … I know that she was the kindest, most generous spirit I have ever known, and what is best in me I owe to her.[18]

Obama's apparent remorse-driven tribute in the reissue of his book was doubtlessly heartfelt, but it too doesn't really capture the full nature of his relationship with her. His mother, like his father, also left him, first when she sent him back to live with his grandparents in Hawaii for almost a year before she rejoined him, and then when she returned to Indonesia for long-term fieldwork and an eventual Asian centered career when Barack was entering adolescence.

His Mother's Choice to Separate and its Impact

Their first separation was his mother's decision. She decided Obama needed an American education; she sent him to live with her mother and father in Hawaii saying that she would join her son, perhaps in a year tops.[19] Obama was ten years old at the time.

Alter sees this decision as an example of his mother fostering Obama's "bracing independence" and further, "forcing on him a sense of responsibility for himself that many indulged and overprotected Americans now lack."[20] Perhaps; but Alter seems on more solid ground when he says, "sending him back from Jakarta to live with his grandparents … must have been a wrenching separation for a nine year [sic] old."[21] That seems not only plausible, but also likely. And notice the words that Alter uses, "sending him back."

Obama too uses those words when he writes of this decision: "But by 1971 my mother—concerned for my education, *sent* me to live with my grandparents in Hawaii."[22] The word "sent," conveys the experience of being sent away. It has echoes of a choice that wasn't Obama's and that he would have preferred not to have been made. Obama writes that, "it hadn't sounded so bad when my mother first explained it me."[23] Yet, just a little later getting off the plane and seeing his grandparents he wrote, "I realized that I was to live with strangers."[24] There is an undertone of resignation and dissatisfaction in that observation.

Obama's mother did move back early that fall and began her graduate work in anthropology. She, Obama, and his younger sister lived together for three years,[25] at which time she returned to Indonesia for fieldwork. Obama writes that when his mother "suggested that I go back with her … I immediately said no."[26]

Obama's Separation Choice

Adolescence is a time of beginning the process of separation and individuation for many and Obama's choice to stay in Hawaii is understandable on many grounds—familiarity, friends, and comfort among them. But the "immediately" of Obama's reaction suggests it was strongly felt, unequivocal, and a reflection of a willingness to live apart from her. She was gone for the next three years.

Obama's mixed feelings towards some of his experiences with his mother emerge from a close reading of what he has said over the years. At one point, Obama said of his mother, "I didn't feel [her absence] as a deprivation to me. But when I think about the fact that I was separated from her, I suspect it had more of an impact than I know."[27] Clearly it did. Obama has told many close friends that he grew up "feeling like an orphan."[28] Elsewhere, commenting on the absence of both his father and his mother, he has said of himself, "At some level I had to raise myself."[29] Interestingly, in Obama's 1979 high school yearbook, "He thanked 'Tut and Gramps,' his nicknames for Madelyn and Stanley Dunham, but didn't mention his faraway mother."[30]

Romance and Recklessness

Obama presents his mother as a bit of a naïve dreamy romantic. He writes of her that, "She gathered friends from high and low, took long walks, stared at the moon and foraged through local markets for some trifle, a scarf or stone carving that would make her laugh or please the eye."[31] Yet, there was another side to his analysis of his mother as well.

Obama told one interviewer that his mother's life reflected a "certain recklessness."[32] She had after all met, become pregnant with, married, and then divorced a man she didn't really know very well. And she then married another man she met at school and moved herself and her young child to Indonesia, a country she knew little or nothing about and which in fact had just gone through a bloody coup. Along with her youthful naïveté, she was clearly impulsive and it was hard for the thoughtful young adult Barack not to notice it. One can discern the impact of that knowledge in Obama's determined deliberativeness.

It seems fair to say that Obama had some conflicted feelings about his mother, just as he did about his father. He loved his mother and as every child does, needed her as well. Yet, she married a man who left her and him and in doing so left an emotional gap that set Obama off on a journey of many years' duration to find his father's real emotional place in his life. One article about her put it very well: "She made risky bets that paid off only some of the time, choices that her children had to live with."[33]

In a twist of irony, his mother's impulsive marriage set her son on a decades-long quest that focused most of his emotional attention on his absent father. As a result, she hardly figures in his autobiography, certainly compared to his father. The occasion for Obama's lament about how he neglected his mother in telling his life's story is clearly stimulated by her death shortly before the book is published. His mother died in 1995 at the age of fifty-two from ovarian cancer while Obama was starting his first campaign for public office. He said that, "his biggest mistake was not being at his mother's side when she died."[34] In typical Obama style he raises his lament in the form of a double equivocal: "I think *sometimes* that *had I known* she would not survive her illness, I would have written a different book." Not, mind you, "I should have written a more balanced book," but rather that he sometimes thinks about having done so.

From Ambivalence to Idealization

More important for Obama's focus on fairness, is what he did when he realized and regretted his mistake. He elevated his mother to idealization, just as he had done before with his father until reality threw him off the pedestal. What is the evidence for this? Obama's own words. He writes that, "she was the kindest, most generous spirit I have ever known, and what is best in me I owe to her."[35]

In those words lie his mother's redemption and the redemption of their relationship. Gone are any criticisms of her "recklessness" in making poor choices. Gone is any resentment about her absences that made Obama feel like an orphan. Indeed, somewhat paradoxically, Obama now writes that he thinks he should have written his book as, "more a celebration of the one who was the single constant in my life." The evidence is that she may have been the "single constant," but she was not consistently present. Obama's posthumous idealization of his mother is a direct result of his neglect of her role and his guilt in having done so, with no chance to make amends while she was alive to receive them.

I think it fair to suggest that both in the case of his father and mother, the animating need to reclaim and redeem his relationships with them and their legacies is very strong. In his father's case, failed transformative aspirations can be redeemed by Obama's successfully following in his father's (failed) footsteps. His mother's case is a bit different.

There, a sense of remorse and guilt coupled with an idealization of her virtues leads naturally to an effort to immortalize her legacy in his efforts, and that means framing his transformational ambitions thorough her values. The chief one of those values was treating people "fairly." Obama's redemptive idealization of his mother through the vehicle of fairness becomes the frame through which Obama views the United States and his aspirations for it.

Obama's Racial/Political Identity and Fairness

Obama ran for president in part as a "post-racial" candidate and there is truth in that claim. He developed very early on a style that made others comfortable with him, and that includes racial matters. There he has been more like Sidney Poitier than Al Sharpton, and that aspect of his racial identity has been instrumental in his political ascent.

There is, however, a less appreciated element of Obama's political identity, and that is his identification with political and racial grievance. Identification with grievance is not synonymous with being consumed by it. Nor does identification require grievance to be an overt, major or defining part of a president's leadership persona, the image he chooses to emphasize and project. It simply means, in Obama's case, that he identifies with and is sympathetic to the historical wrongs that are part of the American racial legacy at home and abroad and believes we should strive to redress them. This leads Obama's presidency to the politics of redemption.

Racial Grievances?

The idea that racial grievance of any sort is *part* of Obama's outlook is likely to be controversial and certainly runs counter to conventional wisdom. After all, Chicago liberals coming to the aid of Alice Palmer, who decided she wanted to run for her old state legislative seat, and wanted Obama to step aside, thought he was "too willing to dismiss the 'politics of grievance.'"[36] Remnick, one of Obama's recent biographers, wrote that, "Obama seemed to promise a new kind of politics or, at least a marriage of conventional liberal positions *to a temperament that relied on reconciliation rather than on grievance.*"[37]

Note that it is Obama's temperament that carries the argument of this conventional wisdom. That is made absolutely clear in a review of Remnick's book by historian

Douglass Brinkley who writes that, "Nobody could ever accurately satirize him as an angry black man. Rage has been *exorcised from his demeanor.*"[38] That fact that any charged feelings have been "exorcised from his demeanor" does not mean that they didn't or don't exist. If they did, what happened to them?

One could argue that such feelings never existed, but that would run counter to what Obama has said of himself. In his *Dreams* book, Obama clearly says that as a young adult he experimented with a more racially charged persona.[39] Although he presents himself as wondering, even while doing it, whether it was just a pose, there is evidence, throughout his later life, including the presidency that he has yet to wholly resolve that question. More specifically, he has yet to resolve the ambivalence that exists between his identification with racial discrimination and grievance and his primary "post racial" developmental experience and style.

The point regarding the evidence that follows is *not* that beneath Obama's calm exterior lies a reservoir of racial animosity, but rather that his racial identity is more complex and emotionally charged than has been acknowledged to date. Reading carefully and taking Obama at his word, we can see that he expresses definite racial ambivalence, annoyance, and even occasional anger throughout the book.

Obama's Racial Ambivalence

The primary origin of ambivalence is the experience that there is more than one feeling associated with a person or a situation. Ordinarily, this is experienced as having "mixed feelings," the origin and nature of which are sometimes hard to discern. In Obama's case, both are quite clear, not only to him but, through his autobiography, to a much larger audience.

It is part of Obama's capacity for self-awareness that he is able to recognize his ambivalence and pinpoint its source—his struggle to forge a racial identity. However, the major question regarding ambivalence of such a central identity element is if and how it is resolved. Keep in mind that both sides of ambivalence hold real feelings. Moreover, holding mixed feelings does not mean that the feelings "cancel out."

Obama writes of his ambivalence in his adolescence that, "I would find myself talking ... about *white folks* this and *white folks* that, and I would suddenly remember my mother's smile. ... "[40] Elsewhere there were less ambivalent expressions of his feelings—"our rage at the white world needed no object."[41] Elsewhere in his autobiography he writes of blacks' redemptive struggles, speaking as well for himself, that,[42]

> had arisen out of a very particular experience with hate. *That hate hadn't gone away*; it formed a counter narrative buried deep within each person and at the center of which stood white people—some cruel, some ignorant, sometimes a single face, sometimes just a faceless image of system claiming power over our lives. *I had to ask myself whether the bonds of community could be restored without collectively exorcising* that ghostly figure that haunted black dreams.

Obama describes one incident when he took two white friends to a party his black friend "Ray" was throwing and attended almost entirely by African Americans. Obama's friends asked to leave the party after an hour saying they felt uncomfortable and Obama writes of his response, "I snorted. 'Yeah. Right.' *A part of me wanted to punch him right there.*"[43] This led Obama to ruminate about a "nightmare vision" in which, according to his friend Ray, "We were always playing by the white man's rules."[44]

It is also during this period that Obama tells us that he gravitated to an older socialist black power activist named Frank Davis. Davis told him that "blacks had reason to hate,"[45] complained that his feet were bad as a result of trying to force African feet into European shoes,[46] and warned Obama that all he would learn in college was about "equal opportunity and the American way and all that sh★★."[47]

These words were written to describe a time in Obama's life, his high school years at Punalou, when he began overtly wrestling with his racial identity. And it's true that of this time he rehashes the gains that African Americans have made and writes, "Maybe we could afford to give the bad-assed nigger pose a rest."[48] This on one side and then the other approach, what might well be termed *equivocal agreement*, is characteristic of Obama in many areas.

The above incidents that Obama describes are part of his adolescence, which is for many people, of whatever heritage, a time to try out and sort through different identity elements.[49] Yet Obama writes about feelings of racial antagonism and anger that extend beyond his adolescence. One of these areas has to do with the complex areas of racial identity and loyalty.

Racial Identity and Loyalty

The issues of identity and group loyalty come up several times in his books. Obama writes, "I ceased to advertise my mother's race at the age of twelve or thirteen, when I began to suspect that by doing so I was ingratiating myself to whites."[50] In college, he writes, "To avoid being mistaken for a sell-out, I chose my friends carefully. The more politically active black students … "[51] Obama was speaking of his first two years at Occidental College when he was in his very late teens.

There he recounts his experience of making somewhat harsh fun of another black student who had asked him for a class assignment:[52] "Tim was not a conscious brother … He wore argyle sweaters and pressed jeans and talked like Beaver Cleaver. He planned to major in business. His white girlfriend was probably waiting for him up in his room listening to country music."

Obama was talking to another black friend of his at the time, and was clearly embarrassed by Tim: "I wanted nothing more from him than to go away." Obama walked Tim down the hall and when he returned to his friend Marcus, a hipper black, Obama said to him shaking his head, "Tim's a trip ain't he? *Should change his name from Tim to Tom,*" an illusion to being a sell out.

Much later, as a young adult, Obama met Marty Kaufman, who interviewed him for an organizing job in Chicago. About him, Obama writes, "he was smart … he seemed committed to his work. Still there was something about him that made me wary. A little too sure of himself, maybe *and white*."[53] Later he muses that the black nationalist "Rafiq," "*was right when he insisted that, deep down, all blacks were potential nationalists. The anger was there* bottled up and often turned inward."[54] Here "all blacks" presumably means Obama as well.

As a twenty-eight-year-old adult, Obama visited Kenya and learned from his step grandmother Sarah Onyango Obama, the third wife of Obama's paternal grandfather Onyango, the real story of his grandfather. Of him Obama writes, "I too felt betrayed … my image of Onyango … had always been of an autocratic man … *but I had also imagined him as an independent man, a man of the people, opposed to white rule.*" Obama learned that wasn't true and that his grandfather had worked as a servant learning to "prepare the white man's food and organize the white man's house."[55] Obama then writes, "what granny had told us scrambled that image completely, causing ugly words to flash through my mind. *Uncle Tom. Collaborator. House nigger.*"[56] Strong, harsh words, and they do not come from Obama as an adolescent, but from him as a grown man well into adulthood.

Racial Assumptions and Historical Grievance

On that same trip, he and his half sister Auma were having lunch and Obama took the opportunity to study the tourists who "were everywhere—Germans, Japanese, British, Americans. Taking pictures, hailing taxis, fending off street peddlers, many of them dressed in safari suits like extras on a movie set." Obama recalls that as a child in Hawaii he and his friends

> had laughed at tourists like these, with their sunburns and their pale skinny legs. … Here in Africa though, the tourists didn't seem so funny. *I felt them as an encroachment; I found their innocence vaguely insulting.* … in their utter lack of self-consciousness, they were expressing a freedom that neither Auma or I could ever experience, a bedrock confidence in their own parochialism, *a confidence reserved for those born into an imperial culture.*[57]

Of course, Obama, having been born in the United States, had also been born into one of the "imperial cultures" he names. What comes through in Obama's vignette is a resentment born of envy regarding attributed traits like "bedrock confidence" that he had no way of assessing. There is anger in his condescending descriptions of those tourists as well.

Tourist Lunch Assumptions

The lunch turned sour when the waiters seemed to be paying more attention to an American family than to Obama and Auma, and they left. Auma began to compare

Kenya with a whore, willing to prostitute itself for anyone with money. At first, Obama tried to dissuade her from that view, but then in a typical Obama maneuver begins to equivocally agree with her. He writes,

> I suspected she was right; not all tourists in Nairobi had come for the wildlife. Some came because Kenya, without shame, *offered to recreate an age when the lives of whites in foreign lands rested comfortably on the backs of the darker races.* … [58]

Of course, like his characterization of "bedrock confidence" in their own "imperial cultures" Obama had no real information about how many tourists supposedly came to relive the glory days of imperial empire and the service condition of the "darker races."

This is obviously a projection, an attribution to others of harsh motives on the basis of a generalization with little evidence to back it up. Certainly, it is unfair to use the attentiveness of local waiters, hoping for a large tip as evidence of the racist motives of the tourists. Here Obama's identification with and anger at past oppression bubbles up to slant his view of an American family clearly on a vacation sitting down to have lunch.

Racism and "Skip" Gates/Cambridge Police Incident

Of course the lack of evidence and the predominant role of assumption is precisely the point here. It is not too far from the underlying dynamic evident in Obama's tourist assumptions and attributions to the situation that developed when Obama took the occasion of a presidential primetime news conference to characterize the arrest of his friend "Skip" Gates as an example of Cambridge police acting "stupidly." Police responding to a call of a possible break-in arrived to find Gates at his front door and asked for identification. Gates responded with increasing belligerency and was arrested, briefly, on a charge of disorderly conduct.

What's interesting about the parallel to Obama's attributions and assumptions about the Kenya tourists is the same lack of information and the basis on which the president reached his conclusions. Obama said,[59]

> Well, I should say at the outset that "Skip" Gates is a friend, so I may be a little biased here. I don't know all the facts … *Now, I don't know, not having been there and not seeing all the facts, what role race played in that,* but I think it's fair to say, number one, any of us would be pretty angry; number two, that the Cambridge Police acted stupidly in arresting somebody when there was already proof that they were in their own home; and number three, what I think we know separate and apart from this incident is that there is a long history in this country of African Americans and Latinos being stopped by law enforcement disproportionately. That's just a fact. …

There is a question regarding whether "any of us" would be "pretty angry" when asked to show identification when it was explained that there had been a call reporting a break-in. And there is the question of how, exactly, Mr. Gates acted and what he said to elicit an arrest for disorderly conduct. Yet what is more striking, but from a psychological standpoint not surprising, is the president's willingness to make the assumptions he did and the basis on which he did so. The "long history" that the president refers to is somewhat vague and not exactly to what he is referring. Is he referring to police weapons searches in minority neighborhoods, stops by police of minority motorists, or cases like those of Mr. Gates where homeowners are asked to identify themselves? A large number of factors shape discretionary police decisions in the first two categories and the methodologies used to assess rates of occurrence often reduce these variables to limited, manageable and therefore not necessarily valid measures.[60] However, even granting the president's past history point does not negate the fact that he went from assumption to conclusion in this particular case while admittedly not knowing any of the facts.

In Obama's long concern with not being a racial turncoat and in both the tourist and Skip Gates episodes, it is obvious that Obama strongly identifies as an African American. And with that also comes an identification with the widespread discrimination they have been subject to in all but the most recent of modern times. Asked in an interview about suggestions that he had not done enough for African Americans he replied,

> Of course, there's grumbling. *We* were some of the folks who were most affected by predatory lending. There's a long history of us being the last hired and the first fired. As I said on health care, *we're* the ones who are in the worst position to absorb companies deciding to drop their health care plans.[61]

Note again the inclusion of himself in the "we" that has defined the historic deprivation and grievance. Obama has said he experienced incidents of prejudice[62] while growing up, but they had nothing to do with predatory lending, employment issues, or companies that decide to drop their health care plans.[63] Here, as in the case of his tourist and Gates comments, he is identifying with the historic record of discrimination and it provides the basis for an implicit premise.

Obama's Grandmother's Racism

Finally, there is Obama's treatment of his grandmother ("Toot") with whom he lived and who helped raise him when his mother was in Indonesia for long periods of Obama's adolescence. In his well received speech on America and race given after he had had to disassociate himself from the harsh remarks of the Reverend Wright whose church he had attended for twenty years, Obama had this to say,

I can no more disown him than I can disown the black community. I can no more disown him than I can my white grandmother—a woman who helped raise me, a woman who sacrificed again and again for me, a woman who loves me as much as she loves anything in this world, but a woman who once confessed her fear of black men who passed by her on the street, and who on more than one occasion has uttered racial or ethnic stereotypes that made me cringe.[64]

Actually, his grandmother did not "confess her fear of black men," at least if what Obama wrote about the incident in his book *Dreams* is accurate.[65] There he related an argument between his grandfather and grandmother over her wanting to be driven to work because she was afraid to take the bus. Obama says:

I took her into the room and asked what had happened.
"A man asked me for money yesterday. While I was waiting for the bus."
"That's all?"
"He was very aggressive, Barry. Very aggressive. I gave him a dollar and he kept asking. If the bus hadn't come, I think he might have hit me over the head."

Obama writes that he returned to the kitchen and said to his grandfather, "Listen, why don't you just let me give her a ride. She seems pretty upset." "By a panhandler?" his grandfather asked. Obama replied, "Yeah, I know—but it's probably a little scary for her seeing some big man block her way." At that point Obama's grandfather said,

She's been bothered by men before. You know why she's so scared this time? I'll tell you why. Before you came in she told me the fella was *black*.... That's the reason she was bothered. And I just don't think that's right.

Those words hit Obama "like a fist in my stomach," he reports. However, he didn't seem to think then, or in writing the book when he was thirty-four years old, or in his race speech given when he was forty-seven years old, that those words had a very different possible meaning.

Toot's "Racism:" Alternative Explanations?

Perhaps the descriptor black was just that, a descriptor not a confession of racial prejudice. It is after all Obama's grandfather who makes the characterization of racial fear and it is he who conveys his interpretation to Obama. His grandmother confessed nothing. Moreover, Obama's grandfather was in many ways a bitter man who resented his wife's success as a bank vice president and it is not far-fetched to consider that those feelings entered into his assessment and that he tried to present himself as being on Obama's (racial) side at the cost of his wife.

Obama's comments about his grandmother caused some controversy and he was interviewed about it later on a Philadelphia radio show. Asked about his comment regarding his grandmother he said,

> The point I was making was not that my grandmother harbors any racial animosity, *but that she is a typical white person. If she sees somebody on the street that she doesn't know—there's a reaction in her that's been bred into our experiences that don't go away and sometimes come out in the wrong way and that's just the nature of race in our society.* We have to break through it. What makes me optimistic is you see each generation feeling less like that. And that's pretty powerful stuff.[66]

Here Obama has widened the racial generalization. Now his grandmother harbors racial prejudice not because she was afraid of an aggressive panhandler who was black, but because "if she sees someone in the street that she doesn't know—there's a reaction in her that's been bred into our experiences that doesn't go away." So now, it is not just a black panhandler that stimulates racial fear and prejudice, but any stranger, presumably black, she sees on the street that she doesn't know. And to complete the linkage of a base assumption with a bald generalization, "she is a typical white person."

This is a startling statement, especially for someone so smart and nuanced in his public policy statements and thinking. It is possible that he misspoke in this interview, but his not wholly accurate retelling of the story in his race speech, his failure to consider other far more likely and simple explanations for what he came to believe, and his willingness to generalize from those errors to "typical white" people suggests something fairly powerful and elemental is at work and more importantly has not been fully resolved.

The Impact of Racial Identification

Obama has written, "I can't help but view politics through the lens of a black man of mixed heritage *forever mindful* of how generations of people who looked like me were subjugated and stigmatized ... "[67] and that is apparently true. But it is hard to believe that what is clearly a basic and important cognitive lens for Obama is not accompanied by some feelings appropriate to it.

This helps to explain the president's somewhat time insensitive, overstated generalization made in his Istanbul speech that he was "President of a country that not very long ago made it hard for somebody who looks like me to vote, much less be President of the United States."[68] It is not clear how recently "not very long ago" is in the president's mind, but it seems to have made it into the top tier of the president's racial availability heuristic. It is also unclear how accurate it is to suggest the whole country "not very long ago" resembled Bull Connor's Selma Alabama.

Obama's Moral Compass Advisor

Obama's identification with past racial discrimination and the lens that resulted also helps to explain Obama's emotional connection to the Reverend Wright's tendentious black liberation sermons repeatedly delivered over the twenty years that Obama and his family attended that Church. They both shared the view that blacks had been grievously wronged in the United States and that America must recognize its past errors, amend its ways, and redeem, through its federal policies, America's promise and debt.

Obama writes in his book of the first Reverend Wright sermon he heard that it contained a ringing denunciation of poverty caused by "white greed."[69] Obama reports the uplifting feeling of hope rising up from within him as a result of that sermon which touched on many subjects including "Sharpsville and Hiroshima, the callousness of policy makers in the White House and the state house" and more prosaic issues like paying the electric bill. Obama become a member, married his wife there, baptized his children there and was a member for over twenty years.

Revered Wright was also a close "spiritual advisor." Obama said of him that, "Wright helps keep his priorities straight *and his moral compass calibrated.*"[70] Given the content of some of Wright's remarks and Obama's aspirations for moral leadership, it makes for an odd fit unless one views it through their shared prism of redemption.

Wright condemned the United States for bombing Hiroshima and Nagasaki, events that formed the basis of Obama's view that their behavior required the United States to take the leadership in abolishing those weapons. Wright also expressed the view that the 9/11attacks were a case of "chickens come home to roost," substituted God *damn* America, condemned the "U.S of K.K.K.A," detailed America's past and continuing racism, and accused the government of giving drugs to black young men.[71] Later, he blamed "Them Jews" for not letting Obama talk with him.[72]

Obama made some effort to make the argument that he wasn't in church on the days that these kinds of sermons were delivered. He told Richard Wolfe, whom Obama had recruited to write about the campaign, that he didn't go to church much. Wolfe says, "And he told me look, 'Yeah,' he said. 'It's true, I didn't go much, I had young kids. The services would go on for hours, if you've ever taken young kids to church, for three hours.'"[73] Obama made the same claim in interviews with the *Chicago Tribune* and *Sun-Times.*[74] But in truth as his sympathetic biographer Remnick points out,

> he had certainly sat through enough radical sermons by Wright—and without protest—so that it would be folly to start trying to make fine distinctions. He knew that that sort of hairsplitting would mean nothing, not after he had repeatedly, in his book and in public remarks, praised Wright as a minister and personal advisor.[75]

Over several decades it is unlikely that the Reverend Wright's strong views escaped Obama's notice. Obama is, and prides himself on being, a close observer of people and circumstances. Therefore, it seems safe to conclude then that the church's basic narrative of white responsibility for problems in the black community and the need for whites to recognize their role and redeem their past and (for Mr. Wright) present behavior was neither foreign nor antithetical to Obama's thinking.

It is true, as others have pointed out, that there were some political considerations in Obama's decision to join a church. As a community organizer and later as an aspiring political leader, black churches were a source of support. And it is also very likely the case that although Obama's spirituality, like his politics, reflects more nuance than perhaps is true of the average believer, joining a black church was an important part of cementing his identity as being an African American. Still there were many black churches on Chicago's South Side to choose from and many of them had as much or more possible political clout. We are left then with the importance of the Reverend Wright's outsized personality and his equally bold redemptive worldview.

The point here is *not* that underneath Obama's calm exterior he seethes with racial resentment. It is rather that Obama's racial identity is more complex than it has been understood and presented and that his identification with African Americans includes the historical legacy of discrimination that is part of the reason that he thinks that America's promise must be redeemed.

Fairness and Redemption: The Political Domain

Obama's ambivalent racial identity would be an important matter in its own right, but it is coupled with another identification that reinforces a critical stance toward the nation's structural arrangements and domestic and foreign policies. In his second year at Occidental College, Obama became part of the South African divestiture movement, and at both Occidental and Columbia his quasi-aesthetic life included association with a number of liberal or progressive groups and causes.

The political premises and *raison d'être* of these groups were and continue to be criticism of the inequalities of the American economic and political system along with a critique of the aims and conduct of American foreign policy. Then, as now, liberals also championed broad compensatory and redistributive policies designed to reduce these inequalities, as well as policies like the "nuclear freeze," that Obama wrote in favor of while at Columbia University, to curb what they see as the misdirected assertion of American power abroad.

It would seem fair to say on the evidence that Obama agrees with the major liberal critiques of American domestic and foreign policies, especially as they relate to the cardinal virtues, in his view, of fairness and level playing fields, where "advantage" is somewhat suspect regardless of whether it was earned, while disparities exist. He has written, "I'm angry about policies that consistently favor the wealthy and powerful over average Americans."[76]

Moral Imperatives and Economic Redistribution

Obama clearly has a preference for redistributive economic policies based on fairness and the need to make up for morally suspect past policies. Asked in an interview about "America's greatest moral failure," he replied,

> I think America's greatest moral failure in my lifetime has been that we still don't abide by that basic precept in Matthew that whatever you do for the least of my brothers you do for me. (Applause.) And that notion of—that basic principle applies to poverty. It applies to racism and sexism. It applies to, you know, not thinking about providing ladders of opportunity for people to get into the middle class. I mean, there's a pervasive sense, I think, that this country, as wealthy and powerful as we are, still don't spend enough time thinking about "the least of these."[77]

"Enough" is one of the elastic words that allow the speaker to hold comparatively high moral ground, without necessarily specifying what more is needed. And one could legitimately dispute the idea that there has not been enough thought devoted to issues of racism, sexism, and wealth. This trinity is, after all, a staple of Democratic policy concern, and has been the subject of continuing policy debates going back to the 1960s and Lyndon Johnson's "Great Society" agenda.

However, the important implication here is that although Americans haven't spent "enough time" thinking about the issues of poverty, racism, and sexism, Obama has. There is the further implication that, having not thought enough about it, Americans haven't done enough about these issues, and Obama intends to do so. All of these implications are, of course, perfectly consistent with the politics of redemption.

Obama's view of America's moral failings and its need for redemption came up as well during the campaign. In a town hall meeting, Obama was asked by a seven-year-old girl why he wanted to run for president. He replied, "America is … , uh, is no longer, uh … what it could be, what it once was. And I say to myself, I don't want that future for my children."[78]

Actually, the complete quote is as interesting as the above sound bite that was widely circulated.[79] Asked the why he's running question, Obama responded by noting his two children and saying, "I think about what kind of America *they're growing up in* and what's life going to be like for them twenty, thirty years from now."[80]

And what kind of country does Obama think his children are growing up in now? Well, it is one where "only a few people are able to make it into the middle class." It is a country so dependent on foreign energy that "our economy is grinding to a halt." Campaign hyperbole? Maybe. A rhetorical misstep brought on by campaign fatigue? Perhaps. But it does fit into the premise of faltering America that must redeem its promise.

The Moral Dimension of Transformative Policy

To an unusual degree, Obama is a president who sees his policy preferences as also being moral imperatives. His cap and trade legislation is, among other things, a way of cutting wasteful energy consumption and ameliorating damage to the environment by those who consumed without responsibility. As Obama said in his United Nations speech, "those wealthy nations that did so much damage to the environment in the 20th century, must accept our obligation to lead."[81] In other words, those countries like the United States that "did so much damage to the environment" must make amends and redeem themselves. They must recognize and acknowledge their errors and enact policies that compensate for them. These are the standard motifs of redemption.

Fairness and Consumption

The moral dimension of Obama's redemptive leadership also comes out quite clearly in his views on economic consumption. The president caused quite a stir when he addressed Wall Street and said,

> We're not, we're not trying to push financial reform because we begrudge success that's fairly earned. *I mean, I do think at a certain point you've made enough money.* But, you know, part of the American way is, you know, you can just keep on making it if you're providing a good product or providing good service. We don't want people to stop, ah, fulfilling the core responsibilities of the financial system to help grow our economy.[82]

Leaving aside the president's seeming misunderstanding of Adam Smith's core insight of the relationship of self-interest to collective economic good, the president here is taking a moral stand against making more than "enough" money. The president does not make clear here how much that is, but this is not the first time he's directly expressed the sentiment.

In the *Audacity of Hope* he had this to say,

> I admire many Americans of great wealth and don't begrudge them their success in the least ... I simply believe that those of us who have benefited from this new economy can best afford to shoulder the obligation of insuring every American child has a chance for that same success. And perhaps I possess a certain Midwestern sensibility ... *that at a certain point one has enough,* that you can derive as much pleasure from a Picasso hanging in a museum as from one hanging in your den, that you can get an awfully good meal in a restaurant for less than twenty dollars, and that once your drapes cost more than the average American's salary, you can afford to pay a bit more in taxes.[83]

Obama is alluding in the last sentence to the ostentatious greed of Dennis Kozlowski, former CEO of Tyco, serving a prison sentence for fraud to finance his spending spree.[84]

The issues raised in the quote are complex. They have to do with the amount of taxes already paid by the "very wealthy," and even the definition of such terms and their conceptual siblings such as "rich," "well-off," "affluent" or "well-to do." It requires us to analyze the number, size, and effectiveness of government programs as well as government economic transfer programs. Obama's phrase "a bit more in taxes," coupled with the singling out of those who buy million dollar drapes or works by Picasso, suggests it is only the very wealthy on whom he will call to fund their responsibilities; but this is not the case.

Fairness = Redistribution

On a campaign stop in Toledo, Ohio, Obama talked on camera with a self-employed thirty-four-year-old working class plumber named Joe Wurzelbacher who was about to try and buy a new business with the money he saved and would borrow. He asked, "Your new tax plan is going to tax me more, isn't it?" Obama first replied that he would get a 50 percent tax credit for health care, but then conceded that Wurzelbacher's income taxes would indeed rise. Obama then said, "It's not that I want to punish your success, I just want to make sure that everybody who is behind you—that they've got a chance at success too." Obama then continued and said, "My attitude is that if the economy's good for folks from the bottom up, it's gonna be good for everybody. ... I think when you spread the wealth around, it's good for everybody."[85]

It is of course a far distance from million dollar drapes and buying Picassos to saving and borrowing money to start your own business. And certainly in the case of this man it was not a question of taxes being the vehicle of redistributing money from the very rich to poor, since he was clearly not at that level. Still, Obama's expressed view is interesting for its premises.

The theme of redistribution equalling fairness came up in a very direct way in Obama's first budget document. There he wrote, "There's nothing wrong with making money, but there is something wrong when we allow the playing field to be tilted so far in the favor of so few. ... It's a legacy of irresponsibility, and *it is our duty to change it.*"[86] And he has tried to do so.

Redistributive economic policies in the pursuit of fairness are evident in the president's health care plan. The *New York Times* notes that the income from the administration's cap and trade legislation and the proposed limiting of tax deductions,

> on top of Mr. Obama's existing plan to roll back the Bush-era income tax reductions on households with income exceeding $250,000 a year, *would be a pronounced move to redistribute wealth* by reimposing a larger share of the tax burden on corporations and the most affluent taxpayers.[87]

Obama is most likely correct when he says that an economy that is "good for the folks from the bottom up" is good for everyone. Yet that is only true if those at the bottom are in a position to take advantage of it. Low education levels, poor work skills, lack of motivation, and spotty employment records are all elements that would lead to being in a disadvantaged position to take advantage of opportunity. In those circumstances, "spreading the wealth around" is not about helping people to be in a position to take advantage of opportunity, but rather a plan to simply take money from one group and distribute it to another.

Obama makes this quite clear in an interview. There he said, "Let's make sure our economy takes into account not just the winners, but also the losers in the economy. Let's make sure that the burdens and benefits of globalization are *fairly distributed*."[88] Of course, if people aren't able to take advantage of the globalization opportunities, then the only way that they can be "fairly distributed" is by redistribution.

When he became president Obama was even more pointed. In his remarks accompanying his first budget he wrote, "While middle-class families have been playing by the rules, living up to their responsibilities as neighbors and citizens, those at the commanding heights of our economy have not."[89]

There is the clear implication in this statement that those who are wealthier than the middle class have been somehow cheating in gaining their wealth by "not playing by the rules" or ducking their responsibilities as citizens. Their wealth and how they accumulated it is, in some unspecified way, therefore morally suspect. And if that is the case, it presents a moral as well as an economic argument for redistribution and "leveling the playing field." Asked about these statements in an interview, Austan Goolsbee, a key member of the White House Council of Economic Advisers, confirmed that the administration thought that those at "commanding heights of the economy" included anyone making over $250,000 a year and that the president's budget statements about playing by the rules did reflect the administration and the president's thinking.[90]

The fairness and redemptive aspects of the president's budget and economic policies are also quite clear. A *Washington Post* analysis of the president's 2010 budget said,

> The blueprint, meanwhile, would overhaul programs across the federal bureaucracy to strengthen assistance for millions of people who have borne the consequences of what Obama called "an era of profound irresponsibility," helping them pay for college, train for better jobs and save for retirement while taking less of their earnings in taxes.[91]

And while millions were bearing the consequences of "profound irresponsibility," who was it in fact that was irresponsible? The very surprising answer is found in the president's official budget proposal transmitted to Congress,

We arrived at this point as a result of an era of profound irresponsibility that engulfed both private and public institutions from some of our largest companies' executive suites to the seats of power in Washington, D.C. For decades, too many on Wall Street threw caution to the wind, chased profits with blind optimism and little regard for serious risks—and with even less regard for the public good. Lenders made loans without concern for whether borrowers could repay them. Inadequately informed of the risks and overwhelmed by fine print, many borrowers took on debt they could not really afford. And those in authority turned a blind eye to this risk-taking ... [92]

In short, the responsibility for that "profound irresponsibility" is widely shared throughout many levels of society, including those toward whom the redistribution is aimed.

Fairness to Obama: Full Credit On his Terms

There is one more, very personal, element to consider in discussing the impact of fairness on Obama's thinking and that concerns his understanding of the term when it comes to assessing his own performance. Obama has a public reputation for equanimity, but a private reputation for being "thin-skinned." Alter presents him as a candidate and president who doesn't hold grudges and "disliked revisiting old grievances that had no clear bearing on the present."[93] His friend and advisor Valerie Jarrett said of Obama, "I've never seen someone so grudge-less."[94] This seems to be another area where it is well to keep in mind the aphorism "still waters run deep" when analyzing Obama.

The reality is that Obama does remember people who have crossed him, in his view, and is perfectly capable of holding grudges. Moreover, given Obama's view of himself he is especially keen to be judged by standards he deems appropriate—his own. Both dynamics have a long history, and have, as a result, found their way into the White House.

The earlier instances for which there is a record go back to Obama's days as a high school student. As an adult, Obama wrote in *Dreams* of himself during that period that he played basketball "with a consuming passion that would always exceed my limited talent."[95] That modest assessment, however, apparently was not what he felt at the time. Nor is it how he described those experiences in a 2004 interview and another interview given while he was running for the presidency.

Obama recalls in *Dreams* that "it was on the court that I could find a community of sorts, with an inner life all its own. It was there that I could make my closest white friends, on turf *where blackness couldn't be a disadvantage*."[96] That was not quite accurate. Much later in an interview during his presidential race he said, "It [basketball] did parallel some of the broader struggles I was going through, because there were some issues in terms of racial identity that played themselves out on the basketball court."[97] And what were these?

Obama spent hours perfecting his game and developed "an idiosyncratic, street style of shooting."[98] His style owed more to the elegant acrobatics of Julius Erving ("Dr. J") who has justly been called "one of the great innovators in basketball history,"[99] than it did to Boston Celtic's ball handling and point guard scoring legend Bob Cousy.[100]

Obama says of his style,

> I had an overtly black game, behind the back passes, and wasn't particularly concerned with fundamentals, whereas our coach was this Bobby Knight guy, and he was all about fundamentals, you know bounce passes and four passes before you shoot, and that sort of thing. So we had a little conflict that landed me on the bench when I argued. The truth was, on the playground I could beat a lot of guys who were starters, and I think he thought, it was useful to have me there in practice.[101]

There is a great deal of interest in this later interview. First, and most obviously, it provides another illustration of Obama's view that he is held to a different, and given his view of his talents, inappropriate standard. On the playground after all he "could beat a lot of guys who were starters." That, however, seems implausible. Remnick notes that three players of the starting five in Obama's senior year went on to play serious college ball.[102] Moreover, however much Obama disagreed with his coach's style, in his senior year at Punahou, that team, using that style, won the state basketball championships.

The quote also reveals that Obama thinks that he landed on the bench "when I argued." The implication here is that he wouldn't have if he hadn't and was penalized for speaking up. Recall that this was the period when Obama had slacked off from his already laid back approach to his school work, was doing a lot of partying, drinking, and smoking marijuana, and that he himself had said that he would have been a better student and basketball player if he hadn't "goofed-off." And of course, there also remains the question of fit between his personal style and the style that the coach used for the team.

What's odd about this is that in *Dreams*, Obama talked about this specific issue, and did so in quite a different way then. In his book Obama recounts his friend "Ray" arguing to him that he didn't get more basketball playing time because he was black, and Obama arguing back that Ray was wrong. Here is Obama, the voice of reason, in his late thirties looking back on that high school conversation:

> I'm saying yeah, I might not get the breaks on the team that some guys get, but they play like white boys do, and that's the style the coach likes to play, and they're winning the way they play and I don't play that way.[103]

Obama wanted to play more and asked his coach for a meeting with him and a few other players who had not broken into the starting five to discuss it. The coach

Chris McLachin was interviewed by two of Obama's biographers and both report that the conversation was respectful with the coach praising Obama's talent and role on the team.[104] Yet, when Mendell interviewed Obama about the incident in 2004, eight years after the publication of *Dreams* and its even-handed treatment of his high school basketball disappointments, another much sharper view emerged.

Mendell writes that when he mentioned to Obama that he had interviewed his high school coach, "His viscerally emotional reaction, even though twenty years had passed, was one of the moments when Obama's short fuse ... slipped out from behind his cool exterior." He quotes Obama as saying, "I got into a fight with the guy and he benched me for four or five games ... and I was furious, you know," and then goes on to add that Obama said this, "with a twinge of unresolved bitterness, along with the implied presumption of 'how dare he bench me.'"[105]

It's difficult, but not impossible to sort through the mélange of different versions of this story and find what seems to be its most likely reality, thus allowing us to draw some implications from it. First, it seems that the resentment that Obama felt in being penalized, as he saw it, for his black street style was real. While he presents himself in *Dreams* as seeing the point of the coach whose game style was much different and successful, in reality Obama clearly felt that an exception should have been made because, in his view, he was better than some of the starters. How the coach could have reconciled having two different playing styles operating in the same game at the same time is left unresolved.

Second, and perhaps of no less importance, is the apparent fact that Obama's presentation of himself in *Dreams* as a person able to see, understand, and to some degree accept his coach's point of view is by no means the whole story. Obama in the two later interviews clearly had strong feelings about not playing more or "being benched for arguing" as he put it. And that calls into question Obama's first presentation of that incident. It is not necessarily the case that the *Dreams* story is wholly constructed to showcase Obama's equanimity and even-handedness. Recall that *Dreams* was written well after Obama had already attended Harvard Law School and had been elected editor in chief of the law review precisely because of his skill at appearing to be understanding of both liberal and conservative positions.

It is also possible that both were true to some degree. That Obama did see his coach's point, but that he also felt the resentment that came with being held to a different standard and one that he thought was unfair and illegitimate. The strength of the last two interview statements, one in 2004 and one in 2009, suggests his ambivalence had never really been resolved. And the longevity of the resentments suggests they weighed more heavily in his feelings than the equanimity he presented as his only response to these events in *Dreams*.

Obama's temperament seems inconsistent with holding a grudge for many years, but if you shift the framework just a little you can see how it is possible. Obama's view of himself is the standard by which he judges what others say about him and his expectations of how others should treat him. And the evidence suggests he can certainly become resentful if he is not treated in accordance with his views and standards.

When he was a college freshman Obama was upset because his political science teacher gave him a B on a paper on which Obama thought he deserved an A. Obama's reasoning, he said in an interview,

> was that I knew that even though I hadn't studied, that I knew this stuff much better than my classmates." Obama then continued, "I went to him and said 'Why did I get a B on this?' and he said 'you didn't apply yourself.' He was grading me on a different curve and I was pissed.[106]

It seems not to have occurred to Obama, even in his retelling of the story as an adult, that the "different curve" the teacher was applying might have had something to do with the quality of the paper. Obama's view was he knew more than his classmates and should get credit for that on his paper, even though it might not by itself, considered alone, merit more than a B.

One can see here the parallels to the basketball conflict, above. There too Obama saw himself as better than those who were chosen over him (to start on the basketball team or in this case receive a better grade) and was angry. And in both cases, it is Obama's view of his talent and knowledge that fuels his resentment.

Remnick recounts a seemingly small incident that took place back at the time that Obama was working in New York at Business International after having just graduated from college. He was having lunch with a colleague when the subject of exercise came up and Obama mentioned that he worked out in Riverside Park after work and on weekends: "'I jog there too,' the colleague said. 'I don't jog,' Obama said, 'I run.'"[107]

What's telling about this is that it's a relatively small matter on which to insist, publicly, on a correction. Moreover, Obama's terseness and tone reflect a desire to be sure that one is given one's due, and especially not to be put in the same lower category being implied by his colleague's remark. It is at the same time a claim to be put in one's proper, better place and with it to insist on one's higher status. It is also exactly the kind of anecdote that is consistent with assertions that Obama can be arrogant as well as extremely self-confident.

Ryan Lizza, who has covered Obama now for a number of years, writes of an incident that took place during Obama's 2007 Senate campaign. Obama was standing around before a rally and saw Lizza approach,

> He sees me approach and suddenly a memory seems to be triggered. "You know, it's like Ryan Lizza," he says, gesturing at me and smiling widely. "Did I tell you the story of when I was sitting there doodling—I'm just drawing a bunch of different faces. And I guess that one face I drew was a long face. So

he just assumed it was me." It's true I once noted that the attention Obama was receiving seemed to be going to his head. *As evidence, I reported that during an interview he doodled a picture of himself. This is the second time in three years Obama has brought up Doodlegate.* At the Democratic convention, he approached me at a press breakfast and gently admonished me for the anecdote, then took out a pen and drew two doodles on a newspaper, one with a narrow face that I instantly recognized from our interview. "You see a picture of a guy with a long chin and big ears and automatically assume it's me?" he asked. It was a light-hearted rebuke, but also a reminder of Obama's reputation for being a little thin-skinned.[108]

This dynamic seems to be at work in Obama's complaint, as president, expressed in several different interviews that he has not been given sufficient credit for his accomplishments. Alter writes that after one year in office, "the president was annoyed by the lack of credit for what he accomplished."[109] He quotes Obama as saying, "I don't think people fully appreciate the degree to which prior to health care, we've had twelve straight victories in a row. These are pieces of legislation that in any normal year would be considered huge accomplishments."[110]

Among those "huge accomplishments" Obama named were financing expanded health care coverage for children (building on the CHIP program), "reining in" credit card companies, regulating tobacco, expanding national service, and banning pay discrimination against women. It is unclear whether independent observers would call all of these "huge accomplishments" or be impressed with the administration's legislative victories on these matters given the fact that his party had a filibuster proof control of both houses of Congress. Moreover, these legislative victories were somewhat peripheral to the public's main concerns at this time, which centered on the economy.

At another point the president complained that health care has so "overwhelmed the debate that people have sort of forgotten what we've done [on a number of other issues]."[111] Of course, Obama's successfully passed health care legislation cannot be considered to be anything other than a "major" piece of social legislation. Yet, the ambivalent reaction to it even after it was passed with 63 percent of the public wanting to repeal it,[112] underscores the distinction between passing legislation and public support of it, to say nothing of whether the legislation accomplishes the purposes that were given as the rationale for writing it.

The same dynamic was on display after the midterm election. In a press conference in South Korea, when the president was asked about his "failure" to accomplish some of the trip's purposes, he had sharp replies. When asked what was the "number one complaint, concern, or piece of advice that you got from foreign leaders about the U.S. economy and your stewardship of the economy?" he snapped back: "What about compliments? You didn't put that in the list."[113]

When Sheryl Stolberg of the *New York Times* asked him if his relations with other foreign leaders were a bit rocky now compared with previous summits when they "maybe were just a teensy bit falling all over you when you first arrived on the world stage," he again responded sharply, "That's not how I remember it. I remember our first G20, you guys writing the exact same stories you're writing now about the exact same issues. Don't you remember that, Sheryl?"[114]

Frustration and disappointment at not getting your due is a chronic condition for many political leaders, though some are able to keep these feelings to themselves. What seems clear is that Obama's Zen-like tranquility does not extend to validation of his view of himself as a successful leader and president.

6

THE QUESTION OF LEADERSHIP INTEGRITY

Among the most important characteristics of a president who is attempting to lead and govern in a politically divided society is *leadership integrity*. The reason is not hard to discern. When a society has gone through decades of political conflict during which almost every aspect of political life—policies, leaders, symbols, and basic assumptions—has become "contested," as the liberal terminology would have it, the reservoir of public trust needed to find common ground is in short supply. In such circumstances, how then might presidents successfully govern?

One possible model is to try and govern by poll-driven consensus, taking the most basic and general common denominator of what the public says it wants and designing and pitching your policies accordingly. This is not a recipe for success for many reasons, among them the fact that on important policies the public is not always well informed and even when it becomes more informed it often holds conflicting views. Moreover, even if it were possible to do so, such a strategy would fail on the grounds that the public now demands "leadership" of its presidents, and those elected to the office are convinced they can provide it.

Another possible model is for the president to govern on the strength of his convictions. Here, a president who has strong policy views and goals, simply does his best to carry them through given the partisan make up of Congress. It helps if you are a *conviction president*, like Barack Obama, to have the public on your side. This was Ronald Reagan's formula for a successful two-term presidency. He had strong and well-known right center convictions, was clear about running and governing on them, and came into office at a time when his basic policy worldview struck a responsive cord with the general public.

Conviction presidents, however, cannot always count on continued public support, even when they start out with it. After 9/11, George W. Bush became a conviction president, whose primary purpose was to protect the United States from another, worse, terrorist attack, perhaps next time using nuclear, biological, or chemical weapons. In that pursuit he enacted a number of very strong, and controversial, domestic and foreign national security policies. These were, and generally still are, supported by the American public.

Yet President Bush also reached the conclusion that Saddam Hussein, Iraq's dictator, was dangerous to the region and to the United States and had to be removed. He did so and the resulting war proved difficult, costly and, over time, controversial. Democratic opposition to Mr. Bush's national security and economic policies and especially the war in Iraq was continuous and ferocious. For complicated reasons including opposition to the president's policies and to the assertion of American military power, public opinion in many parts of the world also turned against Mr. Bush and the United States. That, coupled with the increasingly difficult conduct of the war, begin to drive the president's domestic support down and he ended his second term at a very low level of public support. In this case, the president's convictions did not translate into unceasing public support, nor is there reason to expect that they should have done so.

Leadership Integrity

Leadership integrity develops out of two key elements, one a matter of character, the other a matter of identity. The character element of leadership integrity originates in a president having the courage of his convictions. To qualify a president must not only have discernible ideals or values, but be willing to stand up for them in circumstances where that might involve personal or political loss. This is the element of character integrity.

Leadership integrity also stems from the authenticity of the president's personal and political identity. That requires the president not only to be who he claims to be, but that he also govern in a way that is consistent with those claims. Both of these are important. A president's political identity, especially when he explicitly characterizes and campaigns on it, contains an explicit premise and promise. The premise is that it is real. The promise is it will be the basis of how the president actually leads and governs. Adhering to that premise and keeping that promise is one strong foundation of political legitimacy.

Presidential candidates campaign and in doing so convey to the public who they are and what they stand for. However, to the extent that candidates tell the public what they think it wants to hear, their authenticity and legitimacy are self-undermining. There is a strong element of deception involved in taking this approach and a large element of risk. Running as a pragmatic moderate and governing like a transforming liberal would seem to qualify as the kind of legitimacy gap that can bring a president trouble.

A second strategy increasingly used by modern presidential candidates starting with President Nixon, is to blend and blur the lines of their political identities.

Nixon saw himself as "pragmatic" rather than ideological and his policies tended to follow from that. Was Nixon a conservative anti-communist? Yes, for the most part. Was Nixon prepared to engage in strategic negotiations with his adversaries? Yes, when possible. Did Nixon's anti-communist views keep him from forging a new relationship with China? No, they did not.[1]

Candidates as diverse as Michael Dukakis, who ran on a "competence, not ideology" theme, Bill Clinton, who ran on a "third-way" perspective, George W. Bush, who ran as a "compassionate conservative," and Barack Obama, who ran as a "pragmatic progressive," are all examples of the attempt to by-pass or transcend conventional ideological categories in the search for winning electoral and governing coalitions.

The problem with these ambiguity strategies is that they run the risk of loosening the relationship between character integrity and governing legitimacy. It is, after all, hard for a president to demonstrate that he has the courage of his convictions if, at the same time, he presents himself as having a flexible, open, and "each problem has its own pragmatic solution" approach to questions of policy and governance.

Finally, there is the connection between character integrity and identity authenticity on one hand and actually leading and governing while in office on the other. Basically, presidential campaigns give candidates the chance to showcase who they are and for the public to anticipate *how*, and *on what basis* they will govern. The public does not expect a president to act on principle regardless of costs or circumstances. They expect, and hope, that the president's policy and governing choices will be thought through, responsive to the issues at hand and effective. Yet, they still expect, legitimately, that those choices, within certain broad considerations, will reflect the president's stated ideals and convictions—the ones on which they were persuaded to give him their vote and their trust. They also expect, legitimately, that the president will lead and govern in ways consistent with his professed personal and political identity.

Each and every one of these considerations—character integrity, identity authenticity and their consistency with Obama's governing philosophy and choices—have become troublesome issues for this president.

Obama's Character Integrity

Recall that character integrity involves the development and consolidation of ideals and values into a useful framework that allows the person, or president, to fairly and effectively negotiate the complexities of life's choices. There is no expectation contained in this term that the person will necessarily be a paragon of principle or virtue. Moral, ethical, and political issues are complex, circumstances impose their own imperatives, and a president must balance many factors. Still, the absence of ideals and values means that a person or president is largely motivated by their unanchored and undiluted ambitions.

Such leaders accumulate power for a variety of personal reasons that are rationalized and presented as public purposes. Early on, the psychological analysis of political leaders uncovered the fact that some leaders accumulate power to overcome low estimates of themselves, or in more clinical terms to buttress low levels of self-esteem.[2] In these circumstances, the psychological equation seems to be: I have accumulated power therefore I am a good and important person.

Such persons are skilled at gaining power, but not particularly flexible in exercising it. The reason is that challenges to their power, prestige and policies are often taken personally, and in a psychological sense are personal since they challenge the leader's basic sense of himself. Presidents with this psychological frame of mind don't see politics through the basic paradigm of "give and take" or "win some, lose some," but rather "how dare they!"

During the campaign Robert Samuelson, a respected *Washington Post* columnist wrote that, "Aside from ambition—hardly unique among presidential candidates—I cannot detect powerful convictions in Obama."[3] I think he was mistaken. *It is now very clear that Obama does have both powerful ambitions and powerful convictions.* The ambitions are very clear. Obama wants to be a great president. He aspires to be America's moral arbiter at home and in the world and he seeks to do so through transformative redemptive policies based on his ideas of fairness.

That is why the perhaps well-intentioned, but naïve suggestion, made after the 2010 midterm elections, by two centrist Democrats in the *Washington Post*, wholly misses the point. They subtitled their piece, "To be a great president, Obama should not seek reelection in 2012."[4] Aside from the dire political consequences to his presidency that would ensue,[5] it is absolutely certain that Obama would not view being a modern one-term of the legendary Cincinnatus, Republican leader of Rome, as a suitable model for realizing his transformative ambitions.

The problem for Obama and his presidency, and for increasingly large segments of the American public, is that Obama didn't campaign on his aspirations for transformation. Nor did he make clear to the American public that his desire to transform America at home and abroad would be strongly framed through his ideal of fairness. He campaigned on "hope" and "change," two vague terms that have little direct connection with his ambitions or their enactment.

A plausible case can be made that the American public should have asked more of Obama than campaign platitudes, and to be fair he discussed a great many policies during the many campaign debates and in interviews. But these discussions were, in most circumstances, general and Obama, with one exception—his "spread the wealth around comment"—did not mention, much less discuss, the extent to which his views of fairness require redistribution of resources and opportunities from some groups to others. Nor did he make clear the extent to which he saw the United States as having to redeem itself with new less assertive policies for its past transgressions.

Obama's Identity: Pragmatism vs. Liberalism?

The same set of issues arises with regard to Obama's political identity. He campaigned as a moderate and a pragmatist. In reality, he framed those terms through the lens of his strongly held liberal worldviews (see Chapter 2).

Being either a liberal or conservative has no particular relationship to character integrity. One can be either, so long as you have the courage of your convictions, be they left or right. The issue that arises here is campaigning as a moderate without making clear your pragmatism is framed through a strongly held liberal or "progressive" worldview.

Worldviews supply basic premises and assumptions to how a president frames an issue and thus shapes his response. Consider Iran. Underlying questions at the level of policy towards its apparent nuclear aspirations depend in part on assessments of intentions and assumptions about motivations. Does Iran want the bomb, if it does, for security? Does it want it to gain respect? Regional hegemony?

Yet, underneath these questions lies the sub-strata of assumptions about how the world works. If it is true, as Obama said in his speech to the U.N., calling it a "deeply held belief," "that in the year 2009—more than at any point in human history—the interests of nations and peoples are shared,"[6] policies like engagement should be geared to maximize those possibilities. If on the other hand, nationalism utilized by leaders with hegemonic aspirations trying to reestablish past glories or build new ones, is viewed as a real and present danger, the center of gravity of foreign policies will shift toward a stronger more protective stance.

"The Plan:" Obama's Persona vs. His Political Identity

One of the surprises of the first two years of the Obama presidency is how far and how fast he has fallen in public support, especially among Independents, but also among Republicans. In July 2009, support for Obama was at 90 percent for Democrats, 20 percent for Republicans and 56 percent for Independents. One year later those numbers were 81, 12, and 38 percent respectively.[7] Some perspective on these numbers can be gained by looking at Obama's approval levels on the date he first entered the presidency, January 20, 2009. Those numbers were 88 percent Democrats, 41 percent Republicans, and 62 percent Independents.

What stands out in these figures is the support that Obama drew from those who indentified as Republicans, 41 percent, and majority support from Independents, 62 percent. Obama clearly had the good wishes of a substantial part of the opposition party and a solid foundation with Independent voters.[8] That has obviously dissipated for reasons that can be directly laid at the doorstep of the president's insistence on pursuing his transformative redemptive agenda despite substantial public opposition.

Yet the sharp decline in these figures also suggests that groups that might have been in opposition (Republicans and Independents) were willing to give the

Obama Administration a chance and felt disappointed and perhaps even betrayed by what they saw unfolding. This raises the question of why the expectations of these groups proved so unrealistic. Why was their initial optimism so high?

Part of the answer is to be found in the persona that Obama put forward during the campaign as being moderate and pragmatic. Relevant too is the fact that Obama had a relatively brief career in politics for a major party presidential candidate and so he did not have a long history to research and debate. Yet, he did have a history.

Obama had spent eight years in the Illinois state legislature and accumulated an easily identifiable record as a typical urban liberal from a substantially African American and white liberal district. Any serious inquiry would have easily discovered these facts. He also had a record as a United States senator that was easily identifiable as very liberal. Why didn't people clearly see the real record he had accumulated? Part of the answer has to do with a series of strategic steps that Obama and his advisors conceived and carried out to blunt the impact of Obama's record.

In the beginning there was "The Plan." The plan, it should be emphasized, involves no conspiracy theory from any part of the political spectrum. It was simply the name given to a strategic plan developed by David Axelrod, Peter Rouse (his legislative assistant at the time and later to become Chief of Staff), and Robert Gibbs, senior advisors to the new senator, to prepare for his reelection and whatever other political opportunities might present themselves.[9] The latter possibility, at least according to Mendell, was already on the horizon. He wrote,

> the game plan was to send Obama into the 2007–8 election cycle in the strongest possible position. No politician had gained the sort of attention that he had won so quickly, and his advisors knew that he had a shot at being a vice presidential selection or perhaps an outside chance *at running for the presidency as early as 2008*.[10]

From the outset, "The Plan called for Obama's transition to occur with as little media attention as possible," and toward that end Gibbs, Obama's press advisor and later press secretary, "did everything he could to thwart" a reporter who wanted to write a story on Obama's first year from gaining access to him.[11] The Plan called for Obama to keep a low profile, take care to nurture his relationships with his Illinois constituents, and other obvious prudent steps.

But the key aspect of The Plan,

> frustrated some of his friends, his legislative colleagues, and particularly his devoted liberal followers. *In order to keep himself as unscathed as possible, he became even more cautious in his political approach, avoiding controversy at all costs. In Springfield, Obama had been an unabashed liberal* ... But if he had larger ambitions, his team believed that he could not be fitted too uncomfortably with a liberal straightjacket.[12]

So, the essence of the plan was to suppress situations or information that would reveal Obama's real political identity, as a liberal, and accentuate the construction of his political persona, as a moderate.

One reason then that Obama supporters among members of the Republican Party and Independents were so surprised at the redemptive transformational turn of Obama's first two years in office, was that they had been led to focus on his persona, not on his real political identity.

Bipartisanship Revisited: Health Care

Then there is the issue of leadership while governing. Obama has touted his bipartisan experience and aspirations. As noted, Obama's view of compromise is, "*you have to be the one who's dictating how the compromises work.*"[13] In his *Audacity* book he has more to say about this subject:

> Genuine bipartisanship, though, assumes an honest process of give-and-take, and that the quality of the compromise is measured by how well it assumes some agreed upon goal, better schools or lower deficits. This assumes that the majority will be constrained—by an exacting press corps and ultimately an informed electorate—to negotiate in good faith.[14]

What's interesting about this quote is that it assumes that neither party, if in power, will negotiate in "good faith," being intent to "dictate how compromises work."

Obama then goes on to complain about the bipartisan charade of then ascendant Republicans in Congress:

> the majority party can begin by asking for 100% of what it wants, go on to concede 10%, and then accuse any member of the minority party who fails to support this "compromise" of being "obstructionist." For the minority party in such circumstances, "bipartisanship" comes to mean chronically getting steamrollered, although individual senators may enjoy certain political rewards by consistently going along with the majority and hence gaining a reputation for being "moderate" or "centrist."[15]

Obama's critical comment about "individual senators" belonging to the party out of power does not seem to grant their efforts much credit because he notes they "enjoy certain political rewards." Presumably, this is in place of compromising because they are really searching for common ground. Moreover, his comment does reflect much appreciation of the ways in which parties in power try to tempt at least a few members of the opposition over to their side by offering just enough minor compromises to lure some opposition members to their side and hail the results as "bipartisan."

Obama's Approach to Health Care: Strategic Ambiguity

Obama's complaint about the high-handed tactics of the then Republican majority would seem to apply equally to his approach as president with large Democratic majorities on such issues as health care. And this points to a fundamental issue with all the talk of bipartisanship. Parties in the majority view the term as requiring them to incorporate a few nonessential ideas from the other side while insisting that the legislated policy go down the road they prefer. Parties out of power see bipartisanship as adapting policies that both parties can agree with. This is a difficult proposition since each party's underlying assumptions of how policy and reform are best accomplished differ dramatically.

Democrats are generally in favor of government regulations and mandates in which big social problems are solved by large-scale, mandated government programs. The Democratic health care legislation that passed mandates that the government determine what kinds of health care insurance consumers can buy and what health care insurers must cover. It also mandates what insurance companies may charge for the basic coverage so that costs are held down. Opponents view these features as large steps toward essential government control of the health care market place. Republicans see that approach as unnecessarily limiting individual choice, unlikely to accomplish its purposes, and dramatically expanding the reach of government control. They prefer smaller scale, incremental, market based policies such as allowing families and businesses to purchase insurance across state lines, allowing individuals, small businesses, trade associations to pool together and acquire health insurance at lower prices, and changing the tax code to encourage and not tax these efforts along these lines.

In trying to bridge these policy divides, but on his own terms, Obama is a master of inclusionary rhetoric. As one *New York Times* columnist put it, "For President Obama, being 'bipartisan' means incorporating a few right-of-center proposals into an essentially liberal legislative package."[16] And what right of center proposals did the president incorporate? That's a difficult question to answer directly. I discuss the provisions to cap health care lawsuits below in the next section, but here I want to focus on the so called "public option." The public option would have effectively federalized the entire American health care system with the government directly underwriting and bringing under federal control all health care insurance, what it covered, how it covered it, and who got covered at what cost. This option was extremely contentious and did not appear in the final bill.

The president expressed himself as being both a supporter of the idea, but denying its importance to him. Obama supported the idea, saying, "I continue to believe that a public option within the basket of insurance choices would help improve quality and bring down costs."[17] Later, he backed away from it saying that he had "never campaigned on it,"[18] although it had appeared as part of his campaign's health care proposals, and that "it was not the most important part of the health care bill."[19]

After reviewing all the evidence on both sides of the claim that Obama had or had not championed the public option, two reporters concluded that there was ample evidence on both sides and that, "This all really speaks to what a blank slate Barack Obama was for so many people—liberals, centrists and conservatives alike. Anyone could find something they liked about him and adapt the idea of Obama to what they wanted."[20] This is a good illustration of Obama's strategic inkblot strategy in operation—make so many nuanced, contextually dependent statements on a subject that it is hard to know exactly where the president stands.

In fact, the president's retreat on the public option seems to have little to do with his belief in having free market mechanisms as part of his legislation. It was driven by political need to get the votes to pass the legislation at all. Senator Kent Conrad (D-N.D.), a major player for the Democrats in the Senate, said during the debate, "The fact of the matter is there are not the votes in the United States Senate for the public option. There never have been. So to continue to chase that rabbit, I think, is just a wasted effort."[21] A few days later an editorial in the *Washington Post* put the matter more directly:

> the reality is that, if the Obama administration wants to get health reform done, it's going to have to back away from the public option sooner or later—and it's getting awfully late. This is not a matter of ideology but of political nose-counting. *And there's no way to amass 60 votes with a public option in the bill.*[22]

Pragmatist, Moderate, Or Transformer?

All of these facts raise a very basic set of questions: On what basis can Obama be legitimately called a "pragmatist" or a "moderate," and on what basis is it possible to call health care legislation bipartisan? Can we legitimately say that Obama is a moderate because he jettisoned the public option in order to get his bill passed? We might more correctly associate this with his "pragmatism," except that it's extremely narrow and limited. In order to get his bill passed the president gave up on his preference for a public option which would have put the government almost wholly in charge of every important aspect of American medical care. Instead he threw his support behind a bill that established "health care cooperatives," in which the government was *the* major player that mandated what kinds of health care insurance consumers could buy, what health care insurers must cover and for what price.

The government did not immediately federalize the whole system with this bill but took enormous and unprecedented steps in that direction. Yes, private insurance companies still exist. However, to gain some appreciation of their circumstances imagine if the government passed a law that allowed General Motors to dictate the style, number and price of its competitor's models. In such a case Toyota or other carmakers would essentially continue to exist only at GM's sufferance.

So, yes, Obama did settle for something less than the most far-reaching proposal to nationalize American health care, but he did get something very close to it. How close will only become clear as the policy unfolds, if it is not revised. The point here is not about the virtues or liabilities of the different approaches but whether the final product entitles Obama to claim himself as moderate on the basis of it. A fair appraisal would indicate that he couldn't legitimately make such a claim.

In an early interview as president-elect Obama listed the problems he wanted to work on including health care and said, "I think the Republicans have a lot to offer."[23] What exactly they had to offer he didn't make clear. He further narrowed the grounds by saying, "And if somebody presents to me a plan that they are ideologically wedded to but they can't persuade me that this is actually going to be good for the economy, then we're not going to do it."[24] The problem here of course, is that seems to rule out approaches that Republicans believe because of their worldviews and premises just as Democrats have theirs. As a committed liberal and democrat who is already on record as saying, "I won't deny my preference for the story the Democrats tell, nor my belief that *the arguments of liberals* are more often grounded in reason and fact,"[25] what would it take to convince such a committed liberal that the arguments of conservatives have some, or maybe even more, merit?

At one point in the process after the surprising Republican senate victory in Massachusetts, the president said, "I would advise that we try to move quickly to coalesce around those elements of the package that people agree on,"[26] phrasing that seemed to indicate he was open to a real bipartisan solution that incorporated elements of both parties' perspectives. However, those sentiments were never translated into actions aside from the search for compromises that would entice a minimum number of "moderate" Republicans, so that the bill could be touted as bipartisan.

And what of pragmatism claims? Here too, the facts seem to speak clearly. Obama did not, as Woodrow Wilson did with his League of Nations proposal, fight any changes and help bring about the proposal's defeat. Obama was tactically flexible and willing to concede points where he had to, but the net result was still legislation that was, in almost every one of its particulars, a bill reflecting Democratic assumptions about how best to solve America's health care problems. There seems to be little basis for considering this bill as in any serious way bipartisan, certainly not in the attempt, were it even possible, to really try to blend Democratic and Republican ideas about the best direction and methods for health care reform.

There is nothing novel about the president proceeding as he did, except in so far that he has touted his bipartisan leadership. Did Republicans, even so called moderate ones, vote unanimously against the bill? They did. But that owed less to intransigence than to the fact that with large majorities in both houses, Democrats could, and did, choose to enact legislation that included their views of what was important and how to proceed, and the few options they offered Republicans were narrow and marginal (see below), and in any event did not change the basic nature and direction of the legislation.

In the health care debate, President Obama is revealed as a transformational-minded president who made use of his large Congressional majorities to accomplish his view of "changing America" which he alluded to but did not really describe on the campaign trail. For all the rhetoric about pragmatism, moderation, and bipartisanship, these terms seem to have been limited and very narrowly applied.

Regardless of the realities of the president's bipartisan efforts, he has clearly articulated transformational ambitions and followed through on them. So the question presents itself: Are transformational ambitions consistent with pragmatism? Not really. We are accustomed to think of revolutionary transformations as requiring revolutionary tactics especially in societies in which power arrangements are entrenched. But Obama is no revolutionary in that sense; we will not see him leading his followers in a mass march and storming the barricades. But if the health care legislation is any indication, he will use every, and any legal, political, and parliamentary means to enact his transformative vision. This may be pragmatic in the very limited strategic meaning of that term, but it is by no means a reflection of policy or political moderation.

Character Integrity and Willingness to Stand Up for What You Believe

Ambition bears a strong relationship to character integrity though in politics the two are not necessarily on friendly terms. The essence of character integrity is to be found not only in the development of ideals and values but also in the courage to stand up for them when it might entail real loss. There is no real courage involved in standing up for what most people believe and will reward. Courage consists of taking unpopular stands, sometimes against public belief, but also against the views of those who support you. In this respect, Obama's pursuit of transformation, against public wishes, certainly qualifies as an example of having the courage of your convictions.

This, however, raises another question: just how independent minded is Obama? How far across the aisle is he really willing to reach to find common ground and pragmatic solutions? On what core issues, if any, has he been willing to go his own way and take the consequences of doing so? This latter point is critical. The hallmark of true independence is the willingness to go against those who support you. Mr. Obama was not part of the bipartisan "Gang of 14" that tried to avert a showdown on judicial filibusters; he was not among the sixty-eight senators voting for a bipartisan agreement on the Foreign Intelligence Surveillance Act; and he dissented from the part of the bipartisan immigration deal that displeased unions.[27] He also first joined then withdrew from John McCain's efforts to forge a bipartisan reform of Congressional ethics.[28]

Obama points to a number of areas where he says he has demonstrated his courage and independence. He often mentions his support for better gas mileage in a talk before Detroit automakers.[29] This, however, is a conventional Democratic policy position delivered before a group who are hardly political allies.

He has also touted his support of teachers' merit raises, a position that seems at variance with the position of a key Democratic support group, the National Education Association.[30] Yet a look at his website on the issue of rewarding teachers shows that he emphasizes giving merit pay for mentoring new teachers, serving in underserved places, and only last "if teachers consistently excel in the classroom, that work can be valued and rewarded as well."[31]

David Brooks looked into Obama's education rhetoric and plans and found ample evidence of statements meant to please two distinctive education policy positions *within the Democratic Party* (no evidence was reported of him having considered ideas from across the aisle). Brooks writes that Obama has made numerous statements over time that seem to support first one side, then the other. Moreover as Brooks notes in all of these rhetorical initiatives he,

> doesn't really address the core issues. What do you do with teachers and administrators who are failing? How rigorously do you enforce accountability? Obama doesn't engage the thorny, substantive matters that divide the two Democratic camps. He proposes dozens of programs to build on top of the current system, but it's not clear that he would challenge it.[32]

Character Integrity and the Health Care Debate

A more recent example came up in the health care debate. Among the major ideas that Republicans wanted seriously considered was a cap on health care law suits. The *New York Times* reported that,

> In closed-door talks, Mr. Obama has been making the case that reducing malpractice lawsuits—a goal of many doctors and Republicans—can help drive down health care costs, and should be considered as part of any health care overhaul, according to lawmakers of both parties, as well as A.M.A. officials.

However, were it enacted, that proposal, "could hurt Mr. Obama with the left wing of his party and with trial lawyers who are major donors to Democratic campaigns."[33] Certainly, Obama's expressed interest, even behind closed doors, signaled a public opportunity for demonstrating his independence and willingness to take some political hits in the service of bipartisanship.

As one trade journal noted,

> The possibility that malpractice changes could be part of health care legislation that suddenly seems to have better chances of passing has sent doctors and trial lawyers scrambling. Senators on the Finance Committee are looking at the possibility of special courts in which a judge with medical expertise would hear malpractice cases … Other possibilities include the option of arbitration,

as well as some liability protection for doctors who follow "best practice" clinical standards in treating their patients.[34]

And so what did the president then do? Faced with a furious and successful lobbying blitz from trial lawyers such proposals were dropped from the pending legislation. In the words of a Bloomberg news report,

> The absence of such a provision reflects the clout of trial lawyers, whose PAC contributed $1.1 million this year to Democrats, trailing only the International Union of Operating Engineers and International Brotherhood of Electrical Workers, according to the Center for Responsive Politics, a Washington research group.[35]

Obama did not wholly abandon his stand. He instructed the Department of Health and Human Services to provide $23.2 million in local grants for demonstration projects related to reducing malpractice litigation.[36] These grants will take at least three years to get up and running, after which evaluations will be made.

The grants will cover a number of discrete areas including:[37] health care, early offers for financial settlement, apology programs,[38] and medical review panels. Congress must still appropriate funds and they will have the final word on how they are implemented. Taking part is optional, as is abiding by the results. The more troublesome issue is that the projects are very small, the results will not therefore be easy to generalize, and as is the case in most social science policy research we can expect that the results will be somewhat equivocal.[39] This will provide talking points for those who wish to resist implementing any of these reforms.

Sister Souljah Revisited?

President Obama did not have a Sister Souljah moment with the issue of reducing medical litigation. That name refers to the moment when Bill Clinton spoke out directly and publicly against a "gangster rap" song by that woman that lauded the killing of white cops by blacks. This was considered to be a brave and controversial act of courage at the time. So too when Barack Obama came out against the harsh, racist, anti-American statements of his mentor and church leader Jeremiah Wright, some thought this was a Sister Souljah moment.[40]

But coming out against the idea that blacks should take a week and kill whites (Sister Souljah) or that the U.S. government had infected blacks with the AIDS virus and had brought terrorist attacks on itself by practicing terrorism abroad (Wright) hardly seems to be an example of a courageous political statement for which you might pay at the polls. On the contrary, not to have come out against Reverend Wright's assertions would have disqualified Obama from presidential leadership.

As to the small-scale demonstration programs for medical litigation reform, they appear, given their size, scope, and timing to be more symbolic than substantive. In this they resemble in much reduced and narrower form presidential commissions that are designed to appear to do something about a difficult problem without, however, having to do any particular thing until much later, if at all. In this respect, Obama's follow through to his hints about being open to medical litigation reform follows the same path. They do begin an effort, but that effort is small and unlikely to bear much policy fruit for many years, if at all. Having taken that small step, however, allows Obama to burnish his credentials as someone willing to stand up to his own party, without, however, taking the stronger steps that would have constituted real political courage. It cannot really be counted under the category of having the courage of your convictions. If anything, it reflects a certain timidity in doing so.

The Asterisk** Presidency

Every president knows more than he can safely tell. In times of emergency or in high-stakes domestic or national security matters, the president is hardly obligated to share all of the doubts and reservations that may have been expressed during the course of policy deliberations. On the other hand, if the matter is not an immediate crisis or a high stakes national security question, the weight of argument moves toward fuller and more honest accounting of the advantages and risks of a particular problem.

Presidents, especially smart ones, as Obama clearly is, almost surely know or ought to know, the ambiguities and risks in the policies they propose. It is of course possible that someone so committed to both their own worldview and the solutions they deem appropriate might systematically err on the side of downplaying alternative arguments, even though being perfectly capable of repeating them. This is a particular risk for President Obama.

The leadership legitimacy question at the heart of this dilemma is how honest to be with the public. Every president, and Obama is no exception, accentuates the positive. How could they do otherwise? After all, they have come to the conclusion whether through debate, ideology, or worldview that their proposals are best. Few presidents tout the virtues of opposition policy.

Obama on Obama's Leadership Probity

Still, Obama has gone out of his way, as Jimmy Carter did before him,[41] to emphasize his policy veracity and desire to level with the American public. In a campaign interview he said of himself, "I do think that I have tried to conduct my political career and my campaign in a way that is honest and candid and straightforward and minimizes spin."[42] The night he won the election, he said in a speech, "But I will always be honest with you about the challenges that we face."[43] Later in another interview, he went further,

> But one of the things I've actually been encouraged by—and I learned during the campaign—was the American people, I think, not only have a toleration

but also a hunger for explanation and complexity, and a willingness to acknowledge hard problems. I think one of the biggest mistakes that is made in Washington is this notion you have to dumb things down for the public.[44]

In another interview Obama took up the theme of honesty and said,

> But the second thing that I admire most in Lincoln is that there is just a deep-rooted honesty and empathy to the man that allowed him to always be able to see the other person's point of view and always sought to find that truth that is in the gap between you and me. Right? That the truth is out there somewhere and I don't fully possess it and you don't fully possess it and our job then is to listen and learn and imagine enough to be able to get to that truth.[45]

There are many shades of truth and they lie on a continuum that leads to misrepresentation and onto outright lies. Smart, knowledgeable presidents and leaders don't often lie outright. However, they are tempted to mislead either by omission, tailored representation that does not do justice to the facts, or phrasing that misdirects. All of these are "slight-of-words" rhetorical techniques.

Obama is a very smart well-versed president and can easily be given credit for knowing the difference among all these choices. He has not always chosen to live up to his Lincoln-like aspirations. As the *New York Times* reported,

> During almost two years on the campaign trail, Barack Obama promised to slay the demons of Washington, bar lobbyists from his administration and usher in what he would later call in his Inaugural Address a "new era of responsibility." *What he did not talk much about were the asterisks.* The exceptions that went unmentioned now include a pair of cabinet nominees who did not pay all of their taxes. Then there is the lobbyist for a military contractor who is now slated to become the No. 2 official in the Pentagon. And there are the others brought into government from the influence industry even if not formally registered as lobbyists.[46]

The most recent example is the report that the White House met with lobbyists away from the Oval Office which meant that the meetings would not show in White House logs.[47]

Caveat Civitas?

This is far from the only instance of what might be termed *the asterisk** presidency.* It is not a presidency of outright lies. Rather it is one in which there may well be a technically correct truth in a president's statements, if the somewhat skewed, inaccurate, debatable, or unrepresentative premises are accepted at face value.

Among those areas where there was a substantial gap between promise and reassurance on one hand and reality on the other were:

1. "Obama repeatedly vowed during the 2008 presidential election campaign that he would not raise taxes on individuals making less than $200,000 and households earning less than $250,000 a year."[48] However, taxpayers earning less than $200,000 a year will pay roughly $3.9 billion more in taxes—in 2019 alone—due to health care reform, according to the Joint Committee on Taxation, Congress's official scorekeeper.[49]

2. The president disowned any involvement in the unsavory horse trades that allowed this health care bill to proceed,[50] but his chief of staff was intimately involved with making these deals happen.[51]

3. The president and his administration said repeatedly that the GOP had no ideas on health care.[52] An independent evaluation by Politi-Fact found those and similar statements to be untrue.[53]

4. The president urged Congress to adapt pay as you go which he described as follows: "Congress can only spend a dollar if it saves a dollar elsewhere."[54] Yet, "pay-as you go" does not necessarily require savings, new spending can be offset by taxes, or by ending tax breaks already enacted, and in this case, the proposal excluded the trillions of dollars in new spending mandated by the president's stimulus bills.[55] Nor would the PAYGO law apply to discretionary spending programs, which account for about 40 percent of the federal budget.[56]

5. In his seventh press conference as president-elect Obama said,

    > "Let me repeat what I've said earlier, there is a bipartisan consensus among economists—you can talk to Conservative as well as Liberal economists, that right now our biggest challenge is putting people back to work and stabilizing the economy ... the thing that we have to do right now is to have a bold economic recovery plan."[57]

    In reality, while conservative and liberal economists might agree that putting people back to work is a priority, there is no consensus on what steps to take to do so, much less that the president's "bold economic plan" is an appropriate and effective one.

6. The president has repeatedly pointed out that health care reform of the kind that he proposed would improve the long-term budget outlook.[58] This is not accurate. CBO Director Dr. Douglas Elmendor has written in a report that, "Rising health costs will put tremendous pressure on the federal budget during the next few decades and beyond. *In CBO's judgment, the health legislation enacted earlier this year does not substantially diminish that pressure.*"[59] And indeed, in campaigning for the 2010 midterm elections, "Key White House allies are dramatically shifting their attempts to defend health care legislation, abandoning claims that it will reduce costs and deficit, and instead stressing a promise to 'improve it.'"[60]

7. In speaking of his administration's plan to rescue Chrysler and GM Obama said,

> It's a partnership that the federal government will support by making additional loans that are consistent with what I outlined last month. As part of their agreement, every dime of *new* taxpayer money will be repaid before Fiat can take a majority ownership stake in Chrysler.[61]

Listeners might be excused for failing to catch the importance of the adjective "new" before taxpayer money. In reality, many billions of dollars had already been loaned by the time of Obama's comments and were not likely to ever be repaid.[62]

8. Regarding health care Obama said, "If you like your doctor, you will be able to keep your doctor. Period. If you like your health-care plan you will be able to keep your health care plan. Period. No one will take it away. No matter what."[63] That turned out not to be accurate. An early draft of administration regulations on this matter, "estimates that many employers will be forced to make changes to their health plans under the new law. In just three years, a majority of workers—51 percent—will be in plans subject to new federal requirements."[64] And that is only for the so-called "grand-fathered" plans.

9. With regard to some of his principal core support groups, even as Obama is, "publicly keeping them at arms length and saying little on so-called wedge-issues, he's been quietly advancing their agendas, hitching many of them to the economic crisis that, he's said, is also an opportunity America cannot afford to waste." For example, When Obama ended Bush's ban on funding overseas groups that perform or promote abortion, he did it quietly, on a Friday afternoon, with no popping flashes or handshakes with the directors of women's groups. But the groups say that as long as he keeps pushing the policy—his budget includes more funding for family planning programs, and cuts to abstinence-only programs, for instance—they have nothing to complain about.[65]

10. Obama said, "[My plan] will not help speculators who took risky bets on a rising market and bought homes not to live in but to sell. It will not help dishonest lenders who acted irresponsibly, distorting the facts and dismissing the fine print at the expense of buyers who didn't know better. And it will not reward folks who bought homes they knew from the beginning they would never be able to afford."[66] However, "While the Obama administration initially said it would focus on owner-occupied properties, Fannie Mae and Freddie Mac said they would refinance loans for some second homes and investment properties, too."[67]

11. Obama weighed in, seemingly forcefully, in a highly public venue, on the right of Muslims to build a cultural center at the site of the World Trade Towers,[68] a right that no one disputed. He avoided the question of whether it was

appropriate or sensitive to do so on what he termed "hallowed ground," and when confronted with the view that his strong endorsement of their right would be seen to also endorse their decision to do so, he disclaimed the strong endorsement implied in his first statement, even as he stood by its assertion.[69] The result was that what seemed to be a strong and unequivocal statement became substantially less so and even severely muddled by subsequent "clarifications." As one report put it, "Obama's new remarks, literally speaking, re-open the question of which side he's on,"[70] a not uncommon Rorschach moment for the president.

12. In March 2011 President Obama announced that he had reversed his two-year-old order suspending military trials at Guantánamo,[71] The new Executive Order emphasized the right of review for Guantánamo inmates,[72] along with other procedural privileges such as the ability to call witnesses who are "reasonably available and willing to provide information."

In issuing the Executive Order the president touted the order as furthering our commitment "to bring terrorists to justice consistent with our commitment to protect the American people and uphold our values."[73] Critics on the left were concerned that, "It is virtually impossible to imagine how one closes Guantanamo in light of this executive order."[74] On the right, critics essentially saw the Executive Order, as the *Wall Street Journal* headline announced, as a tactical ratification of the Bush administration.[75]

Less noticed was at the fact that at the same time the administration was publishing the president's Executive Order, it also published a "Fact Sheet" that contained the following revelation not contained in the president's Executive Order, nor his official statement, nor was it discussed by administration aides with the major newspapers that reported the story: "Our adherence to these principles is also an important safeguard against the mistreatment of captured U. S. military personnel. The U.S. Government *will therefore choose out of a sense of legal obligation to treat the principles set forth in Article 75 as applicable to any individual it detains in an international armed conflict*, and expects all other nations to adhere to these principles as well."[76]

What is article 75?[77] It is part of Protocol I of the 1977 amendments to the 1949 Geneva Conventions that grants further procedural redress to those covered by those conventions.[78] It has not been ratified by the United States. Nor is the administration submitting Article 75 to the Senate for approval as constitutionally required. Rather, the president is simply announcing at the end of a "Fact Sheet" that it will now be administration policy.

That policy requires the United States not to engage in "outrages upon personal dignity, in particular humiliating and degrading treatment." It is unclear just what this means and the administration will surely be required to define it. However, it does seem to open up a wide basis on which to challenge any information gained as a result of interrogation, even with techniques sanction by the U.S. Army code of conduct.[79] The protocol under which the administration pledged to make its operating policy also requires that, "Anyone charged with an offence shall have the right to examine, or have examined, the witnesses against him and to obtain the attendance and examination of witnesses on his behalf under the same conditions as witnesses against him." The phrase "have examined" seems to contradict the president's Executive Order that any witnesses called must be "reasonably available and willing to provide information." After all, inmates may now have their representatives depose any witness, residing anywhere and of whatever level in the intelligence, military, or administration with information asserted to be germane to their status.

The thrust and likely result of this little noticed policy initiative, stuck in at the end of a "Fact Sheet" will be to make the military trial system, that the president has opposed since it was first formulated after 9/11 by the Bush administration much more difficult to successfully utilize against those designated as "enemy combatants."

Perhaps that is its purpose and perhaps that purpose is legitimate. However, if both of those are the views of the Obama administration, they would seem to be important enough to be publicly direct about and to mount a public case for their appropriateness and not be placed at the very end of a "Fact Sheet."

Every president must, and should, adjust policies as circumstances change. Every president finds himself in a position in which he cannot follow through on campaign promises. Most, if not all presidential administrations have adjusted the policy numbers to put the best face on their efforts.

The Lincoln Standard

Yet, for the sheer range, number, and tempo of asterisk statements, this president surely stands apart. This partially reflects Obama's role as singular embodiment and spokesman for his many initiatives. In part, it reflects Obama's clear intelligence and his ability, not second to any president including Bill Clinton, to parse words and meaning.

When Obama called attention to his idealization of Lincoln's ability to "find the truth," he went on say that,

> *Most of our other great presidents, there was that sense of working the angles,* and bending other people to their will. FDR being the classic example. And Lincoln just found a way to shape public opinion and shape people around him and lead them and guide them *without tricking them or bullying them* but just through the force of what I was talking about: that way of helping to illuminate the truth. I just find that to be a very compelling type of leadership. *It's not one that I've mastered.* ... [80]

In truth, he has not.

The Paradox of Obama's Convictions

Obama, it is clear, is not a timid president when it comes to his own transformational ambitions. He pursues them to the point of being willing to impose them on an increasingly reluctant and resistant public. As a result, he must now spend the second half of his first term in decidedly less friendly legislative and public support circumstances.

The irony here seems clear. *Obama is a conviction president.* He has strong convictions about the need to redeem the United States through his transformational ambitions and clearly is willing to go to the wall for them. How else can one adequately explain his full speed ahead approach to transformation, after it became clear that the public was resistant and the Democrats had several surprising electoral set backs and were likely to suffer more in the future.

In a meeting with Senate Democrats this exchange took place between Blanche Lincoln (D–Ark.) and the president:[81]

LINCOLN: "I visited with a constituent yesterday, good Democrat, small business owner, who was extremely frustrated—extremely frustrated because there was a lack of certainty and predictability from his government for him to be able to run his businesses … I want to … ask you, in terms of where we are going, what can we tell the people in terms of predictability and certainty in getting this economy back on track? Are we willing, as Democrats, not only to reach out to Republicans, but to push back in our own party for people who want extremes, and look for the common ground that's going to get us the success that we need not only for our constituents, but for our country, in this global community, in this global economy?"

THE PRESIDENT: "Well, the—look, there's no doubt that this past year has been an uncertain time for the American people, for businesses and for people employed by businesses … Well, if the agenda—if the price of certainty is essentially for us to adopt the exact same proposals that were in place for eight years leading up to the biggest economic crisis since the Great Depression—we don't tinker with health care, let the insurance companies do what they want, we don't put in place any insurance reforms, we don't mess with the banks, let them keep on doing what they're doing now because we don't want to stir up Wall Street—the result is going to be the same. I don't know why we would expect a different outcome pursuing the exact same policies that got us into this fix in the first place … And if our response ends up being, because we don't want to—we don't want to stir things up here, we're just going to do the same thing that was being done before, then I don't know what differentiates us from the other guys. And I don't know why people would say, boy, we really want to make sure that those Democrats are in Washington fighting for us."

I want to skip over the caricature that Obama paints of bipartisanship, equating working with Republicans as involving having to not tinker with health care, not "messing with banks" and "letting insurance companies do what they want," and so on. These are not fair or accurate representations of Republican positions on these issues and the president almost certainly knows that.

What is interesting in this exchange is the president's response to a plea for him to focus on the economy. He essentially dismissed Lincoln's plea to focus on the economy by saying that there were many other things he had to do and if he didn't do them people would wonder why they sent him, a Democrat, to Washington.

The Focus of Obama's Character Integrity: Doing Big Things

The apparent discrepancy between Obama unwillingness to stand up to his party and yet push full speed ahead with his transformative agenda that might decimate their power is explained by a very basic fact. Obama doesn't really go against his party in any substantial way because he essentially agrees with its positions. This is after all the candidate who said that, "the arguments of liberals are more often grounded in reason and fact."[82] That is why he could dismiss the concerns of Senator Lincoln, a conservative or moderate Democrat. In Obama's view, conservative centrist arguments, whether from the left or right, simply don't have the convincing legitimacy of reason and facts on their side that liberal arguments do. There is an irony here of course that a president who prides himself on being pragmatic and defines that in terms of taking the best ideas, regardless of their partisan origin, summarily dismisses ideas that come from the center.

But explaining why Obama does not buck the liberal center of gravity in his party doesn't fully help us to understand why Obama's courage of his convictions is focused on transformation. One answer to that is the imperative of redemption. Another is the critical leadership lens of fairness, as Obama sees it. But there is a third aspect to that courage, and it has to do with Obama's desire to do big, even great things.

Using Crisis: The Big Bang Theory

Obama was, from the start, committed to doing many big things. Recall his claim in his speech to a joint session of Congress in February in 2009 that, "at every moment of economic upheaval and transformation, this nation has responded with bold action and big ideas." Among those new ideas were initiatives in the following areas: jobs, a new lending fund for the auto industry, college and small business; foreclosure assistance; bank regulation; a new energy policy

> that places a market-based cap on carbon pollution and drives the production of more renewable energy in America;

> fifteen billion dollars a year to develop technologies like wind power and solar power; advancing the use of bio fuels, clean coal, and more fuel-efficient cars and trucks built right here in America;

Our recovery plan will invest in electronic health records and new technology that will reduce errors, bring down costs, ensure privacy, and save lives. It will launch a new effort to conquer a disease that has touched the life of nearly every American by seeking a cure for cancer in our time;

we are committed to the goal of a re-tooled, re-imagined auto industry that can compete and win;

we must also address the crushing cost of health care;

what we must address is the urgent need to expand the promise of education in America;

I [have] pledged to cut the deficit in half by the end of my first term in office;

we must also address the growing costs in Medicare and Social Security;

we will forge a new and comprehensive strategy for Afghanistan and Pakistan to defeat al Qaeda and combat extremism.[83]

That is quite a list and it is premised on the assumption that in the midst of a severe economic downturn is precisely the right time to take on a number of complex, difficult, contentious, and costly major pieces of social legislation in four or five policy areas. Alter writes of the speech that, "Obama was now fully committed to what some White House aides called the 'big bang' strategy of using the economic crisis to confront long-festering problems in health care, energy and education that were preventing the United States from achieving greatness in the twenty-first century."[84] This concern with those problems keeping the United States from "greatness" is, of course, the view of interviewed White House aides and to Alter's credit his next sentence reads: "It was either visionary and long overdue or reckless and radical, depending on one's perspective."

David Broder wrote that it was, "one of the most ambitious agendas any newly inaugurated president has ever announced." Equally interesting, he also said that, "The size of the gambles that President Obama is taking every day is simply staggering." And Broder ends with a comment worth thinking more about, "When we elected Obama, we didn't know what a gambler we were getting."[85] Obama was not only willing to gamble the country's fortunes, if his policies, if passed, didn't fulfill the claims mounted on their behalf, but also his own presidency. This seemed very inconsistent with the Obama as prudent pragmatist narrative. Indeed, it cast a great deal of doubt on it.

And there is one more element that has emerged with greater clarity in Obama's quest for policy and historic greatness. And that is the cool, some might say cold, ability to use his loyal troops in Congress to advance his plans in the face of growing evidence that in doing so many were going to be committing political suicide.[86] As with the president's July 2010 speech on immigration, touting a "grand bargain" on top of his already large and controversial agenda, the president's self-interest, including reelection in 2012 and his place in history are of more concern to him than to members of Congress.

This, along with his views of "middle America" expressed in the campaign and his decision to ignore widespread and basic public concern with the pace, thrust and implications of his policies suggest that for all Obama's emphasis on his own empathetic abilities,[87] when it comes to advancing his own ambitions, they take a back seat.

Why Be President?

In an interview, Obama was asked what prompted him to run. He mentioned the basic question of whether he could win and would his wife support his run and then he said:

> And the third question, which was the most profound question, and one where probably … in the end I had to answer all by myself was: should I win? Just because you can win doesn't mean you're the person who's best for the country at this moment in time, *and I, I, I actually believe my own rhetoric when I say I think we're in a defining moment*. It's very difficult to think back to a time where we had a bigger series of choices, and obviously WWII maybe, and the immediate aftermath of WWII, the Great Depression, and before that the Civil War … but this country has lots of issues it has to deal with … I felt as if there was the possibility that I could do something that no other candidate in the race could do, whether it was bringing the country together more effectively, [or] building a consensus, [or] reinvigorating the American people's interest in government.[88]

One of the ironies of this statement is that of course Obama has stimulated people's interest in government, but not in the way he had anticipated. The rise of the so-called "Tea Party" and those who associate with some of its concerns definitely has the hallmarks of a grassroots social movement. Gallup found that Tea Party supporters "skewed right but demographically, they are generally representative of the public at large."[89] And that movement has arisen precisely out of concern with and in opposition to the president's transformative agenda.

Nor has Obama succeeded in "bringing the country together more effectively," or "building a consensus." Quite the opposite. As noted at several points, the partisan gap in the president's job approval is the widest in the modern era, and there are widening partisan gaps on his handling of health care and the economy.[90]

Doubtlessly, every candidate who runs for the president thinks they are uniquely qualified for the role, so what is interesting about this statement is not that Obama reached that conclusion, but his expectations in doing so. It is, he says, a defining moment in American history, as important as World War II, the Cold War, the Great Depression, and the Civil War. What makes this period a defining one? Obama doesn't really say except to mention that the "country has lots of problems to deal with."

One wonders what these problems that are on a scale of the ones Obama mentioned might be. Surely the country "has a lot of problems to deal with" but none of them are as immediately dire (World War II, the Civil War, the Great Depression) or potentially catastrophic (the Cold War nuclear stand-off between the United States and Soviet Union) as the ones Obama mentions.

Transformation's Timing: The Use of "Crises"

It is within this context that the origins of Rahm Emanuel's comment about never letting a crisis go to waste acquires fresh meaning. In an interview with the *Wall Street Journal* he said, "You never want a serious crisis to go to waste. ... Things that we had postponed for too long, that were long-term, are now immediate and must be dealt with. This crisis provides the opportunity for us to do things that you could not do before."[91] Among the areas he mentioned were, "energy, health, education, tax policy, (and) regulatory reforms."

The problem with this formulation for the administration is that there is no direct and immediate relationship between the economic downturn and health care reform, or energy policy or education and tax policies for that matter. Nor did the public see any direct relationship. Provisions in the health care legislation and financial regulation would not go into full effect until well after Obama leaves office after a second term, if he has one. The legislation front loads the public benefits and delays those parts to which there are strong objections for periods of up to a decade. So,

> health care reform cracks down on insurers right away but won't force people to buy insurance until 2014. A new consumer financial protection agency kicks in almost immediately under the Wall Street reform bill, but banks won't feel its full force for more than 10 years.[92]

Reform that takes effect in ten years can hardly be considered a timely response to an immediate catastrophic level crisis.

Dire Narratives

The administration tried to encourage the feeling of imminent crisis in the context of the Gulf oil spill. Speaking on the economy at Carnegie Mellon University the president used the oil leak to make a dire case regarding, "our continued dependence on fossil fuels" saying it "will jeopardize our national security. It will smother our planet. And it will continue to put our economy and our environment at risk."[93]

From that dire risk, he transitioned to the need to support his proposed energy policies, "And the time has come to aggressively accelerate that transition. The time has come, once and for all, for this nation to fully embrace a clean energy future." What would these policies entail? Among them, unprecedented effort to make everything from our homes and businesses to our cars and trucks more energy-efficient. It means tapping into our natural gas reserves, and moving ahead with our plan to expand our nation's fleet of nuclear power plants. ... And the only way to do that is by finally putting a price on carbon pollution.[94]

In the president's stated view, there is a relationship between the oil spill and the need for major government control over the energy sector in the form of creating and regulating a market in carbon production. It is that the United States uses lots of energy that is supplied by oil and, as a result, we allow offshore oil drilling, which can result in damaging environmental accidents. Therefore we should reduce our dependence on oil by using less of it and the best way to do that is to tax and regulate every economic activity that uses energy, including those that use oil to force them to become more energy efficient and use less of it. So-called "clean" energy alternatives need large-scale government investments to become economically viable so that money will be obtained by "cap and trade" legislation that will tax business, and ultimately the public to pay for it.

It is clear what the president expects the public to make of his statement that the United States consumes "more than 20 percent of the world's oil, but has less than 2 percent of the world's oil reserves," and because of this we "send billions of dollars of our hard-earned wealth to other countries every month including countries in dangerous and unstable regions." However, other facts undercut the president's dire narrative. The United States actually imports most of its oil from Mexico and Canada.

As to spending our "hard-earned wealth," it is basically to produce energy that in a dynamic and productive economy grows to meet increased demand. Should consumption be dependent on reserves within our territory? It is also unlikely for "alternative fuel sources to be able to provide for more than a fraction of America's energy needs and even then it will take large-scale government incentives or equally large taxes on conventional fossil fuel to make them economically viable." And finally, there is the issue of nuclear power, a relatively inexpensive, cost-effective, environmentally friendly alternative power source that the administration has mentioned, but not put its weight behind.

The dire energy narrative espoused by the president is not a fair or accurate analysis of the issues involved in developing energy policy; it is an advocate's brief.

Obama's Choices

Obama assumed office as the country was in the midst of a substantial economic downturn and faced a choice. He most certainly needed to address the downturn, and did so with the tools available to him, the same ones that his predecessor had used—financial rescues, stimulus policies, and tax incentives. Yet Obama aspired to do more and did so, most obviously in passing major health care legislation, proposing major energy legislation and repeatedly claiming that he wanted to address comprehensive immigration reform.

Only one of these, the economic downturn and the stresses it caused for economic institutions, was immediately urgent. Why then did the president and his administration throw all their weight behind the president's other major legislative initiatives and try to build support through dire narratives? The answer lies in the government's structural architecture that favors incremental policies, Obama's reading of his presidential political calendar and the felt urgency of his redeeming America's promise.

Of the first, little need be said. The country's system of separation and overlapping of powers makes it difficult to politically engineer major, rapid policy shifts. However it is possible to do so when the country faces major crises as it did in 1938 and after 9/11. Arguably, the liquidity freeze that faced the Bush administration qualified as a major crisis, since it put the economy as a whole at risk. The Obama administration necessarily continued and built upon his predecessor's responses, for the simple reason that when they took office the crisis was not over.

Yet, the Obama administration's response to the country's economic downturn and the liquidity crisis that was part of it had little to do with a range of policies that it undertook. Health care, energy policy, and immigration, if it is seriously attempted, have little to do with the immediate economic crises both the Bush and Obama administrations faced. And therein lies the difference between responding to a crisis and making use of one.

Lincoln assumed office and was faced with a civil war. FDR assumed office and faced a great depression and then a world war. In each case these presidents were responding to dire, even potentially catastrophic, events. Having no immediate crisis of comparable magnitude Obama was forced to treat the economic upheaval, and later the Gulf oil spill in stark terms ("it will jeopardize our national security. It will smother our planet") to elevate public concern to the levels that he perhaps felt about our future.

The public did not see the oil spill as a catastrophic disaster on the scale of World War II. Nor did it see the recession, as difficult as it was, as the equivalent of the Civil War. Obama's expressed sense of crisis fell flat with the American public who wanted him to focus on jobs not energy policy, health care, education, or immigration.

In raising these matters as severe crises requiring immediate fixing, Obama ran several large risks. The first was creating a gap between what Obama saw as the important issues to address and what the public thought. A second related issue was the mismatch between Obama's dire language and public views about the severity of these crises and more importantly the rationale for using them to insist on large new government programs that the public could not see as connected to them. These in turn risked the most precious leadership commodity of all, the perception of Obama's leadership integrity.

In the end, Obama's concern about overcoming the role of checks and balances in favoring incremental change and the narrowing window of the November election calendar pushed in the direction of going big early. But none of this would have made a difference without the third and final ingredient, Obama's view of himself as a potentially great leader coupled with his transformational agenda. Jonathan Alter reports in his book that Rahm Emanuel said of the health care legislation, "I begged him not to do this," but "Obama overrode Rahm's advice, privately taking a bit of shot at Clinton by telling advisers that he hadn't been sent to the White House to do 'school uniforms.'"[95] Obama not only wanted to break the conventional rules, but change them.

Jumping Through Windows of Opportunity

Emmanuel's often-quoted remark about crises clearly reflected administration thinking about making use of the economic crisis, but opportunity was not the only rationale. Obama apparently believed that the time frame to attempt transformational change was short; very short. In an interview with Jonathan Alter, Obama made clear that his political capital was already declining as a result of backing a second round of TARP funds and therefore "the only option, he thought, was to power through their issues."[96] At another point, after his victories on the stimulus and the budget, the president felt there wasn't a coherent idea of where to go next and felt he was just "treading water" and in the late winter told his senior staff, "we have to take this thing big."[97]

In an interview with PBS for their *Frontline* behind of scenes analysis of the health care process, White House communications director Dan Pfeiffer, who was present in many of the White House deliberations said,

> And the president was very clear that our first year was our best chance to get it done, because you're not going to get it done in an election year. As soon as the election year is over, we're heading into a Republican presidential primary and a presidential campaign. And then you're a second-term president. In the history of doing huge legislation, the second term is pretty skimpy. So that was how the decision was made.[98]

So, from the president's perspective, he did not really have one or two terms to make his mark, but literally the first twenty months of his administration. The president did not apparently consider, or if he did, chose not to act on the possibility, that each of his major initiatives, "may have been defensible in isolation, but in combination they created the impression of a federal onslaught."[99]

The rapid pace the administration adopted on many major policy matters left the public with feelings that too much was happening too fast. From Obama's point of view, crises need immediate responses, and extraordinary measures. Justifying the recess appointment of Dr. Donald Berwick, without allowing him to testify before Congress, to a major post overseeing the revamping of America's health care system, was justified by senior White House Advisor David Axelrod as "too important" to wait for a Congressional hearing.[100] One logical, and obvious, explanation for this, is that the administration did not want to refight the health care debate during confirmation hearings. Yet, sidestepping the debate in this way, for this reason, adds to the impression that not only is the president trying to do too much, but that he is willing to cut some corners in the process.

7

AMBITION'S CONFIDENCE

One of the most important, obvious, but in some respects still puzzling characteristics of President Obama is his enormous self-confidence. The evidence for it is overwhelming, but its origins and full implications remain unclear. How and when did this young man, who was at best a fair student with modest accomplishments, become a successful presidential candidate who compared himself, not without some truth, to the outstanding world-class basketball player LeBron James? Does he owe that self-confidence to his upbringing, which psychologists usually assert is the primary foundation of self-esteem on which self-confidence is built? And if so, how did that happen with an absent father, a mother who was away from him for long periods of time, and modest academic and personal accomplishments?

Accounting for the origins of Obama's self-confidence is of more than passing interest. Understanding if and how his self-confidence developed provides clues for the firmness of its foundation and also its nature. Personal accomplishments provide the most effective means to earned self-confidence when they are consistent with both effort and results. Ordinarily, when self-confidence develops in the absence of real, commensurate accomplishments, its foundations will be shaky and its manifestations are likely to be compensatory. But what happens when someone is given too much credit for their accomplishments? Is that also a recipe for trouble?

Beyond Obama's self-confidence, lies an array of questions that also have direct relevance for his leadership and judgment. There is a relationship between self-confidence and arrogance. Arrogance can be understood as a person's assumption that a gap or imbalance that exists is based on some assumed virtues that confer superiority on the person who has them. Needless to say presidential arrogance is a recipe for errors in judgment and, if widely perceived, a source of public disenchantment.

There is also an important question to be asked regarding the relationship between self-confidence and actual accomplishments. Of course, even legitimately self-confident people can make mistakes in judgment. However, presidents whose self-confidence exceeds the extent of their real talents or accomplishments are especially prone to this class of errors. The gap between the two can serve as a rough definition of the clinical term *grandiosity*. *Grandiosity* then can be understood as reflecting in the size of the gap between a person's real talents and accomplishments and the level of their sense of a unique obligation, suitability, and expectations to accomplish their ambitions.

The central question here is: Where does Obama stand in relation to these issues?

Obama on Himself

Obama has been in public life long enough, and is smart enough, to recognize that a leader's inflated sense of himself is an occupational hazard in public life. He is on record as noting "the narcissism that is already a congenital defect for a politician."[1] And he has offered his second book, *The Audacity of Hope*, as a meditation on how I, or anybody in public life, can avoid the pitfalls of fame. ... "[2] It is a hazard that he specifically disclaims for himself,

> If you didn't think you should be up on stage then you wouldn't do it. But, if you're going to grow up as a politician or as a person, *then at a certain point the vanity has to fade away*. Then you have to be doing these things for something bigger than yourself.[3]

Of course, vanity doesn't often "fade away" and doing things for "something bigger that yourself" can reinforce it.

As to all the adulation that has accompanied Obama since his 2004 keynote speech at the Democratic National Convention, he says that it hasn't fazed him. He has written, "As a rule, I find it difficult to take all this attention very seriously, there are days when I still walk out of the house with a suit jacket that doesn't match my suit pants."[4] This is the voice of the "I'm just an ordinary person" Obama, but any failures to match pants and jackets are not reflected in Obama's very strategic approach to his political goals. Nor is the evidence to be reviewed shortly consistent with Obama's assertion that he doesn't "take all this attention seriously."

Obama feels that his celebrity is not a particular issue for him. He writes,

> I find comfort in the fact that the longer I'm in politics the less nourishing popularity becomes, that a striving for power and rank and fame seems to betray a poverty of ambition, and that I am answerable to the steady gaze of my own conscience.[5]

Perhaps Obama sincerely believes this, but there is contrary evidence and other explanations for the traits he sees in himself.

It seems true for example that Obama has found popularity less nourishing, but evidence (reviewed in the next chapter, pp. 181–182) for the causes of that seem more connected with Obama's own disappointments with popularity's emotional half-life and the emotional and physical demands it places on him than with any reflective self-insight. Moreover, striving for power is precisely what Obama has done throughout his adult life, first in Chicago as a social worker, then as his chief reason for going to law school, and finally in the fast paced upward trajectory of his political career.

There is nothing suspect about this at all. Obama went to law school to learn about power and make the connections. His subsequent political career has been fueled by an upwardly mobile strategy to be in a position to exercise political power in the service of his policy ambitions framed through the lens of his view of fairness.

It is true that disowning the ample evidence of his own ambition detracts from the confidence we might have in Obama's view of himself. Perhaps what Obama has in mind here is the concern that for some leaders power is accumulated for its own sake, or to make them feel better about themselves. This idea, the compensation hypothesis, has a long history in political and psychological analysis. However, Obama is certain this theory or pattern does not apply to him.

Does the Compensation Hypothesis Apply to Obama? He Says No

At the core of the compensation hypothesis in political leadership theory is the psychological dynamic of gearing important aspects of one's adult life to make up for something that was lacking in early development. Political scientists[6] have singled out the early failures to develop and consolidate self-esteem as a particularly important element in the single-minded search for political power.

Interestingly, President Obama has commented on the applicability of the compensation hypothesis to his ambition. He has said of his own presidential ambition that it was different for him than for the other candidates. He explained it this way:[7]

> I'm pretty well adjusted. You know, you can psychoanalyze my father leaving and this and that, *but a lot of those things I resolved a long time ago. I'm pretty happy with my life.* So there's an element, I think, of being driven that might have operated a little differently with me than maybe some other candidates. *The way I thought about it was more of a sense of duty, in this sense.* I thought to myself: There aren't that many people put in the position I'm put in. Some of it's just dumb luck. Some of it maybe has to do *with me embodying some characteristics that are interesting for the time that we're in.* But when I made the decision to do this, it wasn't with the certainty that I was the right person for the job. It was more the sense of, given what's been given to me, I should probably just give it a shot and see whether in fact there's something real there.

So, to paraphrase, some might think that Obama's presidential ambitions stem from trying to make up for the experience of his father's abandonment, though he does not mention his mother's long absences and his ambivalent responses to them, but that's not the case since he resolved those issues "a long time ago."

Obama's explanation for his political ambitions as originating in a sense of duty is certainly possible, but the question is duty and responsibility to whom? Obama appears to have an odd and somewhat personal understanding of that term. A duty ordinarily implies a responsibility to others, one's family or country for example. Obama's formulation of duty is to himself. He bases his decision on the view that not many people are in his position, and that position reflects in part some characteristics that are "interesting for the time that we're in." That said, Obama opts for a presidential candidacy "to see if there's something real there," that something being the interesting characteristics that he embodies.

When he was considering running for the presidency, Obama told David Axelrod, "I don't really need to do this, because being Barack Obama turns out to be a pretty good gig."[8] Maybe. But there is every indication that he really wanted it.

Obama, Redemption, and the Compensation Hypothesis

Redemption, at its core, shares a theoretical affinity with the compensation hypothesis. Both focus on an effort to make up for some important psychological element or experiences in the person's past, and for political leaders so motivated, the political world becomes the preferred arena for doing so.

At the core of the compensation hypothesis in political leadership theory is the psychological dynamic of gearing important aspects of one's adult life to make up for something that was lacking in early development. And, as noted, political scientists have singled out the early failures to develop and consolidate self-esteem as a particularly important element in the single-minded search for political power.

That formulation, while clearly compelling, in some cases suffers from two potential blind spots. First, it is clearly possible for political leaders to seek power to *validate* high estimates of self.[9] Presidents in this category, like Bill Clinton, grew up being adored and even venerated in their family, even if the venerating parent put pleasure before responsibility as Clinton's mother did. They also accumulated a record of achievement in which their skills mostly outmatched their circumstances and they gained the legitimate expectation of success. In these cases, the attainment and exercise of political power is viewed as a natural consequence of one's skills or other unique qualifications. Presidents with unusually high estimations of their own importance and unique standing are particularly prone to this dynamic.

In certain respects Obama fits the pattern described above. His mother both loved and left him for several long periods while she followed her own internal anthropological muse. Obama writes about how his mother told him how special he was. Remnick says of this that Obama is essentially reporting this while rolling his eyes at his mother's naïve well intentioned efforts, but the fact of the matter is that Obama experienced this as a child and it is as an adult that he takes her no doubt heart-felt views with a grain of salt. One wonders when, and if, the question crossed Obama's mind: If I'm so special, why did she leave?

The other possible defect of the conventional formulation of the compensation hypothesis, one also raised by the Obama presidency, is that whatever other narcissistic elements are involved in the pursuit of power, it can be in the service of some larger set of personal or political goals. In Obama's case, the motivation for redemption has both a triple personal (his own aspirations for greatness, redeeming his father and his relationship with his mother) motivation and a unique redemption motivation for past American policy. I use the word unique here because the idea that American domestic and foreign policies must be framed by, or geared toward, expiation of past errors is a novel stance for a president to hold.

Harold Lasswell wrote of "political men" that they rationalize their pursuit of political power in terms of public interest,[10] and to some extent this seems unexceptional. What president could run and win office on a platform that says he needs power to buttress his low self-worth? Nor would we expect someone like Obama to run for office on the platform that says he ought to be president because it will confirm how smart and deserving he is.

In Obama's case, given that there is no noticeable self-esteem or self-confidence deficit, any appeal to the compensation hypothesis would seem to run aground. Some in Obama's inner circle, including his wife[11] and Valerie Jarrett,[12] have speculated that the loss of Obama's father led to his desire for political acclaim. The assumption there would be that he didn't get enough from an absent father and his peripatetic mother.

This is a possibility, but that suggestion has some problems associated with it, among them Obama's very high self-confidence and the fact that when he had opportunities for activities that increased his visibility and his availability for acclaim, he didn't always seize them directly. For purposes of this discussion though, the important point is that it tends to underestimate the seriousness with which Obama has approached his transformational ambitions. It has if anything damped any adulation that was presumably at the source of any psychological quest for acclaim. It seems quite clear that in this respect for Obama, redemption trumps acclaim.

But redemption, of the country and of his father's and mother's legacy, is also intimately bound up with Obama's own redemption. And a very important element of that is Obama's view of himself as a transformational president of historic proportions and of himself as a moral center for his redemptive efforts. For Obama, as is the case with almost all aspects of his psychology and his presidency, his redemptive ambitions are a complicated form of compensation.

Obama's Self-confidence

One of the reasons that the compensation hypothesis about using political power to overcome low estimates of self does not appear to apply to President Obama is that he most certainly does not seem to have a low estimate of himself to overcome. On the contrary, Obama's self-confidence is legendary and much remarked upon. One of Obama's biographers, who covered him during his time in Chicago, wrote of him that, "He emanates supreme self-confidence at almost every moment,"[13] Obama's very close friend and confidant, Marty Nesbitt, spoke of Obama's "supreme confidence."[14] Peter Rouse, a thirty-year veteran of Capitol Hill recruited by Obama to organize his Senate office and staff said, "that in his thirty years on Capitol Hill, he had never seen anyone with more faith in himself."[15]

News accounts by those who cover the president and his advisors quickly reached similar conclusions. Writing about the efforts that went into the stimulus package, the *Washington Post* reported that the "fledgling administration ... came to Washington with equally high measures of ambition and confidence in its ability to quickly begin remaking the country."[16] Two *Los Angeles Times* reporters covering Obama's meeting with a group of bankers noted, "Direct, assertive and utterly self-assured, Obama has used his broad popularity, a driving ambition and a sweeping agenda to move America in a wholly new direction."[17] Another veteran reporter covering Obama's first thirty days in the White House noted his "serene— self confidence," but worried that "it can cause blind spots," a worry we will take up shortly.[18]

Obama for his part has said of himself, "I have high expectations of myself and I usually meet them."[19] In his book *The Good Fight*, Senate majority leader Harry Reid, D-Nev., recalls a conversation with Obama after a speech. Reid writes:

> "That speech was phenomenal, Barack," I told him. And I will never forget his response. Without the barest hint of braggadocio or conceit, and with what I would describe as deep humility, he said quietly: "I have a gift, Harry."[20]

Let's assume Mr. Reid was correct, that there was no hint of bragging or conceit, although it is hard to see how Obama's comment conjures up "deep humility." Indeed a "deep humility" response might have been a simple "thank you." Yet Obama's response is revealing in another way.

Recall that Obama is a master of preparation. Obama devoted endless hours to practicing his major speech before the Democratic National Convention and made hundreds of speeches at black churches before he mastered the sense of rhetorical (see p. 67) cadence needed for success. If indeed Obama does have "a gift" it is found in the talent he had and worked hard to develop and refine.

There is no ignominy in developing one's talents. Indeed, it is admirable. The disconcerting aspect of Obama's claim is that he would apparently prefer to present himself as pre-naturally gifted rather than someone with talent who worked hard to develop it.

Looking back on the period shortly before he was inaugurated, Obama told David Remnick that, "I wasn't scared. I think *at that point I had a pretty firm grasp on what the moment required.*"[21] Asked in a post-election interview, "Have there been moments when you've said 'What did I get myself into?'" Obama replied, "Surprisingly enough, I feel right now I'm doing what I should be doing."[22] Speaking to his advisor David Axelrod earlier, during the transition period he said,

> The weird thing is, *I know I can do this job.* I like dealing with complicated issues. I'm happy to make decisions. I'm looking forward to it. *I think it's going to be an easier adjustment for me than the campaign. Much easier.*[23]

This quote precisely captures the uneasy relationship between self-confidence ("I know I can do this job") and incipient arrogance, even grandiosity ("it's going to be much easier").

It seems clear that there is ample evidence regarding Obama's substantial level of self-confidence. It takes a substantial amount of self-confidence to seriously consider a presidential race, especially for someone with an unusually thin political résumé, and to survive and eventually win the grueling presidential marathon against formidable opponents and odds. And, as a number of behind-the-scene presidential campaign books make clear, Obama was instrumental in his own campaign strategy and its implementation. Modern presidential campaigns do not favor the weak-willed, or those for whom self-confidence and self-esteem are lacking.

The level of Obama's self-confidence raises a number of theoretical and political questions of interest for his presidency. What, exactly, is the relationship between self-esteem and self-confidence? Are they synonymous or does each have a different relationship to presidential leadership and decision-making? How does self-confidence develop in a political leader and what implications do variations in its levels have for presidential performance? How and on what basis did it develop?

At first glance self-esteem and self-confidence would seem psychologically to be siblings and perhaps even identical twins. Yet, there are differences. Self-esteem is primarily a general and internalized sense of self-satisfaction. It reflects an internal assumption that, in general, you are basically a good person, one who tries to live up to your responsibilities toward yourself and others and that you have developed sufficient proficiency in the skills to allow you to make a viable place for yourself in the world.

Clearly, it is the latter part of this definition that provides the most direct link to self-confidence. Developing the skills that allow you to find your place in the world reflects an important personal accomplishment. Having poor math skills is a bad fit for becoming a nuclear physicist, but having unusually good speaking skills is certainly an advantage for gaining elective office. So the question arises: What is the origin and developmental path of Obama's self-confidence?

The Mysterious Origins of Obama's Self-confidence

One of the mysteries of Obama's very substantial level of self-confidence is how did it develop? He was not a truly good student until he got to law school. He loved basketball and thought of himself as quite good, but he could never break into the starting line up of his high school basketball team. His first real job, a difficult one, as a community organizer, left him feeling so frustrated and ineffective that he changed career paths and applied to law school. He aspired to be a writer, but talked of keeping a journal of daily reflections and "bad poetry,"[24] and none of his short stories were ever published. The reviews on his book *Dreams*, before he gave the keynote address at the Democratic National Convention, "were mildly favorable" when it was first published, but "the sales were underwhelming."[25]

Nor were Obama's family circumstances auspicious. His father abandoned the family and Obama only saw him once before he died. His mother was frequently away pursuing her career interests. And he kept his grandparents, who had a substantial part in raising him, at a distance while he was growing up.

Obama's Confidence: A Variety of Explanations

As befits a mystery, there are many explanations for Obama's high level of self-confidence. Alter says that, "Obama had been so lucky in his personal life and political career that it bred a faith in himself. ... "[26] It's hard to understand just how Obama has been lucky in his personal life given his difficult family circumstances. And as to Obama's luck in his political career, it was certainly true that his first Senate opponent self-destructed and his replacement wasn't up to the race, but other than that, Obama's "luck in his political career" recalls golfing great Ben Hogan's observation: "The more I practice, the luckier I get."

It is possible, in spite of the reality of Obama's family circumstances, to find some support for a family origin theory of Obama's self-confidence. Obama's first biographer wrote,

> This extreme of confidence was something that was ingrained in Obama's psyche early in life. His maternal grandfather would tell Obama that this was the greatest lesson that he could learn from his absent father: "Confidence— the secret to a man's success." That is how Obama's father led his life; and even in times of self-doubt Obama has harkened back to that wisdom.[27]

This theory makes no sense on several grounds. Obama's grandfather was hardly a model of success, regardless of what lessons he might have tried to impart. Obama writes in *Dreams* of listening to his grandfather's attempts to sell insurance over the phone at night. As Obama described in poignant detail in his book, "the work went badly."[28] As to Obama's father's confidence, it is true that it was abundant, perhaps too much so. At any rate, it was in his father's case not the key to his success, but on the contrary the vehicle of his downfall. In a 2006 speech in Nairobi, Obama said that "his father's idea about how Kenya should progress often put him at odds with the politics of tribe and patronage ... " but then he added "and *because he spoke his mind, sometimes to a fault,* he wound up being fired from his job and prevented from finding work in the country for many, many years."[29]

It is unclear just how much of the real story of Obama's father's life "Gramps" (as Obama called his grandfather) knew. Obama learned the tragic reality of his father's life when he was twenty-five years old. Certainly before he learned it, Obama had a romanticized view of his father and perhaps that and his grandfather's homilies on confidence may have created a mental model of confidence. But if so, at the time, it was not supported by any successful efforts on Obama's part that would have translated those homilies into the reality of earned confidence.

Obama's mother has also emerged in some versions as the source of Obama's self-confidence. Mendell says that she "reinforced his self-esteem constantly."[30] Obama said of her, "she would be our biggest cheerleader," "had complete confidence that you were special in some fashion," and "as a consequence, there was no shortage of self-esteem."[31] When it came to race, his mother apparently went farther. Mendell writes, "mostly Barry was given the lesson that he would consume over and over. His unique racial ancestry certainly was not to be ostracized and shunned. Far from it—he was a special person worthy of others' deep admiration."[32]

Leaving aside the question of why someone should be "worthy of deep admiration because of their racial ancestry," Obama has expressed skepticism about his mother's naïve view of his racial inheritance,[33] but that skepticism was the expression of an adult at mid-life looking back on his childhood and adolescence. It is hard to know what he made of it when he was six or seven or older. It is possible that his mother's insistence on his "being worthy of deep admiration" did provide some basis for the development of his self-esteem and self-confidence in later life. But that possibility still does not account for one critical factor. Obama had no substantially self-earned success by which to further develop and consolidate his self-esteem and self-confidence before he arrived at Harvard.

Harvard as the Crucible

If these explanations don't seem persuasive, it is probably best to look elsewhere, most appropriately later in Obama's life. Here one comes across several potentially useful understandings. For example, it seems clear that Obama's relationship with success was equivocal until he got to Harvard Law School. Alter reports that one day over lunch, Newton Minnow, another of Obama's well placed mentors, asked him where his confidence came from. Obama replied that when he got to Harvard he was unsure he was up to the level of his classmates, "But when I was elected head of the *Law Review* I figured I was just as capable. And now that I've been in the Senate I realize the same thing."[34]

Obama's point reflects the fact that self-esteem, far from being an abstract quality instilled by parental or family reinforcement, is best viewed as a relational concept. From this perspective a person compares his sense of himself and his accomplishment with others in similar circumstances and gains a sense of confidence that he can hold his own in his "weight class." That appears to have happened at Harvard for Obama. Not only could he hold his own, but he also excelled.

Moreover, it was at Harvard that he further developed and successfully deployed his rhetorical skills and ability to convince others he stood with them to win a major law school prize: the editorship of the *Law Review*. Remnick writes, "that much of Obama's self-confidence resided in his belief that he could walk into any room, with any sort of people, and forge a relationship and even persuade those people of the rightness of his positions."[35] Implicit in this skill was the assumption on Obama's part that others would see him as he presented himself. That confidence was an important basis of his undertaking the run for president.

Asked what had he learned about the American people from his campaign, Obama replied,

> I have to tell you and this is in no way an indication of overconfidence—I was not surprised by the campaign. I felt that, and I said this on the stump, I felt vindicated in my faith in the American people.[36]

Of what did this faith consist? In one of the campaign analysis books, the reporters write, "Even at the lowest moments of the campaign, *nothing had shaken the conviction that the country would see him in the way he wanted it to see him*. See him as he saw himself. See him as he was."[37] Of course none of these three perceptual lenses were necessarily synonymous with each other. Indeed, the Obama campaign made strenuous efforts to connect the first two in the public mind although their relationship to the last was much more unclear and equivocal.

This was a skill whose origins can be traced to early in Obama's life when he discovered and made use of the technique of *rhetorical empathy* coupled with withholding his own feelings, whatever they might be—his inkblot strategy. It is also now a fully developed mature skill in ample evidence during the campaign and in his presidency.

Obama's Self-Confidence and Success: Beyond Harvard

Along the way in Obama's political career, there were other experiences that went into building his sense of confidence. One was the accumulation of mentors and those straining to ease his path that began to accumulate while he was in law school. All of these people, by their actions and commitments, reinforced the view that Obama was special. They also reinforced his confidence that he did possess something that drew people to him, and further that he could count on it.

Obama's Legion of Mentors

Obama made a number of career critical connections before, during and after going to Harvard. This is also evidenced in the many persons who Obama sought out and who have become mentors to him over his career. A partial list would include: Jerry Kellman, Abner Mikva, Jeremiah Wright, Newton Minnow, Judson Minor, and Valerie Jarrett[38] in Chicago; Laurence Tribe, Christopher Edley and others at Harvard Law School; Senate majority leader Emil Jones in Springfield; and Harry Reid, Richard Luger, Dick Durbin, and others in the Senate.[39]

Very oddly in a 2008 interview, Obama said he felt he never had any such people:

> That doesn't mean there haven't been occasions in my life where the idea of having an older, wiser figure who's been through the ropes before and can avoid having you make the same mistakes he made would not have been nice, *but those just aren't the cards that I was dealt.*[40]

The phase "occasions in my life" coupled with the date (2008) of the interview seems to suggest that Obama is not confining himself to his adolescence, but to his life more generally. Whether this reflects Obama's true feelings, or the wish to further the idea that he is solely responsible for all that he has become, it is patently untrue.

However, it is not an easy matter to discern how reciprocal these relationships were. Obama's ability to emotionally stand apart from others and play his emotion and policy cards very close to his vest, suggests that he was less emotionally involved with others than they were with him. Like most other aspects of Obama's life, the question of his relationship to his mentors has resulted in disagreements. One line of argument has been that, "Those who know Obama say he didn't seem to need a replacement father."[41] Jerry Kellman, who brought Obama to Chicago and trained him in community organizing said of him that he was always good at finding "different kinds of people he could learn from" and that "mentors very quickly ceased to be mentors with Barack, they became collaborators. ... He was able to form intimate relationships with people, but they were friendships. He was not in search of surrogate fathers."[42]

On the other hand Remnick, one of Obama's biographers, says, "Like many young people of promise and ambition, especially ones with absent parents, he had a hunger for mentors."[43] In Remnick's telling Obama was unusual among his peers in that "he sensed he had much to learn from older people who had special knowledge of the ways things worked, and his eagerness to learn brought out their eagerness to teach."[44] This idyllic description defies credulity. In it Obama only wants to learn and grow and his mentors, recognizing his willingness to learn, are eager to teach him. The reality is far more complex and revealing.

One must begin with the fact of the rather large number of Obama mentors. Ordinarily one has, if fortunate, one or a few mentors in professional life, but not dozens. What accounts for this? One element was Obama himself. He was seen, and correctly so, as smart, measured, presentable, unthreatening, verbally fluent, a rhetorically agile young man with a bright future in front of him.

But he was also black, a liberal Democrat, and he had aspirations for a political career. It did not require unusual predictive powers to conclude that this young man would have an important career in politics either at the city (mayor), state (governor) or national level (Member of Congress, Senator, even president). And it would obviously be a liberal Democratic career. Almost all of Obama's mentors once he reached Harvard shared that political perspective whether they were old line Democratic like Abner Mikva or newer ones like Christopher Edley.

His mentors not only saw Obama's admirable intellectual qualities, they also saw someone who had a future that they could help and become a part of. Remnick quotes one of Obama's Harvard mentors, Christopher Edley as saying, "Even as we would talk about career paths, he seemed so centered that, in combination with his evident intelligence, *I just wanted to buy stock in him, I knew that the capital gains would be enormous.*"[45]

Emil Jones, the old time politico who became Senate majority leader when Democrats assumed power in the Illinois Statehouse, did become uncharacteristically emotional for him when being interviewed about Obama. Jones,

> is an older man, very dark-skinned, gruff, and given to referring to politics as "this business." But he got up, walked around from behind his desk, held out his arms, and peered into the middle distance, grinning unself-consciously. We were in a gray-walled office on the sixteenth floor of a building in downtown Chicago. Jones sighed happily. "One day, I want to retire, and sit back and watch him on the national scene."[46]

Certainly Obama sought out these connections, and many had a clear self-advancement element to them. One reporter who covered him wrote that, "Obama has always had a healthy understanding of the reaction he elicits in others, and he learned to use it to his advantage a very long time ago."[47] One example has made the round of Obama stories. Long before one of Illinois' two U.S. Senate seats came up for election in 2004, Obama approached his mentor, Emil Jones, who was preparing to lead a new Democratic majority in the state Senate in 2002:

> "You're a very powerful guy," Obama told Jones.
> "I've got the power to do what?" Jones responded.
> "You could help elect a U.S. senator," Obama said.
> Jones asked his protégé if he had anyone in mind.
> "Yeah," Obama replied. "Me."[48]

Obama approached his possible mentoring relationships with a clear eye on his goals.

When Judson H. Miner, who headed the law firm for which Obama ultimately went to work, took him to lunch to interview him for a position, he found himself being interviewed instead. Obama, made it clear that he was less interested in a job than in learning the political lay of the land from a man who had served at the right hand of the city's first black mayor, Harold Washington. The confident younger man "cross-examined" Mr. Miner about how Mr. Washington had managed to emerge from an election riven by bigotry to form a governing coalition. ... [49]

This anecdote reflects an enormous amount of self-possession on Obama's part and at a very early age.

In Obama's first term in the Illinois State Senate it was former U.S. Senator Paul Simon, who called Abner Mikva and suggested that Mr. Mikva play matchmaker between Obama and Emil Jones. "'Say, our friend Barack Obama has a chance to push this campaign finance bill through,' Mr. Mikva recalled Mr. Simon's telling him. 'Why don't you call your friend Emil Jones and tell him how good he is.'"[50]

There is then a large element of strategic calculation interwoven throughout Obama's many mentor relationships. There is no doubt that earlier in his career, in Hawaii with Frank Davis, in his Chicago community organizing days with Jerry Kellman, there was an element of the obvious, but clearly not fully accurate, Freudian analysis that can be made; to wit—boy without father seeks same.

Yet, Chicago also appears to mark a turning-point in Obama's seeking guidance/ strategic consideration ratio. Obama's decision to join Reverend Wright's church seems to have had a deeply personal dimension—Wright's social gospel message resonated with Obama. But it also seems to have had a strategic dimension associated with it as well. Obama needed to have a religious home if he were going to socially minister to South Side needs and Wright's church was large and influential.

Did Obama need guidance from those who were experienced and successful enough to be in a position to give it? Yes. Did Obama understand that in giving him their guidance, he might also get their help? Yes. Is there anything suspect about a smart, upwardly mobile and ambitious young man thinking along both lines? No.

The only thing that distinguishes Obama in the usual give and take of such relationships is the large number of them that Obama managed to successfully cultivate.

Helping Obama

There is another aspect to Obama's mentoring relationships that begins to shade over into the public's response to him. Obama's Democratic-minded mentors from Harvard onward saw in him a rising star that they wanted to hitch themselves to (Edley), help advance, or both. But Obama also had a pronounced effect on people in a position to help, though not mentor him. As noted, "Obama has always had a healthy understanding of the reaction he elicits in others. ... "[51] And what reaction exactly, was that? Evan Thomas writes, "Barack Obama had a gift, and he knew it. He had a way of making very smart, very accomplished people feel virtuous just by wanting to help Barack Obama."[52] One reporter who followed Obama around during his Chicago campaigning said in an interview, "Obama was somehow all about validating you. He was radiating the sense that 'You're the kind of guy who can accept a black guy as a senator.'"[53]

That experience had actually begun for Obama when he first moved back to Hawaii. His grandmother's job helped to pay the steep tuition costs at Punalou. Mendell writes,

> By living in a modest apartment and sending Obama (and eventually Maya) to private school, his grandmother sacrificed their own prosperity for the sake of Obama and his sister. ... That was a trend that would follow Obama throughout his charmed personal life and into his political career—people going out of their way to clear a path for him to succeed.[54]

It can be argued of course that his grandmother's decision was a matter of family and that others who have helped along the way have not made equivalent sacrifice, and that is true. However, the dual set of elements, wanting to help smooth the way for Obama and feeling that in doing so one is doing something virtuous is part of the complicated relationship between Obama and others, and was very likely an important element of his presidential election. To paraphrase the quote just above: you're the kind of person who could accept a black guy as president.

Drawing Confidence from Political Success

Obama also drew confidence from his successful U.S. Senate run even though his opponent was a very weak one. In an interview with Obama, Balz and Johnson asked what had made him believe that the country was ready for an African American president. They report,

> He cited his run for the Senate in 2004, saying the experience had given him confidence that his race would not be an insurmountable obstacle. "Illinois is a pretty good microcosm of the country, and when I started my U.S. Senate race everybody said a guy with your name, African American, can't win a U.S. Senate race. And we won. And my approval ratings, I think, when I announced for the presidency here in Illinois, were like 70 percent. So I thought to myself, 'If I'm in a big industrial state with 12 percent African American population and people seem to not be concerned about my race and much more concerned with my performance, why would [that not hold true] across the country?'"[55]

And there is finally the spectacular success of Obama as a presidential candidate and his smart, well-run and agile campaign. Michiko Katutani, reviewing one of the many books about the Obama campaign, makes a point worth keeping in mind. He writes, "their retrospective does prove useful in reminding us ... *of the daunting odds that Mr. Obama overcame to win the White House in the first place.*"[56] And winning this very large undertaking, against substantial odds and against a very formidable primary opponent, and then a respected war hero, certainly would legitimately be an example of a very important self-confidence formula in operation: intense and successful effort invested in a high stakes, long odds undertaking and succeeding, thus translating successful effort into well deserved self-confidence.

Looking back, we can see that Obama really began to develop his self-confidence sometime in early adulthood, and that his experiences at Harvard seem central. It is also fair to say that Obama's self-confidence rests legitimately on a core of personal and political skills that have been instrumental in his rise. Obama has a solid basis for his confidence, and the size of his political accomplishments in a very short period of time might well simulate an understandable degree of high, perhaps over-confidence.

The question that arises at this point is whether an understandable surge in self-confidence has not either turned the corner to arrogance or, whether an element of arrogance wasn't present *earlier* on that acted as accelerator to his self-confidence, his ambitions, and his willingness to take risks on their behalf.

Self-Confidence and Arrogance

In drawing a distinction between an understandable surge in self-confidence that comes from having succeeded at a high risk undertaking, and its more arrogant or grandiose counterpart, it is necessary to develop some basis of distinguishing between them. One requirement is to ask a very basic question: Is there any evidence of an arrogant element in Obama's psychology. The answer to that question leads to another, that of timing. *If* there is evidence that arrogance is part of Obama's self-confidence, was it a byproduct of his large-scale successes, or was it present before he legitimately earned his self-confidence? If it was present before his real, earned success, then obviously success can't be the cause. In this case, the large-scale accomplishments act as an accelerant on the arrogance.

And lastly we can look at the questions of magnitude, process, judgment, and levels of risk involved in any undertaking to see whether confidence has overstepped its effectiveness boundary. It is tempting to use magnitude of a presidential undertaking as the sole indicator for overstepping confidence boundaries, and some do. However, magnitude alone is a difficult measure to validate. It is easy to see why.

Running for president is an audacious undertaking of the highest magnitude of difficulty, yet Obama did so and won. Succeeding in passing national health care legislation was also clearly an audacious and difficult undertaking. Yet, Obama also successfully did this. On what basis then could anyone argue that this shows that Obama overreached because of too much confidence that it could be done? That would be a difficult argument to make or sustain. On the other hand, the fact that a president accomplished a goal cannot alone serve as an analytical conclusion that no appropriate confidence levels were breached. How an undertaking was done, at what costs, in what political circumstances, and with what public legitimacy also have to be entered into the analysis.

One of the most damaging consequences of having too much self-confidence is that it retards the acquisition of new information. And when strong self-confidence is also coupled with strong ideological convictions, their joint impact is substantial. One of the by-products of strong ideological convictions is that people who hold them force new discordant information into old categories. Some time ago, in a classic set of experimental studies, Milton Rokeach demonstrated that those who held strong ideological convictions on either the left or the right had a great deal of trouble integrating new information.[57] Those findings are not surprising. After all when you are absolutely certain of your views, it is very hard to accept information that may undermine them. And, it seems quite obvious that a president who combines very high self-confidence in his own views with strong ideological convictions, both being characteristics that fit President Obama, will have trouble integrating new information that challenges their beliefs.

In an interview on July 22, 2008 right after his *New York Times* commentary piece still opposing the surge, after his trip to Afghanistan and Iraq as the Democratic Party nominee, Obama was asked the following question:[58]

Q: Was there anything that you saw on this trip that changed your mind? John McCain, as you know, is saying, "Well, he already knew what he was going to think before he got there."

OBAMA: Well, I thought John also suggested that I'm always changing my mind, so he's got to make up his mind about what he says about my mind.

Q: But is there anything where you really feel like you've changed your mind?

OBAMA: *Look, I feel as if I had a good grasp of the situation before I went. It confirmed a lot of my beliefs with respect to the issues.*

One of the critical ingredients of good presidential judgment is the ability to see problems *and possible solutions*, as they really are and not primarily through the lens of one's prior beliefs. This is a large issue for Obama who not only has very strong views about a great many policy areas, but also because of his enormous confidence in these views.

Arrogance?

The first step in trying to clarify these issues is to ask directly: is there evidence of arrogance in Obama's psychology? Evidence suggests the answer is yes, although his supporters don't think so. Jonathan Alter says of Obama that, "most of the time his refusal to be conspicuous about his superior intelligence lent modesty to what might otherwise have been an impression of cockiness."[59] John Podesta, who served as a Chief of Staff for President Clinton and now heads the progressive Center for American Progress had this to say about Obama's self-confidence: "He has great self-assurance without being egotistical and he's totally Zen-like without being arrogant."[60]

Mirroring the ample evidence of Obama's self-confidence is equally copious evidence that it can veer off into arrogance. Let us begin here, as we did above with what others, all of whom covered Obama for long periods of time, say. Wolffe writes, "He could be self-confident to the point of arrogant. ... "[61] Mendell wrote of him,

> for those who know Barack Obama well, this might sound close to impossible, but the swagger in his step appeared even cockier than usual on the afternoon of July 27, 2004 [the day he gave the opening speech at the Democratic National Convention].[62]

Remnick reports that in his 2000 Congressional race, "even to some allies he seemed aloof to the point of arrogance."[63] Toni Preckwinkle, an alderman in Chicago's fourth ward (Obama's ward) supported him but said that Obama, "was kind of snooty. His head was way up in the air, he acted like he was too good to be there."[64]

The *Newsweek* team that covered the campaign behind the scenes wrote that, "Barack Obama can be cocky about his star power."[65] Alter, whose disclaimer about Obama's arrogance was noted just above, also had this to say: "Obama could occasionally seem cocky to even his most ardent supporters from Chicago, especially when he tilted his head up and bragged that he knew more about organizing, media, political strategy, domestic affairs and foreign policy than the people around him."[66] Alter summarizes an unusual presidential circumstance:

> The president was, by several accounts, his own national security advisor, coordinating the different elements of foreign policy, intelligence gathering and defense to suit his needs. That was the way he wanted it. ... [67]

Indeed one "senior official" went on record to say, "The truth is that President Obama is his own Henry Kissinger—no one else plays that role. Every administration reflects the personality of the president. This president wants all the trains routed through the Oval Office."[68]

The quote that lists all the areas in which Obama believes he has superior knowledge almost seems hyperbolic, but is not. Here in his own words is President Obama. At one point during the presidential campaign he asserted that in picking a vice presidential nominee he doesn't have to worry about foreign policy experience because, "Ironically, this is an area—foreign policy is the area where I am probably *most* confident that I know more and understand the world better than Senator Clinton or Senator McCain."[69] Asked after the presidential campaign about the best advice he had received while running he replied, "Well, I have to say it was the advice that I gave to myself."[70] In July of 2007, he told a group of fundraisers, "I'm the best retail politician in America."[71] In early 2007, when Obama interviewed Patrick Gaspard, who became the campaign's political director, he told him, "I think that I'm a better speechwriter than my speechwriters. I know more about policies on any particular issue than my policy directors."[72]

Alter, writing on Obama's view of his foreign policy said that, "Obama immodestly believed the strategy on proliferation has been 'pretty flawless.'"[73] Writing about Obama's view of his foreign policy he further says, "The president was proud—maybe too proud—of his record abroad. He described what he called a 'pretty flawless execution of what our strategy was at the beginning of the year. ...'"[74]

Much has been made of Obama's deliberative decision style and it was routinely noted in the lead up to his decision to commit more troops to Afghanistan. Yet, there is another less commented upon aspect to Obama's dealing with his own aides. Two reporters noted in their book on the Obama campaign that in campaign meetings with his aides,

> he exerted control over the meeting by interrupting whoever was talking. "Look," he would say—it was his favorite interjection, almost a tic—and then be off to the races, reframing the point, extending it, claiming ownership of it. "Whose idea was that?" was another of his favorites. ... [75]

Obama has said of himself more than once, "I am someone who tends not to have a lot of pride of authorship ... , I would be happy to steal ideas from anybody. Republican, Independent, or Democrat."[76] Yet, this is not wholly accurate, as his behavior in the health care debate demonstrated. For all his success, Obama can be very demanding of receiving all the credit he judges himself to deserve, and as will be detailed in Chapter 9, that amount is substantial. And he can be very prickly about others pointing out mistakes for which he bears some responsibility.

Wolffe reports on a state of the campaign meeting after Hillary Clinton won some state primaries. Obama began by critiquing some of his own mistakes and then invited input from others. He called on Dan Pfeiffer, his deputy communications director, who said, "Frankly, sir I think Hillary worked harder." Obama "bristled. Through the rest of the meeting, he prefaced his comments by repeating Pfeiffer's thoughts. 'Well, Pfeiffer says I'm not working hard enough.'"[77] For all his success, Obama can be remarkably thin-skinned.

Asking for frank comments and then ridiculing those who make them is not a recipe for continued frankness. One is reminded here of an interview in which President Obama was asked,

> Has anybody said to you, No, sir, you can't do that? Has there been a moment in these last six weeks where you tried to do something and somebody said, Sorry, sir, it doesn't work that way? Obama answered: "Well, I mean, I think what we were talking about earlier in terms of Guantanamo.

People didn't have to tell me, No you can't do that. It was simply, Well, sir, here are the challenges that we face in terms of making a decision about that."[78]

Measuring Up to Obama

The last two reported stories speak to something that showed up early in Obama's development, his view that he stood alone as a serious person with the knowledge necessary to address whatever the issue at hand, and those who didn't measure up were to be scolded or disdained. Writing about Obama's monk period in New York, Mendell said,

> Obama's intellectual elitist nature also began to sprout during this period, and he perhaps began to take himself a bit too seriously. Maya, who was in her mid teens at the time, recalled that her brother chastised her for reading a copy of *People* magazine and watching television instead of delving into the novels that he had given her.[79]

In his book *Dreams*, Obama confirms that account but adds another telling detail: "*I instructed my mother* on the various ways that foreign donors and international development organizations, *like the ones she worked for* bred dependence in the Third World."[80] The tone implied by the word "instructed" is one of a superior talking down to someone of lesser rank or knowledge. It is also a frontal attack on his mother's life work. His mother's visit took place the summer before Obama started Columbia University.

It is not hard to envision the link between Obama's growing sense of intellectual superiority reflected in his somewhat presumptuous instruction of his mother and a well-publicized campaign incident in which Obama accused Pennsylvania primary voters of being people who "cling to guns or religion or antipathy to people who aren't like them."[81] David Axelrod, Obama's chief advisor, had this to say about the issue: "Barack is extremely intelligent, and one of the pitfalls of extreme intelligence is you are so accustomed to being right, that you believe you are always right."[82]

Immune to his Own Hype?

As noted in Chapter 2, Obama has said more than once, "We don't buy our own hype,"[83] yet there is ample evidence to the contrary. Mendell reports that, "managing Obama's healthy ego has been one of the more trying tasks for his staff and paid consultants."[84] Mendell found himself in the middle of one such effort during Obama's Senate campaign when the *Chicago Sun-Times* ran a story about a prominent Chicago politician who was said to have the "IT" Factor which it defined variously as "charisma," "packaging," or just plain "sex appeal." Obama was mentioned as one such politician, and Mendell then writes that, "Obama walked through the campaign office with a copy of the tabloid newspaper folded under his

arm and open to the story. He proclaimed with glee, 'See, told you. I've got IT.'"
When Mendell brought up the story to one of Obama's aides, the aide said, "for
god's sake don't mention that story to him. He's walking around here with a big
grin on his face and saying 'I've got It. I've got IT.' He sure doesn't need any
reinforcement in the IT department."

It seems fairly clear that all of the adulation and hype surrounding Obama has
made an impression on him. He likes the spotlight. He likes the adulation. And it
reinforces the idea that Obama holds, in part because of what he has been able to make
of himself, through a great deal of planning and effort, that he is in fact someone special
and thoroughly deserving of the esteem with which he is held by his admirers.

Obama's Confidence in Perspective

There is, then, ample evidence that Obama feels a large degree of self-satisfaction
with the person he has become. And he has every reason to be proud of his
accomplishments. Yet, he also holds the view that he deserves all the accolades that
have been given to him, breaching the barrier that separates self-esteem from vanity.
Moreover, Obama's view of himself as uniquely able to get at the heart of many
matters, whereas others like his mother who spent years in pursuit of her efforts to
help the poor for example, simply don't have his superior perspective, helps push
his self-confidence into the domain of arrogance.

For any president obvious public displays of vanity or arrogance are political
negatives and Obama is no novice at presenting himself as he prefers to be seen.
Nonetheless close observers of Obama along the way have seen what rarely slips
through in most of Obama's public venues. Mendell writes that when Obama first
came to the Senate, he visited with Robert Byrd, who had once been a member of
the Ku Klux Clan. Byrd confessed "the sins of his youth," and Obama replied
"If we were supposed to be perfect, we'd all be in trouble … ," thus providing
Byrd a form of political absolution. Remnick writes that,

> Obama knew that if he made enough of these respectful visits, if he made
> enough gestures of modesty and obeisance to the institution, he would go a
> long way toward forming alliances and ease any jealousies. Obama tried to
> make these *conspicuous shows of humility* … a hallmark of his way of doing
> business. *He did not hesitate to advertise them.*[85]

It also seems clear, to return to a question posed earlier, that a large number of
the factual reports covered above come from the period *before* Obama earned the
self-confidence he so easily displays by investing himself in risky hard work and
ultimately succeeding. The point was that if arrogance was present before legitimately earned self-confidence was established there would be the danger that confidence will be stretched beyond its means. There is some evidence of this in
Obama's vast policy ambitions in the first two years of his presidency.

Michelle as Obama's Anchor?

One of the occupational hazards of being president is the dreaded White House bubble. The term ordinarily refers to something artificial and inflated. In the presidency, the word is generally used in two senses. The first and more frequent use refers to the physical limitations imposed on the president for safety reasons, and the fact that every presidential trip outside of the White House is a major logistical operation.

The second, arguably more consequential, understanding of that term refers to the intellectual, political, and strategic inflation of the president's judgment and preferences by his closest advisors and others because he is president. This is not an issue that is peculiar to President Obama, but it is one that is a particular danger for this president given his high self-confidence in his own judgments and large personal investment in his own ideas.

Michelle: Obama's Reality Check?

David Ignatius in his *Washington Post* column asked,

> Now that the perpetual traveler [Obama] has arrived, who will puncture that bubble of presidential loneliness? Presidents can spin into their own twilight zone, isolated in a crowd of advisers and hangers-on, and become prone to serious misjudgments. Think of Richard Nixon, or Lyndon Johnson, or Bush.[86]

Ignatius answered his own question by looking at the Barack and Michelle Obama interview on *60 Minutes* where he found "an encouraging answer … Obama's reality check will come from his wife, Michelle." He based his optimism on the fact that Michelle contradicted her husband on national television about how he liked washing dishes. She has also done the same on *Good Morning America*, overruling her husband on getting a dog, and insisting it would be his responsibility to walk it. Ignatius concludes that, "you have to believe that a man who can smile while his wife lovingly, genially puts him in his place is a pretty sane guy."

Obama's relationship with his wife Michelle is a lot more complex than her being able to "put him in his place." In fact, frequently being publicly and abruptly brought down to earth might well stimulate the desire for ego elevation outside of the relationship. However the by-play is mostly theater.

The fact of the matter is that, "People forget that Barack himself has been working the hapless-hubby routine for a long time … ."[87] Long before David Ignatius was extolling Michelle's anchoring virtues as Obama assumed the presidency, that by-play had been going on for some time. After Obama gave his 2004 convention speech, he was interviewed on *Face the Nation* and Bob Schieffer said to him "you're the rock star now," and Obama replied, "'talk to my wife and she'll tell you that isn't so,' Obama said in a self-deprecating manner. … "[88] Obama's biographer then continues, "This would become standard routine as his fame grew—using his wife's taskmistress side as a way to display public humility and keep his feet on the ground."[89]

It was and is a bit of a routine meant to disarm and endear. Michelle is not likely to sabotage her husband's political career. Even her supposed "telling it like she thinks it is" comments like "he's a gifted man, but in the end he's only a man" elicited warm applause from the audiences to which she spoke on her husband's behalf.[90]

Michelle: More Like Hillary than Laura

It is clear that Michelle is a smart independent minded woman who politically will occupy a position somewhere between Hillary Clinton and Laura Bush. Unlike Hillary Clinton, she seems to have no overt formal policy aspirations of her own. She will not be heading any White House policy initiatives as Hillary did. On the other hand, it is clear that she has much more pronounced and stronger views on political matters, as evidenced by transcripts of her stump speeches, than did Laura Bush.

It is also clear as one observer noted that Michelle is "a crucial part of the Obama package itself, complementing and shaping her husband in ways that are both politically and personally significant."[91] Valerie Jarrett, who worked for Chicago Mayor Daley and now is a chief advisor to the president, interviewed Michelle for a job in Daley's administration and "That was the start of a long relationship that has paid off politically for Barack Obama, connecting him to Daley's inner circle."[92] In that sense, their marriage has political elements that more closely resemble the Clintons than they do the Bushes, but that is not the focus of this analysis.

Guilt? Yes, but Politics Still Calls

It already seems clear that Ignatius' "encouraging conclusion" about Michelle being the anchor to keep Obama grounded is somewhat misplaced. If anything, the stable core of that relationship given Obama's own family experiences is likely to be in his role as father to his two children, a role that he clearly loves and cherishes. At a picnic thrown for campaign volunteers after he won election to the Senate and realized the demands on his life and time he had acquired, "a tear rolled down his cheek" as he said to his friend Valerie Jarrett, "*I'm really going to miss those little girls.*"[93] He didn't mention his wife.

His relationship with his wife, as would be the case for any two adults who become couples in early adulthood, is more complex and more prone to tensions than the ordinary parent-child emotional bond. We get a hint of this in Michelle's publicly repeated comment that when her husband was advancing his career in Springfield (Illinois), she had not expected to be raising the children alone. These are not atypical tensions in modern marriages when two independent, career-minded people have to adjust to the personal and professional demands of their lives.

However, for all Obama's expressed guilt about the effect his political ambitions were having on his family, he still pursued them, including a grueling two years on the presidential campaign trail. In late August 2005, Obama decided he wanted to speak at the Florida Democratic Party convention. That convention took place on a Saturday, which happened to be the day of his daughter Malia's dance recital in Chicago. When his press secretary Robert Gibbs asked him what he had in mind Obama replied,[94] "I've got some stuff I'd like to try out." And as his campaign chroniclers note,

> And he was so intent on going to Florida—Florida!—that he was willing to leave his daughter's recital, drive out to the airport, catch a charter plane, fly down to Lake Buena Vista, and jet back to Chicago the same night.[95]

Obviously Obama could feel both his ambition and the family regrets associated with it, but the point here is that even his clear and great love for his children had to contend with it.

Obama and Michelle: A Shared Worldview?

A more important question about Obama's marriage is what emotional role each plays for the other. In marriage, husbands and wives attempt to blend together two separate but, ideally, *complementary* psychologies. Couples can share broad cultural or religious perspectives. They can share social, aesthetic, or political interests and views. Or they can share basic identities or worldviews, premises about the world in which they live and how it operates. It is here that some very interesting psychological perspectives, with presidential consequences, emerge.

Obama's search for identity given his mixed race background is obviously a central element of his personal development and in that respect his choice of Michelle Robinson carries some interesting implications. In *Dreams*, Barack tells of dating on his mother's side of his racial identity, and in fact dated at least two white women somewhat seriously. One was a relationship carried on primarily inside an apartment when he lived in New York and was obviously limited.[96] The other was, symbolically enough, an anthropology student at the University of Chicago.[97]

What is interesting, and a somewhat obvious point, about his marriage to Michelle, is that as one person put it, "she is pure Chicago. ... raised in a one-bedroom apartment on the top floor of a classic Chicago brick bungalow, now surrounded by a chain link fence, in South Shore."[98] Her husband has "consistently battled questions from some African-Americans about whether the son of an African father and a white American mother is authentically black."[99] No such question can be asked about his wife, whose great-great grandfather was a slave, and therein is one aspect of the choices that have shaped his identity.

In Chicago, Obama's search for a black identity led to Reverend Wright and his Trinity Church. There was doubtlessly an instrumental aspect to the Trinity-Obama relationship. It was a large well established church, a fact that wouldn't be lost on a politically ambitious newcomer. But it also seems clear that Reverend Wright's strong views about the nature of American society resonated to some degree with Obama. And there is an element here that also connects his wife to the reverend's worldviews.

She had of course been criticized for her remarks about Obama's nomination marking the first time she was proud of her country. Less reported and of more interest are some of her remarks made while stumping for her husband and reported in a feature story in the *New Yorker,* hardly a bastion of conservative views. Among other things she said were that this country was "just downright mean," "guided by fear," and that most Americans' lives have "gotten progressively worse since I was a little girl."[100] In Western Iowa she said, "I'm so tired of fear and I don't want my girls to live in a country, in a world based on fear. That is why, and we have to admit it, we are in this war."[101]

There are others. In a 2007 *Vanity Fair* profile of her, she is quoted as saying,

> I am desperate for change—now, not in 8 years or 12 years, but right now. We don't have time to wait. We need big change—not just the shifting of power among insiders. We need to change the game, because the game is broken. *When I think about the country I want to give my children, it's not the world we have now. All I have to do is look into the faces of my children, and I realize how much work we need to do.*[102]

In one of her presidential campaign speeches, Michelle belittled the idea that the Clinton years were ones of opportunity and prosperity, saying

> The life that I'm talking about *that most people are living* has gotten progressively worse since I was a little girl. ... So if you want to pretend like there was some point over the last couple of decades when your lives were easy, I want to meet you![103]

One might attribute the fear comment as a dig at the Bush administration, a common enough sentiment and not a surprising one for someone trying to help make her husband president. But the other remarks are more puzzling. By most measures, things have not gotten progressively worse for Americans and certainly for Americans of African descent since she was a little girl (she was born in 1964).

Michelle Obama spoke before a number of church groups during the campaign and would begin by saying, "On behalf of my church home and my pastor, Reverend Wright, I bring greetings."[104] She too sat in the pews of Reverend Wright's church with her husband and family. And it seems fair to say that she heard the same controversial views expressed. The question raised by the views expressed in her stump speeches and her apparent comfort with the sermons at Trinity Church raises the question of whether she and her husband share and reinforce that worldview with each other.

A *New York Times* story on the morning after Michelle's speech to the Democratic National Convention noted that for the next ten weeks of the campaign she would have to "refashion her own occasionally harsh public image in warmer tones," and noted that she was, "at the center of a multimedia charm offensive that may be the most closely managed spousal rollout in presidential campaign history."[105] The reasons for this were clear. In focus groups, "voters volunteered their misgivings: that she was unpatriotic, seemed entitled or angry. ... "[106] Remaking spousal images is routine in presidential image management. Still the glimpses of Michelle's worldview before the professional airbrushing advice enveloped her are worth considering.

The interview that Ignatius found reassuring was based on Michelle's ability to remind her husband that, in words she used on the campaign trail, "at the end of the day he is only a man." But does she also remind him of premises that support some of the bleak assessments she made of life in the United States?

8

A ZEN-LIKE PRESIDENT'S EMOTIONAL UNDERCURRENTS

The desire to take on many things is one of Obama's long-standing traits and he is aware that it can bring trouble. In an interview with one of his biographers for a book that was published in 2007, Obama said this:

> There are many times when I want to do everything and be everything ... and that can sometimes get me into trouble. That's historically been one of my biggest faults. I was trying to organize Project Vote and the same time I was writing a book, and there are only so many hours of the day.[1]

Obama neglects to mention that during this period, immediately after graduating law school, he had also started his job as a lawyer at Miner, Barnhill and Galland, a politically well-connected Chicago Law firm.[2] When Obama first took up his role as a U.S. senator, he was also writing his second book. One of Obama's biographers wrote of that, "writing a book is a full time job in itself. And writing one while stepping into a new job is a recipe for burnout." It's also a recipe for commitment juggling and time borrowing. At any rate, his biographer's point was that, "Obama has a history of taking an inordinate number of tasks."[3] One can see this trait at work in Obama's determined relentless pursuit of his transformative ambitions in his first two years of office.

All that determined activity raises a question: Why so much of it? An obvious and plausible answer is that Obama had, and has, a lot that he wants to accomplish. And that is true. However, other evidence suggests that there is more to it than accomplishing ambition's purposes.

Obama's Boredom

Obama has written of his "chronic restlessness" and "an inability to appreciate, no matter how well things are going, those blessings that were right here in front of me." Obama thinks it a "flaw of modern life" and also that it is "endemic in the American character," and that "it is nowhere more evident than in the field of politics." He is puzzled though about whether "politics encourages the trait" or "simply attracts those who possess it."[4]

The answer in Obama's specific case appears to be none of the above. Appreciating what you have and feeling so comfortable with it that you don't want to change is thin fuel for ambition. Frustration and dissatisfaction are more powerful spring-boards for ambition than comfort. And in politics as in life, ambition reflects a desire to do more of what you want to do and to be in a better position to further the views and policies that you think are needed.

Obama shares with every modern president abundant ambition. But not every president's ambition seeks political, economic, and social transformation. And not every president defines success by how many big, important and perhaps even great things can be done in a short time. Obama made it clear from the moment he took up his position as a state senator in Springfield that he would work to accomplish his goals, one of which was to move up the political ladder. One news account of his time there notes that, "During his first week at the state Capitol, he scheduled a meeting with Senate Minority Leader Emil Jones (D) to request a heavy workload and coveted committee assignments."[5] Jones soon became Obama's mentor and when the Democrats gained control of the legislature, he put Obama in charge of numerous important bills, not only because he had confidence in his skills but also to help build his résumé. That story also notes that, "With an eye toward the future, Obama decided to befriend everyone in Springfield who could help him get where he wanted to go."[6]

Bored in Springfield

There is nothing suspect about Obama's dual motivation. He did work hard on behalf of a number of liberal issues, and some other issues like legislative ethics, that were important to him, but he also worked very hard to find a political road out of the state senate. Remnick writes of Obama's time in Springfield, that, "He was also bored with the details of so much work,"[7] which he thought did not really measure up to what he hoped to achieve. Nonetheless, Mendell reports that in his first two years Obama introduced or was the chief sponsor of fifty-six bills, with fourteen of them becoming law. In his third year Obama cosponsored almost sixty bills of which eleven became law. Considering that this was accomplished as a junior representative in the minority party Mendell concludes "it is a rather impressive record" and the evidence would seem to bear him out.[8]

In spite of this relative success, Obama's boredom with Springfield "deepened,"[9] and he looked around for ways to escape and decided his quickest route was to challenge long time Chicago Member of Congress Bobby Rush. All of his closest advisors were dead set against this move, but Obama insisted, a mistake of judgment brought on by the frustrations of his increasingly dammed up ambition, impatience over his ambition's pace, and over-confidence. He lost badly.

Bored in the U.S. Senate

He had to wait four more years for a successful escape. And escape he did. Obama won the U.S. Senate race and exalted, "I'm not a toy senator. I'm not playing Senator. I'm a real Senator now!"[10] However, his pleasure was short lived.

He found the slow pace of the Senate frustrating and complained to one friend that, "It's basically the same as Springfield except the average age in Springfield is forty-two and in Washington it's sixty-two. Other than that, it's the same bullshit."[11] After floor debates, he would leave "shaking his head, rolling his eyes, using both hands to give the universal signal for the flapping of gums, sighing wearily—'Yak, yak, yak.'"[12] The truth, as David Axelrod, Obama's chief advisor, told David Remnick in an interview, was that, "Barack hated being a senator."[13] Remnick notes of this that, "Obama could barely contain his frustration with the torpid pace of the Senate."[14]

As he had in other circumstances, when Obama got bored, he arranged his time so that he could work on something meaningful to him. One detailed examination of his Senate career reported that, "He spent long days in his Senate office and long nights toiling on his book [*The Audacity of Hope*], sometimes e-mailing chapters to friends and members of his Senate staff for fact-checking at 3 or 4 a.m."[15] Obama had done the same thing at his first Chicago law firm job at Miner, Barnhill and Galland, with the agreement of Mr. Miner, who had recruited Obama. Allison Davis, one of the partners in the firm, said in an interview, "He spent a lot of time working on his book. Some of my partners weren't happy with that, Barack sitting there with his keyboard and his feet up on the desk writing the book."[16]

Obama, as noted, was doing others things as well. He had signed on as director of "Project Vote," a voter registration drive. And he was also a lecturer at the University of Chicago Law School. The high pace of activity reflected in all these efforts is a reflection of Obama's tendency to take on a lot. But it is also reflective of not being fully present and engaged in any of these projects. This is not to say that Obama didn't manage to do them all well, though he seems to have devoted the least effort to his legal work. It reflects the fact that each one of these by itself was a major and arguably full time commitment, and to do all three at the same time, at the same level of personal investment and intensity, simply seems implausible.

Being Of, But Not In

It is just this implausibility that led David Brooks to make the interesting comment that Obama was a sojourner. He writes, "There is a sense that because of his unique background and temperament, Obama lives apart. He put one foot in the institutions he rose through on his journey but never fully engaged."[17] An extensive review of his time at the University of Chicago Law School concluded, "The young law professor stood apart in too many ways to count." He was "well liked at the law school, yet he was always slightly apart from it, leaving some colleagues feeling a little cheated that he did not fully engage."[18] Obama made five political races during his twelve years at the school and, as noted, was a practicing attorney in a law firm as well among other efforts. And as was the case when he was editor of the *Harvard Law Review*, Obama never committed any of his legal theory ideas to paper. One of his mentors from this period said that Obama, "was impatient with academic debates over 'whether to drop a footnote or not drop a footnote.'"[19]

In fact, the University of Chicago Law School, Springfield, and Washington were not the first places that didn't live up to his expectations and left Obama feeling unengaged. Remnick notes that Obama grew weary of the small college environment at Occidental College that he attended for two years before transferring to Columbia.[20] Things weren't much better at Harvard where he attended law school. Obama wrote of his time at Harvard,

> The study of law can be disappointing at times, a matter of applying narrow rules and arcane procedures to an uncooperative reality; a sort of glorified accounting that serves to regulate the affairs of those who have power—and that all too often seeks to explain, to those who do not, the ultimate justice and wisdom of their condition.[21]

Here Obama writes as if he chafed both at the narrow tedium of the law and its role as an instrument of subjugation. As to the latter, Remnick notes, this harsh language "was not far from the left leaning instruction on campus."[22]

Adulation Can Be Disappointing Too

Obama's disappointment also extended to the crowd adulation that others have said he craved because he had grown up without a father. As to the latter, Mendell writes,

> there was a part of Obama, whose father abandoned him as a child and whose mother traveled to faraway places and left him with his grandparents, that clearly fed off the public adulation. Nothing nourished him more than connecting emotionally and intellectually with an audience.[23]

Obama's closest advisor, Valerie Jarrett, agrees. Asked whether his father's abandonment contributed to Obama's desire to seek public attention she answered, "Absolutely, having a parent who leaves you makes you particularly energized for approval."[24] "His wife Michelle, and close friends would later speculate that his isolated childhood and parental loss had played a significant role in feeding his desire for public attention."[25]

This bit of instant psychoanalysis has initial plausibility, but there are some issues with it. One, as noted in the last chapter, is that given a choice between adulation and transformation, Obama has clearly chosen the second at the expense of the first in his first two years as president. Another is that it may be validation rather than approval that is the issue. When a candidate or leader *needs* approval, it suggests that the crowd provides buttressing to someone with low or uncertain self-esteem. There is no evidence that this is the case for Obama, and in fact the evidence points directly in the other direction. He has an abundance of self-esteem and self-confidence. In these circumstances, crowd response would provide validation of a candidate's already high level of self-regard. And if public adulation provides any emotional buttressing for Obama, it is as a validation of his own self-image as a unique and historical transformative political figure.

A third issue is that it falters on the grounds of timing in relation to cause and effect. Recall that Obama's first brush with the power of his own voice took place at an anti-apartheid rally when he was a freshman at Occidental College. Yet, immediately after that he went to New York and began his monk-like phase, and after that he went to Chicago to work as a community organizer where as Remnick notes, "When Obama did have free time, he usually liked to spend it alone."[26] Nor was Obama active in a public way at Harvard on the large issues, many racial, that divided law school students. He preferred then, as in his presidency, to exert his authority in small group settings where he was in charge.

The set speeches at this point in his presidency are mostly in front of supporters. They most likely provide some measure of relief from the complex and paradoxical realities of a presidency in which major legislation passes, but public approval sinks further. There is an artificiality to these kinds of audience friendly speeches for any president.

In any event, the satisfaction that Obama drew from his public adulation had a short half-life. Mendell writes of Obama on the campaign trail,

> that after a couple of days of fighting the crowds, Obama was starting to grow more weary of the speeches and the people—especially the people. ... With the sheer number of people he had to greet, the worshipping crowds became less ego gratifying and more of a burden.[27]

The truth of Obama's emotional interior is that the people demands of the presidency and of public life exhaust and deplete him. Peter Baker, who conducted a substantial pre-midterm election interview with the president wrote that,

> Insulation is a curse of every president, but more than any president since Jimmy Carter, Obama comes across as an introvert, someone who finds extended contact with groups of people outside his immediate circle to be draining. He can rouse a stadium of 80,000 people, but that audience is an impersonal monolith; smaller group settings can be harder for him. Aides

have learned that it can be good if he has a few moments after a big East Room event so he can gather his energy again.[28]

Bored in the Presidency?

Obama won the Democratic Party nomination for president after a very long and bruising battle against Hillary Clinton. Upon winning the nomination he had done what many thought impossible, beat a formidable, well established, well financed nominee who had acquired decades of key relationships at the national, state, and local levels. By doing so, Obama had also taken a very large step to becoming president. It was a moment of hard earned victory and a reason for satisfaction and even pleasure, but Obama seems not to have felt that.

Interviewed by Charlie Gibson after winning the delegates necessary to clinch the nomination, there was this exchange:[29]

GIBSON: I watched closely your countenance last night, your mien, as you stood in that hall. *You didn't smile much. Has the joyfulness of this hit home yet? Do you take joy from it?*

OBAMA: You know, I'll tell you where I feel joyful. I feel joyful when I think about all those young people who volunteered for our campaign, and I see them high-fiving and seeing the work that they put into this thing bear fruit. I feel joy when a woman, this morning, tells me that her son teaches in an inner city in San Francisco and that during the course of this year, he's seen the behavior of the African American boys he's teaching change and them start thinking about their options and hitting the books a little harder. I take joy in that. *But—but, look, there's no doubt that, you know, I tend to always be thinking a few steps ahead.* I've been thinking about all the work that needs to be done. And I think it's good advice that I've received from several quarters to, sometime in the next couple days, sit back and reflect a bit.

It's certainly possible that Obama is trying here to make some personal or political points about how his feelings of joy are for other people, but it is equally clear that he allows none of that to be said publicly for himself, and perhaps even experienced privately for himself. He is, by his own words, already looking ahead to the next battle, thinking about the work to be done. And he clearly values the advice to sit and reflect. Taking some time to feel satisfied with what he and his campaign have accomplished doesn't even merit an answer to a direct question about it.

Obama has called the presidency "the best job in the world,"[30] but it is also a frustrating one about which Obama has expressed his doubts. In a speech commemorating Martin Luther King at a Washington church, Obama echoed King's self-doubts, "There are times when it feels like all these efforts are for naught, and change is so painfully slow in coming, and I have to confront my own doubts."[31] It is true that here Obama is consciously picking up King's mantle, but it is also true that it is precisely these circumstances of too slow a pace of getting what he wants done that caused Obama to very much want to move on from his time at Harvard Law School, the Illinois State Senate and the United States Senate.

In an interview about Obama's schedule, David Axelrod said,

> There are certain things that are sacrosanct on his schedule—kids' recitals, soccer games, basketball games, school meetings … .These are circled in red on his calendar, and regardless of what's going on he's going to make those. *I think that's part of how he sustains himself through all this.*[32]

The "all this" seems to refer to the increasing public resistance to Obama's agenda and frustrations with Congress. The use of the words "sustain himself" reflects a depth of frustration or difficulty that it takes some substantial effort to overcome. And that is precisely the point at which Obama has, in the past, looked to move on.

The dynamic is well summarized by Gwenn Ifill: "Lacking power, Obama is shown to be the ultimate pragmatist. If he can't be in control, he is ready to move on."[33] Asked by Diane Sawyer "Ever in the middle of all of this do you think one term is enough?" Obama answered equivocally, "You know, I—I would say that when I—the one thing I'm clear about is that I'd rather be a really good one-term president than a mediocre two-term president. And I—and I believe that."[34]

Apparently though, he is willing to give a second term a shot. In mid-October, even before the midterm elections Vice-President Joe Biden revealed that the president had asked him to stay on for his reelection campaign in 2012.[35]

The question has begun to be asked, "Has Obama become bored with being president?"[36] One might be tempted to dismiss this question since it is raised by a clearly conservative commentator, but it is not only the "right" that is asking this question. Fred Hiatt, editorial page director of the *Washington Post*, wrote of Obama that, "He doesn't seem all that happy being president."[37] David Ignatius reports,

> A man who knows Obama well speculated a few months ago that this president isn't in love with the White House. The Post had run an article saying that with his dry intellect, Obama would be happier on the Supreme Court than in the Oval Office. The insider nodded his head. "That's true."[38]

The Meaning of Obama's Boredom

Perhaps the most startling observation regarding Obama's boredom came from Valerie Jarrett, his closest friend from Chicago and one of his very closest advisors. Speaking of him, she said, "He's been bored to death his whole life. *He's just too talented to do what ordinary people do.* He would never be satisfied with what ordinary people do."[39]

And why does she think Obama has been bored his whole life? She says,

I think Barack knew that he had god-given talents that were extraordinary. He knows exactly how smart he is ... He knows how perceptive he is. He knows what a good reader of people he is. And he knows that he has the ability—the extraordinary uncanny ability—to take a thousand different perspectives, digest them, and make sense of them, and I think that he has never really been challenged intellectually.[40]

This, remember, is from the person whom Remnick describes as "personally closer to the Obamas than *anyone* in his political circle,"[41] and whose formal title, Senior Advisor and Assistant to the President for Intergovernmental Affairs and Public Engagement, doesn't truly convey her central role as an Obama advisor on myriad issues. Aside from being mistaken on factual grounds, Obama's meandering performance up until Harvard Law School appears to have nothing whatsoever to do with boredom brought on by his brilliance; it is the startling level of idealization that stands out. Jarrett is the closest personally to the president and his wife and she also serves at the very highest level as one of his chief advisors. Yet, it would seem very difficult for her to envision thinking, much less saying to Obama, whom she sees as extraordinary in every way, that he is wrong. Given her view, how could he be?

The origins and meaning of boredom can vary. Valerie Jarrett's view is that Obama is so smart and talented that he has never really been challenged. That view flounders on the fact that Obama has yet to demonstrate the extraordinary brilliance that Jarrett attributes to him, and gave no evidence of it developmentally. This is not to say, as already noted, that the president isn't very smart, talented, and accomplished. It is only to say that a large gap between his supposed brilliance and the lack of challenges along the way is unlikely to provide a satisfying understanding of why he is bored.

Boredom's Explanation? Expectations vs. Accomplishments

During the presidential campaign in the period that Obama was drawing large enthusiastic crowds and adding delegates to his count at a rapid pace, he was interviewed and had this to say:

We had an enormous run through February, where we won eleven straight, and at that point all cylinders are clicking. That's when we had the huge rallies and filling every auditorium. My speeches are, I think full of energy and people. We're just on a roll.[42]

So, by all rights this should be when Obama is most satisfied. He is not just sitting around debating; he is out on the stump and in constant motion. Moreover, he is having success, by his own admission. So is he satisfied? No; disappointment and dissatisfaction begin to creep in, even in these circumstances: "But that's eleven victory speeches; thirty huge rallies. *Everything gets stale after a while.* So at a certain point it starts losing its spark, its freshness."[43]

It's possible to adopt Jarrett's theory and say that Obama simply didn't feel challenged by the life or death nomination struggle with Hillary Clinton, but this is a difficult argument to take seriously in these circumstances. The fact that it was a struggle that would determine whether Obama was in a position to carry out his transformational agenda suggests that it should have had deep importance to him, and winning should have been satisfying in a way that being either a "toy" or a "real" senator was not. Yet, the satisfaction soon faded into ennui.

Certainly, repetitious experience, even winning, can lose its luster. Yet, recall that at this point the final battle was not won, there remained a long fight ahead for Obama. So the feeling of having advanced far toward your goal might have carried more weight than the drag of repetition. This suggests something is operating underneath Obama's boredom.

Achievement Gaps and Obama's Boredom

Another obvious candidate to explain his boredom is the gap between what Obama hoped to accomplish and what was possible in the settings in which he became bored. Harvard Law, Springfield, and the U.S. Senate all failed to quiet Obama's sense of disappointment. It raises the question of whether these kinds of feelings will eventually attach themselves to his presidency, and there is some evidence that they have done so already.

If there ever was an office that would allow Obama to feel that he has finally achieved the impact that he has long sought, the presidency is surely it. And at first, it seemed like the office was everything Obama might hope it to be. He won the office with a resounding victory, brought about by assembling a new and formidable coalition of supporters, including many independents. He entered office on an almost unprecedented wave of public pride in his historic candidacy, even among those who didn't support him, and an outpouring of rapturous support worldwide.

Once in office, and with the help of substantial Democratic majorities in both the House and Senate, Obama compiled a major record of policy accomplishment. Yet the presidency is an office of enormous power, but also of limits. This has surprisingly proved to be the case in spite of, and perhaps because of, Obama having overwhelming majorities in both Houses of Congress. Paradoxically, it seems as if the more major legislation the Obama administration passed, the more uneasy and unsupportive the public became.

On the left, Obama was criticized for not passing a larger stimulus, pushing for greater financial regulation and enacting a fully nationalized health care system. On the right he was criticized for over involving the government in the country's economic life and trying to change the United States from a country best characterized by free market capitalism with a safety net and necessary government oversight to a European style social democracy in which the government heavily regulated most aspects of social, political, cultural, and economic life.

What became clear in the aftermath of the midterm elections was that Obama's liberal base stayed with him though in diminished numbers, and Republicans, and those who leaned right-center, voted against him in substantial numbers. But the real source of the major Republican victory was provided by independents.

Obama will face rough sledding after the 2010 midterm elections. Republicans, having gained control in the House and narrowed the Democratic majority in the Senate, will dramatically curtail Obama's transformational leverage. And this in turn is likely to increase the level of his dissatisfaction and heighten the level of his failure to achieve the goals he has set for himself. This has, in the past, been Obama's formula for boredom.

The Origins of Boredom: Obama Alone

Obama's peripatetic transformative redemptive policy ambitions and his determined pursuit of them recall the equally, almost frenzied, pace of personal activity that characterized Bill Clinton. His famous cardinal words were "What next. What next."[44] There was and remains a relentless, driven quality to Clinton's high activity levels. Whether he was staying up late at night after a grueling day of campaigning to search for more people to meet, engaging in speed diplomacy, or frenetically relaxing on vacation, Clinton was and is not only a man in motion, but also a man for whom motion is clearly an important psychological element.

The evidence is that Bill Clinton had trouble being alone, and that constant motion especially around people was a result.[45] Speaking of Clinton's aversion to spending time at Camp David, John Brummett, who covered Clinton as both governor and president, observed that, "The quiet (at Camp David) bothered him too. Clinton is not proficient at being alone; if nothing else he'll pick up a telephone."[46] Another biographer noted that Clinton,

> is almost compulsive about seeking people out; many of those midnight calls for which he is famous have no bearing on politics or business of any kind. Sometimes he has no more on his mind than contact with another human being, as evidenced by the time he called a local reporter whose father had just died. Clinton moved through the entire conversation without ever offering his condolences or even indicating any specific reason for having called, but rather giving the bereaved journalist a summary of a book he had been reading.[47]

Psychologically, boredom reflects the existence of some internal void or missing personal resource. Clinton and Obama differ here in several important outward respects, but not in something far more emotionally fundamental. Clinton entered the presidency with no grand plans to transform the country; Obama did. Clinton's time was focused more on people and contact with them; Obama's time is much more taken up with forwarding his own policies. Clinton's need for other people clearly contrasts with Obama's distant stance toward personal relationships, with the exception of his family and especially his children.

Frenzied activity is not a term that you would think legitimately applies to Obama personally given his "preternatural calmness,"[48] a phrase that at least on the surface seems well suited to the president. However, the president has displayed an intense focus and determined persistence in advancing his transforming agenda. While Obama doesn't give the impression of being in a what next, what next "frenzy," he is in a rush and his intensity operates below the public persona that gets picked up or understood by those observing him.

While Clinton and Obama share high activity levels (though Clinton's was more publicly obvious than Obama's), and they are dissimilar in important respects in how they approach the presidency's policy opportunities, there is one very important experience that both presidents share. They were both left on their own as children and growing up. Clinton's real father died before he was born and he was raised by a mother who had very strong interests in having a good time—and that included men, drinking, and gambling.[49] She adored him, much like Obama's mother adored him. However, both parents followed their own stars; in Clinton mother's case her north star was pleasure; in Obama's mother's case it was her wanderlust. Obama too, like Clinton, lost a father and had a stepfather. And Obama, as did Clinton, had grandparents who stepped into the parenting breach and tried to provide some physical and emotional stability.

In these similarities of having been left to a large degree on their own growing up, and of having therefore been on their own to an unusual degree lies a *possible* answer to the question of Obama's tendencies towards restlessness, boredom, and dissatisfaction. The word *possible* is italicized here to emphasize the provisional nature of the argument. Let me try to explain this formulation here as directly as possible.

The primary question at issue is to account for Obama's repeated boredom even, perhaps especially, after he has been successful. One possible theory is that he has never been adequately challenged, but it is hard to think of his grueling presidential nomination fight in this way. There is too the idea that many of his successful accomplishments proved disappointing because they failed to give him the political clout to command policy changes that he wanted. But if that's true he should not have been disappointed with all the victories that put him on the road to becoming president—a position that would enable him to do just that.

That leads us to consider that Obama's dense policy workload is meant to be the vehicle for his full emotional engagement and a hedge against the boredom he has so often experienced, unexpectedly one might add, after he has reached the positions that he thought he wanted. Obama's relentless policy activity is, as I have argued, a byproduct of his sense of himself as a transcending, perhaps great historical figure and his fervent belief in the necessity of America's transformation.

To that analysis, I want to add here the formulation that Obama's intense surge of transformational policy activity is an extremely important form of emotional investment to him, a vehicle for the emotional attachment that others might feel for their friends, their jobs or perhaps their possessions.

The origin of this intense investment lies in his early experience of not having had a father and having had a peripatetic mother who loved him, but often did so from a geographical distance. Obama's grandparents loved him, but by his own account, they were not good resources to help navigate the adolescent identity struggles he had to undertake on his own. He was forced to rely on his own counsel and doing that became consolidated as an emotional habit. Others, as noted, had little idea of what was going on underneath Obama's seemingly mellow surface. Moreover, he developed what I have termed *Rorschach strategies* to further cloud where, exactly, he stood and what, really, he thought. Obama's famously cool demeanor and the accompanying capacity to stand apart and sometimes beyond other people appears to be a clear reflection of those developmental experiences and Obama's reaction to them.

Obama's Emotional Demeanor: A Key to a Pragmatic Style

If there is one thing that observers, those who have spent time with him, and Obama himself all agree about it is that he has a decidedly cool, some would say detached temperament. Calm-tempered, cool, deliberative, and laid-back are all terms that have been used to describe Obama by people who have known him at various periods in his life.[50] These adjectives and descriptions are so widespread and behaviorally obvious that it seems fair to have confidence in them. Yet, beyond noting this characteristic there has been little effort to examine its origins, its impact on his leadership or the public's response to it other than the more recent complaints that the president ought to show a little more emotion. There has been even less analysis of how and why this style developed—whether its origins can be found in the need to bridge different racial worlds or the emotional impact of his father's absence, or some other set of factors. More basically, no one has bothered to ask or analyze the extent to which it is true.

Headlines like "Calmer Obama ushers in new age"[51] or "Mr. Calm"[52] trumpeted the earlier conventional wisdom. Naturally, Obama has been compared to Spock, the television character in Star Trek. In the words of one commentator, many are "drawing parallels between the dependably logical half-Vulcan and another mixed-race icon: Barack Obama," representative of a race where "logic would reign over emotion, and rational thought triumph over blind faith."[53]

Conservative columnist Kathleen Parker,[54] writing about her experience with the president on an Air Force One trip wrote,

> What struck me most was his immense calm. I kept looking for fissures in the façade, some signal that the cool cat is a defense mechanism or some tactical

ploy to deflect or defuse an opponent. Nary a crack. You may as well try to find the Dalai Lama's Achilles heel. I suspect that if you cut Obama open, you'd find a little Buddha sitting inside, smiling.

David Brooks, commenting on the president's "resolved, but reserved" speech on his new Afghanistan policy noted that overall "Obama's emotional coolness remains a signal feature" of his presidency.[55]

Even those very close to Obama have noticed his tendency to put thinking above feeling. His wife Michelle is quoted as having yelled at her husband during a debate practice session, "'Barack,' she interjected, 'Feel—don't think!' Telling her husband his 'over-thinking' during past debates had tripped him up with rival Hillary Clinton, she said: 'Don't get caught in the weeds. Be visceral. Use your heart—and your head.'"[56]

And the president has said of himself, "There's a certain ambivalence in my character that I like about myself."[57] Asked by a supporter whether all the attention he was receiving was making him sweat, he replied, "Nah, I don't sweat. You ever see me sweat?"[58] In another interview, Obama has said of himself, "one of my strengths is I don't get too up when we're up and I don't get too down when we're down."[59] In his second book Obama wrote, "My wife will tell you that by nature I'm not somebody who gets real worked up about things."[60]

These characterizations are true, to a point. Yet, these raise a number of questions. What is the psychological nature of Obama's calm? Is it a matter of biology (temperament), or is it something Obama learned to do with his emotions? And what does the president do with the normal range of emotions that most people experience—the surge of pleasure at success, the disappointment at setbacks. And finally, the important question arises as to the impact of "calmness" on his leadership and the deliberation of policy choice.

The Emotional Origins of a Zen Style

While one cannot definitively answer the nature or nurture question concerning Obama's emotional style, it seems clear that experience has played a substantial role in its development. Recall James David Barber's idea that style develops as the future president "moves beyond the detailed guidance of his family." In Obama's case, his family provided him no detailed guidance for two very good reasons. First, as noted, he was searching for the elements of a black identity and his mother and grandparents with whom he lived were Caucasian. And second, Obama grew up without the ongoing guidance of either his mother or his father. His father's absence is a well-known fact, and his mother too made choices that resulted in their separation.

There is also another less well known fact about Obama's mother. She wore her emotions on her sleeve, or in more clinical terms we might say they were labile. Her daughter (Obama's half-sister) Maya Soetoro-Ng said of her mother,

"She cried a lot, if she saw animals being treated cruelly or children in the news or a sad movie—or if she felt like she wasn't being understood in a conversation."[61]

Obama has already written of his annoyance at his mother's clumsy attempts to find common ground with him, "You know, I don't feel White."[62] As Obama relates his mother's approach to his racial heritage,

> Every black man was Thurgood Marshall or Sidney Poitier; every black woman Fannie Lou Hammer or Lena Horne. To be black was to be the beneficiary of a great inheritance, a special destiny, glorious burdens that only we were strong enough to bear.[63]

Of this, Remnick notes that you can almost see Obama "rolling his eyes."[64]

In short, his mother was given to emotional excess and had a tendency toward effusive and naïve views. It is likely that herein lies one source of Obama's disciplined self-containment. As noted in Chapter 5, the first separation from his mother occurred when she sent Obama to live with his grandmother and grandfather when he was ten years old and she stayed behind in Indonesia for a period. Obama's mother did move back the following fall shortly before his one and only visit from his father but then returned to Indonesia.[65] In 1974, she returned to Hawaii and she, Obama, and his younger sister lived together for three years,[66] after which time she returned to Indonesia for fieldwork. Obama was quite unequivocal that he did not want to join her. She returned from her fieldwork in 1978 at the start of his senior year in high school,[67] a three-year absence, and the following fall Obama headed to Los Angeles to start his freshman year at Occidental College.

Obama, writing in a new preface to his *Dreams* book, laments that he didn't focus more on his mother, who died in 1995 and was according to him, "the single constant of my life."[68] The evidence already reviewed suggests otherwise, and this probably accounts for Obama's stated feelings of "having a sense of abandonment."[69] Elsewhere he has said, "Away from my mother, away from my grandparents. ... I was trying to raise myself to be a blackman. ... "[70] And recall that in another interview, he said simply and more generally, "At some level, I had to raise myself"[71] and that "he had often described himself as an 'orphan'. ... "[72] Obama himself has written of "the sense of abandonment I'd felt as a child."[73] His wife Michelle told one of Obama's biographers that, "Barack spent so much time by himself that it was like he had been 'raised by wolves.'"[74]

It's worth noting the distinction above between "raising myself as a blackman" and having to "raise myself" and the metaphor of being an "orphan." It is one thing to have to navigate developing a specific racial identity on your own, it is quite another to feel that you have to navigate your whole identity and life on your own. Conventional wisdom focuses on the first, but in fact both were true, in Obama's view. So, Obama was not only on his own about his racial identity, but also more generally.

Nor were his grandparents, with whom he lived during his high school years, and who clearly loved and tried to guide him, of much help. Obama writes of them, "I'd arrived at an unspoken pact with my grandparents: I could live with them and they'd leave me alone so long as I kept my trouble out of sight."[75]And keep it out of sight he apparently did.

In *Dreams* Obama tells the story of going to an all-black party with two white friends who asked to leave early because they felt uncomfortable. That night made Obama "furious" because one of his friends said it made him realize how Obama might feel at school, and this in turn made Obama realize how much power whites had over blacks. But that friend Greg Orme said in an interview, "I never knew, until reading the book later, how much that night had upset him."[76]

Using unadorned language, you could legitimately say that Obama was abandoned by his father and left alone by his mother too for significant periods. As a result, Obama was left on his own, and he apparently felt alone. He certainly was and is not a loner, but his friends were apparently not very aware of the internal turmoil that Obama writes of himself having gone through in *Dreams*.

Obama kept his feelings to himself, and that became a life-long pattern. However, the pattern goes beyond keeping his feelings to himself. Obama apparently decided early on to actively foster a style that not only kept people from really knowing what was going on inside him, but of fostering an erroneous impression. I refer to this as Obama's Rorschach strategy, one that when coupled with Obama's uncanny chameleon-like ability to blend into diverse settings has made him the mystery to many people that he continues to be.

Obama Redeems Himself

When Obama moved to New York he experienced a period of doubt and temptation. He worried that his old habits of avoiding working hard and taking drugs would reassert themselves and that he would succumb to their temptations and the temptations of wealth and fortune that he saw all around him. To forestall those temptations, Obama undertook a form of personal withdrawal that also could not help but further consolidate the emotional self-sufficiency that he had adopted as a result of his father's abandonment and his mother's long absences before and during his adolescence in Hawaii.

Obama's biographer notes that during this period he chose to live a "monastic existence, spending time alone in his spare Manhattan apartment and digesting the works of Nietzsche, Hermann Melville, and Tony Morrison, as well as the Christian Bible."[77] Of his self-described "monk-like" period, Obama says, "I had tons of books. I read everything. I think that was the period when I grew as much as I have ever grown intellectually. *But it was a very internal growth.*"[78]

Obama further says of this period,[79]

So there's a phrase, which I wrote about in my first book, where, for whatever reason, a whole bunch of stuff that had been *inside me*—questions of identity, questions of purpose, questions of, not just race, but also the international nature of my upbringing—all these things started converging in some way. And so there's this period of time when I move to New York, and go to Columbia, where I pull in and wrestle with that stuff, and do a lot of writing and a lot of reading and a lot of thinking and a lot of walking through Central Park. *And somehow I emerge on the other side* of that ready and eager to take a chance in what is a pretty unlikely venture: moving to Chicago, and becoming an organizer.

In another interview he said, "Those two years were extremely important to me. I just stripped everything down and sort of built things back up. For about two years *there I was painfully alone and really not focused on anything, except maybe thinking a lot.*"[80]

What's striking about these remembrances, other than their aesthetic quality and their relationship to fighting off the temptations that allowed Obama to feel he had surmounted them and been redeemed, is their utterly self-accomplished nature. Recall that Obama was a student at Columbia University during this period, taking courses in political science and other departments. Yet, in his view, he read and digested all those works on his own. He figured out all those personal questions by himself. He grew as much as he had ever grown intellectually, but it was in his own words "a very internal growth." His biographer, discussing this period, says, "Obama focused on himself and did not give much credit to his college professors in his book … ,"[81] and one might add, to anyone else either.

The importance of this period then, is not only Obama's temptation and redemption, and not only his intellectual growth, but also that he presents himself as, and believes himself to be, the sole author of both developments. In Obama's view, it was a soliloquy, not a dialogue of any sort. This is clearly one source of Obama's enormous self-investment in his own ideas. It is, after all, a large and unusual accomplishment to have successfully mastered philosophy, politics, religion, and race, not to mention sorting through the dilemmas of your own racial and personal identity all by yourself. So when Kloppenberg argues that "ideas matter to Obama," he is right.[82] However, he misses the point that it is Obama's own ideas that are paramount.

That accomplishment is also one key building block to Obama's enormous self-confidence. It is true that his self-confidence received a strong boost from his comparative success at Harvard. But the building blocks of that success were, in Obama's view, self-taught and singularly his own. And of course, in this self-taught theme, lies another parallel with Lincoln who taught himself the law and much else.[83]

Obama: Self-contained, but not Isolated

The word that seems to most legitimately suit Obama's emotional style is *self-contained*.[84] Emotionally, there is no doubt that he can connect with people, perhaps the most vivid examples of which are his clear emotional attachment to his children and his wife. They represent the intact family and stability he never had growing up and it is not unusual for experiences seen as important that are missing in a person's developmental experience to become an important focus in adult choices.

Obama's commitment to wife, children and family are the most self-evident evidence of his ability to make strong emotional connections. His love and connection to his children is palpable and not surprising given his experiences with his parents and especially his father. In an early biography, David Mendell characterized Obama's father's relationship with women as being in "a constant state of disarray— by most counts he fathered nine children by four wives."[85] Obama told Mendell at one point that his father's "family life was unstable and his children never knew him well."[86] That was true as far as it went, but it hardly went far enough.

In a later interview Obama was more direct. He said,

> My father was a deeply troubled person. My father was an alcoholic. He was a womanizer. He did not treat his children well. I think that even my mother, who loved him and was always very generous toward him, said to me once that I probably ended up benefiting from not having grown up with him because he was very hard on those children who were in his household, and in a lot of ways he was a tortured soul.[87]

These were difficult, hard truths and all the more impressive for having replaced a foundation of earlier idealization that his mother had fostered.

It is not unusual for children who live with, or in Obama's case, learn about a missing parent's large parental imperfections to, as a result, make strenuous efforts to avoid those in their own lives. And this Obama clearly did in his personal life. Obama's marriage to his wife Michelle and her deep roots in the South Side Chicago community reinforced and consolidated Obama's own search for his black identity and the community in which it could be validated and enacted.

The Mystery of Obama's Empathy

When the histories of the Obama presidency are written, one of the puzzles that will need to be addressed is how this smart, very knowledgeable, and at least at first, engaging president so misjudged the relationship between his ambitions and the public's appetite for them. Part of the answer surely has to do with Obama's enormous confidence and investment in his own ideas (see Chapter 7). Part of it is clearly a by-product of the president's redemptive and transformative ambitions. A president with large ambitions that are coupled with high self-confidence can be very prone to minimizing or trying to suppress the heart-felt and legitimate concerns of those who don't share his perspective.

In a 2009 interview with Steve Kroft, Obama acknowledged the public's emotional fatigue with all of his initiatives, but indicated that he felt that he had no choice but to continue with enacting his policies:[88]

KROFT: As I said, there was an unusual set of circumstances. But after doing all this, and continuing the policies, and spending incredible amounts of money I mean, amounts of money that people couldn't even get their mind around a few years ago. Now, you're changing the health care system. I get the sense out there politically that some people are just sort of worn out. I mean, there's been so much change.

PRESIDENT OBAMA: Look ...

KROFT: And so much that people have—people are fatigued. And yet, you have to do all of this.

PRESIDENT OBAMA: I think you are absolutely right. That this is a very difficult economic environment. *People are feeling anxious ... And I think it is absolutely fair to say that people started feeling some sticker shock.* After a while, they just sort of felt like, "Gosh, you got the banks, you got the autos, you got AIG, you got, you know, two wars that we're still paying for. And it just seems like an awful lot." And so, there is an argument to be made out there that maybe health care can just wait. Because, you know, we've had to absorb a lot. The system's gone through a shock. Maybe we should just hold off until some other time.

KROFT: People ask you this question. And I probably asked you this question when you first came in. Look, things are really difficult. We don't have as much money as we had. Do we need to do all of this? Can't we scale some of this back? And you could've said, "Let's scale it back." But you didn't.

PRESIDENT OBAMA: The problem I've got is that the only way I can get medium- and long-term federal spending under control is if we do something about health care.

Obama clearly recognizes that he has asked the American people to absorb a lot of policy change in a very short period, too short to truly educate the public in the midst of raging political battles about the legislation's passage. He acknowledges that the public is anxious and having "sticker shock." Yet, he also argues that he has no choice since controlling health care costs in the short and long term are essential to budget control. Yet, there is ample evidence that this is not the case.[89] The president's push to immediately make a large legislative down payment on his transformative ambitions, including health care, owes more to his view of his own historical and presidential role than immediate policy necessity.

Empathy and Fairness

So in part, the solution to the puzzle of Obama's empathy rests on excess—too much ambition and too much self-confidence. But it also reflects a psychological deficit, an emotional blind spot. And that brings us to the question of the nature of empathy.

Empathy can be viewed as the quality of being able to genuinely appreciate and sympathize with another's perspective and feelings. Some, including the president, have suggested this involves an ability, "to stand in somebody else's shoes and see through their eyes."[90] It is wholly unclear how really possible this is given the ubiquitous and often hidden emotional weight of self-centric assumptions and perspectives. That is why it is easier to empathize with those with whom we share common perspectives and experiences. This is no indictment, just a psychological fact, against which empathy must struggle.

Like many virtues that the president finds in himself, Obama has written on empathy and how he obtained it. He writes that, "Like most of my values I learned about empathy from my mother."[91] He writes about his early arguments with his grandfather in a way that echoes more present, presidential experience, "With a certain talent for rhetoric, as well as an absolute certainty about my own views, I found I could generally win these arguments. ... "[92] But these adolescent empathy lapses became "less satisfying" and "I realized that sometimes he really did have a point and that by insisting in getting my way all the time, without regards to his feelings or needs, I was in some way diminishing myself." Obama said of this "awakening" that there is "nothing extraordinary about it," "in one form or another, it is what we all have to go through if we are to grow up." Having done so, Obama says of himself, "I find myself returning again and again to my mother's simplest principle—'how would that make you feel?' as a guidepost for my policies."

Redemption and the American Empathy Deficit

Among the deficits that Obama sees the United States as having is that of empathy. He says that "the how would that make you feel question," is "not a question we ask ourselves enough." More directly he says, "as a country we seem to be suffering from an empathy deficit." As evidence he notes that Americans, "wouldn't tolerate schools that don't teach, that are chronically underfunded and understaffed and underinspired [sic] if we thought that the children in them were like our children." He further raises the issues of CEOs getting million dollar bonuses while cutting health care for workers and leaders launching wars "if they envisioned their sons and daughters in harm's way."

For such a strong moral indictment, Obama is surprisingly cavalier in dispensing with some perspectives and facts. Most Americans send their children to be educated in public schools, about which there are widespread concerns at all levels of society. That is why support for increases in state education budgets, often resulting in higher taxes, has been the norm not the exception in most localities, until recent revolts over lack of actual academic performance results from all the money spent.[93] Some schools may be underfunded, though it is not clear what that means in practice. Urban public schools for example spend an enormous amount of money per student, but that seems not to translate into student academic progress. It is also unclear why presumably countenancing under-inspiring teachers is a reflection of America's empathy deficit.

Obama believes that "a stronger sense of empathy would tilt the balance of our current policies in favor of people who are struggling." Then, in typical Obama fashion he also argues that, "this does not mean that those who are struggling—or *those of us* who claim to speak for those who are struggling—are thereby freed from trying to understand the perspective of those who are better off."[94] This seems to be another example of Obama's tendency towards even-handed *rhetorical empathy* (see Chapter 7), but that doesn't mean he lacks the real thing.

Obama's Empathy?

How is it possible for someone as widely and legitimately known as emotionally calm, tempered, cool, deliberative, and laid-back[95] to develop empathy? After all, doesn't empathy require and reflect *emotional* attachment? And if so, how did Obama, who prides himself on his emotional equilibrium, develop it?

One easy, but erroneous, answer is that Obama's emotionally even keel precludes having empathy because his laid-back temperament precludes real emotional attachment. Empathy requires both an ability to imagine, though not necessarily to inhabit, another's perspective, and to draw the appropriate emotional lessons from the experience. Emotional equanimity, to the extent that it actually exists, is no barrier to the first or to the second, although a tight band of equanimity may narrow the impact or range of that experience. This formulation neglects the clear evidence that Obama has shown himself more than capable of forming emotional attachments to others, for example his family and especially his children. Such attachments are the emotional foundation of the capacity for empathy, and Obama has demonstrated at least in this one very important area that he has it.

Another, more plausible, but still mistaken answer to the question is that Obama's high self-regard and self confidence drains all the empathetic attachment from the situation. This formulation would seem to carry more weight since it is built on the undeniable evidence of Obama's elevated views of himself and his capacities. Yet, it too neglects a very strong piece of counterevidence.

Obama spent three long, very hard years as a community organizer trying to help those who were, to use his own word, "struggling." Obama is not someone who just gave political lip service to helping those having trouble making a go of their lives; he pitched in at the ground level and tried to help. The reality of Obama's empathy is found in that commitment to which he dedicated three years of his life.

A Narrow Empathy

Establishing a case for the reality of Obama's empathy does not resolve all the presidential leadership issues that arise from it. In the quotes above about the need of both those who speak for those who are struggling and those who are better off to understand each other's perspective lies the key to Obama's real empathy deficit. It is cramped and constricted.

There is little doubt that Obama *identifies* with the plight of those who are "struggling," but that word identifies carries with it a large cerebral component.

When his wife yells out to him during a practice debating session, "Barack, Feel don't think!" she is zeroing in on a very basic element of Obama's psychology—his tendency to prefer what he thinks to how he feels. As a result, most of his attachments, whether to ideas or to people, carry with them a high proportion of thinking and a much lower proportion of feeling.

It is tempting to laud Obama on precisely these grounds and many have. Deliberative, calm, and systematic are all words that have been used to describe Obama's "Spock-like" approach, and there is much to recommend that, at least to some degree. Yet, feelings provide emotional checks on ideas that don't give sufficient voice to the experience side of abstract formulations. And that can be dangerous for a president and a country.

No one is suggesting that a president give in to the momentary surges of emotion that often accompany presidential experience. John F. Kennedy was very angry that the Russians had lied to him about putting offensive missiles into Cuba, but he did modulate that anger in favor of thinking through his circumstances over the next thirteen days. And that anger was not wholly lost or unhelpful in resolving the crisis since it helped to buttress his determination not to let their attempts stand.

The constructed nature of Obama's empathy can be seen in his campaign encounter with Joe Wurzelbacher (Joe the Plumber) and his famous share the wealth remark, and his remarks about people in small towns:

> And it's not surprising then they get bitter, they cling to guns or religion or antipathy toward people who aren't like them or anti-immigrant sentiment or anti-trade sentiment as a way to explain their frustrations.[96]

In both these cases, what appears to be lacking is an understanding and appreciation of something basic that the president says he learned back in adolescence from arguments with this grandfather, namely that "I realized that sometimes he really did have a point. ... "

Whatever the points that Joe the Plumber or the small town Americans had on their side, they clearly had little standing with Obama. One might say both were related to a lack of personal familiarity with such people and their circumstances, except that his grandmother and grandfather worked hard and especially his grandfather had his share of "struggles." And recall that Obama prides himself on having rejected the temptations associated with economic advancement in the business world after he graduated from college.

Obama clearly doesn't identify with or have much sympathy for these people and their hopes and ambitions. He has trouble seeing that someone working hard and taking economic risks to advance his and his family's circumstances might have legitimate feelings about having the government take a not inconsiderable portion of it from him and his family for purposes and for people he felt were undeserving. Similarly, Obama has difficulty seeing that some people's religious beliefs were a legitimate and important part of their lives, even aside from their economic circumstances. In both cases, Obama had reached his own conclusions about whose points were deserving of consideration and whose could be discarded.

What emerged during the campaign as a tendency to be aware of, came into sharper focus after Obama became president. Obama's decision to go full-speed ahead with his "big bang" theory of transformation, regardless of the fatigue or anxiety of the American public is a classic case of empathetic failure. This is not only the case of one man trying to build a new business, or some people in small towns, but for a large and growing cross-section of the American public urgently asking the president, with all the means available to them, to slow down and reconsider his ambitions.

Obama's answer in a word has been: No! His empathy for those who are upset about the direction he is leading the country and the possibility that they, like his grandfather, might "have a point' is very limited. His confidence in his plan being the best and necessary one is unshakable. And that of course limits the extent to which he can truly hear what others are asking of him.

Chameleon?

In reviewing David Remnick's biography of Obama, Walter Russell Mead comments on the way in which presidents must develop their own identities and transcend them in order to connect to America's larger cultural and social traditions. He gives Bill Clinton, whom he calls "the great chameleon of modern American political history" as an example of a good ole boy who, after "returning to Arkansas after his years as a Rhodes scholar and Yale law student ... had to reconnect with an American vernacular."[97] The point is well taken and you can see it in operation with presidents as diverse as Dwight Eisenhower, whose genial persona masked an incisive mind and in Richard Nixon whose every man persona belied a brilliant geo-political mind. Yet, it is mildly ironic to call Bill Clinton "the great chameleon of modern American politics" when Mead was reviewing a book about a man who is much more deserving of the title.

Obama, the Adaptor

Barack Obama has, from very early in his adolescence, had to learn to navigate different racial, class, cultural, and geographical worlds. *He has become so adept at it, that it is the capacity to adapt, itself, that is a basic and unrecognized core element of Obama's real identity.* In analyzing Obama's core adaptive identity, and using the word chameleon, there is no implication that he doesn't stand for anything. The analysis to this point has made quite clear that Obama is a conviction president. Nor in using that word is there any presumption that this style has been adapted to intentionally mislead.

On the contrary, that part of Obama's psychology and identity is very authentic, having developed early in Obama's life and having becoming consolidated over time. Somewhat paradoxically, therefore, his adaptive capacities are an important part of who he really is. This is bound to create confusion, and that paradox is partially behind all the "where does he stand" questions that are repeatedly asked of him. His adaptive style and capacity seem to reflect less of who he really is and more of who he has had to become.

The word chameleon denotes a capacity to change in relation to the environments in which one finds oneself. Of course, every president does this to some degree and Obama is certainly no exception. He is, however, unusual in not only acknowledging that, but also justifying it. He is also unusual in that what is in most presidents a situational strategy to be deployed as needed, is for Obama much more of a core characteristic.

Obama has said,

> The fact that I conjugate my verbs and speak in a typical Midwestern news-caster's voice—there's no doubt that this helps ease communication between myself and white audiences, and there's no doubt that when I'm with a black audience, I slip into a slightly different dialect.

Obama absolves himself of any charges of pandering or misleading by saying

> *I don't feel the need* to talk in a certain way before a white audience. And *I don't feel the need* to speak in a certain way in front of a black audience. There's a level of self-consciousness about these issues the previous generation had to negotiate that I don't feel I have to.[98]

Obama's point seems to be it's not an issue because he doesn't feel as if he has to talk differently to different audiences, yet he chooses to do it because it helps each audience think of him as one of them, and he's just decided that's alright. And perhaps he's right. But there is much more to this issue and it lies much more deeply in Obama's psychology and identity than speaking in different dialects to different audiences.

Adaptability's Emotional Origin

The term chameleon reflects an ability to adapt in relation to changes in environment, but in evolutionary terms it has a purpose—protection. So the question then arises here, what is the purpose of Obama's deep capacity for adaptability? The easy answer is that it furthered his political career, and that is doubtlessly true. However, Obama began to develop his adaptive skills very early on in his life.

In his *Dreams* book, Obama writes of himself at seventeen reassuring his mother after a friend, named Pablo, had been arrested,

> I had given her a reassuring smile and patted her hand and told her not to worry I wouldn't do anything stupid. *It was usually an effective tactic, another one*

of the tricks I had learned: People were satisfied as long as you were courteous and smiled and made no sudden moves. They were more than satisfied; they were relieved—such a pleasant surprise to find a well mannered young black man who didn't seem angry all the time.[99]

The use of the phrasing "effective tactic" and "tricks" suggests that they were consciously adapted, not wholly felt and this is apparently the case. It also probably marks the beginning of Obama's inkblot ambiguity strategy.

Here Obama was negotiating several things. He was keeping his mother's questions to him at bay, preserving his own independence of action, but he places that in the larger context of presenting himself as whites would like him to be and reaping the rewards, while all the time hiding his true feelings. We know that at this time, according to Obama himself his feelings were inconsistent with that "well mannered black man who didn't seem angry all the time." It was during this period as well that Obama wrote, "I learned to slip back and forth between white and black worlds. ... "[100]

One of Obama's heroes Malcolm X appealed to him precisely because "his repeated acts of self-creation spoke to me. ... forged through sheer force of will."[101] Obama has attempted to do the same thing. Still, by the time he reached Occidental College, Obama writes that he was gripped by,

> The constant, crippling fear that I didn't belong somehow, that unless I dodged and hid and pretended to be something I wasn't I would forever remain an outsider, with the rest of the world, black and white, always standing in judgment.[102]

Here the main theme seems to be fitting in and worrying about being adversely judged because he didn't belong. Notice how his rationale has echoes from learning and displaying the "effective tricks" that kept his mother's questions and others' adverse judgments at bay in high school. Remember too that Obama not only made use of the tricks he developed, but that they also served as a façade behind which no one knew what was going on. Recall too, that none of his friends in high school or college knew about the turmoil that Obama described himself as going through in his book and in interviews.

It is a trait that remains to this day. Obama is well known for holding things close to his chest.[103] At the University of Chicago Law School where he taught for twelve years he often left, "fellow faculty members guessing about his precise views."[104] Eric Holder, who became Obama's Attorney General, and worked closely with him during the transition, said that at the end of many meetings "you didn't know where he stood."[105] Remnick writes of Obama's rhetoric in the U.S. Senate that it, "sometimes left even sympathetic colleagues and critics frustrated and wondering what he really believed in, what was essential to his view of the world."[106] And of course the public has increasingly been wondering the same thing.

Learning Along the Way

What Obama didn't know along the way he learned. One account noted that, "Fitting in, for Obama, had never been a natural process so much as a learned skill—something that required adjustment and work."[107] Terry Link, a senior State Senate Democrat said of Obama, "One thing that Barack has is the ability to adapt. ... "[108] There are many examples at both a personal and political level; in Springfield, he decided he needed to play golf. Democrats who felt useless in the legislative minority sometimes left the session to play 18 holes in the early afternoon, and their on-course conversations ranged from meaningless trash talk to political deal making ... [Terry] Link [a senior democrat] invited Obama to play and watched the beginner hack his way around the course. Frustrated by his incompetence and worried he might not be invited again, Obama signed up for lessons,[109] and became reasonably proficient. Another account noted that Obama had watched others and taught himself a number of things that had helped advance his career, among them "how to play poker, golf, and even church pastors' patterns of speech, how to take people up the [rhetorical] ladders."[110]

Obama even taught himself how to behave. Remnick writes that when Obama first arrived in the state senate, "he struck his colleagues as stiff, academic, arrogant. Over time, he became friendlier, more congenial. He didn't radiate, as he once had, a sense of superiority."[111] Or, as Alter writes in his book Obama, "leavened his enormous self-confidence *with an acute self awareness of how reasonable and wise people should act.*"[112]

Obama's conscious decision to shape himself into the person he wanted to be and the persona he wanted to present began early. Obama's math and science teacher in high school, Pal Eldredge, said in an interview that during that period the way in which Obama "carried himself changed," "His gait. The way he walked changed. And I wasn't the only one who noticed."[113] This observation from Obama's high school years, made by one of his teachers, echoes another made decades later by Bobby Rush, the black Congressman who defeated Obama in his 2000 congressional race. During an interview, Rush said,

> It's amazing how he formed his black identity ... " rising from his desk and starting, theatrically, to sashay around his office, mimicking Obama's sinuous walk. "Barack's walk is an adaptation of a strut that comes from the street. There's a certain break at the knees as you walk and you get a certain *roll* going. Watch. You see?"[114]

Rush was a successful rival of Obama's, one of the few, and in the above quote he is clearly having some fun with his former opponent, but he does then turn to analysis that is worth considering. Speaking of Obama he says:[115].

> But this isn't new. I really admire the way he's learned. I don't denigrate it. *He's been adapting all his life. He had the discipline to accomplish it, and the foresight*

to see what his vision of himself required. ... Barack's calculating in almost every decision in terms of how he wanted to present himself. Life is not a bunch of accidents, especially for someone with a huge vision of himself. He planned it out. *If you desire to be great, the projectile of your life, you have to map it out. And that's what he did in every sense.*

Of course, some things could not have been planned out, Obama's luck with his Senate opponents who either self-destructed (Peter Fitzgerald) or were not up to the challenge (Alan Keyes), being an example. Yet, Rush's point is consistent with a great deal of other evidence about Obama's conscious efforts to make himself into the man he wanted to become, and present the results as part of the seamless essence of who he is. Again, I want to underscore that while his construction and presentation of his persona as his essence is somewhat misleading, it is unclear, to me, if it is at some level intentionally dishonest. It is the stance with which Barack Obama chose to confront the world; it is, in a word, part of his basic character. Whether Obama simply acts that way because it is basically who he is and has become over time, or whether at some level he is aware of this and allows himself to make use of it, is unclear.

Robert Putnam, the Harvard political scientist who ran a three-year-long seminar that Obama attended, is quoted as saying that,

Obama is the same person all the time. When we see him in public, it is not a face he is putting on—it's him. There is no mask, or at least the mask is so well integrated in his life that it's disappeared.[116]

9

PSYCHOLOGY IN THE WHITE HOUSE: LEADERSHIP AND JUDGMENT

A president's history and psychology cannot help but be expressed in his presidency. It is in the presidency that personal ambition, style, and politics coalesce. And it is in the presidency that we get the fullest expression of how these elements are understood and acted upon by the president. For a mysterious president like Obama, who is aware of and makes use of a long developed Rorschach strategy, his actual behaviour in office itself provides an important reality check to those who study them.

Obama's Search for Policy Command

Obama's disappointment in the two political positions he held before becoming president had to do with the slow pace of policy change. But it also had to do with Obama being one of many. Being a legislator in the minority party as he was when he first came to both the Illinois State Senate and the U.S. Senate would be very frustrating to someone who wished to be at the forefront of transformational policy. Even when the Democrats became the majority party, and Obama became a very visible celebrity political presence in the U.S. Senate, he was still one of many. In the presidency, Obama has a policy importance and singularity in the American political system and he has moved to capitalize on that position.

The range of responsibility is large for any president and the amount of work that could, and arguably should be done, matches and doubtlessly exceeds the hours available in the day. Aside from the economy, the winding down of the war in Iraq and the surge taking place in Afghanistan, Obama has undertaken a number of large new domestic and foreign policy initiatives. All of these require the president's time and attention.

Building on and extending similar efforts by his two predecessors in office, Obama has concentrated a great deal of power in the White House. This has also doubtlessly added to a constant, fast policy pace as well. As one report notes, "President Barack Obama is taking far-reaching steps to centralize decision-making inside the White House, surrounding himself with influential counselors, overseas envoys and policy 'czars' that shift power from traditional Cabinet posts."[1]

Obama has made no secret of where this trail of accumulating power in the White House leads. At his third news conference during the transition he said, "Understand where the vision for change comes from, first and foremost. It comes from me. That's my job, is [sic] to provide a vision in terms of where we are going, and to make sure, then, that my team is implementing."[2] Or as an analysis of the same issue one year later put it, "it is clear that the center of Barack Obama's administration will be Barack Obama himself."[3]

The Puzzle of Obama's Policy Engagement

There can be little doubt that Obama has concentrated a great deal of power over his executive agencies in the White House. There is also no doubt that he has initiated some of the largest policy initiatives since Lyndon Johnson's "Great Society." What is not clear is how much Obama himself is personally invested and involved in the design or in bringing them to legislative victory. The two are not the same.

Obama could be invested in the bill's success without necessarily doing much conceptually besides agreeing to its broad contours. And that seems to be Obama's pattern in his first two years as president. He will agree to the general framework favored by those in his party who have worked on these measures in Congress. For example, he will agree there will be some kind of government mandated market for taxing carbon pollution or that there will be a large scale government option in setting health care costs and regulating them. He will then leave it up to Congress as to what the final bill might actually contain.

So, in the case of Congress's climate bill,

> In the hour-and-a-half meeting Tuesday, Obama urged the 23 senators to "aim high," several lawmakers said. But the president also made it clear that "he wasn't putting out a particular recipe for a bill," said Sen. Jeff Merkley (D-Ore.). "The Senate is going to have to figure this out."[4]

In the debate on the health care bill,

> Obama has also proved frustrating to moderates, who simply wanted to know where Obama's core principles on health care stood, all the better to cut a deal to the president's liking. Time and again, he rebuffed Democrats' requests to speak up more forcefully about what he wanted—a strategy that allowed Obama to preserve maximum flexibility to declare victory at the end of the process, no matter what the final bill looked like.[5]

Another report noted that, "What has fueled the lobbying surge is that President Barack Obama has left the details of the health overhaul to Congress."[6]And on the Stimulus Bill, the president's first victory in Congress, "Barack Obama let congressional appropriators write the stimulus package."[7]

The public pattern seems clear, but it seems best not to take the conventional wisdom here fully at face value. There is a great deal of presidential involvement behind the scenes, for example,

> In pursuing his proposed overhaul of the health care system, President Obama has consistently presented himself as aloof from the legislative fray, merely offering broad principles. Prominent among them is the creation of a strong, government-run insurance plan to compete with private insurers and press for lower costs. Behind the scenes, however, Mr. Obama and his advisers have been quite active, sometimes negotiating deals with a degree of cold-eyed political realism potentially at odds with the president's rhetoric.[8]

This public-private gap makes good sense for a president heavily invested in passing his transformative redemptive legislative agenda. With a Democratic majority in Congress and the leadership and rank and file of most of its members on the solid left side of the political spectrum, there is no danger that the bill will not almost wholly reflect that group's ideological perspectives, and the president's. As a result, Obama doesn't need to "lead" very much on the direction of the bill or its major elements, it's center of gravity and major thrust is already a given. The president can be confident that after all the wrangling about the bill's details are done, the bill will reflect his positions on the most basic and important matters.

No wholly run government insurance (single payer) plan? The health care legislation passed by Congress makes the government *the* major payer in the health care system though regulation is surely good enough. And in not pursuing the so-called "single player option" in which the government directly controls all health care insurance, Obama gets credit for his moderation, angers those who wanted a complete government take-over, thus adding to his moderate credentials, while still getting almost all of his major goals met and still ensuring that the government exercises *de facto* control through regulation.

One other aspect of Obama's investment and involvement in his legislative agenda merits at least a mention. That is that the president himself has not contributed any new ideas of his own to any of the legislation he has championed. He has in every case pushed other people's ideas. This is not unexpected because the economic stimulus, health care, and energy policies have long debate histories and a president, any president, comes in long after the major arguments have been debated for a long time. Still there is no record of a unique, creative, or different Obama position on any of the issues. He can be eloquent about those positions he favors and knowledgeable about others' positions, but he brings no unique ideas, arguments, or understanding.

In this, Obama's presidential legislative career much resembles his time as Editor in Chief of the *Harvard Law Review*. He ran it well and effectively, was himself a sounding board that absorbed and synthesized various points of view, but made no unique or innovative contribution of his own either regarding the organization or in works or views that he published in the *Review*.

The same can be said of his book *The Audacity of Hope*. That contains Obama's views on a variety of subjects: Republicans and Democrats, the Constitution, Politics, Values, Opportunity, Faith, Race, Foreign Policy, and Family, and there is not an original thought in the book. Rather, it takes an "on one hand, but then on the other hand" approach to each of these issues areas. For example Obama makes what some might see as a bold statement: "Not so far beneath the surface, I think we are becoming more not less alike." But this is immediately followed by a disclaimer: "I don't mean to exaggerate here to suggest that pollsters are wrong and that our differences—racial, religious, regional or economic—are somehow trivial."[9] Or,

> In every society (and in every individual), these twin strands—the individual and the communal, autonomy and solidarity—are in tension, and it has been one of the blessings of America that the circumstances of our nation's birth allowed us to negotiate these tensions better than most.[10]

True? Probably. Profound? Not really. Innovative? No.

During the presidential campaign, Richard Wolffe, who covered Obama and wrote a book about it, said of Obama's policy ideas that they were "Democratic boilerplate."[11] Those looking to tout the president's brilliance will have to look elsewhere.

The Rhetorical Presidency Revisited

The Obama administration is a presidency of words. This follows from the fact that words have been the instrument of this president's political success and they are the frequent and most public skill that Obama uses. In that respect, to an extent that surpasses the administration of the smart and loquacious Bill Clinton, Obama's is a rhetorical presidency.

The cascade of Obama's words both conceals and reveals. The concealment is found in the many varied and seemingly distinctive views of the same policy issues that Obama's words reflect. It is often unclear that his words add up to a particular position. The revelations are found in the fact that Obama's words often seem at variance with what he and others say about himself and certainly some important aspects of conventional wisdom.

A Calm Exterior, but also a Capacity for Rhetorical Harshness

Obama's calm external demeanor leads to the question of what he does with the normal passions that animate people. I raise this point not to suggest that buried underneath that calm exterior is a seething cauldron of intense emotions, but to simply ask the question as it has been stated. Some, like Jonathan Alter, have claimed, "It wasn't in Obama's nature to lash out."[12] The evidence suggests this view is very mistaken.

It is clear from other evidence presented earlier that Obama can be angry at criticism that doesn't accept his views as the starting point for any assessment of him, and he can also hold a grudge. Moreover, Obama's seemingly detached equanimity does not mean that he is incapable of tough, even harsh attacks on others. The sheer number and nastiness of these attacks raise some clear questions about Obama's real temperament, style, and the accuracy of his claims to be a bridge builder that rest on his inclusionary rhetoric (see below). One observer of his political attack style noted a number of examples and said, "The response was signature Obama: Attack first, sort out the details later, if at all. No apology, no immediate regret, just a sharp counterattack."[13] The political worldview premises of this characterization seem inconsistent with building bridges or finding common ground.

The first recorded example of this rhetorical tendency is found in Obama's famous 2002 anti-war speech. Obama framed his criticism of the war with direct personal attacks on members of the Bush administration and their motives.

> What I am opposed to is the attempt by political hacks like Karl Rove to distract us from a rise in the uninsured, a rise in the poverty rate, a drop in the median income—to distract us from corporate scandals and a stock market that has just gone through the worst month since the Great Depression.[14]

His personal attack raises the question, of whether the basis of his good judgment is prescient geo-strategic analysis or a liberal or progressive's animus toward a conservative agenda?

Of Hillary Clinton, Obama said that she "says and does whatever it takes to win the next election."[15] Towards Republicans he has been even harsher. In a 1995 interview, speaking of the success of Christian conservatives in building communities he said, "it's always easier to organize around intolerance, narrow-mindedness, and false nostalgia."[16] Eight years later, in speaking of Republicans more generally he said,

> What I'm certain about is that people are disenchanted with a highly ideological Republican Party that believes tax cuts are the answer to every problem, and lack of regulation and oversight is always going to generate economic growth, and unilateral intervention around the world is the best approach to foreign policy.[17]

Depending on your political point of view Obama's characterizations are either truthful essence or partisan hyperbole. However, which they are is not the point here. The point is that Obama's calm exterior does not inhibit his tough-minded defense of his own interests, sometimes in very harsh ways.

The president has not shied away from singling out, often in a very personal way, those who have opposed or raised questions about his policies. The *New York Times*, no critic of the president or most of his policies, had this to say about his treatment of health care insurance companies:

> President Obama *whose vilification of insurers helped push a landmark health care overhaul through Congress,* plans to sternly warn industry executives at a White House meeting on Tuesday against imposing hefty rate increases in anticipation of tightening regulation under the new law, administration officials said Monday.[18]

Samuelson writes that, "Obama has made vilification of oil and the oil industry a rhetorical mainstay."[19] And this was before the horrific Gulf oil well spill. Bankers are another group that have been a useful political foil used by Obama to gather support for his policies. At a meeting with them Obama warned them that, "My administration is the only thing between you and the pitchforks."[20] At the same time he took to the public pulpit to blast "fat cat bankers."[21] In a major economic address, Obama had this to say: "[I]f you're a Wall Street bank or an insurance company or an oil company, you pretty much get to play by your own rules, regardless of the consequences for everybody else."[22] Even reliable allies on the left like Mark Ambinder have wondered why, "Obama's winning, and he has plenty of political enemies. Why the need to find them where they aren't?"[23]

Among those the president has directly criticized are Republicans Mitch McConnell ("in bed with Wall Street movers and shakers and fronting cynical and deceptive arguments for them"), John Boehner ("mocked for predicting Armageddon if the Democrats' reform bill passed"), Sarah Palin ("not exactly an expert on nuclear issues"),[24] and Eric Cantor.[25]

Obama has taken personal swipes at Fox News, Rush Limbaugh, and Glenn Beck.[26] The White House has also directly taken on *Politico*[27] and a CNBC commentator, Rick Santelli, who voiced criticism of Obama's economic policies.[28] And at one event, "President Obama took a shot at Rep. Pete Hoekstra during an event here Thursday, subtly taunting the Michigan Republican—who was seated in the front row—as among those who 'opposed the federal stimulus package but showed up at a groundbreaking ceremony funded by it.'"[29]

Obama can also be harsh to those who hold different policy views. In a speech advocating his proposals for nuclear proliferation Obama said, "to denounce or shrug off a call for cooperation is an easy but also *a cowardly thing to do.*"[30] Pushing his health care initiative Obama said of doctors,

You come in and you've got a bad sore throat, or your child has a bad sore throat or has repeated sore throats, the doctor *may look at the reimbursement system and say to himself,* "*You know what? I make a lot more money if I take this kid's tonsils out.*"[31]

In speaking of those who oppose what they consider to be amnesty for illegal immigrants, Obama said of them, "There are going to be demagogues out there who try to suggest that any form of pathway for legalization for those who are already in the United States is unacceptable."[32]

In a campaign radio interview on Univision meant to mobilize Hispanic voters on the Democrats' behalf the president said,

> If Latinos sit out the election instead of saying, "*We're going to punish our enemies* and we're gonna reward our friends who stand with us on issues that are important to us," if they don't see that kind of upsurge in voting in this election, then I think it's going to be harder and that's why I think it's so important that people focus on voting on November 2.[33]

In response to criticism, the president later equivocally backed off his words, saying "I *probably* should have used the word 'opponents' instead of enemies."[34]

Obama's embrace of political populism has been a staple of the administration since his first State of the Union Address where he said,

> Americans are angry at "bad behavior on Wall Street." It is time to "slash the tax breaks for companies that ship our jobs overseas." Lobbyists are trying to "kill" financial regulation. American "cynicism" is the result of "selfish" bankers, CEOs who "reward" themselves "for failure" and lobbyists who "game the system."[35]

During the campaign the president accused the Chamber of Commerce of a crime and worse.[36] A *New York Times* news report described the effort this way: "With his party facing losses in next month's election, President Obama pressed his argument Sunday that *the opposition is trying to steal the election* with secret special-interest money, possibly including money from foreign companies."[37] The report goes on to note dryly,

> The Democrats have offered no evidence that the chamber is using foreign money to influence the elections. The chamber has overseas affiliates that pay dues to the main organization but says it has a process to segregate those funds from any used for electioneering.[38]

And there is also Obama's unprecedented "high-profile rebuke" of a Supreme Court decision directed specifically to the justices who attended his State of the

Union Address.[39] Democrats stood up and cheered. Linda Greenhouse noted that in reality, "Mr. Obama's description of the holding of the case was imprecise. But this was a populist night and the target was irresistible."[40] When the Chief Justice said later

> "The image of having the members of one branch of government standing up, literally surrounding the Supreme Court, cheering and hollering while the court—according to the requirements of protocol—has to sit there expressionless, I think is very troubling."[41]

In response, the White House press secretary directly criticized the Chief Justice.[42]

And finally, at a Labor Day rally, the president singled out for criticism House Minority Leader John A. Boehner (R., Ohio), who stood to become majority leader if Republicans retook the House, by name eight times during his speech.[43] Yes, this was the traditional Labor Day kick off to the fall election campaign. Yes, the strategy of trying to find and create a recognizable "enemy" on which to frame the political debate was obvious. But that last is just the point. As the above list makes clear, it has been more of a general rule than an exception for this president, who has a history that precedes his time in the White House.

In a post-election *60 Minutes* interview, the president had this to say about the subject:[44]

> PRESIDENT OBAMA: Okay, during election season, I think the rhetoric flies. And by the way, I've been guilty of that. It's not just them. And you know again, this is an example, you asked me earlier, of what I reflect on. I reflect on the fact that part of my promise to the American people when I was elected was to maintain the kind of tone that says we can disagree without being disagreeable. And I think over the course of two years, *there have been times where I've slipped on that commitment*. And that's something that I've got to make sure that I'm checking on an ongoing basis, making sure that my rhetoric matches up with my expectations for myself and the expectations of my supporters.

The phrasing, "there have been times where I've slipped on that commitment" ("to disagree without being disagreeable"—itself a soft characterization of the harsh language that has been used) seems hardly adequate to the directly personal and harsh language that has frequently been used by the president. That phrasing seems to suggest that it has happened only a very few times but this is not accurate.

The point of this listing is not to demonstrate that the administration is capable of engaging in political combat; it is obvious that they are. What is striking is the extent to which the president personally delivers the attacks, the number of targets against whom they are directed, and the personal nature of many of them and the length of time they have been going on, since Obama's first major speech in 2002 against the war.

Ordinarily, presidents get their surrogates to do this kind of work, but because the Obama presidency is so singularly focused on the person of Obama, he has in fact become his own Spiro Agnew.

A Rorschach Rhetorical Style in the Presidency

If you delve into Mr. Obama's pronouncements on a variety of subjects, the challenge of nailing down where Obama stands will soon become obvious. One of the president's rhetorical tells are the words "having said that." These words signal that the point that the president had just endorsed will now be followed by endorsement of its counter point. So when Obama was delivering a sermon remembering Martin Luther King he said,

> the trials we face today are very different from the ones that tested us in previous generations. Even after the worst recession in generations, life in America is not even close to being as brutal as it was back then for so many. That's the legacy of Dr. King and his movement. ... *Having said that, let there be no doubt the challenges of our new age are serious in their own right,* and we must face them as squarely as they faced the challenges they saw.[45]

At a town hall meeting one participant raised the issue of the difficulties of persons with criminal records getting jobs, to which the president replied by listing his programs in education and job creation and then said,

> So that I want to make that point first, because, frankly, it would be so much easier to work with your brother, if he hadn't gone to jail in the first place, to get a job. ... I'm just being realistic. If I'm a business owner, and I'm saying to myself, right now the unemployment rate is 10 percent, so there are a whole lot of folks who have never been to jail who are looking for a job—it's hard for me to say, I'll choose the guy who went to jail instead of the person who never went to jail and has been laid off. *Now, having said that,* what is also true—what you say is exactly right, that if we can't break the cycle, then all we're doing is just churning folks in a revolving door—through the jail system, back on the streets, back to dealing drugs, back to—and this is part of my faith, my religious faith, but you don't have to be religious to, I think, believe in the idea of redemption, that people can get a second chance that people can change (Applause).[46]

In an interview, Joe Klein asked the president about the economy:

During the transition period last year, it became apparent very quickly that we were going to have to make some fast, tough and in some cases politically unpopular decisions to make sure the financial system didn't melt down and we did not spiral into a second Great Depression. We made those decisions and executed them, and I am absolutely convinced that had we not acted the way we did that the situation would've been far worse. *Having said that*, we've still lost 7 million jobs over the last two years. People who are out of work or have seen their 401(k)s diminish or their hours reduced understandably are frustrated when they see big banks getting money for a problem that they helped cause. And when you see the unemployment rate spike to 10%, it was inevitable and justifiable that the political climate would become very difficult.[47]

And finally, asked about the release of Bush administration interrogation memos, the president said,

On the one hand, we have very real enemies out there. And we rely on some very courageous people, not just in our military but also in the Central Intelligence Agency, to help protect the American people. And they have to make some very difficult decisions because, as I mentioned yesterday, they are confronted with an enemy that doesn't have scruples, that isn't constrained by constitutions, aren't constrained by legal niceties. *Having said that*, the OLC memos that were released reflected, in my view, us losing our moral bearings. That's why I've discontinued those enhanced interrogation programs.[48]

Of course reality is complicated. It is true that the United States race relations have progressed substantially, but there are still serious problems to address. And it is true that business people would rather hire someone who has stayed in school rather than been sent to jail and it would be good if the cycle of criminal recidivism could be broken. And yes, some of our enemies are without scruples and that doesn't mean we have to lose ours.

Yet somewhere within the boundaries contained within those multiple truths lay the more specific views and underlying beliefs that are the ultimate sources of presidential judgments and the policies that are chosen as a result. What are America's race issues and how does the president propose to address them? What policies can square the circle between an employer's reluctance to hire a convicted felon and the applicant's bad choices? Granted that the president had to make hard economic choices in the face of a deep recession, is public discontent with his economic policies primarily a consequence of the stimulus or TARP programs, or are there other elements operating as well? And finally, as the controversy about extending Miranda Rights to the terrorist who tried to blow up an airliner on Christmas Day, is weighting anti-terrorism and domestic terrorism toward a law-enforcement model really likely to keep the country as safe as it would be if the tilt were the other way?

The problem with Obama's policy fluency is that recognizing the many sides of an issue does not nullify the necessity to frame specific choices, weigh options and risks, make a specific policy decision, and clearly communicate that decision and its reasoning to the American public. It may well be that an understanding of the many sides of complex issues might result in less risky or more successful policies, but it is also possible that hedging too many bets may dilute the elements that are instrumental for policy success. We will discuss a case, Afghanistan, shortly that seems to underscore this issue.

It is also true that being able to see many sides of an issue does not guarantee a person will either select or focus on the ones that are most likely to produce good policy outcomes. The question of whether a president has done that in a specific policy area or case can only be answered by examining the contours of the problem and the president's policy thinking and solutions.

A Question of Judgment

If there is one thing that Obama is certain of, it is that he has good judgment. Of this he has said,

> as an adult I made a series of choices that I'm very proud of. I got to work on behalf of people who needed help, to advocate for the dispossessed, and [took] a lot of risks when a comfortable path was before me. *So I think my judgments over the last 25 years indicate somebody who handles just about anything that is thrown at him.*[49]

Whether that is true is exactly the question in assessing Obama's first two years of his presidency. Obama made an early decision to push his initiatives on energy and especially health care immediately on entering office and in the face of a severe economic recession. He might have chosen to focus on the economy, and assuming some success there could have then pressed for his other initiatives. The decision to go full-steam ahead on many fronts, even in the face of public opposition and election losses in NJ, VA, and MA certainly reflects the scope and depth of the president's policy ambitions and his determination to achieve them; but it also reflects something else about his governing psychology. He is a president with supreme self-confidence in his convictions that he is right. And he is willing, indeed determined, as a result, to take large risks on his behalf and ours. And in doing so his ambition undercut his persona as a pragmatic moderate.

That willingness to assume substantial risk, both for himself and on the public's behalf with his transformational policies is one of the most under analyzed aspects of the Obama presidency.

Good Foreign Policy Judgment?

Obama is especially sure that he has good judgment in foreign policy: "One thing I'm very confident about is my judgment in foreign policy is, I believe, better than any other candidate in this race, Republican or Democrat."[50] It's true that this remark and some of the others quoted earlier were made in the context of a campaign in which Obama's foreign policy experience was being questioned. Yet, there is still the absolute and unequivocal way in which they are expressed. I'm "better than any other candidate in the race" of either party of course includes John McCain who specialized in foreign policy as a senator for decades. And there is the fact that Obama expresses pretty much the same level of self-confidence in his foreign policies ("flawless") now he has become president.

In many of his foreign policy campaign quotes, Obama is calling attention to the difference between experience and judgment, and he is right to do so. Long experience can be a hedge against poor foreign policy judgments but not necessarily. Similarly, John Kennedy was still young and inexperienced when he was forced to confront the Cuban Missile Crisis, and that is generally considered a textbook case of a high-quality decision and good presidential judgment. Yet, it is also true that presidential self-confidence in making decisions can be both an advantage and a source of worry. Too little confidence can leave a president insecure and at the mercy of his advisors. Too much confidence can leave a president committed to his own views, regardless.

Invading Iraq

For Obama, the archetypical example of his good judgment concerned his anti-war speech in 2002 and he has repeatedly touted the high quality of his own judgment in that matter. That positive self-review rests on what he sees as his prescient opposition to the war; "on the most important foreign policy issue of a generation, I got it right and others did not."[51] It is somewhat unclear however just how strategically accurate the basis of his opposition was. He said at the time,

> I also know that Saddam poses no imminent and direct threat to the United States, or to his neighbors, that the Iraqi economy is in shambles, that the Iraqi military is a fraction of its former strength, and that in concert with the international community he can be contained until, in the way of all petty dictators, he falls away into the dustbin of history … I know that even a successful war against Iraq will require a U.S. occupation of undetermined length, at undetermined cost, with undetermined consequences. I know that an invasion of Iraq without a clear rationale and without strong international support will only fan the flames of the Middle East, and encourage the worst, rather than best, impulses of the Arab world, and strengthen the recruitment arm of al-Qaeda.[52]

Obama argued that Saddam posed no imminent threat to the United States or its neighbors, but Iraq had already invaded Iran and Kuwait, and clearly had aspirations for regional hegemony that would have posed a threat to vital American and allied interests in the region. Obama's opposition was also premised on the view that Saddam could be contained; others made strong arguments that containment was failing.[53]

It is true that an occupation would be of uncertain length, costs, and consequences but that is true of every war and represents no unique insight. It is also the case that a U.S. "occupation" was not part of President Bush's plan and that in fact Bush ordered that sovereignty turned over to the Iraqi government as quickly as possible to avoid precisely the problem of being viewed as an occupier. The failure to do that apparently rested in decisions made by Paul Bremer that held up the transition till the occupation perception took hold.

As to "fanning the flames of the Middle East," what American invasion of a Middle Eastern country wouldn't? Would it have made a difference in the Middle East if France and Germany had been enthusiastic public partners in the war instead of giving unpublicized support? Clearly the war "fanned the flames of the Middle East," but so did Saddam. Yes, for a time the war did seem to strengthen the recruitment arm of Al-Qaeda, but their substantial setbacks in Iraq as a result of the surge and change in American strategy seem to have dampened recruitment enthusiasm. And of course there is always Afghanistan, Israel and a host of other purported grievances for them to try and exploit. The real point here is the question that follows the truism that any action against these enemies will inflame some parties in the Middle East and elsewhere: Should we therefore cease taking them?

These are now old arguments, as direct military involvement in Iraq winds down. But that 2002 speech is the basis of Obama's reputation and self-perception of having prescient and superior judgment. It is therefore important to keep in mind that the arguments that Obama raised were matters of debate then and now and that opponents could marshal plausible, and in some cases persuasive evidence and points, against them. In this case at least, Obama's claim to superior and prescient judgment is, in every particular, debatable.

Obama's Iraq Surge Judgment

The surge of American forces in Iraq begun in January 2007, by all accounts tipped the balance away from defeat and bought time for the United States to correct a deteriorating situation. Most discussions mention an increase in the number of troops as the key element of Bush's initiative, but there were two other factors present that were central to the surge's success. First, the army had recently completed a new field manual for counter-insurgency that laid out a new doctrine, the first changes to the doctrine in twenty years. General David Petraeus oversaw the revision of that manual, and he was also selected by Bush to oversee the surge and implement the new counter-insurgency strategy.

If Obama's judgment about invading Iraq is more problematic than he sees and presents it, then his judgment on the surge of American troops there seems clearly to shift to the error side of the continuum. Bush announced the surge in early January 2007. In response, Obama said: "I am not persuaded that 20,000 additional troops in Iraq is going to solve the sectarian violence there. *In fact, I think it will do the reverse.*"[54] Within weeks Obama introduced legislation in the Senate to withdraw all American troops, with certain limited caveats, by March 31, 2008.[55] In mid-March, 2007 he voted against a bill authorizing funding for the war,[56] saying he was registering his objection to there being no date or timeline for withdrawal.

This was a position he maintained throughout 2007, as evidence that the surge and the strategy it was meant to bolster was taking hold. In responding to Bush's State of the Union message Obama said,

> I don't think the president's strategy is going to work. We went through two weeks of hearings on the Senate Foreign Relations Committee; experts from across the spectrum—military and civilian, conservative and liberal—expressed great skepticism about it. My suggestion to the president has been that the only way we're going to change the dynamic in Iraq and start seeing political commendation is actually if we create a system of phased redeployment.[57]

In July of 2007, Obama said, "My assessment is that the surge has not worked."

In November 2007, two months after General David Petraeus testified before Congress about the progress that had been made because of the surge, Obama said,

> Finally, in 2006–7, we started to see that, even after an election, George Bush continued to want to pursue a course that didn't withdraw troops from Iraq but actually doubled them and initiated a surge and at that stage I said very clearly, *not only have we not seen improvements, but we're actually worsening, potentially, a situation there.*[58]

Obama did say that, "there's no doubt that additional U.S. troops could temporarily quell the violence," but that admission came at a Democratic presidential candidate debate[59] in January 2008, almost a year after the surge was announced and implemented. And in acknowledging the success of the surge to bring down levels of violence he also said: "What we have to do is to begin a phased redeployment to send a clear signal to the government that we are not going to be there in perpetuity. ... We should start negotiating now. That's how you change behavior." Finally on July 14, 2008 Obama wrote in a *New York Times* op-ed that, "the same factors that led me to oppose the surge still hold true."[60] Obama named a number of considerations for this view but chief among them was that, "they have not reached the political accommodation that was the stated purpose of the surge."

In many ways this was not surprising. After decades of brutal dictatorial rule, two wars with the United States, one with Kuwait and another with Iran, and being in the middle of brutal insurgency that almost toppled the government and forced the defeat of the allied occupation force, the failure to reach an acceptable political accommodation on all of the many very tough and divisive problems that Iraq faced is not surprising? And didn't the stated purpose of Obama's legislation to quickly remove American forces communicate a "wait us out" invitation to those we were and are fighting there? And finally, doesn't a definite and clear cut withdrawal date indicate to our allies that they had better begin to cut whatever deals are possible, given the withdrawal dates are to a large degree dependent on the Iraqi government's ability to meet its security needs on its own?

This is exactly the same box that Obama placed himself in with regard to the long and detailed review of the Afghanistan war. There too, he insisted on having a withdrawal date firmly set at the same time that he committed more American troops.[61] Alter reports that Obama said at one meeting, "I am not going to do a ten year, one trillion dollar Afghan plan. It's not required and not in the public interest."[62] And that assertion essentially ended that option.

Obama's rationale for limiting American involvement in Afghanistan is the same as it was for him regarding Iraq. If we set a firm date for leaving, the government there (Iraq or in this case Afghanistan) will get the message that they can't depend on us forever and thus be highly motivated to do all the things that they need to do which would allow us to leave their country in good shape and in good hands. Of course, it is also quite possible that the Afghan government would get the message that they can't depend on the United States, period, and the opposition forces might understandably feel that time is on their side.

Shortly after his *New York Times* commentary piece, in an interview with Katie Couric, Obama gave a different set of reasons having to do with where else the money for the Iraq war could be spent,[63]

COURIC: But yet you're saying ... given what you know now, you still wouldn't support it ... so I'm just trying to understand this.

OBAMA: Because ... it's pretty straightforward. By us putting $10 billion to $12 billion a month, $200 billion, that's money that could have gone into Afghanistan. Those additional troops could have gone into Afghanistan. *That money also could have been used to shore up a declining economic situation in the United States. That money could have been applied to having a serious energy security plan so that we were reducing our demand on oil, which is helping to fund the insurgents in many countries.*

Here Obama seems to be echoing George McGovern's campaign theme of "Come Home America." Of course money spent for war can always be used for other things, however, it is not clear why establishing a viable stable pro-Western government in Iraq is not worth the investment. Having stabilized the military situation in Iraq with the surge, isn't working further on the development of an Iraqi state that can be a partner with the United States worthwhile? And indeed, by limiting his commitments to Afghanistan to defeating Al Qaeda,[64] Obama seems to suggest that Afghanistan's importance is limited to not again becoming a safe haven for planning an attack against the United States. If the military situation in Afghanistan stabilized to that point, would they be as important and useful an ally to the United States as a pro-Western Iraq would be? It would appear that the answer to that question is no, but then again it is another matter of judgment.

Obama's long-standing criticism of the Iraq surge did not keep him from claiming credit for its results. In his speech to call attention to the Iraqi drawdown,

> Mr. Obama hailed the improved security in Iraq, without mentioning that he opposed the troop buildup ordered in 2007 by his predecessor, President George W. Bush, that along with a strategy change is credited by many with turning the war around.[65]

Afghanistan

In Afghanistan, Obama has sought to hedge his bets, but he has done so in an odd way. President Obama's decision to commit substantially more American troops in addition to the 17,000 troops he had previously committed has been characterized by those in a position to make that judgment as "among the most important decisions of his presidency."[66] There is no doubt that it is consequential.

This decision process has also been unusually public. Starting with the leak of General McCrystal's dire assessment,[67] the leaks that followed,[68] White House descriptions of the process,[69] an unusually detailed set of news analysis post-mortems,[70] interviews with key players,[71] the president's public speeches on the Afghan issue,[72] and the president's own on-record reflections immediately before the announcement,[73] the decision process has been unusually accessible, which is not to say necessarily accurate.

However, what can be gleaned about the arguments made, the political and military considerations that framed them, the process that led to the president's choices and his own role in reaching them provides a window into Obama's search for the elusive "golden mean" as a method by which diverse, strongly held views regarding policy options were narrowed to find unanimous agreed upon common ground.[74] So, after, a very long and much reported set of deliberations, Obama decided to commit 34,000 additional troops to Afghanistan to reverse a deteriorating military and political situation. But this was a compromise figure between a much higher one of 40,000,[75] which was later reduced and a lower one which would essentially reflect a decision that would provide only minimal opportunity to arrest, much less reverse a deteriorating situation. Obama also declined to consider total immediate withdrawal, but this was hardly a viable political or strategic option. There was also a debate about a full scale counter-insurgency strategy that required many more troops to protect the civilian population and hold and expand such territory so that the Afghan government could be brought in to take control and demonstrate its effectiveness.

Oddly, although Obama opted for a substantial increase in the number of troops, it was barely enough to undertake a modified counter-insurgency strategy. However, Obama also opted to narrow the goals of his strategy to "degrading, not destroying"[76] the Taliban as a military threat. In Obama's words,

> What we're looking to do is difficult—very difficult—but it's a fairly modest goal, which is: Don't allow terrorists to operate from this region. Don't allow them to create big training camps and to plan attacks against the U.S. homeland with impunity.[77]

In essence, Obama had agreed to a number barely sufficient to put into place a modified but still plausible version of a full counter-insurgency campaign to stabilize Afghanistan, while committing himself to a very narrow goal and setting in motion a July 2011 date for beginning to withdraw American forces,[78] a point on which the president was highly insistent.

This was an unusual split the difference decision. *It was a combination of two very different plans.* One plan, the McCrystal plan, called for enough troops to mount a real counter-insurgency strategy (COIN), but he got enough troops only to carry out a limited version of that strategy, but not an endorsement by the president or a commitment to the strategy itself, or time enough to successfully carry it out. Those who opposed a robust counter-insurgency strategy got a narrowing of the goals and a shortened timetable.

A fair look at this composite decision would lead to the conclusion that those who opted for a minimal commitment won the day, with those wanting a more robust strategy fighting for a come from behind acceptance of their views. If American troops do begin to withdraw before the Afghan government or the military and political situation are stabilized, the chances that the government will actually survive or effectively govern the country are much reduced.

And there is the added question of how long it would take to put into effect a really effective program to reform and recast the Afghan government, its army and political institutions. That undertaking is best measured in multiple years, but it does not necessarily need close to 100,000 allied troops stationed in Afghanistan to carry it out. Yet, in Afghanistan as in Iraq, the military situation must be stabilized to some degree if political and economic development is to make progress. How that is consistent with a specific set of drawdown dates is unclear. A firm withdrawal date certainly sends a signal to allies and enemies having an interest in the question about American commitments and reliability.

It is clear that the president is not committed to a strong long-term American presence in either Iraq or Afghanistan. He is clearly anxious to downsize American commitments in both countries and attend to transforming and rebuilding at home. Yet, there are great risks in removing American presence and influence from Iraq at too fast a pace. And in Afghanistan by opting for more troops, but less time to use them effectively, Obama tried to square that circle by narrowing the goal.

It is an elegant perceptual solution giving the appearance of commitment (more troops), while limiting their utility by beginning the process of withdrawal before it is possible to have really stabilized the country. Obama may have come to a composite solution that cuts American losses and investments, but does so at a potentially high cost.

Obama: A Monumental Risk Taker

Obama has a reputation as an extremely deliberative decision maker. This is generally true, but as with so many aspects of this president and his presidency, it is not the full story. The secret, hidden in plain sight, of the president and his administration is its propensity for taking high-risk initiatives, often in the face of public disapproval and even opposition. These high-risk ventures are not confined to either domestic or foreign policy, but on the contrary can be discerned in both.

Melody Barnes, one of the president's domestic policy advisers, noted that,

> after eight years of Bush, Obama's supporters were very eager to change everything right away. The pent-up demand across every issue area—around science, around education, around health care, immigration, you name it— there was a lot of desire to finally get these things done. Every segment of the population had something that was very important to them that they really wanted to put over the finish line.[79]

The president used the "big bang" theory, making use of the economic crisis to push a number of supporters' long delayed projects.

The result, as one decidedly centrist Democrat and political scientist noted eighteen months before the dramatic midterm election, was that Obama

> wagered his presidency on the proposition that the US budget and political system can simultaneously absorb an economic stimulus, bail-outs of financial institutions, the housing sector and the automobile industry, comprehensive regulatory reform ... and a social-democratic program not seen since the days of Lyndon Johnson, perhaps even Franklin D. Roosevelt (FDR).[80]

The results of the midterm election, to be considered in the next chapter, suggest that Obama lost his bet. What's more he went "all in" for immediate transformation, when a more prudent approach might have given better overall results over the long-term, thus raising questions about his ambitions trumping his judgment. Obama's determination to bet all his chips on transformation reflects his willingness to embrace enormous risk not only to the future of his presidency, but also his relationship with the American public. Moreover, there were risks to enacting large-scale untested programs like his health care reform plan, about which much remained unknown about how they would actually work. The president was clearly willing to take on all these risks, but especially regarding the policies themselves; the only risks the president discussed were the ones regarding not adopting his proposals.

Obviously, there are risks in every consequential decision a president makes and Obama is no exception to that norm. What sets Obama apart is the number of such high-stakes, high-risk initiatives, their rapid introduction and implementation, his willingness to go against public sentiment, and the wholly unknown consequences of much of what he proposed in his domestic and foreign policies.

Obama Rash? Sometimes

The conventional wisdom on Obama's decision-making style is that it is extremely deliberative, dispassionate, and thoughtful. Less appreciated is that Obama is very capable of making rash decisions on what amounts to impulse. An impulse need not be quick and momentary like a flash of lightning. It can also be a reoccurring desire that keeps making itself known until it is satisfied. Such was the case with Obama's ill-conceived and impatient decision to take on Bobby Rush for a congressional seat against the strong advice of almost all of his advisors.

Obama's biographer wrote of that failed effort that in undertaking the race, "he made his first major political miscalculation. The cause of this misjudgment: unbridled ambition."[81] Obama has acknowledged this if only indirectly. Later he said, "there was *no great external imperative* for me to be a congressman at that stage. *It really had more to do with me feeling anxious to be in the mix.*"[82]

Having strong views in a variety of policy areas and also having such high self-confidence in them can sometimes lead Obama to make quick, one might even say rash decisions. One anomaly of President Obama's seemingly deliberative, cool decision-making style occurred when he announced two days after taking the oath of office that he was shutting down the facility at Guantánamo. At the time he made that announcement, he had not yet had a formal review completed about what his options were on the many major issues that remained. That resulted in the administration missing its own self-imposed 2010 closing deadline. More recently a *New York Times* review of the administration's stance was titled, "Closing Guantánamo Fades as a Priority."[83]

Obama could have chosen to handle the matter differently. He could have announced his intention to close it down after those reports were given to him and reviewed. Or (less likely) he could have waited to say anything definitive. He chose to make a bold statement, without the underlying analysis that would help resolve the issues involved. One can summon up many explanations for his acting so quickly, the most obvious of which is to make a dramatic, immediate break with the policies of his predecessors (while retaining some rights to act as his predecessor had). Whatever else one may say about this decision it cannot be said to have been deliberative.

Another slightly different example comes from the president's decision to weigh in on the placement of a mosque very near the site of the former World Trade

Towers. Several days before he announced his position at a Ramadan dinner and speech, he had been discussing "how or whether to publicly address the issues." At a meeting,

> [a] few days before, Obama erased any doubt. He *opened* his weekly Oval Office senior staff meeting by informing the group which included Jarrett, Axelrod, Senior Adviser Pete Rouse, Press Secretary Robert Gibbs, Communications Director Dan Pfeiffer and Chief of Staff Rahm Emanuel of his plans to go public. "*He made his position clear, and no one dissented*," said a senior administration official.[84]

Once the president *opens* a meeting by giving a strong statement of his preferences, it would take brave advisors indeed to buck him.

That report continues, quoting a source that took part in those meetings: "There was no [other] meeting or big internal debate." Once Obama had stated what he had decided to do there was apparently no further need felt to discuss it. Yet it is interesting that this report does not mention any debate on what emerged as the most critical element of Obama's decision to go public, not whether Muslims had a right to build, but whether it was appropriate. Obama's forceful public stand at a high visibility event implied that his ringing affirmation of the first, implied agreement with the second. The next day he clarified by saying the two were unconnected, yet it reflected a surprising lack of preciseness on Obama's part not to have made that distinction clear from the start on an issue his advisors knew would be controversial.

The Nature of Obama's High-stakes, High-risk Propensities

One of the most obvious, important, and so far under-appreciated aspects of Obama's psychology and his presidency is the degree to which he is a monumental risk taker. His risk taking propensities have been commented upon primarily in terms of the "audacity" of his presidential run, but the characteristic goes well beyond that. It is an absolutely essential key to this man and his presidency. And therefore it is important to be clear just what is and is not meant by characterizing him in that way.

Obama is fully capable of hedging his bets. The first and most obvious instance of this was running for the presidency at all given his age, background, and experience. It was an audacious move, but one with an enormous upside even if he didn't win. Obama would have established himself as a national figure at a new level, becoming in the process one of his party's chief spokesmen. He could have parleyed a defeat into a vice presidential slot, and bided his time for eight years, when he would have been a presumptive front-runner. In short, running for the presidency was an audacious long shot, but given the public mood (see Chapter 1) and the potential upside of even losing, it had a lot to recommend it.

Where Obama's policy audacity and real risk taking shine through very clearly is in his approach to domestic and foreign policy. As one reporter put it, if Obama wasn't comfortable with a high level of risk,

> he would not have sought $1 trillion from affluent Americans and a similar sum from businesses to finance health care, education and energy initiatives. All that while simultaneously trying to save the auto industry, revive financial markets, end the Iraq war and redouble efforts to battle Islamic extremists in Afghanistan.[85]

His closest aide and campaign manager David Plouffe said, given the issues that Obama wishes to address, "Political calculation and risk aversion really have to take a back seat."[86]

Plouffe's statement is an interesting one on closer inspection. He is making the case that given all the major problems confronting Obama, he and the country could not afford to let political calculations or concerns with risk keep them from making what they saw as necessary policy decisions. His use of the words "political calculations" seems to reflect the decision that presidents often make between doing what's right and doing what's politically best for them. Here the implication is that Obama had to worry about the country and not himself.

But there is also another reality in which the words "political calculations" play a large role and that is in the public receptivity to what the president undertakes. Public receptivity is one basic and legitimate element of "politics," and it can operate to endorse or inhibit presidential ambitions. In Obama's case, it is very clear that substantial sections of the public have soured on the president's leadership and in particular his decision to move full-speed ahead on his own agenda. That agenda does not match up well with what the public wants the president to concentrate on—mainly the economy. And the public has, for the most part, not accepted Obama's argument that health care and a new cap and trade energy initiative are critical to the economy and creating jobs. Nor is the public convinced that the enormous amount of stimulus spending on the president's favored projects and supportive constituencies is very helpful or is consistent with what they would like to see the president focus on. The result is a large and widening presidential legitimacy gap.

This gap reflects Obama's propensity to take very large risks, both for himself and the public. The "never let a crisis go to waste" mentality suggests that the president made a decision very early on to try and fold in a number of his policy ambitions to his ostensible response to the economic "crisis." Crisis is placed in quotes here because the real crisis of liquidity took place during the waning days of the Bush administration and Bush set in motion the mechanisms that addressed and began to resolve those problems. Obama faced a substantial economic recession, but not the same crisis of liquidity that his predecessor faced and which would have seized up the whole economy. The Obama administration's theory was simple, "though always freighted with risk: "Use a season of economic anxiety to enact sweeping changes the public likely wouldn't stomach in ordinary times."[87]

This point is central to the critical distinction between responding to a real crisis and using a sense of crisis to further your own agenda. The latter of course is misleading, though the president has so far escaped the consequences of widespread understanding of how this distinction played out in the president's choices. Yet, that choice and the decision to keep going full-speed ahead with the administration's "big bang" theory says a great deal about the president's pursuit of high-stakes, high-risk strategies and policies.

Policy Risks

Every major decision a president makes is fraught with political and policy risk. The political risks revolve around the fact that presidential policies are likely to cheer some supporters while alienating opponents. The policy risks are that the rationale for policies won't be realized or that there will be unintended but substantially negative consequences. In short, the danger here is that policies won't work as advertised. This is an especially acute issue for very large-scale never before tried policies of the kind that Obama has staked his reputation and presidency on.

Health Care

Obama's health care legislation makes three very high-stakes-high-risk bets: (1) that rising health care costs can be contained justifying a new 1 trillion dollar entitlement program; (2) that the benefits of extended coverage (via the mechanisms contained in the bill) outweigh the dangers of restructuring a very large segment of the economy and placing it under *de facto* government control; and (3) that the Obama bill is the best vehicle to realize the goals of cost containment and coverage.[88]

No one can address these risks with any certainty. What is certain is that these policies and their risks have already resulted in a very heated debate about whether this legislation will produce the results that were its rationale, without resulting in major economic, personal, and policy dislocations. What is also absolutely clear however is that Obama is so certain of the correctness of his views that he is willing to take those risks. These risks, it should be noted, are not necessarily to Obama politically. Many of the most difficult measures are scheduled for enactment after he leaves office, even if he gains a second term.[89] There was the risk of course that he would lose Democratic control of one or more Houses of Congress, and he did.

However, the biggest bearers of risk are the American public. It is they who will see the results of government control over vast portions of health care decision-making. That risk too Obama is not only willing to take on, but also to a large degree impose on a public that is increasingly unsettled and upset about the possible changes to the health care they have and favor. The sum total of all the policy risks that Obama has pledged his administration to make is "a dramatic reminder of the unbelievable stakes he has placed on the table in his first month in office, *putting at risk the future well-being of the country* and the Democratic Party's control of Washington."[90] That is a quote by David Broder who was an extremely center of the road non-partisan columnist.

Foreign Policy

We can see Obama's willingness to embrace risk in his foreign policies as well. His outreach to America's enemies and rivals was a calculated risk based on the assumption that a less assertive and more understanding United States would reap policy rewards in the shape of shared policies. This was certainly behind Obama's early and strong outreach to Muslim nations. It was also the basis for reaching out to and "resetting" relations with rivals (Russia, China) and enemies (Iran). It is also behind his attempt to be seen as less of a reliable ally of Israeli policy preferences in the Arab-Israeli conflict.

The risk of engagement is that it may wind up passing valuable time without much to show for it. Certainly, the two-year pursuit of an agreement with Iran over their nuclear weapons programs has allowed them to make use of that valuable time to continue their quest. Obama's "reset" with Russia has so far brought few tangible gains on major policy issues, and relationships with China remain equivocal.[91]

The Risk to Obama's Leadership Integrity and Reputation

Among the risks that Obama has apparently embraced is the risk to the public view of his leadership integrity and his reputation. Passing policy over the strong objections of substantial portions of the public is a recipe for their alienation and even anger. Yet, "White House officials say they never seriously considered a more incremental approach to the year. ... "[92] David Brooks, a repeated supporter of the president and his political style wrote a column immediately before Martha Coakley lost the Massachusetts Senate race to her Republican opponent, Scott Brown. He wrote,

> Some believe they can still pass health care even if their candidate, Martha Coakley, loses the Senate race in Massachusetts on Tuesday. That, of course, would be political suicide. *It would be the act of a party so arrogant, elitist and contemptuous of popular wisdom that it would not deserve to govern.* Marie Antoinette would applaud, but voters would rage.[93]

One might add here that it was the act not only of a party but also of its president. "Doing something about health care" did not necessarily require Obama's specific legislation. His legislation is however "historic," and it is the largest new social entitlement program since Lyndon Johnson's "Great Society." The vast scope and reach of his program is certainly consistent with a president who aspires to do "great" things, and sees himself as doing them.

So Obama's sense of what he must do is to place his bets on an untried and unprecedented restructuring of the American health care system, regardless of what Americans might feel about those efforts. If there ever was a textbook case of the relationship of high, perhaps extraordinary self-confidence and the embracing of risk for all Americans, regardless of their understandable concerns and clear anxieties, this is surely it.

A Highly Confident President, with Transformational Aspirations, Approaching a Stark Fork in the Road

As the 2010 midterm elections approached, a majority of American voters expressed the view that Obama had fallen short of expectations on each of twelve major issues tested in an August 2010 NBC/WSJ poll including:[94] the economy, the war in Afghanistan, the situation in Iraq, reducing government spending, the federal budget deficit, changing business as usual in Washington, standing up to big business and special interests, health care, the environment, improving race relations, improving America's image around the world, and improving oversight of Wall Street and the banks.

That's quite a litany of disappointment and disapproval. Some of the disapproval is factually wrong, America's image abroad has improved, but it is not less politically powerful for being misplaced. Some of it has to do with the enormous expectations that surrounded Obama's candidacy and which his campaign and the candidate encouraged. Some of it no doubt stems from a general dissatisfaction with the state of the economy and, importantly, the view that the president has not done enough about it, while pursuing his own transformative agenda.

Douglas Schoen, a Democratic pollster, has argued that,

> There is a fundamental problem with the way President Obama has governed. Since taking office, he has systematically put forth policies the American people do not want. The net result is a crisis of confidence and legitimacy in the American political system and our institutions.[95]

That gap has eroded the confidence and good will in the president himself and his leadership and judgment.

Yet the president presses on secure in his views and convinced that he is right. On the Congressional campaign trail he said,

> You know, sometimes these pundits, they can't figure me out. They say, "Well, why is he doing that?" That doesn't poll well. Well, I've got my own pollsters, I know it doesn't poll well. But it's the right thing to do for America.[96]

In another interview the following exchange occurred:[97]

STEPHANOPOULOS: So, just existentially, you don't think there's anything that maybe you did that contributed to those feelings [public's dissatisfaction]?

OBAMA: ... If you're asking have we made the decisions that are the right decisions to move this country forward after a very devastating recession, then the *answer is absolutely.* (crosstalk)

STEPHANOPOULOS: So, you know, we've talked about this a couple times in the last year. And so, you have conceded you could have found better ways to communicate. But *it sounds like you're still saying no fundamental rethinking of your approach to the country's challenges.*

This is possibly the last defense of a president who has lost the public's confidence, a reflection of how the president really feels, or more likely both.

But it is a highly risky and a potentially self-destructive approach to his leadership responsibilities that can't help but summon associations to his father's similarly failed "big bang" approach to his transformational ambitions. Charles Cook, a political poll watcher for many decades and "perhaps the most respected crystal-ball gazer in politics,"[98] wrote of Obama, "At the risk of sounding like an unlicensed psychoanalyst, it seems that President Obama is so supremely self-confident, so self-assured of the righteousness of his positions, that perhaps he believes if he does what he thinks is best and lets the chips fall where they may, everything will eventually work out.[99]

As someone trained in the field, I think Cook is on to something here. However, it is not only that Obama is supremely self-confident, although that is certainly true. It is not only that he thinks he is right, although he certainly does think so. It is that the president is also self-assured regarding the *righteousness* of his positions. His positions are not only politically superior to the positions of his opponents, but morally correct and virtuous.

With such a view, it is easy to look down on and askance at those who haven't reached that level of morality or virtue, especially if you believe that holding those views elevates you above those who don't. Indeed, this is precisely the understanding that some supporters give. In speaking of the mosque proposal for the site of the World Trade Center attacks Margaret Carlson, a liberal columnist, asked, "How can President Barack Obama be so right about the mosque and yet get it so wrong?" She then answered, "Here's how: He is so supremely confident in his intellect that he forgets, on his way to the correct decision, to slow down and pick up not-so-gifted stragglers."[100]

This is a witches' brew worldview for any president. That seething cauldron of troubles mixes rectitude, arrogance, determined ambition, and self-certainty and is a recipe for political disaster.

Part III
THE FUTURE OF THE OBAMA PRESIDENCY

10

TRANSFORMATION'S COLLAPSE AND THE REDEMPTION OF THE OBAMA PRESIDENCY

In November 2010, two years into his presidency, voters went to the polls and delivered their judgments about the direction and adequacy of Barack Obama's presidential leadership. The results strongly suggested that they found both questionable.

The *New York Times* delivered this sweeping judgment on the president: "The verdict delivered by voters on Tuesday effectively put an end to his transformational ambitions."[1]

With this historic vote, Obama's life-long redemptive odyssey came full circle and presented him with the most profound personal and political questions of his life. He had matured, searching for an understanding of his complicated relationship with his father and had then sought through his own successful ambitions to redeem his father's failed legacy. Yet, before he could accomplish that, he first had to redeem himself and his own ambivalent identity and equivocal ambition and settle on an emotional resolution of his complicated relationship with his mother, and her legacy.

Obama was tempted in high school and his first two years of college by a stance of lassitude in the face of questions about what, if anything, he would do with his life. Later as a student and in his first job, the riches of a surging New York economy sorely tempted him. In response, Obama withdrew into his own self-contained world of political and cultural exploration, and successfully resisted New York's material temptations. He emerged from this quasi-monastic period ready to pursue a life devoted to achieving political "fairness." This was his mother's legacy and its pursuit—first as a community organizer and later as a lawyer, professor, state senator, U.S. Senator, and now president—was Obama's means of redeeming his ambivalent relationship with her.

Beyond his own earlier redemption as a young man in New York, Obama as president was in a position to bring to fruition the larger cultural, economic, and political redemption he had sought. Through his own transformational presidency he could redeem his father's failed dreams of national and historical significance. Through the idealized legacy of social, economic, and political fairness as the framework for his historic policy ambitions, he could redeem his failure to resolve his conflicted feelings about his mother, who both loved and repeatedly left him. And ultimately, through his own view of his moral standing and leadership destiny, and the redistributive policies that flowed from them, he could redeem the promise of his own country that had repeatedly failed to live up to its moral and political premises.

Obama won the presidency with a resounding victory, brought about by assembling a new and formidable coalition of supporters, including many Independents. He entered office with many well wishers, even among those who didn't support him. Many Americans expressed public pride in his historic candidacy and there was an outpouring of rapturous support worldwide when he won.

Once in office, and with the help of substantial Democratic Congressional majorities, Obama compiled a major record of passing domestic legislation: continuing the TARP programs that President Bush had initiated that helped to bring the American economy back from the brink of collapse, passing a major economic stimulus package, intervening to keep two major automakers economically afloat, changing the structure of the student loan industry, initiating programs to help homeowners in danger of defaulting on their mortgages to achieve government aided refinancing of their debts, passing major financial regulation legislation, and passing very major national health care legislation. And those are only a partial list of Obama's domestically fulfilled legislative ambitions.

In foreign policy the president was equally active and ambitious. His foreign policy initiatives included a "reset" of U.S.–Russian relations, a highly visible and concerted outreach effort to Muslims, a decided push to break the long-standing impasse in the Middle East between Israel and the Palestinians, an attempt to develop a dialogue with Iran over its nuclear and regional ambitions, and an effort to move toward a "nuclear-free" world, among other things.

Given the number and range of these policy initiatives, it also seems an understatement to say, as one writer did, that "In the year since he was elected president, Barack Obama has revealed himself as one of the boldest leaders to occupy the Oval Office in the modern era."[2] Yet, there is a profound paradox at the center of Obama's transformational efforts. These efforts, especially the domestic ones, can be counted as "accomplishments" in the sense that these policies were enacted or became laws. However, the public does not uniformly regard them as accomplishments. There is weak and conflicted support for many of these policies, and majority opposition to some. Indeed, paradoxically, it seems that the more major legislation the Obama administration passed, the more uneasy and unsupportive the public became.

The 2010 midterm election stopped Obama's transformative and redemptive policy ambitions cold, at least as they are embedded in the vehicle of major congressional legislation. Ironically, in the aftermath of this extraordinary election, it is the Obama

Presidency itself that is in need of redemption. How, exactly, that could be accomplished and whether Obama is psychologically capable and politically willing to do what might be necessary to accomplish this task remains an open question.

A Consequential Election

If there were ever an off-year election that might be characterized as immediately consequential, the 2010 election certainly would seem to qualify. The concrete political results of the election were easily discernible. Republicans picked up at least sixty-two seats in the House of Representatives and gained control there. They picked up six Senate seats—not enough to gain a majority, but enough to be an even more formidable power in the policy debates over the next two years and beyond. They gained six new governorships, several in the important bellwether states of Michigan, Ohio, Pennsylvania, and Wisconsin. And perhaps most unexpectedly, because there had been little attention paid to the state level of government, Republicans won 680 State Legislature seats nationally with "all legislative chamber switches in the 2010 election ... going from a Democratic majority to a new Republican majority with one going from Dem to tied."[3]

An Election Fraught with Meanings

These were the clear post-election political facts. But what did these figures mean? That was not so clear.

Apocalyptic and pointed hyperbole abounded. Some thought the election a "great repudiation,"[4] a "devastation,"[5] a "Democratic bloodbath,"[6] "an earthquake,"[7] a "blowout,"[8] a "crossroads election,"[9] "a perfect storm for Republicans,"[10] a "Democratic Apocalypse,"[11] a "sizable landslide,"[12] an "historic upheaval,"[13] an election in which the "tide turns sharply,"[14] "a convincing rejection of Obama's policies,"[15] "[a] no-confidence vote in Obama,"[16] "a broad rebuke to President Obama's agenda,"[17] "a vote to end the excesses of the Obama administration,"[18] a vote on Obama's ideology—"It's the Ideology, Stupid,"[19] an "election debacle,"[20] or as the president himself put it "a shellacking."[21]

Support for the rebuke theory came from several polls. For example a CNN poll asked the following question to half its sample:

> As you know, as a result of the election which was held earlier this month, the Republicans will control the U.S. House of Representatives. Do you think the Republican victories in the House races are more of a mandate for Republican policies or more a rejection of Democratic policies?

Seventy percent answered that their vote was a rejection of Democratic policies. When the question was revised and asked to the other half of the sample to include specific mention of President Obama, 35 percent answered that their vote was a rejection of Democratic policies and 44 percent said it was to register disapproval of the president. Adding the president by name increased the overall disapproval of Democrats and the president to almost 80 percent.[22]

Others were not so sure. Some saw the election as a "return to the norm (a sea of interior red, bordered by blue coasts and dotted by blue islands of ethnic/urban density);"[23] "a setback for progressives, not a permanent defeat;"[24] or "hardly an order from the American people to discard the progress of the last two years and start over again."[25]

Other characterizations aimed to be more descriptive: "a remarkable comeback for Republicans two years after they suffered a crushing defeat in the White House and four years after Democrats swept control of the House and Senate;"[26] "a referendum on President Barack Obama's first two years, a period notable for its ambitious agenda but also for the administration's missteps in the face of evidence ranging from eroding public opinion to town hall meetings gone wrong to unfavorable outcomes in three bellwether elections last fall and winter;[27]" "less a mandate for Republican ideas than a brake on Obama's;"[28] "A Vote Against Dems, Not for the GOP,"[29] "revealed that 'the Bush majority' is still alive and well—and strong enough to sweep the Republican party to its largest House majority in several generations;"[30] that the "country remains highly polarized and unsettled in the center,"[31] or that the administration lacked "a compelling, easily grasped narrative that offered a theory about our challenges and unified his [Obama's] recommendations for addressing them."[32]

After the election the president first tacked to the center. However, when ballooning spending and deficits became the focus of public concern and the GOP presented a comprehensive plan to reduce both, the president tacked strong left. How this would sit with the independents who had abandoned him was unclear.[33]

Whatever the characterizations of the election, two major questions immediately arose for the president and his presidency. The first was: How did the president understand the meaning of the election? Was it "the natural and unavoidable backlash in a time of historic economic distress, or was it a repudiation of a big-spending activist government? Was it primarily a failure of communications as the White House has suggested lately, or was it a fundamental disconnect with the values and priorities of the American public?[34]"

The second question arose naturally from the answer to the first: How would the president proceed given this understanding? Would he follow Bill Clinton's path after his 1994 midterm election setback by lowering his sights and appealing to suburban swing voters with priorities like promoting school uniforms, and V-chips to block offensive television content.[35] Would Obama follow Clinton down the path of "triangulation," "trying to play off both his own party as well as the empowered opposition"?[36]

Or, might Obama opt for the "Truman model"? Though very unpopular in 1948, Truman called a special summer session and dared Republicans to pass the more liberal reform platform adopted by its own party's nominating convention. When Republican lawmakers refused, "Mr. Truman campaigned against Congress and beat the odds to win the election."[37]

These two models, though widely discussed, were not the only ones available to the president. He might choose a *strategic accommodation model* that combines centrist rhetoric espousing the language of common ground while fiercely defending the political territory he has won through legislation, executive decisions, and personnel choices from any retrenchment, while looking for opportunities to advance his policy preferences and his reelection prospects. He might also resort to the use of multiple messages, some for public consumption, some for the private understanding of his base as he did recently with proposed changes to the health care law that the public embraced.[38]

Strategic Accommodation

And that is precisely what the president did. He borrowed GOP language to discuss tax reform, saying it should be "simplifying—eliminating loopholes, eliminating deductions, eliminating exemptions in certain categories."[39] He launched a "charm offensive" reaching out to the new Republican leaders in Congress, "promising cooperation and straight dealing with the GOP power players," yet in doing so was also "seeking political high ground and trying to position the Obama administration as willing to work with Republicans rather than succumb to partisan gridlock."[40]

The president also made some very visible personnel changes. He replaced his assertive chief of staff Rahm Emanuel with William Daley, who helped President Clinton pass the North American Free Trade Act. David Plouffe replaced David Axelrod who left to head the president's reelection campaign. And Jim Carney replaced Robert Gibbs as press secretary.

Karl Rove, no supporter of the president's policies, praised the selection of Mr. Daley saying he "will probably streamline the West Wing's unwieldy decision-making structure while expanding the range of opinions the president hears."[41] Perhaps. But it is the president who ultimately makes the decisions that set his policy priorities into motion, and it has been very clear that this president has not only centralized policy decisions in the White House, and enjoys making decisions, but also thinks he is quite good at it.

On the policy front, the president instituted a partial two-year wage freeze for some federal workers. It did not affect step increases within GS levels, new hiring, nor did it affect bonuses.[42] The president also issued an executive order[43] for a "government-wide review of federal regulations" and published an op-ed piece in the *Wall Street Journal* extolling the virtues of his new outlook toward reducing them.[44] Yet the story behind the headlines announcing a new more centrist leaning administration was more complicated than it appeared.

This post-election initiative is prudently viewed in the context of the president's early regulatory blitz that the *New York Times* described as initiating "hundreds of new mandates, while also stepping up enforcement of rules by increasing the ranks of inspectors and imposing higher fines for violations" and calling it "A new age of regulation ... in Washington."[45]

Moreover, as the *New York Times* reported, the president's executive order, "exempted many agencies that most vex corporate America."[46] But perhaps the largest caveat to the president's efforts to decrease burdensome federal regulations was a little-noticed provision in his executive order requiring all government cost-benefit analyses to include "values that are difficult or impossible to quantify, including equity, human dignity, *fairness, and distributive impacts*."[47] Here was Obama's attempt to institutionalize his mother's legacy of "fairness" and his redemptive ambitions to equalize "distributive impacts" across the thousands of areas in which the government affects American economic and political life.

Tax Cuts: Optics and Reality

Perhaps the most commented-upon legislative initiative was the president's acceptance of the extension of all the Bush tax cuts, including those for the "wealthy." In the past, the president had vigorously and consistently opposed these particular tax cuts.[48] The strategic rationale for his agreement however was quite clear. Not only had Republicans signaled unified opposition to any tax increases, but they were also joined by a number of Democrats (139 of whom voted for the measure in the House).[49] Moreover, from the standpoint of *strategic accommodation* the political optics were obvious:

> White House officials say this is a deliberate strategy: to demonstrate his ability to compromise with Republicans and portray the president as the last reasonable man in a sharply partisan Washington. The move is based on a political calculation, drawn from his party's midterm defeat, that places a premium on winning back independent voters.[50]

Options and strategic calculations aside, the president undercut his new partnership message at a news conference ten days before he signed the bill to announce that tax agreement had been reached. There, Obama railed against the bill he and his party had just agreed to.[51] The news conference however was much more petulant than is evident from the transcript.[52] In it he directly criticized the news media for their depictions of him as having not stood up for what he said he believed in or, alternatively, in their view of being too flexible (question by Ben Feller, Chuck Todd). He also criticized members of his own party (question from Jonathan Weisman) for not recognizing how much of his and their progressive agenda he had fought for and won. One is reminded here of Obama's insistence many years earlier as a young lawyer in getting full credit for the fact that he "ran" and didn't just "jog" (see p. 121).

Obama was so upset at the tax extension bill he felt that he had to sign that after a private meeting with former president Clinton he convened an impromptu press conference with Mr. Clinton by his side, said a few words, and then left to attend a holiday party leaving Mr. Clinton to defend his tax signing decision.[53] As one reporter noted, "their public appearance will be long remembered. The sight and sound of Clinton going solo in the White House briefing room, as Obama slipped away to a holiday party, was certainly a head-turner on a slow Friday afternoon."[54]

The Budget: Clarifying Obama's Strategy

Perhaps the clearest indication of the limits of Obama's strategic accommodation to his new political circumstances was to be found in his 2012 budget. That budget calls for spending a record 3.7 trillion dollars.[55] That includes, "$53 billion over the next six years on high-speed rail, and proposes spending $15.7 billion to build a nationwide wireless network for emergency workers and to widen access to mobile high-speed Internet,"[56] plus additional funds for education[57] and energy area spending.[58]

Any national budget can be viewed through multiple and conflicting frames of analysis and this one is no exception. According to the administration, its budget "*can* reduce projected deficits by $1.1 trillion over the next decade,"[59] although these, like all other multi-year projections, are uncertain.[60] Yet it is also true that under the 2012 Obama budget, "interest payments on the national debt will quadruple in the next decade and every man, woman and child in the United States will be paying more than $2,500 a year to cover the nation's past profligacy."[61] Or, you could look at the significant new increases in government spending contained in the budget; "Obama's budget would have the federal government spend *twice* in 2012 what it did just 12 years before. Even after accounting for inflation, that's a 57 percent increase."[62] Or perhaps the most pertinent fact is that, "at no point in the president's 10-year projection would the U.S. government spend less than it's taking in."[63]

Of course the truth of the matter is that no matter how one frames Obama's budget, it is the first move in a debate that he will have with Republicans and members of his own party over the nation's priorities and its available resources. What is clear is that the president has signaled his commitment to preserving as much of the substantial increase in government spending that has characterized his first two years in office as he can. In doing so, he underscores the point that he made to liberal members of his party in the petulant press conference noted above.

His budget strategy also underscores the president's insistence during an interview with Bill O'Reilly that he really hadn't changed at all after the midterm elections.

When "pressed Sunday during a live interview with Fox's Bill O'Reilly on what political analysts say is a clear sprint toward the center, Obama dismissed the notion with a 'no'. 'I haven't—I didn't move to the centre. I'm the same guy,' he said."[64] It seems fair to view the president's insistence as reflecting the truth of his political identity and ambitions.

The Political and Emotional Limits of Strategic Accommodation

As a tactic, strategic accommodation may be the most obvious and possible response to the president's new, weaker political position after the midterm elections. But it is clearly not without costs, both political and emotional. The political danger to the president is that his strategy will be seen for what it clearly is, a strategy and not a change of heart or a narrowing of his transformative and redemptive ambitions. The gap between the president's strategy and what the public expressed in the 2010 midterm elections will be hard to reconcile by rhetoric, symbolic steps, or by grudging incremental accommodation. The president may get some mileage out of portraying his opponents as being against everything he wants to do to help the country, and he may be able to generate some public pressure for "compromise" that allows him some measure of success, and perhaps even reelection. However, that strategy, even if successful, will come at an emotional cost to the president because of what it means for his transformative ambitions.

The enormous and often contradictory public expectations that accompany any presidency have been a long recognized fact of modern political life.[65] Still, it is somewhat startling to learn from the *New York Times* that, "Mr. Obama has told people that it would be so much easier to be the president of China. As one official put it, 'No one is scrutinizing Hu Jintao's words in Tahrir Square'."[66] The frustrations of presidential leadership in a system in which political power is dispersed are legion. And this would especially be the case for a president whose ambitions are transformational.

The remark suggests that Obama believes the Chinese president rules by something closer to fiat than consultation and perhaps this is true to some degree. Still, while the wish that one would be able to accomplish one's presidential purposes more easily is understandable, it is an unsettling identification on the president's part. And that identification is a very far distance from the president's usual public identifications with President Lincoln or Martin Luther King.

Even if, as seems likely, the president positions himself to win some of these debates, the rest of his presidency is very unlikely to resemble the grand, forceful and successful march toward the country's transformation and redemption that the president envisioned after his historic election. How this forced curtailment of the president's ambitions will play out for the president's resilience and determination over the longer run is an open and critical question.

Smaller Government, Redux

One result of the election was an immediate reappearance of themes that had surfaced earlier in the Obama presidency. For example, earlier we noted elected President Obama's rhetorical argument about having smart effective government rather than "big government."[67] In a post-midterm election interview, the president said this: "But I think most Democrats and Republicans, they want a government that works, but they want one that's lean. One that's not wasting money. One that is looking after their interests, but isn't engaged in a whole bunch of giveaways."[68] In between those two rhetorical commitments to smaller, smarter, and more effective government, the Obama administration policies unfolded.

It is hard to know how much to credit the president's post-election return to virtues of a smaller government. As noted this president is unusual in being so well versed on the issues that he is at ease not only with his own arguments, but those of his opponents. Yet, being able to give public voice to more than one side of a policy debate is not the same as being clear about how you assess their relative weight and legitimacy in actually making a decision. Understanding your opponents' policy positions is not the same as thinking that they have valid points. Nor, as noted, is it the same as actually taking them into account.

The president's "I see, understand and even agree with some of your points" meme has a decades-long history, dating back at least to his time in law school. And that meme may well be intellectually true for the president, but it has often proved in the past to be a rhetorical understanding without practical political consequences.

Obama's Understanding of the Election

Facts do not speak for themselves in large part because there are so many of them and their meaning and implications are a matter of interpretation and judgment. This is no less true for President Obama than for the American public, as they try to make sense of this election's meaning and adjust their expectations for each other accordingly. Moreover, the understanding of these many facts, and their interpretation at this present time, are dependent in part on the political and policy choices that unfold as a result. And here, as is the case for any presidency, President Obama will not be the only player trying to accomplish their purposes.

That said, it would be foolish not to assign a central role in how Obama's presidency now unfolds to Obama himself. He has, as documented earlier in this analysis, centralized power in the White House to an unprecedented degree, amplifying the historical trends of modern presidential centralization. Moreover, as president, he has proven to be much more of a decider than a delegator. This is not surprising given that Obama has made very clear that it is he who is the radiating core of the ideas and actions that animate his presidency (see Chapter 9, p. 204) and also the enormous amount of confidence he has in his own abilities (see Chapter 7, p. 153) and views (see Chapter 8, pp. 192–193).

Therefore, to a considerable extent, the president's personal understanding and response to the midterm election is very likely to be his administration's as well. The critical question then obviously is: How did he understand it?

The president gave his personal understanding of what was happening in the election process both before and after the election took place. It is useful to distinguish these understandings from the more partisan rhetoric that the president used during major campaign events to arouse his base and push independent voters to be leery of his Republican opponents. These sometimes harsh characterizations and accusations may reflect a bit of what a president actually thinks, but in the rough and tumble of a hard fought election campaign, they are not likely to be reliable guides to what he is able to do as opposed to what he might like. More reliable guides can be found in smaller group contexts or in the quiet of one-to-one interviews, of which he gave a number, and they help open a window in the president's thinking.

In September 2010, before the final campaign swings and the election, the president sat down for a long interview with Peter Baker of the *New York Times*.[69] The president had "muscled through Congress perhaps the most ambitious domestic agenda in a generation," but found himself, "vilified by the right, castigated by the left and abandoned by the middle." He was "facing likely repudiation, with voters preparing to give him a Congress that, even if Democrats maintain control, will almost certainly be less friendly to the president than the one [with which] he has spent the last two years." The report noted that, "Obama has already begun thinking about what went wrong—and what he needs to do to change course for the next two years."

Obama as a "Tax and Spend Liberal Democrat"—Wrongly Labeled or Self-Defined?

Baker reported that during the interview, although the president said, "he had no regrets about the broad direction of his presidency,"[70] he "did identify what he called 'tactical lessons.'" He had, he said, "let himself look too much like 'the same old tax-and-spend liberal Democrat.'" David Brooks had raised the same point in the same passive manner. Brooks wrote of Obama, "Then he got defined as an orthodox, big government liberal who lacks deep roots in American culture."[71] The passive phrasing implies that this was something that was done to Obama, rather than something for which Obama himself bears major responsibility.

The question then arises: How did this happen? Part of the answer must lie in the choices that Obama made. The president's decisions to provide more TARP money to stabilize financial institutions and to rescue GM and Chrysler to save jobs had some economic policy logic behind them. However, the large stimulus and enormous health care plan touted as an eventual vehicle for major savings were, and proved to be, more economically questionable. They were in the first case based on the assumptions built into the economic models that the administration used to make their case, and in the second instance were based on assumptions, that have already been shown to be in error.

The three factors that effect the impact of any economic stimulus are that they be targeted in focus, rapid in getting money into the economy and substantial enough to make a difference. There seems little doubt the president's economic stimulus plan was substantial, though some on the left thought it should have been much larger. Where it lost traction was in the first and second requirements—focus and speed. Many of the stimulus projects, like the seed money for a high-speed rail line, will take many years to complete, if they ever are, and will need continuing government subsidies to be economically viable. Cost overruns and construction delays have dimmed the economic viability of these kinds of projects both in the United States[72] and abroad.[73] The stimulus also provided 20.8 billion dollars for improved health care technology like electronic health care records, but that too will take many years to complete, and its impact on health care costs is unclear. Overall, the Congressional Budget Office estimated that over 200 billion stimulus dollars would be spent in 2011, or later—very late to have a targeted immediate impact.[74]

The stimulus was designed by a Democratic Congress wishing to use that bill to further a number of their political priorities. These may or may not have been economically meritorious, but each specific program could not easily be considered "targeted" or likely to have an immediate impact. Republicans complained about the political framing of stimulus projects and this in turn forced the administration to tout immediacy of the stimulus' impact.

Obama has said that one of the "tactical" lessons from his first two years in office was that he "realized too late that 'there's no such thing as shovel-ready projects' when it comes to public works."[75] It's unclear though just when the president learned this lesson. More than a year before the Baker interview, the president said in a July 2009 interview with *ABC*'s Jake Tapper that he knew that, "infrastructure projects were always going to take "six months to eight months to get that money actually into the ground because that's the nature of big infrastructure projects."[76] Yet, a few months earlier he was touting the 150,000 "shovel ready" jobs and saying, "We are seeing shovels hit the ground."[77] He had been using that term for months.[78]

A question arises here as to how a very smart, policy detail oriented president like Obama didn't know that "shovel ready" projects took time, or didn't ask how long it would take for their economic impact to be dramatically felt. It's hard to conceive that the president did not know that building high-speed rail lines would take time or that roads are not built in a day.

Three Million Jobs Created: Statistical Models Vs. Reality

At that same ceremony, the president also "claimed today that 150,000 jobs will be created or saved by the end of next year with the road-building provisions of the $787-billion economic stimulus that he signed."[79]

Did the stimulus create or save millions of jobs? Not exactly. The White House first put forward a claim that its stimulus package had "saved a million jobs."[80] An *Associated Press* analysis however suggested that some of these figures were inflated. It

> found job counts that were more than 10 times as high as the actual number of paid positions; jobs credited to the stimulus program that were counted two and sometimes more than four times; and other jobs that were credited to stimulus spending when none was produced.[81]

The White House responded that the *AP* study covered only a fraction of the jobs that had been created.

The White House next said that the stimulus had "saved or created about three million jobs,"[82] and produced a report by the White House Counsel of Economic Advisers to support their claim.[83] That White House Report correctly noted[84] that the Congressional Budget Office had used similar models to arrive at its estimate of "as many as 3.3 million jobs."[85]

So the White House seemed to be on solid ground in quoting the CBO figures, yet at the same time it was touting having "saved or created 3.3 million jobs," the economy had actually lost, in reality, 3 million net jobs and unemployment had risen to record levels. How was this possible?

The answer is to be found in how both the White House and the CBO made their *estimates*. The estimates were not actual real jobs that were created, but rather an assumption, built into the calculations that so much government spending would produce a specific number of jobs. What did these estimated figures have to do with the actual number of jobs really being created in the economy? Nothing. The amount of money the government spent was an actual figure but the number of jobs created was a pre-determined artifact of the formula, not an actual count of any jobs being created. CBO Director Doug Elmendorf confirmed this in a speech to the National Association of Business Economics.[86]

So, the administration put itself in the position of touting the millions of new jobs that it said stimulus spending had created based on assumptions that were hard wired into the estimation formulas, while, in real life, Americans were facing increasing unemployment and the businesses' failure to hire at anywhere near the rate needed to absorb new labor market entrants, much less those who had lost their jobs.

Here again, it's hard to understand why the president did not ask his economic advisors why the job growth model he had relied on in pushing his stimulus package wasn't working as advertised. Here is one of those forks in the road where presidents can choose between disingenuousness and candor. As late as September 2010, nineteen months after the American Recovery and Reinvestment Act of 2009 was signed in February 2009, the president called on Congress to vote for another 50 billion dollars in stimulus funds that would be used for building roads and railways.[87]

In a post-election interview, Obama made this somewhat confusing point: "Well, it wasn't because the Recovery Act didn't work; it's because the modeling, in terms of what to expect where unemployment would go to, turned out to be wrong."[88] So the continued downturn in employment "wasn't because the Recovery Act didn't work," it was because the model on which it was based didn't work! That raises the question of why, if the model underlying the policy was proven wrong, the president would ask for additional funds based on the exact same set of assumptions already proven wrong.

Politically and psychologically, the public was forced to choose between the administration's view of the robust job-creating results of its very large stimulus bill, and the everyday evidence that employment prospects were dismal and getting bleaker. The president, in turn, doubled down on a stimulus model that clearly wasn't working as advertised.

The president gave many speeches, interviews, and appearances arguing for the correctness and effectiveness of his chosen policy. Yet the public facts were inconsistent with his reassurances and arguments. Words, fluency, and intelligence—woven together in a narrative of success—key elements of Obama's leadership skills, failed the president here. But that is not how the president saw and understood it.

Too Busy to Lead?

Two of the oldest clichés about presidential leadership are that governing is different than campaigning and that leadership in a democracy requires public persuasion. Both are partially true. Mobilizing potential supporters is important for both winning campaigns and winning support for governing policies once in office. And persuasion is important for successful presidential leadership but so are the actual policies the president is trying to persuade people to support.

"Campaigning is different than governing," the president told reporters in offering advice to the Republicans after their congressional victory, thus confirming his knowledge of conventional wisdom.[89] But exactly what understanding of the difference he had developed was unclear.

In a post-election interview with Steven Kroft, there was this exchange:[90]

KROFT: People have made the argument you lost control of the narrative. You've let other people define you. *That you haven't sold your successes well enough.*

PRESIDENT OBAMA: I think that's a fair argument. I think that over the course of two years—and I mentioned this during the press conference—*we were so busy and so focused on getting a bunch of stuff done* that we stopped paying attention to the fact that we yeah, *leadership isn't just legislation. That it's a matter of persuading people. And giving them confidence and bringing them together.*

Notice the premise of the question that the president readily accepts, that Obama hasn't sold his successful policies well enough. Notice also Obama's point that leadership is a matter of persuasion and giving people confidence. The question here is the relationship, if any, between the two.

Is it the successful persuasion that gives people confidence? Or is it the demonstrated success of the policies that raises confidence? And what exactly is persuasion? Is it simply presidential assertion backed up by narrow finely tailored arguments? Or does it consist of laying out the issues carefully, respectfully considering alternative arguments and making clear the basis of your own thinking?

These are important questions. If it's a matter primarily of narrowly based "persuasion," then the midterm results are not about policy or leadership direction, but about the failure of the president to be sufficiently convincing and persuasive about the virtues of what he did. This is essentially the president's basic take on the meaning of the election.

At a back-yard gathering in Seattle during part of the midterm campaign, Obama had this to say:

> I think that one of the challenges we had two years ago was we had to move so fast, we were in such emergency mode that *it was very difficult for us to spend a lot of time doing victory laps and advertising exactly what we were doing*, because we had to move on to the next thing.[91]

He made the same point in an interview with two *National Journal* reporters: "If you think about it, the amount of work that should have gone into communicating just what was in the stimulus might have taken six months. *We didn't have time*. Because right away we had to figure out how do we apply a stress test to the banking system that stabilizes it and what are we going to do about autos?"[92]

In his interview with Peter Baker of the *New York Times*, Obama said, "I think anybody who's occupied this office has to remember that success is determined by an intersection in policy and politics and that you can't be neglecting of *marketing and P.R.* and public opinion."[93]

The emphasis on "advertising," "marketing," and "P.R." by the president reflects a campaign mind-set about persuading others of the correctness of the president's policy initiatives. President Obama is not the first president to use "advertising," "marketing," and "P.R." to sell his policies, but recall these questions are in response to inquiries about what he might have possibly done wrong. The president's answer seems to suggest that he thinks he needed more and better "advertising," "marketing," and "P.R." rather than any rethinking of his actual policies.

Too Correct to Change?

The president was willing to admit during his interview with Peter Baker that, "given how much stuff was coming at us, we probably spent much more time trying to get the policy right than trying to get the politics right." To this observation, Baker dryly observed, "that presumes what he did was the right thing."[94] And did the president "do the right thing" and "get the policy right?" In his mind the answer is an unequivocal "yes."

At his post-election press conference the president, on three separate occasions, was asked directly whether the election reflected dissatisfaction with his policies and each time he answered no.[95]

Representative was this Q&A:[96]

Q: Just following up on what Ben just talked about, you don't seem to be reflecting or second-guessing any of the policy decisions you've made, instead saying the message the voters were sending was about frustration with the economy or maybe even chalking it up to a failure on your part to communicate effectively. If you're not reflecting on your policy agenda, is it possible voters can conclude you're still not getting it?

THE PRESIDENT: Well, Savannah, that was just the first question, so we're going to have a few more here. I'm doing a whole lot of reflecting and I think that there are going to be areas in policy where we're going to have to do a better job. I think that over the last two years, we have made a series of very tough decisions, *but decisions that were right* in terms of moving the country forward in an emergency situation where we had the risk of slipping into a second Great Depression.

Asked by White House correspondent Jake Tapper in April 2009 whether he would have done anything differently regarding the stimulus, the president replied, "So, there's nothing that we would have done differently."[97] And recall that he told Peter Baker in his *New York Times* interview that, "he had no regrets about the broad direction of his presidency."[98] Even the unseemly process by which Obama's health care legislation made it through Congress, which he called an "ugly mess," was worth it because "the outcome was a good one."[99]

These quotes, all from different time periods, point to one seemingly correct fact—the administration and specifically the president began his presidency with high confidence in the correctness of his decisions and he has not changed his mind. There is, to be sure, some political mileage to be gained by admitting one needed to "do better," as the president did several times in these interviews and in his news conference. And there is a decided downside in acknowledging that you made mistakes of policy judgment and that your critics were correct. So in that respect it is hardly surprising that Obama would not admit to having made mistaken policy judgments on such large and consequential presidential decisions. It would be especially hard for someone like this president who has such high confidence in his own judgments.

Obama himself indirectly and obliquely acknowledged that difficulty. He told Peter Baker,

> There is probably a perverse pride in my administration—and I take responsibility for this; this was blowing from the top—that we were going to do the right thing, even if short-term it was unpopular.[100]

"Perverse pride" is an interesting phrase and is consistent with the president's view that if he can be faulted for anything, it is for being so concerned with getting the policies right, which he thinks he did, that he didn't pay as much attention to "politics" as he might have to persuade the public that his policies were right. Of course, not paying enough attention to "politics" because "[i]n that obsessive focus on policy, I neglected some things … ,"[101] as Obama said to reporters on his way back from his November trip abroad, is to admit to a fault as a vehicle for underlining your virtue.

"Hardwired" for Fear?

In a small fundraiser several weeks before the election Obama offered the several dozen donors his "view from the oval office." He said that "fear and frustration" were behind the public's disaffection. The downturn was responsible for Americans' inability to "think clearly." And then linking his party's declining prospects to a theory of evolutionary psychology he said,

> Part of the reason that our politics seems so tough right now and facts and science and argument does not seem to be winning the day all the time is because *we're hardwired not to always think clearly when we're scared. And the country's scared.*

The president then outlined two responses to this evolutionary and political dilemma in response to the economic crisis:

> You can respond in a couple of ways to a trauma like this. One is to pull back, retrench and respond to your fears by pushing away challenges, looking backwards. Another is to say we can meet these challenges and we are going to move forward. And that's what this election is about.[102]

It's an odd theory to put forward as an explanation for voter dissatisfaction since it seems to suggest that fear has selectively rendered ignorant those who have indicated they might vote against Obama's party in the elections. Presumably members of Obama's party, and Obama himself, have already overcome this evolutionary hurdle. It is also somewhat condescending to suggest that voters are approaching their election choices with the most primitive parts of their brain, and that if they could only break through their temporary fear-induced stupidity, they would vote Democratic. And of course, it makes no room for the explanation that perhaps it is the president's policies that are invoking the very discontent (fear) that voters in opposition are said to be experiencing.

Obama's theory of evolutionary based, hard-wired primal fear as an explanation for voter behavior is primarily of interest, not because of its plausibility, but because it leads directly to the question of the president's ability to emotionally connect with those who don't wholly share his views. That question is raised directly in the title of a *Washington Post* news story: "Assessing midterm losses, Democrats ask whether Obama's White House fully grasped voters' fears."[103] The central question raised by the story is contained in the following observations:

> In his own assessments of what went wrong, the president has lamented his inability to persuade voters on the merits of what he has done, and blamed the failure on his preoccupation with a full plate of crises. But a broad sample of Democratic office holders and strategists said in interviews that the disconnect goes far deeper than that. "There doesn't seem to be anybody in the White House who's got any idea what it's like to lie awake at night worried about money and worried about things slipping away," said retiring Tennessee Gov. Phil Bredesen (D). "They're all intellectually smart. They've got their numbers. But they don't feel any of it, and I think people sense that."

The seeming obvious contrast here is between Bill "I *feel* your pain" Clinton and Barack "I *know* the source of your pain" Obama. Yet, there is more to it than that. Obama is a person and a leader who approaches issues with a strongly analytical bent, and that includes the many interpersonal relationships that are a critical part of a president's leadership role. Chapter 8 covered a great deal of evidence documenting that Obama grew up and became used to being on his own and "being apart" from others. It is an interpersonal style that has had many years to develop and consolidate and, not surprisingly, has followed him into the White House.

The question here is what does this have to do with Obama's emotional connections with groups and people other than his family, with whom he is clearly very emotionally connected? The president's widely noted and much praised Zen-like emotional qualities are not the unalloyed virtue that some have taken them to be. The *Washington Post*'s Joel Achenbach for example, argued during the presidential campaign that Obama's even temperament contributed to his "uncanny knack for avoiding mistakes."[104] Perhaps. However, the president's emotional distance, coupled with his high confidence in his own judgments and his self-image as a transformational political leader are a recipe for a mismatch between the president and the public. And that mismatch is one obvious source of the president's political difficulties.

The President's Emotional Connection with the Public

Obama's meteoric political rise and startling fall from the heights he was instrumental in helping himself achieve provide several cautionary lessons. It provides a stark reminder that the emotional connection between the president and the public is a crucial element of successful presidential leadership. It is also a cautionary tale about the half-life of charisma, the dangers of mixing celebrity and authority, and the limits of progressive political transformation in a right-center country.

Obama's View of his Connection to the Public and its Problems

Obama's view of the nature of his relationship with the public was given in response to a question in his post-election interview and is worth considering in some depth:[105]

Q: Thank you, Mr. President. How do you respond to those who say the election outcome, at least in part, was voters saying that they see you as out of touch with their personal economic pain? And are you willing to make any changes in your leadership style?

THE PRESIDENT: *There is an inherent danger in being in the White House and being in the bubble.* I mean, folks didn't have any complaints about my leadership style when I was running around Iowa for a year. And they got a pretty good look at me up close and personal, and they were able to lift the hood and kick the tires, and I think they understood that my story was theirs. I might have a funny name, I might have lived in some different places, but the values of hard work and responsibility and honesty and looking out for one another that had been instilled in them by their parents, those were the same values that I took from my mom and my grandparents.

And so the track record has been that when I'm out of this place, that's not an issue. *When you're in this place, it is hard not to seem removed.* And one of the challenges that we've got to think about is how do I meet my responsibilities here in the White House, which require a lot of hours and a lot of work, but still have that opportunity to engage with the American people on a day-to-day basis, and know—give them confidence that I'm listening to them. ... So I think there are more things that we can do to make sure that I'm getting out of here ... the responsibilities of this office are so enormous and so many people are depending on what we do, and in the rush of activity, sometimes we lose track of the ways that we connected with folks that got us here in the first place. ...

But I do think that this is a growth process and an evolution. *And the relationship that I've had with the American people is one that built slowly, peaked at this incredible high, and then during the course of the last two years, as we've, together, gone through some very difficult times, has gotten rockier and tougher.* And it's going to, I'm sure, have some more ups and downs during the course of me being in this office.

In this detailed answer the president touches on a number of elements important to the relationship with the public. These include the impact of the presidential bubble and the nature and evolution of his relationship with Americans. In the president's mind they are related. He's right. But let's examine them one at a time.

The White House Bubble as a Cause for Obama's Public Estrangement

The question was asked whether the public thought him "out of touch with their economic pain." The president's immediate and direct response was to talk about the dangers of "being in the White House and being in the bubble," which he directly follows with an observation that this out of touch criticism was not a complaint when he ran for office. This leads him to the conclusion that "the track record has been that when I'm out of this place, that's not an issue." His conclusion: it's the bubble's fault because "When you're in this place, it is hard not to seem removed."

The president's view of his relational dilemma is that his job requires lots of hard work and long hours in the White House and

> we've got to think about … how do I meet my responsibilities here in the White House, which require a lot of hours and a lot of work, but still have that opportunity to engage with the American people on a day-to-day basis, and know—give them confidence that I'm listening to them.

Perhaps it's the case though that the president doesn't have to visit thousands of Americans in their backyard to give them confidence that he is listening to them. He can build that confidence by knowing what's on their minds and responding in press conferences, speeches, and above all policies.

It is very hard to take seriously the idea that the president was not aware of the many concerns that the direction of his administration and specific policies like the stimulus and especially his health care initiatives were raising among a wide swath of the public. This is, after all, a president who when Peter Baker complimented him on the new White House look, replied that he was, "happy with the redecorating of the office. 'I know *Arianna doesn't like it*,' [referring to *Huffington Post* creator Arianne Huffington] he said lightly. 'But I like taupe.'" Baker then notes evenly, "there was something incongruous about the president of the United States checking out reviews of his décor by Arianne Huffington. … "[106] A president who does so, one might add, can surely keep up with public concerns about the direction and nature of his agenda.

The president believes that the answer to this problem, at least as he has framed it, is to find "more things that we can do to make sure that I'm getting out of here … " and at this point he mentions again that "the responsibilities of this office are so enormous and so many people are depending on what we do, and in the rush of activity, sometimes we lose track of the ways that we connected with folks that got us here in the first place."

Marketing as Public Persuasion

The president is absolutely right that his office is one of enormous responsibilities. And yes, the rush of activities might lead a president to "lose track of the ways that we connected with folks that got us here in the first place." Those activities, the president has already told us, have to do with all his efforts to make sure his policies are right, which led him to neglect the "politics," which the president understood as meaning, "you can't be neglecting of *marketing and P.R.* and public opinion."

This is a somewhat startling admission. It suggests that in the president's view the way in which "we connected with the folks that got us here in the first place" was the "advertising," "marketing," and "P.R." efforts that originally were part of the Obama campaign, but had to be cut back once the crises came on rapidly and the president had to spend most of his time arriving at the right answers.

To the extent to which this is accurate, the president appears to have stumbled across another critical similarity and important difference between campaigning and governing. "Advertising," "marketing," and "P.R." are clearly part of both the campaign and governing process since mobilizing support is a key element in both circumstances. Yet, mobilizing supporters and convincing ordinary Americans of the soundness of presidential policies require different tools and in different proportions. "Advertising," "marketing," and "P.R." are more appropriate for political campaigns than for building support for complex, difficult issues of policy and governance.

The president seems to have missed that difference in his remarks. And so has his closest political advisor, David Axelrod. He sits in on many substantive policy meetings, including national security meetings, and in his own weekly political meetings, is reported by Joel Benenson, a pollster for Mr. Obama who also attends those meetings, to always ask: "How do we make sure that the arguments from the president's agenda are made in the most persuasive way?"[107] This political impulse is understandable, but it is not the same as mounting a fair debate in which you have confidence in the superiority of your position.

There is another large inconsistency with the president's understanding as he presents it. In his view he was focused on doing the right thing and lost track of the political aspects of his decisions. Yet even a cursory glance through the *Daily Compilation of Presidential Documents*[108] that, among other items, lists the complete texts of all presidential speeches, interviews, press conferences, and remarks shows that the president devoted enormous time in Washington and outside of it to pushing his agenda. Mark Knoller, CBS radio correspondent and a well-known keeper of presidential statistics[109] had tabulated that by "the end of his first year in office the president had made/given 411 speeches, comments and remarks, 42 News conferences, and 158 interviews."[110] Writing fifteen months into the Obama Presidency, Knoller noted "that since taking office, Obama has logged only seven days without a media appearance—and all but one of those days was a Sunday."[111] This is hardly the record of a president chained to his White House desk.

Moreover, it is also true that in addition to Obama's very substantial agenda promotion efforts, this president has embraced America's celebrity culture to an unprecedented degree. The list of entertainment venues in which the president has appeared and the list of non-political subjects on which the president has offered his views, as has been noted (see pp. 37–39), is quite large.

Obama defends these cultural forays as political outreach to audiences that might not watch *Meet the Press*, or perhaps even his press conferences, and he has a point. Still, the number and range of the various venues, some clearly not in any way message related, suggest that the president enjoys this aspect of his role. There is nothing wrong with that but it is hard to argue the president received his midterm election set back because he did not make more appearances on *The View* or *The Daily Show*, shows that are more aptly seen as base mobilization than a chance to reach the broad range of those concerned about his policies.

The Real Nature of Obama's White House Bubble

The presidency is in an enormously powerful position in the American political system, but it is even more emotionally powerful for those who work close to him. A president's key advisors have often been with him a long time and have developed strong feelings of attachment, loyalty, and dependence. His personal and political well-being reflects and influences theirs. They share the president's worldview and his wishes frame their policy advice. They are in the White House because they helped the president transform his vision into an electoral win, and they will remain there to the extent that they successfully continue to do so.

These kinds of emotional attachments between the president and his closest advisors are the rule and therefore an occupational hazard of the office. It is a particular hazard for a president that has extraordinarily high confidence in himself and in his own views as this president does. The potential for trouble here is magnified when the president is swept into office on a euphoric wave of this president's uniqueness and transcendence, which his chief advisors share.

Already noted is one of his closest personal and political advisors Valerie Jarrett's comment that the president has "been bored to death his whole life. *He's just too talented to do what ordinary people do*. He would never be satisfied with what ordinary people do."[112] More recently his vice president speculated in an interview about why the president seems so distant and aloof to ordinary Americans. Biden's view is that it is because, "he's *so* brilliant. He *is* an intellectual."[113] These observations seem fairly consistent with the impression the president apparently has of himself.

It is not only very close high-level advisors that reflect this danger in the Oval Office, but myriad aides and somewhat lower level advisors as well. One good example comes from the recent trip that the president took abroad, which included a stop in India. The media focused on the president's inability to sign a trade pact with South Korea and in the course of touting the president's accomplishments on the trip the president's chief National Security Advisor Tom Donilon[114] had this to say about the president's trip, "From the first day in Mumbai to today in Japan, I think that the United States *has dramatically* advanced its critical goals and its strategic interest in the region." As to the president's accomplishment in India, "I do think when historians look back *it will be one of those seminal moments, one of those iconic moments* in the relationship between countries when historians look back on it."[115]

The first of these statements can be understood as conventional political spin; the second exceeds the boundaries of historical fact and hyperbole. It was George W. Bush who developed and pushed a special U.S.-Indian relationship as "global partners."[116] This included an historic nuclear power technology sharing agreement between the two powers. And again, this is from the president's chief national security advisor.

The real White House bubble does not stem from the difficulty of getting the president out and about in the country to meet ordinary Americans. It is not getting out of the Washington bubble, but an advice bubble that reflects the range of views that the president hears and is willing to listen to. Both of these elements are important.

The sycophantic impulse is powerful among advisors, and is reinforced by the reality that the president was elected and given political license to exercise his judgment and pursue his agenda. When the president repeatedly said he had come to Washington to do big things, that amounted to a very large framing rubric for the debates on the stimulus, energy policy, health care legislation, and immigration policy that took place. In some respects, arguing against the president's policy wishes is an argument against allowing him to do what the country said he could and should do. It takes a powerful sense of self and responsibility to push such disagreements at all when the president's wishes are known, and an unusual and very rare ability to stand apart from the president and continue to argue against him.

But the advice that the president gets must travel through a president's open ears and receptive worldview frameworks. This is the hardest part of receiving advice for any president. It is a particularly difficult issue for a president as smart and successful as Obama has been by charting his own path in his own singular way.

Getting to Know the President

While registering a complaint about the lack of public comment about him being out of touch when he was running for president, Obama said,

> I mean, folks didn't have any complaints about my leadership style when I was running around Iowa for a year. And they got a pretty good look at me up close and personal, and they were able to lift the hood and kick the tires.

Did people really get to know Obama during the campaign? In some respects they did. The saw a candidate who was smart, verbally fluent, and seemingly at ease in the high stakes presidential campaign. The president campaigned on "hope and change" general themes designed to allow the public to provide their own meaning to the terms. Obama campaigned relentlessly against the "failed policies of the past" without however devoting much time to the specifics of what he wanted to do. As detailed earlier, questions regarding "where does he stand" and "what does he really stand for" abounded and still do. Appendix B contains dozens of quotes starting in 2006 and extending through the present from all points on the political spectrum—left, right, and center that essentially all ask the same basic question: Who, really, is Barack Obama?

In that respect Obama's Rorschach strategy was ironically spectacularly successful and ultimately self-defeating. It certainly helped him win the presidency. But it set the stage for the political equivalent of emotional shock when he began to translate his transformative ambitions into large-scale policies that placed the federal government in control of substantial new areas of personal and economic life.

That shock can be seen in some representative polling data.[117] In early September 2010, 50 percent of a national random sample of American adults said that the president "understands the problems of people like you." Forty-eight percent of that sample said he didn't. Yet, in January of 2009, those numbers were 72 percent who agreed that he did and 24 percent who said he did not. In September 2010, 49 percent of the sample agreed that the president "shares your values," and 50 percent did not. In January 2009, those numbers were 67 percent thought he did and 30 percent thought not. In January of 2009, 29 percent thought that Obama's "views on most issues are too liberal for you;" by September 2010 that figure had risen to 45 percent. An Associated Press/GfK poll put those numbers even more starkly. It found that in January 2009 when Obama took office, 81 percent of respondents said he understood the problems of ordinary Americans very well or somewhat well, and by September of 2010, that figure had fallen to 54 percent.[118]

Obama's American Narrative

In that same post-midterm press conference the president said:

> and I think they understood that my story was theirs. I might have a funny name, I might have lived in some different places, but the values of hard work and responsibility and honesty and looking out for one another that had been instilled in them by their parents, those were the same values that I took from my mom and my grandparents.

In this observation, as he did throughout the campaign, the president skillfully blended his narrative story with the iconic themes of American life—hard work and responsibility—and in a general sense those two narratives do fit. Obama came from a middle-class background, had grandparents who helped raise him and certainly loved and were willing to sacrifice for him. His mother, a more distant and equivocal presence in his life, nonetheless tried to steer him in the right direction. And Obama did eventually invest in making something of himself and obviously succeeded to an extent that is possible in few other places in the world.

Yet, while the general lines of the two narratives blend, Obama's real life story is much more complex, psychologically, socially, and politically than the iconic American narrative to which he laid claim. His real life history contains an edge to it—of being a black youth raised in a white family caught between the lingering racial grievances of the 1960s and his own primarily "post-racial experience" as a talented minority young man in a society eager to make amends for its past racial transgressions.

The other edge to Obama's real coming of age narrative, also strategically hidden, was his wholesale acceptance of the liberal democratic policy agenda and worldview. This element, too, involved grievances, though of a political nature, about the past domestic and international policies of the country and the need to change and make up for them. Both the racial and the political worldview were instrumental in forging this president's transformative and redemptive ambitions.

It seems safe to say that not many Americans realized the relationship in Obama's mind between redemption and transformation. Hope and change might conceivably have been linked to "transformation," but since Obama never provided much detail every voter was free to fill in the empty frame himself. Had Obama overtly expressed his view that America had committed racial and political sins, and that it therefore needed to be redeemed, through his political, economic, and cultural transformative policies, framed by fairness, he would have never been elected.

In that profound sense the public did not really know Obama at all. Once they did begin to gain some measure of the president's intentions, though not necessarily of their sources in his worldview and psychology, they became alarmed—and voted accordingly.

The Reality of the Obama-American Public Relationship

Obama followed up the comments about his personal story with this observation:

> And the relationship that I've had with the American people is one that built slowly, peaked at this incredible high, and then during the course of the last two years, as we've, together, gone through some very difficult times, has gotten rockier and tougher. And it's going to, I'm sure, have some more ups and downs during the course of me being in this office.

The president's understanding is that the public had ample opportunity to get to really know him in Iowa, and perhaps by extension elsewhere during the campaign, and didn't "have any complaints about my leadership style" then. And this leads him to express the view that his relationship with the American people has been a long one that "built slowly" and was presumably deeper for having been through that process. After slowly building, it then "peaked at this incredible high and then in the last two years, as we've gone through some very difficult times, has gotten rockier and tougher."

The reality is quite a bit different. Obama was elected to the presidency on a dual tidal wave of fatigue, anger, and disappointment with the Bush administration and its direct and related counterpart, a buoyant sense of hope-induced optimism that the election of Barack Obama would represent a transforming emotional event. This transformation was not about policy, since the public had little to go on regarding what, specifically, Obama would do, other than the campaign mantra of "hope and change." Rather it represented the wish, among Democratic loyalists to be sure but also among the significant numbers of independent voters that Obama won over, that his election would represent a turning point in bringing the country back to an imagined politics that was less partisan and less divisive.

It is an observation, not a criticism, to say that this hope represented a great deal of very understandable wishful thinking, that was doomed to disappointment because of the president's transformative and redemptive agenda, and also surprisingly, his repeated use of harsh rhetoric to demonize those who disagreed with him.

During his election campaign the president and his advisors amped up public expectations, and it worked. Baker notes of this that it is Obama himself, and not just his supporters, who cast his presidency in grandiose terms.

> As he pleaded with Democrats for patience at another fund-raiser in Washington two weeks later: "It took time to free the slaves. It took time for women to get the vote. It took time for workers to get the right to organize."[119]

In his interview Peter Baker recalled to the president that when he secured the Democratic nomination in June 2008, he told an admiring crowd that someday "we will be able to look back and tell our children that this was the moment when we began to provide care for the sick and good jobs to the jobless; this was the moment when the rise of the oceans began to slow and our planet began to heal; this was the moment when we ended a war and secured our nation and restored our image as the last, best hope on earth."[120]

Baker continued, "I read that line to Obama and asked how his high-flying rhetoric sounded in these days of low-flying governance. 'It sounds ambitious,' he agreed. ... "[121] Not excessive. Not overreaching. Not grandiose. Ambitious.

The president then proceeded to claim that he had more than lived up to all the promises he had made:

> "But you know what? We've made progress on each of those fronts. ... But the prose and the poetry match up," he said. "It would be very hard for people to look back and say, You know what, Obama didn't do what he's promised. I think they could say, on a bunch of fronts he still has an incomplete. But I keep a checklist of what we committed to doing, and we've probably accomplished 70 percent of the things that we talked about during the campaign. And I hope as long as I'm president, I've got a chance to work on the other 30 percent."

Conclusion: The President's Understanding as Prologue?

The president, as noted consistently in this analysis, is a very smart man. And this raises an issue regarding the president's response to the election. The president has repeatedly refused to entertain the idea, in public, or even in private, as reported by his advisors, that his policies and the public's reaction to them had any part in the election's results. The most he has been willing to say is that going forward the result of the election "requires me to make some midcourse corrections and adjustments."[122] But he has also made very clear that, "If the question is, over the next two years do I take a pass on tough stuff, *the answer is no.*"[123]

This suggests that the president's approach will be one of *strategic accommodation*, making rhetorical moves to the center and finding some areas like extending the Bush tax cuts on a temporary basis that are unavoidable accommodations. The president's post-election outreach to the Chamber of Commerce, whom he branded during the campaign as "a threat to democracy,"[124] seems to fit this effort.

So does the president's suggestion that, "it is going to be important for Democrats to have a *proper and appropriate sense of humility* about what we can accomplish *in the absence of Republican cooperation.*"[125] As always with the president, it is important to pay close attention to his words. The sense of humility he recommends for Democrats is not because he thinks that he and they have overreached, but rather because Republicans will keep them from continuing to build on the agenda they pursued in his first two years in office.

His stance raises several crucial questions. Does the president really and sincerely believe that the content and direction of his policies played no important role in the results of the midterm elections? Or, is this merely a political stance adapted to avoid blame, which would in turn require the president to publicly admit that he was wrong? One could understand a president's ordinary reluctance to publicly admit mistakes, but in this case the consequences of doing so would be dramatic. It would call into question President Obama's judgment in insisting on mistaken policies, made worse by the fact that he did so over the clear objection of a substantial portion, over time, of the American public.

It's possible that going forward the president might well act on the knowledge that he was mistaken, without necessarily publicly admitting it. If this were the case we would look for a more heart-felt embrace of finding real common ground—ground more consistent with the right-center views of a majority of the American public on the various issues that might come up. We can call this outcome *real, though tacit, acknowledgment.*

That outcome is unlikely.

No political scientist, and especially one trained in psychology, can rule out the likelihood that this president—ambitious, risk embracing, highly confident in his assessments and judgments, and motivated by a life-long quest for redemption (his and ours as a country)—clearly believes what he has said. The election was a matter of not having sold his policies effectively enough, their positive effect having not reached people soon enough, and the climate of fear because of which the public misperceived what he was accomplishing.

Early on in his development Obama developed the emotional style of being able to stand apart from others. Others are ordinarily more connected to him than he is to them. As a result, Obama shows almost none of the need to be liked that is so often found in politicians seeking public favor and office. Yet, Obama does have an Achilles heel in this area and it revolves around his desire to be validated as the person he aspires to be—the transformational leader with the stature of a Lincoln and the moral authority of a Reverend King.

Interestingly, "In their darkest moments, White House aides wonder aloud whether it is even possible for a modern president to succeed, no matter how many bills he signs."[126] But of course bill signings, as noted, may not be the best measure of successful presidential leadership. Moreover,

> White House aides who were ready to carve a new spot on Mount Rushmore for their boss two years ago privately concede now that he cannot be another Abraham Lincoln after all. In this environment, they have increasingly concluded, it may be that every modern president is going to be, at best, average.[127]

This seems like a premature judgment on the possibilities of the modern presidency and it is certainly inconsistent with the president's view of himself and the redemption and transformation he hopes to accomplish.

Up until this election, Obama had received enormous validation of this self-image in ways too numerous to repeat here again. Yet, this midterm election, whatever else it proves to be politically, was a stinging rebuke to that self-image. That was, no doubt, behind Obama's unusually direct answer to the question "What does it [the election results] feel like?" He answered simply: "It feels bad" before going on to claim that those Democrats who had lost their reelection on his behalf said it was worth it.[128]

In 2000, Obama, impatient with his progress up the political ladder, decided to run for Congress against an incumbent Bobby Rush. Obama was soundly beaten and wrote of that experience years later, "I still burn ... with the thought of my one loss in politics, a drubbing. ... "[129] He went on to say, "no matter how much you tell yourself differently—no matter how convincingly you attribute the loss to bad timing or bad luck or lack of money—it's impossible not to feel at some level as if you have been personally repudiated by the entire community, that you don't quite have what it takes, and that everywhere you go the word 'loser' is flashing through other people's minds."[130]

Four years later he was a U.S. Senator from Illinois. The lesson here is that Obama is a resilient man and his ambitions buttress that trait. He did not give up his ambitions after losing badly to Bobby Rush then and he is unlikely to do so now, especially while occupying the only office capable of translating his transformative ambitions into actual political fact. Vindication of one's original premises about oneself after a setback is a powerful motivation. This is especially true for a president whose view of himself is much more consistent with the early response of the American public to him than its later one.

Barack Obama, recall, is also a person with unusually well developed and refined adaptive skills. He relentlessly practiced and mastered the art of preacher talk at African American churches and now slips into and out of that vernacular effortlessly. He learned how to play golf and poker in order to become one of the boys as a state senator in Springfield. And there is no doubt that Obama's now fully mature, extremely malleable, and self-protective persona will be able to devise and execute a plan that will allow him to successfully preserve and marshal his resources to await the next transformative opportunities, should they present themselves.

One thing though is clear. If real redemption requires a public acknowledgement of an error, a commitment to change your ways and some evidence of that in the form of helping to make whole those you have harmed by your behavior, then whatever subdued feelings Obama showed at his post midterm news conference, he was not repentant and was clearly not seeking redemption. The fault, if any, lay in the economy,[131] his own concentration on doing what was right and his neglect of "politics."

There is an irony and not a little poignancy in Obama's present circumstances. This very talented late bloomer, the author of his own redemption, was determined to redeem his deceased father's failed legacy as a transformative leader by redeeming the country he now leads, by insisting that it live up to his and his mother's ideals by becoming "fairer." Now though, after the midterm election vote, Obama finds himself faced with a stark choice.

Is he willing to redeem his presidency by renouncing our country's transformation? Or, as seems more consistent with his psychology and worldview, is Obama biding his time awaiting the next redemptive opportunity—to resurrect the transformative presidency that is so central to what he sees as his own unique historical mission?

APPENDIX A: ANALYZING BARACK OBAMA

A Note on Theory, Method, Evidence, and Inference

An analysis of a sitting president, especially one not fully through his first term, framed by the perspectives of political psychology raises a number of clear and legitimate questions. The most obvious and immediate are: Isn't it rather early to pursue such a project and won't there be much more information available after the president has left office? The answers to these questions are, respectively, as will be made clear, no and yes.

Those are not the only questions that could be legitimately asked. Others concern such a study's concepts (how valid?), its methods (which one(s)?), its evidence (what and from where?), and the nature and validity of the inferences that are being made (how valid are any conclusions drawn and what is the basis and nature of the underlying reasoning?).

These are all reasonable questions and they deserve, indeed require answers. Those answers are not only relevant to the legitimacy of the analysis. They also represent a roadmap for conducting it, or at least the framework for the analysis employed in this study. No representation is made here that it is the only or the best roadmap available. It represents only the one I have developed and found useful in over a decade of working on presidents, candidates, and leaders. Of course, its usefulness cannot depend on my testimonial, but also on a transparent and ultimately convincing explanation of its procedures and, of course, the quality of its results.

This work on Barack Obama is, as I mentioned in the Preface, my third book-length analysis of a sitting president. The subject of the first was Bill Clinton[1] and the second was of George W. Bush.[2] These books were preceded by another, *The Psychological Assessment of Presidential Candidates*.[3] That book laid out the theoretical template for the two presidential studies that followed, and this one as well. It developed and applied a psychological theory of character made up of three core elements—ambition, character integrity, and relatedness, and examined their relationship to what I posited were the two key performance elements of the modern presidency—presidential leadership and presidential judgment.

A Blended Deductive/Inductive Analysis

That framework, as it developed, incorporated aspects of both an inductive and deductive approach at the two different theoretical levels at which it operates. The first level concerns the relationship of the biographical and political data to the character and performance elements of the framework. The second concerns the relationship of the analysis of a specific president, in this case Mr. Obama, to the usefulness of the framework for other presidents.

So for example ambition is one of the three key elements of any person or president's character. Yet, presidents differ in their level of ambition, the quality of the skills they bring to bear on being able to realize it, whether it is anchored by ideals and values, and what its purposes are. Information relevant to these core building blocks is to be found in the detailed analysis of biographical and behavioral data.

The same is true of the character integrity elements. Here the analyst must become immersed in the facts surrounding the development of a president's core political beliefs and worldview and then closely examine his personal and professional life to see if and when he has been clearly identified with those views and stood up for them in circumstances where doing so might result in personal or political loss.

The third basic character element, relatedness, reflects a president's approach to dealing with the range of his relationships—mentors, advisors, confidants, supporters, critics, and adversaries. Here again, the analyst must delve deeply in the president's developmental and political experiences to gather data that would allow an assessment of these relationships and draw some general conclusions from them.

In short then, the basic elements of this framework are themselves conceptually stable, but their exact nature for a particular president vary. In developing the data that fill in the specific nature of the character elements and their effect on presidential leadership and judgment for Mr. Obama, we are essentially developing a theory of the Obama presidency. Yet, this framework has now been applied to three quite different presidents, and that raises the possibility that it may be useful for the analysis of modern presidents, in general. That is, although modern presidents like Clinton, George W. Bush and Obama might, and do, differ with regard to the nature of the three character elements and how each plays out in relation to the two key elements of presidential performance, it is possible that these character and performance elements and the relationships among them might have some general applicability. It is then, the difference between a theory of the Obama presidency and a theory of modern presidential performance, with the comparative case studies of the individual cases helping to develop the more general applicability of the theoretical framework.

One critical caveat that needs to be underscored here is that the above framework is not premised on the assumption that "character explains all." Every president, and Obama is no exception, comes into an office that has an institutional history and as a result, operates within a developed set of leadership opportunities and constraints. Leadership itself is a transactional word that requires paying close attention to public issues and psychology. And judgment can only be applied to the choices that a president faces, not all of which are of his own choosing. The president's choices in the mix of his own ambitions and values, the circumstances that he confronts, and the results of his own decisions and those of others define the arena in which this framework seems to hold the most promise.

The Developmental Path of a Research Agenda

The theoretical work described above covers, at this point, over a decade of analysis on conceptual and methodological issues arising in the psychological assessment of presidents and candidates, as well as the analysis of specific candidates and presidents. The *Assessment* book began down that path by taking up the issue of the ethics of undertaking a psychological analysis of a sitting president at a distance[4] and an appendix that took up issues of method including selection of cases, data, and analysis.[5] That book also undertook analyses of several presidents and candidates, among them, the 1964 *Fact Magazine* psychological assessment of presidential candidate Barry Goldwater,[6] Thomas Eagleton (George McGovern's vice presidential choice) who was forced from the ticket because he had undergone shock treatments for depression,[7] and Senator Gary Hart who was forced to resign as a presidential candidate over character allegations in 1987.[8] It also contained a before-after analysis of Bill Clinton as a candidate and then four years into his first term as president.[9]

The purpose of that analysis was to examine how well the character-presidential performance framework developed in the book and applied to candidate Clinton actually captured his leadership and decision judgment as president. After he left office, I published another paper that compared my earlier pre-presidential analysis with his leadership and decision-making during the two terms of his presidency.[10] Again, the purpose was to see to what extent the analysis of President Clinton as a presidential candidate was useful in anticipating his actual behavior as president.

In addition, my book-length study of the Clinton presidency (*High Hopes*), contained an appendix, as this book does, specifically focused on methodological issues encountered in undertaking a book-length psychological framed analysis of a president's developmental history and its relationship to the twin pillars of presidential performance.[11] I've also published papers on John McCain and the limits of trait theory,[12] on analyzing presidential candidate Robert Dole at a distance,[13] a comparative analysis of Bill Clinton and George W. Bush that focused on methodological issues,[14] and a book chapter specifically devoted to further addressing the theoretical and methodological issues connected with the psychological analysis of presidents.[15]

Finally, and immediately relevant to this analysis, is that shortly before he took office, I published a prospective analysis of Barack Obama and John McCain based on their life histories and presidential candidacies which sought to lay out some contours, baselines, and parameters of a possible Obama or McCain presidency.[16] This book represents another chance to check that preliminary baseline analysis of Mr. Obama against the early unfolding of his actual leadership and judgment as president.

The interested reader is invited to examine those book chapters and papers for more detailed consideration of the theoretical, methodological, and inferential issues that arise in the course of such work. However, here, I want to focus on some of the specific issues that are relevant to this president, Barack Obama, including some that seem to be unique to him or future leaders like him. I will, for the most part, not repeat in detail the analyses to be found in the above referenced books and papers, and will only note their major points when they bear on this analysis.

What Kind of Analysis?

One important set of distinctions to draw at the outset concern exactly what kind of analysis this is, and what it hopes to accomplish. The answer to the first question is that it draws on Mr. Obama's developmental history, including his adulthood, to illuminate his leadership style and decision choices as president.

I use the phrase "an analysis of Mr. Obama and his presidency from a political psychology perspective" to describe this and my other analyses of aspiring and sitting presidents. In both separating and linking the man and his presidency, I am underscoring the point that while this analysis draws on Obama's biographical history, it is not strictly speaking a biography. I am not interested in all the details or aspects of Obama's early or later life, only those that when they have been examined and compared with other evidence, help us understand his presidency. This is not an *a priori* process. In other words, I have not started with a theory of what themes are important in Obama's life, but rather have carefully read his books, interviews, and others' recollections to develop a set of themes that appear to merit attention.

Some of these themes emerge with great clarity and obviousness. His father's abandonment of his family and Obama's reaction to it, as well as the theme of finding a fitting racial identity are two such obvious themes. Other themes, like his mother's time away from the family and Obama's apparently self-conscious development of a style and persona have received less attention, but are nonetheless evident in any careful consideration of his developmental history.

Note that to have uncovered an important theme is not to have understood its meaning or its relationship to other elements in the "should analyze" package assembled by the research. The themes are possible building blocks to an understanding of Mr. Obama and his performance as president, not a theory of it.

The psychoanalytic or "psychodynamic" perspective involves the search for patterns, the relationship of patterns to other patterns, and then developing theories that help to make sense of them, while linking all these patterns to the crucial questions of Obama's presidency. And that raises an important point about the limits of the focus of this analysis; an examination of developmental elements involved is limited by their demonstrated connection to Obama's presidential judgment and leadership. I have argued elsewhere that these twin elements are the essential core of presidential performance,[17] and will not repeat that analysis here. The point here is that many elements of Mr. Obama's life might conceivably have an impact on these two key presidential performance elements, however it is the analysts' responsibility to make a strong, logical, and convincing case for the elements he includes.

Here again, some key relationships form a strong prima facie case for inclusion. Mr. Obama's intellectual dexterity and rhetorical poise are clearly relevant to the public leadership role that he has taken for his administration. Mr. Obama's calm, deliberative style is clearly linked to his presidential leadership, the process through which he reaches decisions, and finally, the quality of his judgments, although describing the nature of the linkages and assessing their implications, and evaluating their consequences are separate matters.

Even a clear and demonstrable link between an element of Mr. Obama's psychology and presidency does not end the analysts' responsibility or work. This was brought home to me rather directly when I shared a draft of my book proposal with my son Jonathan, who is writing his dissertation in Harvard's Government Department. In it, I had made the somewhat obvious point that Obama's self-defined racial identity was a clear theme in his development and part of his racial reconciliation appeal to many American voters. My son agreed with the point but urged upon me a higher standard of inclusion in this case, namely that the theme of racial identity should have some direct relevance not only to Obama's persona as a post-partisan leader, but also to policy premises and choices. That conversation set off a train of thinking that culminated in my linking of Obama's racial identity and history with the theme of redemption that is part of the title and a theoretical framework for the analysis of this book.

The Meaning of the Term "Political Psychology"

A point needs to be clarified here about the several levels of meaning of the word "psychology" in the phrase "political psychology analysis." At the most basic level this phrase reflects an important understanding, whose implications are easy to lose sight of. First, this analysis is both psychological *and* political. This is not the result of any pro forma efforts to be theoretically even-handed, but rather flows from the nature of the relationship of the person to the presidency and the elemental core requirements of that office; leadership and decision judgment. These are the "dependent variables" of this presidential analysis that we want to be able to understand and account for. These two are obviously not the only elements of a presidency that one might study, but having selected these on the basis of their substantial claim to relevance, it is equally clear that psychology will play an important role in helping us to gain substantive and theoretical traction.

Just how much traction psychological or political theory and analysis can provide is also not an *a priori* matter. The phrase *political psychology* denotes a framework for analysis that takes both of its elements seriously, as it must in studying presidential leadership and political judgment. The presidency is at once a very deeply political and psychological office and nowhere is this fusion more evident than in a president's leadership and judgments. Yet, how much psychology and how much politics depend on the specific president and his political and policy circumstances, and the specific issues or questions that are the focus of analysis.

Leadership for example, seems ordinarily to have more of a political component than judgment since it involves assessing and responding to public views of policy appropriateness, legitimacy, and desirability. Decision judgments, on the other hand, ordinarily involve us more deeply in how the president frames and understands a particular policy problem, how he weighs the information available and according to what criteria, and how skillfully he is able to explain his thinking and persuade others of its net advantages. This last element of course, returns us directly to the question of presidential leadership.

Which Psychology?

Beyond trying to ascertain the right mixes of psychological and political elements in a particular aspect of the overall analysis, lies the question of which kind of psychology seems indicated. Here it pays to be conversant with the range of psychological theories available for use and their appropriateness for the problem at hand. The analyst who wants to explore presidential judgment had better be conversant with a range of cognitive theories focused on framing and the information processing heuristics that follow, as well as the nature of belief systems and the use of analogies and metaphors. Psychoanalytic theories of character might well add value to the analysis. However, they are no substitute for analyzing the cognitive processes that are instrumental as leaders try to weigh options and information to reach sound and feasible policy judgments.

A focus on the president's leadership skills and style moves us away from an emphasis on the theoretical tools of cognitive psychology and toward the domains of character, persona, and group psychology. Here again, the analyst must be conversant with the range of theoretical tools available. A president's leadership is directly related to his ambitions, the persona and style he has developed, the ideals and values he pursues, and the personal skills he can bring to bear on this critical presidential task.

A focus on ambition requires knowledge of the various theories that purport to account for and explain it. This would point the analyst toward theories that link levels of ambition with the dynamics of narcissism—the nature and importance of ambition to self-regard, confidence, and risk taking, all of which have obvious linkages to presidential judgment and decision-making. For a president like Barack Obama, the analyst cannot help but see his enormous ambitions, his substantial self-confidence, and the well-honed personal tools like his strong intelligence, rhetorical presence, and cool demeanor that he developed in the service of achieving his goals.

A focus on the president's leadership also requires, and this is especially the case with President Obama, some knowledge of the theories that help us to understand the public's response to events and presidential attempts to address them. The president has said more than once that, "I am like a Rorschach test,"[18] a point that emphasizes both the opaque nature of Obama's leadership style and its role in allowing the public to attribute their hopes, aspirations, and preferences to him. Yet, here too, the political element of the phrase political psychology presses for attention since Rorschach-like campaign terms such as "hope" and "change" must eventually give way to the requirements of governing on the basis of concrete policies.

The two years plus of Obama's presidency have been characterized by his decision to simultaneously pursue a number of large complex domestic and foreign policy initiatives. Domestically, those areas include enormous infusions of new money for an array of social and political programs, health care, and energy policy. In foreign policy, the president is seeking to resolve the Arab-Israeli conflict, reset relationships with allies and enemies alike, move toward a nuclear-free world, and resolve the tendentious issues of Iran, Iraq, and North Korea. The decision to set all these large policy initiatives in motion not only reflects the size and range of Obama's policy ambitions, but also represents a clear test of his political judgment, and is as well an enormous test of his leadership skills, and a reflection of his willingness to take very large risks on behalf of the country.

While the president is a smooth, knowledgeable, and articulate champion of his preferred policies, his initiatives like health care are large, complex, and consequential in ways that no one in his administration has tried to, or perhaps is capable of predicting. This has created a substantial degree of public ambivalence and anxiety. This set of circumstances provides a test not only of President Obama's leadership skills but also of our theories of what it takes to succeed in the circumstances that characterize Obama's ambitions and the response of the public to them.

Adequately understanding the unfolding relationship between the nature of a president's ambition, skills and leadership style, along with the objectives he hopes to accomplish, and the public's response to them is simply not possible without the clarifying tools of both psychological and political theories. Yet, neither is it possible without delving into the details of the policies that the president is pursuing. This takes us some distance away from the strictly psychology part of the term political psychology, but it is an absolutely essential requirement for understanding the leadership and choices before the president.

The wide ranging health care, economic, and foreign policy initiatives that the president is undertaking involve interventions in very large and complex systems that have complicated histories and may well be responsive to a number of policy options. No presidential scholar is likely to be expert in all these areas; this one certainly is not. That said, it is the responsibility of the analyst to be conversant, though not necessarily expert, in the basic elements of the issues that he makes use of in analyzing a president.

And finally, there is the question of the president's political judgment. The president made a decision to push his initiatives on immense spending, health care, and energy policy immediately on entering office and in the face of a severe recession. He might have chosen to substantially focus on the economy, and assuming some success on addressing the range of issues associated with not only preventing catastrophic damage, but also helping economic recovery. He could then have pressed for his other initiatives. The decision to go full-steam ahead on many fronts certainly reflects the scope and depth of the president's policy ambitions; but it also reflects important aspects of his governing psychology. It suggests that the president is willing to take large risks, on his own behalf and on ours. And that fact brings the analyst face to face with the vexing problem of reaching conclusions.

Reaching Conclusions

At some point the analyst of any presidency is faced with a choice. He or she can keep their analysis at the level of description and explanation or can draw on it to make what amounts to a net assessment, a characterization of the president's efforts, the skills and means enlisted in these efforts, and the relative success of these efforts in accomplishing their purposes. The analyst would have to reach some judgment about a president's efforts and their success.

Obviously, the ability of a book written while the president is still in the first years of his term to provide a useful judgment of this presidency's overall success or likely historical standing is a large risk in itself. In politics, as in life, circumstances can rapidly change, and the unexpected can rapidly reframe a presidency for better or worse. George H. W. Bush was much acclaimed because he brought together a large international coalition to reverse Iraq's invasion of Kuwait, but became a one-term president because the economy soured. His son began his presidency as a "compassionate conservative" but spent almost all of his two terms in office dealing with the consequences of the 9/11 terrorist attacks.

So too, the effects of many large-scale policies of the kind that President Obama is attempting will take years to fully bring to fruition. And that assumes they become law and work as planned or hoped. A key rationale for the president's health care initiative is it will eventually lower health care costs. Yet one analysis noted, "No one knows precisely how to fix the problems that lead to runaway costs, and even if solutions become apparent, they would take years to implement."[19]

And finally, assessments of a president and his policy initiatives are themselves responsive to unfolding historical circumstances and debates long after he leaves office. Harry Truman left office vilified in many quarters and with very low public approval ratings. Yet, his muscular response to Soviet ambitions in Western Europe is now lauded on a bi-partisan basis as iconic. Americans are still arguing about the lessons and meaning of Vietnam,[20] and even the somewhat iconic "New Deal" response to the 1930s economic depression has been the subject of a revisionist analysis.[21] All of these considerations make reaching any definitive judgments about the Obama presidency or its policies an exercise fraught with difficulty and potentially rife with error. Accordingly, no such effort will be made.

That said, it is still possible to attempt some tentative assessment of specific elements of a president's approach or judgments. What can we say, on balance, about the president's leadership approach and its consequences, at least in so far as we have observed them? How well does his leadership style address the tendentious issues of ideology and governance that have come to dominate American public life? And finally, how well do his judgments reflect a fitting solution to the problems he addresses?

Any presidential analyst wishing to make even these minimal assessments cannot be content with knowledge of either politics or psychology at the conceptual or theoretical level. As noted, any analyst of presidential leadership should be conversant with the policies that the president has chosen so that informed judgments can be made about what the president emphasizes, neglects, misrepresents or chooses to focus upon. Certainly, any presidential analyst assessing the president's judgment on a particular policy matter must himself be aware of the debates surrounding those issues, the weight of evidence on one or another side, and have developed a substantive basis for being able to weigh these elements.

In the past some have thought it sufficient when analyzing a large presidential initiative, like the president's health care proposals, to talk in general about the president's ambition, or to encapsulate their understanding with a few summary statements. Given the complexities that become clear if one spends sufficient time with the substantial flow of information now available, this should no longer suffice. Again, this does not require the analyst to become an expert in micro or macro economic theory, health care policy, or the nuances of missile defense. It does require that if the analysts' assessment of a president's leadership or judgment hinges in some substantial part on these policy matters, it is necessary to become conversant, not simply acquainted, with them.

All of these elements must be attended to for even a *preliminary* analysis, and that obviously is the farthest reach of this book's evaluative ambitions. A detailed knowledge of a president's developmental history, his personal and political trajectory before reaching the presidency, the revealing rigors of a presidential campaign, and a substantial period of time as president can allow baseline judgments and analysis to be made, against which the fuller record can be assessed at some future point in time.

Interview the President?

A question that frequently arises for analysts of presidents in office is whether you have interviewed the president. It is not impossible to do. Bob Woodward of the

Washington Post interviewed President Bush and his chief foreign policy advisors, repeatedly, for his books on the Iraq War.

Robert Draper, a reporter for the *Texas Monthly* who first met Bush when he came to the paper's editorial office for an interview in 1996, then spent more time with him for a profile to appear in GQ. Later, in order to get to conduct a series of interviews for a book he was doing on the then president, he went through the West Wing office of Bush's counselor Dan Bartlett to discuss his project, who was very discouraging, though allowing him to interview a series of White House officials. Draper did this for close to two years, before he was finally given limited access to the president. After that it took four more months before the president decided to give him time for a real interview. Thereafter, the president warmed to the project and Draper was able to gain five more interviews. It's worth noting that the president and his advisors changed their minds about the project after the costs of the president's decisions on Iraq, Katrina, and others had taken their toll on his standing and it was clear that he would leave office deeply unpopular.[22] As a result, he was interested in someone whom he, and his advisors thought, could present a fair and, in their view, more balanced picture.

The problems of access are real and difficult to surmount, but there are other considerations as well. The Woodward books focus on a major and controversial war. The president, confident in the judgments he felt he had to make, wanted someone privy to them, and Woodward had a highly successful publishing history of such works. Draper was allowed access when it suited the president's need for someone who might be fair, or at least wasn't clearly oppositional, to present his case. Presidential time and access is a leadership asset deployed for a purpose—the administration's.

Then, consider a project like this focused on a president's developmental history, character, and psychological development, and their impact on his leadership and judgment. What president would accede to help such a project? Any serious consideration of these issues would, at a minimum, require probing that takes the subject beyond the conventional narratives established by the president and his advisors to gain office and maintain political leverage.

A biographer interested in sorting out the psychological issues of the president's early life might well wish to inquire about his ambivalent feelings toward his father who abandoned him and whom he idealized at first, only to be disappointed by learning of the reality of his life. He or she would also have to deal with the president's clear slighting of the impact of his mother on his life in his first book, his feelings about her abandonment of him several times as a young boy and then an adolescent, and the subsequent migration of his idealization to her after he had become disappointed with his father.

These are obviously profoundly personal issues and professional and personal tact would require anyone interested in asking these questions to do so only with the advanced consent of the person being interviewed. And why would the president offer that? Obama has already, in his own mind, settled those matters. He is quoted as saying, "*There was a time in my life* when I had that feeling, because of an absent father, of always being a little bit of an outsider—you can psychoanalyze me and say 'Here's why he's a driven person.'"[23] Elsewhere he has said while discussing his father,

> I can't guarantee that my interpretation of him is the right one, *but in my own mind at least I am at rest with the idea that this was someone who made an awful lot of mistakes in his life*, but at least I understand why.[24]

So having settled the matter in his own mind, the president would be on solid ground in asking from his perspective: what's the point of revisiting them?

Even on subjects much less personal and charged than the president's deepest feelings about his parents and himself, a biographer fortunate to get interview time would have enormous barriers to surmount in order to get anything very useful. Michael Powell, a *New York Times* reporter who interviewed Obama and was himself interviewed about that experience had this to say: "Obama's a very challenging cat to cover. He's a writer himself, and a quite perceptive writer. So he tends to look at himself and everything around him with a writer's eye. And *also therefore tends to have defenses up in interesting ways.* Interviewing him is a challenge, trying to pull him out of that and get him talking about something."

Powell goes on to relate that a subject came up by "luck" since they both had been on the same grueling campaign schedule and began to talk about how it was possible to get in any reading. Powell goes on to say, "I just went with it because it's far more interesting to use your time that way than to try to get him to talk about Pakistan. *Then he's going to retreat into talking points.*"[25]

And there is finally, what may appear to be a somewhat odd, but nonetheless relevant question of what might the president contribute. Obviously, it is the president's life being discussed, but people are not always aware of their beliefs and the feelings that accompany them, or the effects they exert. This is not only an understanding of psychoanalytic theory,[26] but of cognitive psychology as well.[27] Discussing the nature of beliefs, Bob Jervis noted that,

> the reasons we give for many of our beliefs are sincere in that we do believe them, but these are stories we tell ourselves as well as others because *we understand as little about what is driving our beliefs* as we do about what is driving others.[28]

A researcher would be on firmer ground in limiting his or her questions to the president's views and enactment of leadership and the ways in which he understood and acted on his choices. Yet, a number of familiar issues arise. Assuming access and this more narrow focus, the potential for gaining new information would have to be weighed against the fact that the president is often asked about his leadership and his policy judgments in numerous news interviews and Q&A sessions. Moreover, every modern president has many key advisors who are well aware of the importance of these conceptual and political categories, and spend a great deal of time constructing and disseminating a favorable presidential narrative on these matters.

When President Obama was making his decision about whether and how many troops to commit to the war in Afghanistan "senior officials" repeatedly provided commentary on his decision-making style.[29] These narratives were designed to showcase the calm, deliberative, and comprehensive nature of the review process, and the president's key role in encouraging and maintaining that approach. A great deal less information was forthcoming around the nature of the alternatives considered, the assumptions underlying them, and the arguments made for or against them—all central concerns in assessing the range and quality of the options considered and the judgments made. It is possible, but not likely that a president would be candidly willing to discuss these matters.

The president himself has opined on his own qualities as a decision maker. He has said of himself, "What I do have confidence about is that I am a good listener, I'm good at synthesizing advice from a range of different perspectives. ... "[30] He has described himself as a "pragmatist," a decision maker who doesn't approach

> problems by asking myself, is this a conservative—is there a conservative approach to this or a liberal approach to this, is there a Democratic or Republican approach to this. I come at it and say, what's the way to solve the problem, what's the way to achieve an outcome where the American people have jobs or their health care quality has improved or our schools are producing a well educated workforce of the 21st century.[31]

Whether, and to what degree these self-observations are accurate is not the point here. They clearly reflect the president's and his advisors' views of the qualities that make the president a good decision maker. Equally important, those views are central to the public's view of the president's leadership qualities and their assumption that these qualities are positive and lead to good decision-making. Decision-making theorists understand that these two elements *may* be related, but that the latter do not necessarily follow from the former.

At any rate, these views are strongly held by both the president and his advisors. They are important public leadership tools for maintaining and extending their political leverage. Moreover, no modern president gains office without the ability to defend his views and positions, including most importantly his views of his own qualifications for office. The idea that a president would welcome the opportunity for a series of extended discussions on the advantages and disadvantages of his leadership or decision style, along with a frank conversation about how they have played out with regard to significant issues like the war in Afghanistan or the decision to pursue a comprehensive rather than more limited presidential agenda is implausible.

Psychologically minded presidential analysts do not have x-ray vision with which they can divine the president's "real" views or interior emotional life with the aid of a skilled and subtle interview. In real life, in therapeutic settings, such information emerges over time, in response to in-depth probing of both experience and understandings and even then it can sometimes remain hidden for years.

The reality is that in some ways the presidential analyst has an advantage over the psychoanalyst because the latter is ordinarily confined to what the patient chooses to tell. A presidential biographer who is also a psychoanalyst operates under no such limitations and has the advantage of being able to cast a wide net. He can include what the president and others have said about his life and policies. He can gather data across developmental periods and across time and policies within a presidential administration. He can read the policy papers that define the arguments on topics that the president must or chooses to address. And if he has done other in depth work on particular presidents that can operate to provide alternative frames of reference they can act as both a stimulus and a check to the explanations developed for this particular president.

The Dilemmas of Analyzing President Obama

The presidency is a singularly powerful, important, and iconic office in American political life. It has also over time become the epicenter of policy initiatives. Partially as a result of that and the increasingly strong voices raised in defense of or in opposition to these policies, the person occupying that office is the object of strong emotions. The last two presidents, William J. Clinton and George W. Bush, aroused extraordinary passions from the right and left respectively, but President Obama presents a truly unique manifestation of this issue.

He is, of course, a major historical figure by virtue of being the first American of African descent to run for and win the presidency. His election also unleashed an unprecedented level of expectation both in the United States and abroad. For a substantial number of people, Obama has assumed iconic status, a status that is infused with powerful feelings of affection and even adulation.

Yet, at the same time, his presidency has, very early on, become highly polarized. Even after the tumultuous presidencies of his two predecessors, a Pew Research Center poll found Obama's approval rating among Democrats was an astronomical 88 percent and among Republicans a dismal 27 percent, for a gap of 61 percent, characterized as "the most polarized early job approval ratings for a new president in 40 years."[32]

Transparency and Transference

These strong emotional and political currents require caution on the part of the Obama analyst in several respects. There is, of course, in every instance of scholarship the issue of how fair, dispassionate, and accurate the analysis is. There is no sense in pretending that most social science analysis is "value free" as the "behavioral revolution" once aspired to, and perhaps some still do. Rather, it seems to be a matter of fairly considering evidence and transparency in the data analysis and the inferences derived from it. One essential aspect of analytic fairness is consideration of alternative facts and explanations.

Anyone, analyzing the president's leadership judgment and first two years of office, for example, would have to address his Afghanistan engagement policy, and the war against al-Qaeda. To take the latter briefly, for purposes of illustration, you would not have to read widely to come across the view that the administration mishandled the questioning of Farouk Abdulmutallab, the man who tried to blow up a plane on Christmas day.[33] That event triggered a rhetorical policy war, conducted on major Sunday news programs between the former and present vice presidents on the administration's approach to a critically important set of national security issues.[34] Conservatives emphasize the failure to designate Abdulmutallab an "enemy combatant," a symptom of overall weakness in the administration's approach to the war on terror. Yet, any analysis in this area would also have to take into account some very robust actions on the part of the Obama administration. These would have to include the fact that Obama has ordered a dramatic increase in the pace of CIA drone-launched missile strikes into Pakistan in an effort to kill al-Qaeda and Taliban members in the ungoverned tribal areas along the Afghan border,[35] and that he is also seeking the authority to monitor all cell phones, a key element in tracing and preventing terrorist plots.[36]

The point here is that any analyst trying to reach a judgment in this area would first have to be aware of the *range* of evidence on this issue and then grapple with the relative weight to be given to each, and provide a transparent accounting of the reasoning by which any conclusion was reached. Sometimes the exception supports the rule, but sometimes there are enough exceptions to require a revised view. In this respect good social science and good political psychology overlap when they are properly used in the psychological analysis of presidents.

The psychoanalyst undertaking a presidential analysis is also very much aware of the possible impact of transference, the views that an analyst brings to the analysis and their possible distorting effect if they are not careful. Fairness and transparency with data and inference help to mitigate an impulse toward "my side" political reductionism. Also having a real set of substantive questions takes the lead in a study rather than taking a back seat to whatever side of the political spectrum the analysts' preferences lie, also help to mitigate these tendencies, where they exist.

The Problems of Obama's Policy Fluency

For Obama, words are the vehicles of his transformative ambitions and he uses many of them. This is consistent with his stated view that this is "the power of the Presidency that I don't see used enough. The capacity to explain to the American people in very prosaic, straightforward terms: here are the choices we have."[37]

Obama's words don't speak for themselves. If you delve into Mr. Obama's pronouncements on a variety of subjects, the challenge will soon become obvious. One of the president's rhetorical tells are the words "having said that." These words signal that the point that the president had just endorsed will now be followed by endorsement of its counter point. It is often difficult to know just where Obama stands on an issue. And this may be part of the president's strategy.

Strategic ambiguity leaves the president room to maneuver, but it also leaves large and difficult questions about the reality of his professed political identity. Ironically, from a leadership legitimacy perspective, the more maneuvering room the president attempts to give himself, the less latitude over the long run he may have.

Dreams and the Limits of Self-reflection

Obama is among our most self-reflective presidents. By the time he was thirty-four he had published a biographical narrative and meditation on his own life's development. Yet, self-reflection, especially that shaped by the psychological pressures of trying to come to terms with a complex and unusual set of family experiences while growing up and the legacy of his hybrid racial identity, has its limits. As noted, theorists from diverse psychological traditions have concluded that we know much less of ourselves than we think we do, and Obama is no exception. So when Obama says in an early 2004 interview, "I think, particularly during my teenage years, I engaged in a lot of antisocial behavior that can't all be explained by the absence of a father, but I think that was partly accounted for by it,"[38] we must both tentatively take him at his word, and look beyond it.

In the preface to the 2004 edition of his autobiographical book, *Dreams from My Father*, Obama laments the fact that he so neglected the large role that his mother, who had died the year before, played in his life. There, he wrote, "I know that she was the kindest, most generous spirit I have ever known, and what is best in me I owe to her."[39]

Yet, Obama has told many close friends that he grew up "feeling like an orphan."[40] Elsewhere, commenting on the absence of both his father and his mother, he has said of himself, "At some level I had to raise myself."[41] Here his posthumous idealization of his mother and Obama's view of the facts of their relationship seem to be on a collision course.

Obama's apparent remorse driven tribute in the reissue of his book was doubtlessly heart-felt, but it too doesn't really capture the full nature of his relationship with her. His mother, like his father, also left him, first when she sent him back to live with his grandparents in Hawaii for almost a year before she rejoined him, and then when she returned to Indonesia for long-term fieldwork and an eventual Asian centered career when Barack was entering adolescence.

This and other instances caution us against assuming that this self-reflective president is the most reliable guide to understanding his own psychology, the forces that shaped it, or their implications for his presidency. This is no criticism. It is extraordinarily hard to stand outside yourself and dispassionately gain an accurate understanding of the complex experiences that shaped you and be aware of how they play out in your life as it is unfolding. Obama's often thoughtful meditations on his background, political views, and their relationship must be the starting point of any analysis, but they cannot be the last word.

On Relying on Obama

Obama's thoughtful, searching autobiography *Dreams from My Father*[42] received outstanding reviews, once he became a public figure. Michiko Kakutani writing in the *New York Times* said the book provided,

> a revealing, introspective account of his efforts to trace his family's tangled roots and his attempts to come to terms with his absent father, who left home when he was still a toddler. And it was equally candid about his youthful struggles: pot, booze and "maybe a little blow ... [could] push questions of who I was out of my mind, flatten out the landscape of my heart, blur the edges of my memory. ... "

Most memorably, the book gave the reader

> a heartfelt sense of what it was like to grow up in the 1960s and 70s, straddling America's color lines: the sense of knowing two worlds and belonging to neither, the sense of having to forge an identity of his own.[43]

Others called it "a remarkable story, beautifully told," and a book of, "exceptional grace of Obama's prose, its honesty and freshness."[44] Still another review said that it was, "a beautifully written personal memoir steeped in honesty."[45] Over the years however, reporters and biographers tracking down the details of the stories and facts that appear in *Dreams* cast some doubt on their objective authenticity.

David Remnick's careful new biography[46] suggests that Obama's *Dreams* book is "a mixture of verifiable fact, recollection, recreation, invention and artful shaping." Obama, Remnick points out, ended each section with climactic, somewhat over-wrought descriptions of himself in tears—as he sees his father in a dream, discovers his spiritual roots in church, visits his father's grave. It is a dramatically literary device, but not necessarily reflective of the real arc of Obama's biographical and emotional life.

David Maraniss has written, *Dreams from My Father* is

> as imprecise as it is insightful about Obama's early life. Obama offers unusually perceptive and subtle observations of himself and the people around him. Yet, as he readily acknowledged, he rearranged the chronology for his literary purposes and presented a cast of characters made up of composites and pseudonyms.[47]

Another pair of reporters found that,

> several of his oft-recited stories may not have happened in the way he has recounted them. Some seem to make Obama look better in the retelling, others appear to exaggerate his outward struggles over issues of race, or simply skim over some of the most painful, private moments of his life.[48]

Among these were highly charged racial conversations he reports having with a good friend in high school which that friend disputes and Obama's self-stated mastery of the Indonesian language and culture in "less than six months"[49] whereas "Teachers, former playmates and friends recall a boy who never fully grasped their language and who was very quiet as a result."[50] And then there is Obama's story in *Dreams* about being a nine-year-old and seeing a story in *Life Magazine* about a man who destroyed his skin with powerful chemical lighteners that promised to make him white.[51] Yet no such *Life* issue exists, according to historians at the magazine. No such photos, no such article. When asked about the discrepancy, Obama said in a recent interview, "It might have been an *Ebony* or it might have been … who knows what it was?" (At the request of the *Tribune*, archivists at *Ebony* searched their catalogue of past articles, none of which matched what Obama recalled.)[52]

The thoughtful reflective nature of Obama's autobiography makes it hard to keep in mind that the book was published in 1995 when Obama was thirty-four years old. So the book's narrative and stories are reflections on Obama as a child, a young adult and growing up, and are written from the perspective of a man well into adulthood who had graduated from Columbia University and Harvard Law School, worked for years as a community organizer and as a lawyer, and gotten married. None of these life achievements ensure thoughtfulness, but they do suggest accomplishment, the passage of time and with it some perspective.

As a result, the book's reflective depth leads some to confusion. David Maraniss,[53] an excellent reporter and biographer says of Obama that, "By the time he was 6, Barry Obama was a hyper-aware boy with much to think about." It is not clear that young six-year-old Obama was "hyper-aware." Indeed commenting on Obama's story of the *Life Magazine* article and its effects on his racial consciousness two reporters write, "In fact, it is surprising, based on interviews with more than two dozen people who knew Obama during his nearly four years in Indonesia, that it would take a photograph in a magazine to make him conscious of the fact that some people might treat him differently in part because of the color of his skin."[54]

Indeed, Obama himself writes in the Introduction to his book that he has spent much of his life trying to "rewrite" the stories that he was told.[55] He talks further there of

> the dangers inherent in any autobiographical work: the temptation to color events in ways favorable to the writer. … selective lapses of memory … the distance that can cure one of certain vanities. I can't say I've avoided all, or any of these hazards successfully.[56]

How then should a political psychologist, trained in psychoanalysis, and interested in the impact of a president's developmental experiences on his psychology and the exercise of his presidential responsibilities approach such an autobiography? Cautiously. *Dreams* is not presented as, nor is it meant to be, a factually correct chronological depiction of interior development in relationship to external circumstances. It is Obama's meditation, his reflection, on those events and what they meant to him. They are the emotional and biographical facts of his life as he remembered, experienced, and preferred them, when he wrote the book.

They are a construction, but as with all constructions, they serve a purpose. In this case the purpose was to try to make sense of his life and identity. It is honest in that important way, even if some of the events are condensed, shaded, or simply factually suspect (the *Life Magazine* story). Understood in that way, the book has enormous relevance to understanding Obama's developmental history and its consequences for his presidency, but it cannot stand on its own or be taken wholly at face value.

The analyst faced with such a book must approach it as he would any evidence. He must establish its usefulness by placing it in the context of other known evidence, and seeing how it holds up. Other evidence must also support the concepts and theories that rely on it in any way. And he must be careful not to commit the twin errors of reductionism, trying to explain too much with too little evidence, or making too few (psychological) elements carry disproportionate explanatory weight for complex concepts like presidential performance.

The same approach is necessary in dealing with the many, sometimes conflicting things Obama has said about himself, or the explanations he has provided. Over time, the diligent researcher will learn that there are many such instances and they don't always add up. For example, Obama has offered many hints, even explanations of his self-contained nature. He has spoken a number of times of feeling like an "orphan" and about having to "raise himself." He has also alluded to the effects of being raised primarily as an only child. Speaking of the difficulties in his marriage Obama has written,

> Partially because I was still working on my first book, and perhaps because I had lived much of my life as an only child, I would often spend the evening holed up in my office in the back of our railroad apartment; what I considered normal often left Michelle feeling lonely.[57]

The analyst must make some effort to answer the question: Which, if any, of these explanations ought to be accorded most weight? This can only be done by sorting through and weighing all the evidence that is relevant and available.

Know the Players and the Debates

Any presidential analysis that relies primarily on open sources requires that the person doing it become very familiar with the stance of the persons, news outlets and institutions that provide the basic information that goes into it. Presidential scholarship has received an enormous information boost from the explosion of web-based information and analysis. Official reports, interviews with major players, commentary, news sites, and YouTube and Facebook linked video clips of events are now widely and easily available on the president and the range of issues he faces. There are major news websites that now track the president on a daily[58] and hourly basis.[59] And there is one that promises "Politics up to the Minute."[60]

There are also numerous major blogs that note and link to news major stories.[61] The advantage of these compilation blogs is that they link to a variety of major news stories from diverse sources which, when taken together, can often add information and help in developing a fuller picture of the event and its meaning. This facilitates the following of stories over time, which adds to the researcher's ability to gain substantive traction on an issue. And, of course blogs of the left[62] and right[63] that provide their own more narrow perspective and links to an event or what they view as an important administration initiative or misstep.

These are clearly emblematic samplings of the wide range of material available to a presidential researcher. They reflect the fact that the operating political environment has changed dramatically for presidents regarding their twin essential tasks. Yet, it also reflects changes that affect scholarship of the presidency. One obvious concern is the sheer amount of information available. It requires substantial effort if these rich vanes of basic data are to be effectively tapped just to keep up, and this does not take into account the effort necessary to read, compare, and evaluate them.

No scholar can totally keep up with the torrent of information available, but there are ways to manage this flow. And all of them require some element of selectivity and, ultimately, evaluative judgment.

A president must address a wide range of issues, and each of those has its own complexities, policy history, and key players with their own policy or partisan perspectives. No presidential researcher can hope, much less claim, to have gained real substantive traction on these varied elements in more than a few areas. And even then there will be clear limits.

A scholar who wants to examine and evaluate the president's approach to Iran, for example, will have to become broadly familiar with that policy's history, the political and scholarly debates regarding strategic options and their implications, and the perspectives of the institutions and persons contributing to those debates. None of this will make the presidential researcher an Iranian expert, but it will enable that researcher to be an informed consumer of information and perspective and to go from there to form their own essential judgment and understanding of the president's approach.

The same is true of approaches to the president's leadership. Here the researcher must begin with an understanding of what that term means, its basic elements, and the issues concerned with its exercise. That foundation of scholarship allows the researcher to analyze the president's style and approach across different policy domains, most helpfully those with which the researcher has become familiar (as above). Given that leadership is a transactional concept, the researcher will have to become familiar with the public's expectations, hopes and fears since they provide one key element through which presidential leadership must be framed.

In the end, there is no escape for the scholar from knowing the sources on which he relies. A researcher interested in understanding the sources and strength of Obama's presidential leadership, and utilizing "insider accounts" of the campaign might well examine *Newsweek*'s book-length account of their campaign reporting.[64] Yet, a prudent researcher would also want to know that Evan Thomas, the book's chief author and head of the *Newsweek* research team in response to a question about the president's Cairo speech, gave his enthusiasm free reign and likened the president to a deity—"I mean in a way Obama's standing above the country, above—above the world, he's sort of God. ... He's going to bring all different sides together."[65]

Or, a researcher might want to get an insider's account of the campaign from the perspective of the successful candidate and turn to former *Newsweek* reporter Richard Wolffe's book which is, as the front jacket states, "Based on Exclusive Interviews with Barack Obama."[66] Yet, a prudent researcher would want to know that according to Wolffe, it was Obama who approached him with the idea of writing a book about his campaign "Like Theodore White."[67] White, of course, was the legendary journalist whose book *The Making of the President*[68] was the first insider account of the Kennedy campaign, became an instant classic and won a Pulitzer Prize, while helping to advance that president's preferred heroic narrative. Wolffe says that at first, he dismissed the idea, thinking that Obama "was surely trying to nudge me into his own game plan."[69] Yet, several weeks later Wolffe said yes, convinced there was a vital story there "that could only be told by someone who was there to witness it firsthand." It didn't quite turn out as Wolffe had hoped. As one account of the ensuing controversies noted, "Obama provided the insider access. And Wolffe lavishly delivered on the heroic-light end of the bargain."[70]

Still, even with those whose balance seems decidedly compromised there are things to learn. In one of his reported interviews, Wolffe asked whether the president felt constrained by the system, size of the government, or by fate and the president replied,

> So I don't think in terms of trying to avoid fate; I think in terms of what's within my control. And that's why,—so far, at least—I feel pretty calm on the job. We've got these huge problems—not of my making—they're global in scope.[71]

Wolffe reports this without comment, but it is an interesting perspective on presidential responsibility and anxiety management.

Conclusion

In the end, there is no eluding the researcher's responsibilities to be informed about the sources he uses, the issues he addresses and the materials that constitute his evidence. At their best, these materials should not be single sources, and should be evaluated comparatively. The weight of evidence can legitimize a conceptual or theoretical claim, but any such claim will gain in stature by being compared to other rival claims, and while a president's words and actions do not speak for themselves, if enough of them begin to accumulate on one side of a debate or another, our confidence is increased. That is why it is preferable to focus on a president's words and actions and analyze those, rather than wholly rely on characterizations about the president made by others.

In relying on public sources and allowing presidents and events to be able to be heard in their own voice, one or another of the issues raised in this book can be found, in some form, in the public domain. For example, I report that Obama himself has used the aphorism about every man trying to make up for his father's errors, and I quote from Obama speeches and Q&A's to establish the redemption theme in foreign and domestic policy. These are of course reported in the *New York Times* and other public venues.

However, one of the functions of theory is to gather disparate and unconnected data pieces and where possible weave them together in an explanation that makes sense of them, furthers our theoretical understanding, and provides a basis for anticipating future behaviors. A mention here or a mention there of a characteristic is just that, and not an effort to take a fuller measure of the man, his psychology, and his presidency.

Analyzing the psychology of any president as it plays out in their leadership choices is a labor intensive theoretical and factual undertaking, filled with ambiguity, complexity, and ultimately uncertainty. It is possible, through patient and careful exploration of a president over time and across circumstances to draw a theoretically useful and factually plausible picture of a president, especially with the many and varied sources now available to us to do so. We can chart the nature and development of his ambitions and skills, the ideals and purposes that his ambitions serve, and the nature of the relationships he establishes as president.

And to the extent that we have done so successfully, we will have succeeded in taking the psychology measure of the man and his presidency. It is not by any means the only measure, but it is, especially for the study of the presidency, an indispensable one.

APPENDIX B: A MYSTERIOUS PRESIDENT

Puzzlement from the Left, Right, and Center

"His entire political persona is an ingeniously crafted human cipher, a man without race, ideology, geographic allegiances or, indeed, sharp edges of any kind. You can't run against him on the issues because you can't even find him on the ideological spectrum."

> Matt Taibbi, "The Low Post: Between Barack and a Hard Place,"
> *Rolling Stone*, February 15, 2007

"He is a study in dichotomy, bold yet cautious, radical yet pragmatic, all depending on whose prism you use."

> Peter Baker, "No Walk in the Park: For Obama One Year Later,
> It's the Slog of Governance," *New York Times*, November 4, 2009

"Sixteen months after announcing his candidacy, and after twenty-six presidential debates, and thousands of public speaking engagements, Obama remains a puzzle to many voters."

> Dorthy Wickenden, "Talk of the Town—What's The Big Idea?"
> *New Yorker*, June 30, 2008, p. 21

"A complicated man, this new president. Opaque, contradictory and subtle."

> Charles Krauthammer, "Obama's Inaugural Surprise,"
> *Washington Post*, January 23, 2009

"On this much, President Obama's friends and foes could agree: He eludes simple labels. Yes, he's a liberal, except when he's not. He's antiwar, except for the one he's escalating. He's for bailouts, but wants to rein in the banks. He's concentrating ever-more power in the West Wing, except when he's being overly deferential to Congress. He's cool, except when he's fighting-hot."

> Richard W. Stevenson, "The Muddled Selling of the President,"
> *New York Times*, January 29, 2009

"He remains hard to read or label—centrist in his appointments and bipartisan in his style, yet also pushing the broadest expansion of government in generations. He has reached across old boundaries to build the foundation of an administration that will be charged with hauling the country out of crisis, but for all the outreach he has made it clear he is centralizing policy making in the White House."

> Peter Baker, "Transition Holds Clues to How Obama Will Govern,"
> *New York Times*, January 20, 2009

"Well short of Obama's first hundred days, the dominant characteristic of his Presidency is clear: activist government, on every front. It's harder to make out the contours of the philosophy at the core of this dazzling blur of action."

> George Packer, "Obamaism," *New Yorker*, April 13, 2009

"if the first 100 days of President Obama's term have proven anything, it is that he is a hard man to classify."

> Gerald F. Seib, "An Engaged, Yet Elusive President,"
> *Wall Street Journal*, April 29, 2009

"Will the Real President Stand Up?"

> David S. Broder, "Will the Real President Stand Up?"
> *Washington Post*, October 4, 2009

"But almost a year into his first term, there's something particularly elusive about Barack Obama's political identity. He's a bipartisan bridge-builder—unless he's a polarizing ideologue. He's a crypto-Marxist radical—except when he's a pawn of corporate interests. He's a post-American utopian—or else he's a willing tool of the national security state."

> Ross Douthat, "The Obama Way," *New York Times*,
> December 26, 2009

"What's striking about this inside look at Obama [the HBO documentary 'By the People: The Election of Barack Obama'] is how being inside gets you nowhere. It is virtually the same as being outside."

> Richard Cohen, "Obama's Identity Crisis," *Washington Post*,
> October 20, 2009

"So who is Barack Obama? The simple answer is: We don't know, at least not yet."

> Joseph Joffe, "Who is this Guy?" *American Interest,*
> January–February, 2010

"President Obama's true nature—radical or pragmatist, partisan or conciliator—is a subject of endless debate. No doubt it will be still a century from now."

> Fred Hiatt, "Obama's Empathy Meets the Politics of Governing,"
> *Washington Post,* March 1, 2010

"Who is Barack Obama? If you ask a conservative Republican, you are likely to hear that Obama is a skilled politician who campaigned as a centrist but is governing as a big-government liberal. He plays by ruthless, Chicago politics rules. He is arrogant toward foes, condescending toward allies and runs a partisan political machine. If you ask a liberal Democrat, you are likely to hear that Obama is an inspiring but overly intellectual leader who has trouble making up his mind and fighting for his positions. He has not defined a clear mission. He has allowed the Republicans to dominate debate. He is too quick to compromise and too cerebral to push things through."

> David Brooks, "Getting Obama Right," *New York Times,*
> March 12, 2010

"It is essential, though, that he show us who he is. As of now, we haven't a clue."

> Richard Cohen, "President Obama's Enigmatic Intellectualism,"
> *Washington Post,* June 22, 2010; A19

"If Obama doesn't want to be seen as a socialist who coddles business, he needs to be more persuasive in telling Americans who he actually is."

> E.J. Dionne Jr., "What is Obamaism? President Must Do Better
> in Explaining His Policies," *Washington Post,* July 19, 2010

"Before Americans can give him credit for what he's done, they have to know who he is. We're waiting."

> Richard Cohen, "Who is Barack Obama?"
> *Washington Post,* July 20, 2010. A21

"He has left wide swaths of the Democratic Party uncertain of his core beliefs."

> John F. Harris and James Hohmann, "Dems Urge Obama to
> Take a Stand," *Politico,* August 23, 2010

"It [The White House] should be concerned that, after watching the president in office for a year and a half, many Americans still don't know who Obama really is—and that a growing number have concluded that he does not believe what they believe."

Marc A. Thiessen, "Democrats and the 'Evil Eye'",
Washington Post, August 23, 2010

"At bottom, this president is still a mystery to many Americans. During the campaign, he sold himself—or the idea of himself—more than any particular policy, and voters filled in the lines as they chose. He was, as he said at the time, the ultimate Rorschach test."

Peter Baker, "Education of a President," *New York Times*,
October 13, 2010

"Obama rarely reaches outside the tight group of advisers like Emanuel, Axelrod, Rouse, Messina, Plouffe, Gibbs and Jarrett, as well as a handful of personal friends. 'He's opaque even to us,' an aide told me. 'Except maybe for a few people in the inner circle, he's a closed book.'"

Peter Baker, "Education of a President." *New York Times*,
October 12, 2010

"Obama needs to redefine his identity. Bill Clinton gave himself a New Democrat label. Obama has never categorized himself so clearly. This ambiguity was useful in 2008 when people could project whatever they wanted onto him. But it has been harmful since."

David Brooks, "The Next Two Years," *New York Times*,
October 28, 2010

"He's too cool a customer, a beguiling construct more than flesh and blood, an empty vessel for a misplaced idealism, a politician averse to pressing the flesh (and what else is politics?), a man who—not for nothing—tilts his chin upward when he speaks."

Ed Cohen, "Get Bold, Barack," *New York Times*,
November 1, 2010

"But at the heart of that incoherent performance stands the President, as opaque a character as we've seen in the Oval Office in a great while."

Joe Klein, "Where Obama Goes From Here," *Time*,
November 4, 2010

"the American people still don't really feel we know this president the way we, for better or worse, knew George Bush."

Carol Marin, "President's Connection to Voters Broken,"
Chicago Sun-Times, November 17, 2010

"Just where Mr. Obama actually lives on the ideological continuum—that is, exactly what kind of Democrat he sees when he looks in the mirror ... —is the most vexing question of his November 30, 2010."

> Matt Bai, "Debt-Busting Issue May Force Obama Off Fence,"
> *New York Times*, November 30, 2010

"Obama is an undefined figure to much of the country, and to his fellow Democrats."

> Eleanor Cliff, "Halfhearted Soul-Searching at the White House,"
> *Newsweek*, November 21, 2010

"His reserved approach came at a time when he is being pressed as never before to define what American liberalism means for the 21st century ... And yet he seemed reluctant to be drawn out too much as he confronted challenges that were never part of his original agenda."

> Peter Baker, "Obama, Searching for a Vision,"
> *New York Times*, April 9, 2011

"Americans may ask which is the real Obama, the politician who embraced the biggest stimulus package in the nation's history, a bailout of the banks and a takeover of the automobile industry, or the one who on Friday hailed the new budget deal as including 'the largest annual spending cut in our history.'

> Dan Balz, "Can Obama Cut the Budget and Keep Democrats Happy?"
> *Washington Post*, April 10, 2010

"he's a man of many pieces and many parts and not all of which I understand or I think anybody understands."

> David Brooks interview on *CNN*, April 24, 2011

"Nobody at this point really knows what the President stands for—at home or abroad. He is not George W. Bush and he is not Bill Clinton, but who is he and where is he taking us?"

> Walter Russell Mead, "Can This Presidency be Saved?"
> *The American Interest*, June 17, 2011

OBAMA AND HIS FAMILY: AN ANNOTATED TIMELINE

Obama: Father's Family

Onyango Obama (Barack Obama Jr.'s grandfather) b. 1895 in Western Kenya
Second wife, Akumu Nyanjoga: mother of Barack Obama Sr. b. 1936
1956   Obama Sr. marries first wife, Kezia
There are two children from that marriage, Roy and Auma

Obama: Mother's Family

Stanley Armour Dunham b. 1918; died 1992
Married Madelyn Lee Paine b. 1922/married 1939
Obama's mother (Stanley) Ann Dunham born, 1942; died 1995 at age fifty-two

Family Chronology

1959: Obama Sr. leaves his wife (Kezia) who is pregnant with their second child
and Roy, his first son, to take up a fellowship at the University of Hawaii.

1960: Obama Sr. meets his future wife, Obama's mother (Stanley) Ann Dunham
in a Russian language class at the University. She is not yet eighteen, he is
twenty-five years old.

February 2, 1961: Obama's parents married. Ann Dunham is eighteen years old.

August 4, 1961: Barack Obama, Jr. born in Hawaii.

June 1962: Barack Obama Sr. leaves for Harvard University, never to return to his wife Ann Dunham and their child.[1]

1963: Barack Obama Sr. returns to Kenya[2] with an American named Ruth Nidesand, who becomes his third wife.

January 1964: Obama's mother Ann Dunham files for divorce from Obama's father.

1967: Barack moves to Indonesia with his mother and her new Indonesian husband Lolo Soetoro, whom she also met at the University of Hawaii. Obama is six years old.

January 1, 1968: Barack enters 1st grade at start of the school year at Bekusi School. He later attends Santo Fransiskus Asisi, a Roman Catholic school.[3]

1970: Barack's half sister Maya Soetoro (now Soetoro-Ng) is born. Barry is nine years old and in the 3rd grade.

Fall 1970: Lolo Soetoro's economic circumstances improve and Obama's family moves to a much more elite neighborhood several miles from his old one where Obama enters a new, primarily Muslim school for the 4th grade.

Summer 1971: Obama finishes 4th grade in Jakarta and returns to Hawaii to live with grandparents, to begin 5th grade at Punahou School. Obama is ten years old.[4]

December 1971: Father visits Obama and his mother for first and only time. Mother returns briefly to Hawaii during the period of his father's visit.

1974 (?): Obama's mother and her second husband separate[5] and she returns to Hawaii and begins a graduate program in Anthropology at the University of Hawaii. Obama is thirteen years old.[6]

1976–77: Obama's mother returns to Indonesia for fieldwork. Obama declines to join her and lives with his grandparents. Obama is sixteen years old.

1978–79: Obama is second stringer on State High School basketball championship team.

1979: Obama graduates from Punahou High School.[7]

September 1979: Obama moves to Los Angeles to attend Occidental College. He is eighteen years old.

1980: Obama's mother files for divorce from her second husband Lolo. They have however, been separated since the time Obama's mother returned, briefly, from Indonesia in 1971.

February 18, 1981: Obama speaks at anti–South African divestiture rally (first experiences with the power of his rhetoric).

Summer 1981: Obama travels through Asia for three weeks, visits mother and sister.

August 1981. Obama moves to New York to attend Columbia University. He is twenty years old.

November 24, 1982: Father dies in car accident. Obama is twenty-one years old.

1983: graduates Columbia with B.A.[8] in Political Science. Obama is twenty-two years old.

Summer 1983: Obama visits mother and sister in Indonesia.

1984–85: Works in New York (Business International Corporation and then NY Public Interest Research Group). Obama is twenty-three years old.

June 1985–88: Moves to Chicago to become community organizer (Development Community Project)

1986: Visit from sister Auma in Chicago; first learns true story of father's decline.[9] Obama is twenty-five years old.

Summer 1988: Trip to Kenya to research family background; emotional epiphany at father's gravesite. Obama is twenty-seven years old.[10]

September, 1988: Enters Harvard Law School.

June 1989: Meets future wife Michelle at summer law firm placement.

1990: Elected editor of the *Harvard Law Review*.

June 1991: Receives JD degree, magna cum laude, from Harvard University.

1991: Returns to Chicago from Harvard.

1991: Obama becomes engaged to Michelle Robinson.

1992 (October 18): Obama marries Michelle Robinson.

1992: Obama's mother turns in PhD dissertation.

1992: Obama takes position in Miner, Barnhill and Galland Law firm and becomes a lecturer at the University of Chicago Law School.

1992: Obama agrees to lead a voter registration drive (Project Vote).

1995: Mother returns to Hawaii ill with cancer. She has lived abroad for eighteen years.

November 7, 1995: Obama's mother dies of uterine cancer at the age of fifty-two.

1995: *Dreams from My Father* published. Obama is thirty-four years old.

1996: Wins election to Illinois State Senate. Obama is thirty-five years old.

1996–2004: Serves as Illinois State Senator.

1998: First child, Malia, born, baptized at Trinity Church.

1999: Obama writes article for *Punahou Bulletin* detailing his "budding awareness of life's unfairness" and his own "resentments."[11]

March 21, 2000: Obama runs against Bobby Rush in Democratic primary for Congress, and loses. Obama is thirty-nine years old.

2001: Second daughter, Natasha, born.

October 2, 2002: Obama gives anti-Iraq war speech in Chicago.

2003: Democrats take over Illinois State Senate. Obama is forty-two years old.

2004: *Dreams from My Father* reissued with new Preface lamenting his lack of attention in first edition to his mother. Obama is forty-three years old.

March 16, 2004: Obama wins Democratic Primary for Senate.

July 2, 2004: Obama delivers keynote address at Democratic National Convention.

November 4, 2004: Obama elected to U.S. Senate; thanks Reverend Wright.[12]

October 17, 2006: *The Audacity of Hope* is published. Obama is forty-five years old.

November 7, 2006: Democrats gain control of Congress.

November 8, 2006: Obama and his advisors meet to discuss running for president.[13]

November 28, 2006: Detailed memo prepared for possible presidential run.[14]

January 16, 2007: Obama files notice of presidential exploratory committee.[15]

February 10, 2007: Obama announces his candidacy for president in Springfield, Illinois.

November 4, 2008: Obama elected president. He is forty-seven years old.

NOTES

Front Matter

1 "NPR Interview: Barack Obama Discusses His Background, Career and His Future Political Plans as He Prepares to Give Tonight's Keynote Address at the Democratic National Convention," July 27, 2004. Available at: www.nacdl.org/sl_docs.nsf/free-form/Mandatory:306 (accessed June 6, 2009).

2 Quoted in Richard Wolffe, *Renegade: The Making of a President*. New York: Crown, 2009, p. 67.

3 Peggy Noonan, "We Just Don't Understand," *Wall Street Journal*, August 27, 2010.

4 Stanley A. Renshon, *High Hopes: The Clinton Presidency and the Politics of Ambition*. New York: New York University Press, 1996 (1998 paperback edition, with afterword, published by Routledge).

5 Stanley A. Renshon, *In His Father's Shadow: The Transformations of George W. Bush*. Palgrave/Macmillan, 2004.

6 David Broder, "The Obama Effect—Are You With Him or Against Him?" *Washington Post*, May 23, 2010.

7 Janet Hook, "Democrats in Congress Fail the Sales Pitch," *Los Angeles Times*, June 2, 2010.

8 Michiko Kakutani, "Books of the Times; Seeking Identity, Shaping a Nation's," *New York Times*, April 5, 2010.

9 Douglas Brinkley, review of "'The Bridge: The Life and Rise of Barack Obama' by David Remnick," *Los Angeles Times*, March 28, 2010.

10 Michiko Kakutani, "Penetrating the Process of Obama's Decisions," *New York Times*, May 12, 2010.

11 Peggy Noonan, "We Just Don't Understand," *Wall Street Journal*, August 27, 2010.

12 Kakutani, "Seeking Identity, Shaping a Nation's."

13 James T. Kloppenberg, *Reading Obama: Dreams, Hope, and the American Political Tradition*, Princeton, N.J.: Princeton University Press, 2010, p. xi.

14 David Brooks, "Getting Obama Right," *New York Times*, March 12, 2010.

15 Stanley A. Renshon, *The Psychological Assessment of Presidential Candidates*, New York: New York University Press, 1996 (1998 paperback edition, with afterword, published by Routledge).

16 Quoted in Bob Secter and John McCormick, "Portrait of a Pragmatist," *Chicago Tribune*, 30 March 2007; see also Obama, *Dreams from My Father*, New York: Crown, 2004, pp. 39, 344.

17 "NPR Interview: Barack Obama Discusses His Background;" see also David Mendell, *Obama: From Promise to Power*, New York: Harper Collins, 2007 p. 40; Barack Obama, *The Audacity of Hope*, New York: Three Rivers Press, 2006, p. 11.

1 The Early Obama Presidency: From Campaigning to Governing

1 Don Lee and Jim Puzzanghera, "Obama Critics Say his Economic Vision is Hazy," *Los Angeles Times*, January 25, 2010.

2 Obama quoted in David Morgan, "President Vows to Press Ahead on Big Challenges," *Reuters*, March 30, 2010.

3 David Axelrod, Obama's chief advisor, prepared a November 26, 2006 memo on exactly this point. Dan Balz and Haynes Johnson, *The Battle for America 2008*, New York: Viking, 2010, p. 29.

4 Axelrod quoted in Ryan Lizza, "Battle Plans: How Obama Won," *New Yorker*, November 17, 2008.

5 Jon Cohen and Dan Balz, "U.S. Outlook Is Worst Since '92, Poll Finds," *Washington Post*, May 13, 2008. That poll can be found at: http://www.washingtonpost.com/wp-srv/politics/documents/postpoll_051208.html?sid=ST2008051201102 (accessed July 5, 2010).

6 For an argument that expectations for presidential actions have exceeded both the bounds of reasonableness and constitutional limits see Gene Healy, *The Cult of the Presidency: America's Dangerous Devotion to Executive Power*. Washington, D.C.: CATO Institute, 2008.

7 Lydia Saad, "Disapproval of Bush Spans the Issues," *Gallup*, February 20, 2008.

8 Frank Newport, "Bush Job Approval at 28%, Lowest of His Administration," *Gallup*, 11 April, 2008.

9 NBC News/*Wall Street Journal* Survey, November 2007. Question 12. The poll is online at: http://msnbcmedia.msn.com/i/msnbc/sections/news/071107_NBC-WSJ_Full.pdf (accessed July 6, 2010).

10 Cf. NBC News/*Wall Street Journal* Survey, December 2007. Question 17b asks respondents: Which of the following qualities is most important to you in choosing between the presidential candidates? Thirty percent choose being a "strong and decisive leader," the item chosen by the highest percentage of respondents. Not surprisingly, "good values and character" (25 percent) and "knowledgeable and experienced" (21 percent) were the second and third most important attributes to respondents. Interestingly, given the way in which the primary campaign has developed, "being forward looking and inspirational" was important to only 8 percent of the respondents. The poll is online at: http://online.wsj.com/public/resources/documents/wsjnbcpoll20071219.pdf (accessed July 6, 2010).

11 NBC News/*Wall Street Journal* Survey, November 2007. Question 22 reads: "I'm going to read to you several short phrases that describe qualities that someone might be looking for in the next president. Which one or two of these qualities do you feel are most important?" The poll is online at: http://msnbcmedia.msn.com/i/msnbc/sections/news/071107_NBC-WSJ_Full.pdf (accessed April 19, 2010)

12 Adam Nagourney, "Obama Elected President as Racial Barriers Fall," *New York Times*, November 5, 2008.

13 Andrew Kohut, "Americans Are More Skeptical of Washington Than Ever," *Wall Street Journal*, April 19, 2010, emphasis added. For the survey data that Kohut refers to see Pew Research Center for the People & the Press, "Distrust, Discontent, Anger

and Partisan Rancor: The People and Their Government," Washington, D.C., April 18, 2010. Available at: http://people-press.org/reports/pdf/606.pdf (accessed July 6, 2010).

14 Dorthy Wickenden, "The Talk of the Town: What's The Big Idea?" *New Yorker*, June 30, 2008, p. 21.

15 Richard W. Stevenson, "The Muddled Selling of the President," *New York Times*, January 29, 2009.

16 Fred Hiatt, "Obama's Empathy Meets the Politics of Governing," *Washington Post*, March 1, 2010.

17 Carrie Budoff Brown and Patrick O'Connor, "New Plan, Same Old Problems," *Politico*, February 22, 2010.

18 Kathy Kiely, "Obama Urges Expansion of His Agenda," *USA TODAY*, June 2, 2010.

19 Peter Wallsten and Eliza Grey, "Confidence Waning in Obama, U.S. Outlook," *Wall Street Journal*, June 23, 2010; see also Marist College Poll, "Turning Tides … Half View Obama as Not Meeting Expectations," June 30, 2010. The full NBC News/*Wall Street Journal* Survey can be found at: http://online.wsj.com/public/resources/documents/wsjnbcpoll-06232010.pdf (accessed July 3, 2010). The complete Marist College poll can be found at: http://maristpoll.marist.edu/wp-content/misc/usapolls/US100617/Obama_Oil_Spill/Complete%20June%2030,%202010%20USA%20Poll%20Release%20and%20Tables.pdf (accessed July 3, 2010).

20 Obama quoted in Carla Marinucci, "On S.F. Tour, Obama Takes On the Clintons," *San Francisco Chronicle*, January 18, 2008.

21 These terms are developed in Stanley A. Renshon, *The Psychological Assessment of Presidential Candidates*. New York: New York University Press, 1996 (1998 paperback edition, with afterword, published by Routledge), pp. 226–28.

22 Richard Rose, *The Post Modern President: George Bush Meets the World*. 2nd Ed. New York: Chatham House, 2000.

23 Cf., Douglas Holtz-Eakin, "The Real Arithmetic of the Health Care Reform," *New York Times*, March 21, 2010; see also Douglas W. Elmendorf, "An Analysis of Health Insurance Premiums under the Patient Protection and Affordable Care Act," *Congressional Budget Office: Director's Blog*, November 30, 2009; Robert Pear, "Health Care Costs Increase is Projected for New Law," *New York Times*, April 23, 2010; Richard S. Foster, "Estimated Financial Effects of the 'Patient Protection and Affordable Care Act,' as Amended," Center for Medicare and Medicaid Services, April 22, 2010. The analysis by Foster, Medicare's chief actuary can be found at: http://graphics8.nytimes.com/packages/pdf/health/oactmemo1.pdf (accessed July 6, 2010).

24 Kevin Sack, "Massachusetts: Insurers Sue," *New York Times*, April 5, 2010.

25 Anemona Hartocollis, "New York Offers Costly Lesson on Insurance," *New York Times*, April 17, 2010.

26 Health care is not the only legislative initiative for which this is true. Sen. Christopher J. Dodd (D-Conn.), who as chairman of the Senate Banking Committee led the effort in the Senate for legislation regulating America's financial sector, said of his bill, "*No one will know until this is actually in place how it works.*" See David Cho, Jia Lynn Yang, and Brady Dennis, "Lawmakers guide Dodd-Frank bill for Wall Street reform into homestretch," *Washington Post*, June 26, 2011 (emphasis added).

27 Cf. Morris P. Fiorina, and Samuel J. Adams, "Political Polarization in the American Public," *Annual Review of Political Science*, 11 (2008), pp. 563–88.

28 Fiorina and Adams, "Political Polarization," p. 56l. See also Figures 1 and 2 on that page.

29 Michael Powell, "For Obama, a Pragmatist's Shift Toward the Center," *New York Times*, June 27, 2008.

30 Howard Kurtz, "Pretzel Logic," *Washington Post*, June 27, 2008; see also Liz Sidoti, "McCain Backs Gun Decision, Obama Straddles Issue," *Associated Press*, June 26, 2008.

31 Jose Antonio Vargas, "Obama Defends Compromise on New FISA Bill," *Washington Post*, July 4, 2008.

32 Nina Easton, "Obama: NAFTA Not so Bad After All," *Fortune*, June 18, 2008.

33 David S. Broder, "Getting to Know Obama," *Washington Post*, June 22, 2008.

34 Jonathan Weisman, "Obama May Consider Slowing Iraq Withdrawal," *Washington Post*, July 4, 2008.

35 Daniel Dombey and Edward Luce, "Obama Camp Signals Robust Approach on Iran," *Financial Times*, July 1, 2008.

36 Jonathan Karl, "Obama's Evolving Position on Iran," *ABC News*, June 4, 2008.

37 Teddy Davis, Sunlen Miller, and Gregory Wallace, "Obama Kisses Millions Goodbye," *ABC News*, June 18, 2008.

38 Ruth Marcus, "Patriot Games," *Washington Post*, June 25, 2008.

39 Jonathan Weisman, "In Campaign, One Man's Pragmatism Is Another's Flip-Flopping," *Washington Post*, June 28, 2008.

40 Teddy Davis, "Obama Dubs Himself a 'Pragmatic Progressive.'" *ABC News*, January 8, 2009.

41 Walter Russell Mead, "Liberal Internationalism: The Twilight of a Dream," *The American Interest*, April 1, 2010.

42 Robin Wright, "'Progressive realism:' In Search of a Foreign Policy," *New York Times*, July 18, 2006.

43 Lydia Saad, "Americans Unsure About 'Progressive' Political Label," *Gallup*, July 10, 2010. Available at: http://www.gallup.com/poll/141218/americans-unsure-progressive-political-label.aspx?version=print (accessed July 23, 2010).

44 Karl Rove, "It's All About Obama," *Wall Street Journal*, June 26, 2008.

45 Lydia Saad, "In U.S., Majority Now Say Obama's Policies 'Mostly Liberal'," *Gallup*, November 4, 2009.

46 Susan Paige, "1-year Poll Shows Changed View on Obama," *USA Today*, November 28, 2009.

47 Pew Research Center for the People & the Press, "Obama's Ratings Little Affected by Recent Turmoil," June 24, 2010. Available at: http://people-press.org/reports/pdf/627.pdf (accessed July 3, 2010).

48 Jill Lawrence, "Poll: Americans Have High Hopes for Obama," *USA TODAY*, November 12, 2008.

49 Lexington, "The Obama Cult: If Barack Obama Disappoints His Supporters, They Will Have Only Themselves to Blame," *The Economist*, July 23, 2009.

50 Pew Research Center for the People & the Press, "Obama's Approval Ratings Slide: By the Numbers," September 4, 2009.

51 Wallsten and Grey, "Confidence Waning in Obama,"

52 Scott Wilson, "The Change Agenda At a Crossroads: From Health Care to Wars to Public Anxiety, Obama's Strength as a Leader Is Tested," *Washington Post*, September 6, 2009; see also David Brooks, "The Obama Slide," *New York Times*, September 1, 2009.

53 Tom Jensen, "Obama's December Standing," *Public Policy Polling*, December 9, 2009.

54 CNN/Opinion Research Poll, February 17, 2010. Available at: http://i2.cdn.turner.com/cnn/2010/images/02/16/rel4a.pdf (accessed July 6, 2010).

55 Jeffrey H. Anderson, "Comprehensive Failure," *Weekly Standard*, February 22, 2010.

56 Paul Krugman, "What Didn't Happen," *New York Times*, January 18, 2010.

57 Douglas E. Schoen, "Voters to Democrats: Jobs, Jobs, Jobs," *Wall Street Journal*, February 18, 2010.

58 John F. Harris and Jim VandeHei, "Why Obama Loses by Winning," *Politico*, July 15, 2010.

59 Pew Research Center for the People & the Press, "Partisan Gap in Obama Job Approval Widest in Modern Era," April 2, 2009.

60 Jeffrey M. Jones, "Obama's Approval Ratings More Polarized in Year 2 Than Year 1," *Gallup*, February 4, 2011.

61 *C-SPAN* Interview Transcript, "President Barack H. Obama," May 22, 2009. Available at: http://www.c-span.org/pdf/obamainterview.pdf (accessed July 6, 2010).

62 Fred I. Greenstein, *Hidden-Hand Presidency: Eisenhower as Leader*, New York: HarperCollins, 1982.

63 Shailagh Murray, "Obama to Accept Nomination at Broncos' Stadium," *Washington Post*, July 8, 2008.

64 Joan Vennochi, "The Audacity of Ego," *Boston Globe*, July 20, 2008.

65 George C. Edwards III, *On Deaf Ears: The Limits of the Bully Pulpit*, New Haven, Ct.: Yale University Press, 2003.

66 Peter Nicholas and Janet Hook, "Obama the Velcro President," *Los Angeles Times*, July 30, 2010.

67 Stephen Wayne, "Barack Obama: Character and Temperament for the Presidency," paper prepared for delivery at the annual meeting of the American Political Science Association, Boston Massachusetts, August 28–31, 2008, p. 25.

68 Eamon Javers and Zachary Abrahamson, "Obama's Words Downplay Wars," *Politico*, August 13, 2009.

69 Mark Knoller, "Obama's First Year: By the Numbers," *CBS News*, January 20, 2010.

70 Andrew Malcolm, "Top of the Ticket," *Los Angeles Times*, April 2, 2010.

71 Anne E. Kornblut, "Obama's 17-minute, 2,500-word response to woman's claim of being 'over-taxed,'" *Washington Post*, April 2, 2010.

72 Roger Simon, "It's All Obama, All the Time," *Politico*, April 6, 2009.

73 Obama quoted in David Remnick, "Testing the Waters," *New Yorker*, November 6, 2008.

74 Robin Toner, "Obama's Test: Can a Liberal Be a Unifier," *New York Times*, March 25, 2008

75 Quoted in Jonathan Weisman, "Obama May Consider Slowing Iraq Withdrawal: Candidate Says He Remains Committed to Ending War," *Washington Post*, July 4, 2008.

76 Quoted in Ron Fournier, "Essay: Obama's Transcendence is Beyond Race," *Associated Press*, November 5, 2008 (emphasis added).

77 Dan Balz and Jon Cohen, "Confidence in Obama Reaches New Low, *Washington Post*-ABC News Poll Finds," *Washington Post*, July 13, 2010. The complete poll results may be found at: http://www.washingtonpost.com/wpsrv/politics/polls/post-poll_07132010.html?sid=ST2010071300027 (accessed July 12, 2010).

78 Andrew Malcolm, "New Poll to Obama: It's the Economy, Stupid," *Los Angeles Times*, July 13, 2010.

79 Fournier, "Essay: Obama's Transcendence is Beyond Race."

80 The figures and characterizations that follow are drawn from: The Pew Research Center for the People & the Press, "Trends in Political Values and Core Attitudes: 1987–2007," March 22, 2007. Available at: http://people-press.org/reports/pdf/312.pdf (assessment July 6, 2010).

81 Jeffrey M. Jones, "Party Affiliation Gap in U.S. Narrowest Since 2005: Democratic Advantage Shrinks as More Independents Lean to the Republican Party," *Gallup*, April 23, 2010. Available at: http://www.gallup.com/poll/127499/party-affiliation-gap-u.s.-narrowest-2005.aspx?version=print (accessed April 25, 2010).

82 Jones, "Party Affiliation Gap."

83 William J. Clinton, "State of the Union Address," January 23, 1996.

84 Obama quoted in Balz and Johnson, *The Battle for America 2008*, p. 377.

85 Pew Research Center for the People & the Press, "Distrust, Discontent, Anger and Partisan Rancor: The People and Their Government," Washington, D.C., April 18, 2010, p. 7. Available at: http://people-press.org/reports/pdf/606.pdf (accessed July 6, 2010).

86 Pew, "Distrust, Discontent Anger and Partisan Rancor," p. 7.

87 Pew, "Distrust, Discontent Anger and Partisan Rancor," p. 8.

88 Pew, "Distrust, Discontent Anger and Partisan Rancor," p. 8 (emphasis added).

89 Quoted in Toner, "Obama's Test."

90 "Remarks by the President on Comprehensive Immigration Reform," The White House, July 1, 2010. Available at: http://www.whitehouse.gov/the-press-office/remarks-president-comprehensive-immigration-reform (accessed July 5, 2010)

91 Quoted in Toner, "Obama's Test."

92 Kenneth P. Vogel, "Obama: Change Agent Goes Conventional," *Politico*, June 27, 2008.

2 The Puzzle of Obama's Political Identity

1 Barack Obama, *Dreams from My Father*, New York: Three Rivers Press, 2004, pp. 29–30; Kirsten Scharnberg and Kim Barker, "The Not-so-simple Story of Barack Obama's Youth," *Chicago Tribune*, March 25, 2007.

2 Michiko Kakutani, "Obama's Foursquare Politics: With a Dab of Dijon," *New York Times*, October 17, 2006.

3 Laureen Korneich, "Obama: New Dog Could Be 'Mutt Like Me,'" *CNN News*, November 7, 2008.

4 Obama quoted in Sam Youngman, "President Obama Calls African-Americans a 'Mongrel People,'" *The Hill*, July 29, 2010.

5 Obama quoted in Bridget Johnson, "Obama: Critics 'Talk About Me Like a Dog,'" *The Hill*, September 6, 2010.

6 Daniel Kahneman and Amos Tversky, "Prospect Theory: An Analysis of Decision Under Risk," *Econometrica*, 47: 2 (1979), pp. 263–92.

7 Amos Tversky and Daniel Kahneman, "The Framing of Decisions and the Psychology of Choice," *Science*, 211: 4481 (1981), p. 453.

8 W. L. Benoit, "Framing Through Temporal Metaphor: The 'Bridges' of Bob Dole and Bill Clinton in Their 1996 Acceptance Addresses," *Communication Studies* (Spring 2001), pp. 70–84.

9 George Lakoff, *Don't Think of an Elephant! Know Your Values and Frame the Debate*. Vermont: Chelsea Green Publishing, 2004.

10 Cf. Stanley A. Renshon, *The Psychological Assessment of Presidential Candidates*, New York: New York University Press, 1996 (1998 paperback edition, with afterword, published by Routledge), pp. 38–40.

11 See for example, Michael Luo and Jeff Zeleny, "Obama, in Shift, Says He'll Reject Public Financing," *New York Times*, June 20, 2008. For an example of the charges see David Brooks, "The Two Obamas," *New York Times*, June 20, 2008.

12 Michael Powell, "For Obama, A Pragmatist's Shift to the Center," *New York Times*, June 27, 2008.

13 Robin Toner, "Obama's Test: Can a Liberal Be a Unifier?" *New York Times*, March 25, 2008.

14 Brian Friel, Richard E. Cohen and Kirk Victor, "Obama: Most Liberal Senator in 2007," *National Journal*, January 31, 2008.

15 Alec MacGillis, "In Obama's New Message, Some Foes See Old Liberalism," *Washington Post*, March 26, 2008, A01.

16 Michael Powell, "Man in the News: Calm in the Swirl of History," *New York Times*, June 4, 2008.

17 Frank Rich, "The Up or Down Vote on Obama's Presidency," *New York Times*, March 7, 2010.

18 Jon Taplin, "Obama's Victory Strategy," *TPM*, February 12, 2010.

19 George C. Edwards III, *On Deaf Ears: The Limits of the Bully Pulpit*, New Haven: Yale University Press, 2003.

20 Rich, "The Up or Down Vote."

21 As one observer put it, "Barack Obama has gone from being historic to being ubiquitous. He doesn't just control the news cycle, he is the news cycle." See Roger Simon, "It's All Obama, All the Time," *Politico*, April 16, 2009. The president has, for example, expressed himself publicaly on the following, which is only a partial list: whether college football should adopt a playoff system, who would win the college basketball tournament, whether he favored Michael Jordan over Kobe Bryant when asked who was the better professional basketball player. See Peter Baker, "A Presidential Pitfall: Speaking One's Mind," *New York Times*, July 27, 2009; see also Karen Travers, "Overachiever-in-Chief: Is There an Issue the President Won't Weigh in On?" *ABC News*, July 28, 2009.

22 One measure is the sheer amount of words the president has publicaly spoken since entering office. From his inaugural address through his July 22, 2009 press conference that number was 670,000. See Eamon Javers and Zachary Abrahamson, "Obama's Words Downplay Wars," *Politico*, August 13, 2009.

23 Editorial, "Barack Obama for President," *Washington Post*, October 17, 2008 (emphasis added).

24 John Heilemann and Mark Halperin, *Game Change: Obama and the Clintons, McCain and Palin, and the Race of a Lifetime*, New York: Harper Perennial, p. 32; see also John Avlon, "Irrational Obama Exuberance," *Daily Beast*, November 26, 2008.

25 Quoted in David Mendell, *Obama: From Promise to Power*, New York: Harper Collins, 2007, p. 7.

26 Eleanor Cliff, "Halfhearted Soul-Searching at the White House," *Newsweek*, November 21, 2010.

27 Lexington, "The Obama Cult: If Barack Obama Disappoints His Supporters, They Will Have Only Themselves to Blame," *The Economist*, July 23, 2009.

28 Sasha Johnson and Candy Crowley, "Winfrey tells Iowa crowd: Barack Obama is 'the one,'" *CNN*, December 8, 2007.

29 Judith Warner, "Sometimes a President Is Just a President," *New York Times*, February 5, 2009.

30 Jeffrey Goldberg, "Is Obama God?" *The Atlantic*, June 8, 2009.

31 Carrie Budoff Brown and Nia-Malika Henderson, "Paparazzo Snaps Shirtless Obama," *Politico*, December 23, 2008; see also Daniel Libit and Jeffey Ressner, "Obama's Paparazzi Presidency," *Politico*, January 1, 2009; Judith Warner, "A Hot Time in Washington," *New York Times*, May 14, 2009.

32 Touré, "And Next: Mt. Rushmore?" *Daily Beast*, November 11, 2008.

33 "Planning Under Way for Obama Holiday," *Topeka Capital-Journal*, November 9, 2009.

34 American Society of Magazine Editors, http://www.magazine.org/asme/2009-best-magazine-cover-winners-finalists.aspx (accessed March 10, 2011).

35 Jay Cost, "The Celebrity-in-Chief," *RealClearPolitics*, February 3, 2009.

36 "Obama Talks LeBron James Free Agency During Marv Albert TNT interview," *Huffington Post*, May 23, 2010.

37 Josh Gerstein, "Obama, Gibbs Split Over Perfect Game," *Politico*, June 6, 2010.
38 Jessica Derschowitz, "'The View:' Obama Not Invited to Chelsea Clinton's Wedding," CBS, July 29, 2010.
39 Derrik J. Lang, "Obama Appears on George Lopez's Late Night Talk Show," *Huffington Post*, July 29, 2009.
40 Jim Rutterberg, "The Tonight Show With ... President Obama?" *New York Times*, June 3, 2009.
41 Elizabeth Williamson and Sam Schechner, "Obama Reinforces Policy Messages on Letterman's 'Late Night,'" *Wall Street Journal*, September 22, 2009.
42 Helene Cooper, "For Obama, Talk About Economy Goes Into Late Night," *New York Times*, March 20, 2009.
43 Laura Meckler, "On 'Tonight Show,' Obama Urges Steadiness in Face of Crisis," *Wall Street Journal*, March 19, 2009.
44 Dan Loumena, "President Obama a Hit as a TV Broadcaster," *Los Angeles Times*, January 30, 2010.
45 Lisa de Moraes, "John Walsh to Interview President Obama on Fox's 'America's Most Wanted,'" *Washington Post*, March 4, 2010.
46 Michael Humes, "President Obama Fills Out Men's & Women's Brackets in Exclusive ESPN Interview," *ESPN*, March 16, 2010.
47 Michael D. Shear, "Obama to Appear on the 'Daily Show,'" *New York Times*, October 27, 2010.
48 Frazier Moore, "Obama to Appear on ABC's 'The View' on Thursday," *Associated Press*, July 26, 2010. John McCain also appeared on "The View," but as a presidential candidate. See Robert Barnes and Michael D. Shear, "McCain Gets an Earful on 'The View,'" *Washington Post*, September 12, 2008.
49 Peter Nicholas and Janet Hook, "Obama the Velcro President," *Los Angeles Times*, July 30, 2010.
50 Peter Wallsten and Faye Fiore, "Getting to Know the Obamas, on their Terms," *Los Angeles Times*, April 30, 2009.
51 Peggy Noonan, "Look at the Time," *Wall Street Journal*, January 30, 2009 (emphasis added).
52 Robert Dallek, "Obama's Historic Health Care Victory," *Wall Street Journal*, December 29, 2009.
53 "Niall Ferguson on Obama and the Global Crisis," *Der Spiegel*, November 11, 2008. Available at: http://www.spiegel.de/international/world/0,1518,druck-589735,00.html (accessed July 6, 2010).
54 *Charlie Rose*, "Historians on Obama," November 7, 2008. Available at: http://www.charlierose.com/view/interview/9389 (accessed August 8, 2010).
55 Nicholas D. Kristoff, "Franklin Delano Obama," *New York Times*, March 1, 2009.
56 Katharine Q. Seelye, "The Abraham Lincoln Analogy," *New York Times*, February 12, 2009.
57 Joe Klein, "Obama's Team of Rivals," *Time*, June 18, 2008; see also Joe Klein, "National Security Team of Rivals," *Time*, November 21, 2008.
58 Jake Tapper, "Obama Proposes 'Team of Rivals' Cabinet," *ABC News*, May 22, 2008.
59 David Greenberg, "Playing the Tolerance Card: How Obama is like JFK," *Slate*, April 20, 2007; Toby Harnden, "Barack Obama is JFK Heir, Says Kennedy Aide," *Telegraph*, October 12, 2007.
60 Howard Fineman, "Channeling the Gipper," *Newsweek*, November 30, 2009; see also Jeffrey Hart, "Obama is the New Reagan," *Daily Beast*, November 4, 2008; Darrell M. West, "Is Obama the New Reagan?" *Brookings Institution*, July 8, 2008; and Diane Winston, "Obama is the New Reagan," *Politics and Society*, June 27, 2008.

61 Melik Kaylan, "Obama: More Like Nixon Than Carter," *Daily Beast*, September 25, 2010.

62 John Fund, "The Carter-Obama Comparisons Grow," *Wall Street Journal*, September 22, 1010.

63 PBS Transcript, "Lincoln, Roosevelt Presidencies Offer Lessons for Obama," *PBS News Hour*, November 27, 2008. Available at: http://www.pbs.org/newshour/bb/white_house/july-dec08/historians_11-27.html (accessed February 19, 2011).

64 Richard Kirsch, "What Obama Can Learn from Reagan," *Huffington Post*, December 10, 2010.

65 H.W. Brands, "What Obama Can Learn from FDR and Reagan," *NPR*, November 20, 2008.

66 Julian E. Zelizer, "What Obama Can Learn from Clinton, Reagan," *CNN*, January 24, 2011.

67 John O'Boyle, "The Professor and the Prosecutor," *Newsweek*, November 29, 2010.

68 The complete set of rankings can be found at: http://www.siena.edu/uploadedfiles/home/parents_and_community/community_page/sri/independent_research/Presidents%20Release_2010_final.pdf (accessed March 10, 2010).

69 This survey is a particularly questionable example of these kinds of rankings since we are not told how many persons were asked to participate, but only how many had. The survey "is based on responses from 238 presidential scholars, historians and political scientists *that responded* via mail or web to an invitation to participate. Respondents ranked each of 43 (sic) presidents on a scale of 1 (poor) to 5 (excellent) on each of twenty presidential attributes, abilities and accomplishments." See Siena Research Institute press release, July 1, 2010. Scroll down to July 1, 2010 and click on "rankings" for complete rankings: http://www.siena.edu/pages/3390.aspqs=irhttp://www.siena.edu/uploadedfiles/home/parents_and_community/community_page/sri/independent_research/Presidents%20Release_2010_final.pdf (accessed March 10, 2011).

70 John Fund, "Obama the Great?" *Wall Street Journal*, July 3, 2010.

71 Peter Baker, "Transition Holds Clues to How Obama Will Govern," *New York Times*, January 20, 2009.

72 For an explanation and examination of the positivity bias in political life see Richard R. Lau, David O. Sears, and Richard Centers, "The 'Positivity Bias' in Evaluations of Public Figures: Evidence Against Instrumental Artifacts," *American Journal of Public Opinion*, 43 (1979), pp. 347–58.

73 Howard Kurtz, "Missing the Mark in Massachusetts: Honeymoon is History," *Washington Post*, January 25, 2010; see also Center for Media and Public Affairs, "Obama Media Coverage Sours," September 14, 2009.

74 Howard Kurtz, "A Giddy Sense of Boosterism," *Washington Post*, November 17, 2008.

75 Robert J. Samuelson, "The Obama Infatuation," *Washington Post*, June 1, 2009.

76 Pew Research Center for the People & the Press. "Obama at 100 Days: Strong Job Approval, Even Higher Personal Ratings Better Ratings for Foreign Policy than Domestic Issues," April 23, 2009. Available at: http://people-press.org/reports/pdf/509.pdf (accessed July 8, 2010).

77 Center for Media and Public Affairs, "Obama's Media Image: Compared to what?" January 25, 2010. Available at: http://www.cmpa.com/media_room_press_1_25_10.html (accessed July 6, 2010); see also Center for Media and Public Affairs, "Media Boast Obama, Bash His Policies," April 27, 2009.

78 Chris Cillizza, "White House Cheat Sheet: Obama Beloved, Policies Be-Liked," *Washington Post*, April 30, 2009.

79 Obama quoted in Powell, "Calm in the Swirl of History,"

80 Obama quoted in Mendell, *Obama*, p. 12 (emphasis added).
81 E. J. Dionne Jr., "Audacity Without Ideology," *Washington Post*, January 15, 2009, A19.
82 Lydia Saad, "In U.S., Majority Now Say Obama's Policies 'Mostly Liberal,'" *Gallup*, November 4, 2009; see also Rasmussen, "More Voters Than Ever See Obama As Partisan Democrat," March 29, 2010.
83 Anne E. Kornblut, "Obama Holds Traditional News Conference to Talk Bipartisanship," *Washington Post*, February 10, 2010, A06; see also Shailagh Murray and Paul Kane, "Obama Meets with Republicans to Bridge Partisan Divide," *Washington Post*, February 10, 2010, A01.
84 White House, "Remarks by the President Before Meeting with Bipartisan Leaders of the House and Senate," February 9, 2010. Available at: http://www.whitehouse.gov/the-press-office/remarks-president-meeting-with-bipartisan-leaders-house-and-senate (accessed July 5, 2010).
85 Matt Bai, "Debt-Busting Issue May Force Obama Off Fence," *New York Times*, November 30, 2010.
86 Garance Franke-Ruta, "Obama tells blogger he's a progressive," *Politerati*, October 27, 2010.
87 Obama quoted in Jonathan Martin and Carol E. Lee, "Obama: 'I am a New Democrat,'" *Politico*, March 10, 2009.
88 Peter Baker, "The Limits of Rahmism," *New York Times Magazine*, March 14, 2009; see also Elizabeth Drew, "The Thirty Days of Barack Obama," *New York Review of Books*, March 26, 2009.
89 Peter Baker, "Education of a President," *New York Times*, October 12, 2010.
90 Paula Dwyer, "How the Political Gridlock in Washington Might End," *Bloomberg-Business Week*, February 24, 2010. Confirmation of Obama's comment that "I won" during the meeting can be found at Jonathan Martin and Carol E. Lee, " Obama to GOP: 'I won,'" *Politico*, Janaury 23, 2009.
91 Sheryl Gay Stolberg, "Obama's Playbook After Nov. 2," *New York Times*, October 24, 2010.
92 Obama quoted in David Remnick, "Testing the Waters," *New Yorker*, November 6, 2008 (emphasis added).
93 Obama quoted in Ronald Brownstein, "An Eternal Optimist—but Not a Sap," *National Journal*, February 14, 2009.
94 Obama quoted in Richard Wolffe, *Renegade: The Making of a President*, New York: Crown, 2009, p. 67.
95 *C-SPAN* Interview Transcript, "President Barack H. Obama," May 22, 2009. http://www.c-span.org/pdf/obamainterview.pdf (accessed March 5, 2011).
96 Karen Tumulty and David Von Drehle, "Obama on His Veep Thinking," *Time*, August 20, 2008.
97 Ruth Marcus, "President Obama Is Making Nobody Happy," *Washington Post*, April 3, 2010.
98 David Brooks, "Getting Obama Right," *New York Times*, March 12, 2010.
99 Brooks, "Getting Obama Right."
100 Jon Meacham, "What He's Learned: A Conversation with Barack Obama," *Newsweek*, May 25, 2009. http://www.newsweek.com/id/197891/page/1 (accessed)
101 See Jodi Kantor, "In Law School, Obama Found Political Voice," *New York Times*, January 28, 2007.
102 Brownstein, "An Eternal Optimist—but Not a Sap" (emphasis added).
103 Balz and Johnson, *The Battle for America 2008*, p. 305.
104 Remnick, *The Bridge*, p. 430.
105 Peter Slevin, "Obama Forged Political Mettle in Illinois Capitol," *Washington Post*, February 9, 2007.
106 Eli Saslow, "From Outsider to Politician," *Washington Post*, October 9, 2008.

107 Mendell, *Obama*, p. 7.

108 The composite reflects 99 key votes and assigned scores in three areas: economic issues, social issues, and foreign policy. See Brian Friel, Richard E. Cohen, and Kirk Victor, "Obama: Most Liberal Senator in 2007," *National Journal*, 31 January 2008.

109 Toner, "Obama's Test: Can a Liberal Be a Unifier?".

110 Remnick, *The Bridge: The Life and Rise of Barack Obama*, New York: Knopf, 2010, p. 433.

111 Barack Obama, *The Audacity of Hope*, New York: Three Rivers Press, 2006, p. 29.

112 Obama, *Audacity*, p. 10.

113 Obama, *Audacity*, p. 24 (emphasis added).

114 Obama quoted in Sam Youngman, "Obama boasts of most 'progressive' political triumphs in decades," *The Hill*, August 17, 2010.

115 Jann S. Wenner, "Obama in Command: The Rolling Stone Interview," *Rolling Stone*, October 15, 2010.

116 Liza Mundy, "A Series of Fortunate Events," *Washington Post*, August 12, 2007.

117 Stephen F. Hayes, "Obama and the Power of Words," *Wall Street Journal*, February 26, 2008.

118 Hayes, "Obama and the Power of Words."

119 "The second thing I admire most in Lincoln is that there is just a deep-rooted honesty and empathy to the man that allowed him to always be able to see the other person's point of view and always sought to find the truth that is in the gap between you and me."

   (Obama quoted in Balz and Johnson, *The Battle for America 2008*, p. 380)

120 Jon Meacham, "A Highly Logical Approach," *Newsweek*, May 25, 2009 (emphasis added).

121 I am indebted to Richard Friedman, MD for pointing out this question to me.

122 Larissa MacFarquhar, "The Conciliator," *New Yorker*, May 7, 2007.

123 Obama, *Dreams*, pp. 80–81, 100, 105.

124 Obama, *Dreams*, p. 79.

125 Mendell, *Obama*, p. 75.

126 Obama, *Dreams*, p. 293.

127 Obama quoted in Bob Secter and John McCormick, "Portrait of a Pragmatist," *Chicago Tribune*, March 30, 2007 (emphasis added).

128 Cf., Derek Kravitz and Keith B. Richburg, "Obama Quits Longtime Church Over Inflammatory Comments," *Washington Post*, June 1, 2008.

129 Quoted in Evan Thomas, *A Long Time Coming: The Inspiring Combative 2008 Campaign and the Historic Election of Barack Obama*, New York: Public Affairs Press, 2009, p. 69. The article in question is Ben Wallace-Wells, "Destiny's Child," *Rolling Stone*, February 22, 2007.

130 Oscar Avila, "Obama's Census Choice: Simply African-American," *Chicago Tribune*, April 2, 2010.

131 Abigail Thernstrom, "Obama's Census Identity," *Wall Street Journal*, April 16, 2010.

3 The Arc of Ambition and the Development of a Style

1 This portion of the chapter draws on Stanley A. Renshon, *The Psychological Assessment of Presidential Candidates*, New York: New York University Press, 1996 (1998 paperback edition, with afterword, published by Routledge), chapter 7.

2 Dan Balz and Haynes Johnson, *The Battle for America 2008*, New York: Viking, 2010, p. 28; see also John Heilemann and Mark Halperin, *Game Change: Obama and the*

Clintons, McCain and Palin, and the Race of a Lifetime, New York: Harper Perennial, 2010, pp. 30–31.

3 Balz and Johnson, *The Battle for America*, p. 29.

4 Her father had fervently wished for a son. Useful profiles of his mother are: Janny Scott, "A Free Spirited Wanderer Who Set Obama's Path," *New York Times*, March 14, 2008; Tim Jones, "Barack Obama: Mother Not Just a Girl from Kansas," *Chicago Tribune*, March 27, 2007; and Amanda Ripley, "The Story of Barack Obama's Mother," *Time*, April 9, 2008.

5 Judith Kampfner, "The untold story of Obama's mother," *Independent*, September 16, 2009.

6 Attempts to follow up with Ms. Kampfner have been unsuccessful to date.

7 Barack Obama, *Dreams from My Father*, New York: Crown, 2004, p. 47.

8 Cf. David Remnick, *The Bridge: The Life and Rise of Barack Obama*, New York: Knopf, 2010, pp. 77–78; see also Kirsten Scharnberg and Kim Barker, "The Not-so-simple Story of Barack Obama's Youth," *Chicago Tribune*, March 25, 2007.

9 William Finnegan, "The Candidate," *New Yorker*, May 31, 2004.

10 David Mendell, *Obama: From Promise to Power*, New York: Harper Collins, 2007, p. 63.

11 Remnick, *The Bridge*, p. 135. During this period Obama sent several of the short stories he had written based on his change experience to his friends and shared them as well with Kellman.

12 Quoted in Bob Secter and John McCormick, "Portrait of a Pragmatist," *Chicago Tribune*, 30 March, 2007.

13 Mendell, *Obama*, pp. 16, 62; see also Remnick, *The Bridge*, p. 113.

14 Obama, *Dreams*, p. 336.

15 Remnick, *The Bridge*, p. 51.

16 Remnick, *The Bridge*, p. 52.

17 Abercrombie quoted in Remnick, *The Bridge*, p. 52.

18 Obama, *Dreams*, p. 27.

19 Ann Dunham quoted in Remnick, *The Bridge*, p. 53.

20 Ann Dunham quoted in Obama, *Dreams*, p. 6.

21 This is one of the stories that Obama's grandfather and his mother told him of his father. See Obama, *Dreams*, pp. 6–7.

22 Scharnberg and Barker, "The Not-so-simple Story of Barack Obama's Youth."

23 Obama, *Dreams*, p. 53.

24 Scharnberg and Barker, "The Not-so-simple Story of Barack Obama's Youth,"

25 Scharnberg and Barker, "The Not-so-simple Story of Barack Obama's Youth,"

26 Remnick, *The Bridge*, pp. 75–76.

27 Remnick, *The Bridge*, p. 93; Alter characterizes Obama as a "casual student." See Jonathan Alter, *The Promise: President Obama, Year One*, New York: Simon and Schuster, p. 144.

28 Quoted in Mendell, *Obama*, pp. 46–47.

29 Quoted in Mendell, *Obama*, p. 32; see also Remnick, *The Bridge*, p. 93.

30 Mendell, *Obama*, p. 45.

31 Quoted in Obama, *Dreams*, p. 95.

32 Obama, *Dreams*, p. 95.

33 Obama, *Dreams*, p. 95.

34 Obama, *Dreams*, p. 95.

35 Quoted in Kevin Merida, "The Ghost of a Father," *Washington Post*, December 14, 2007 (emphasis added).

36 Quoted in Merida, "The Ghost of a Father."

37 Obama, *Dreams*, p. 115.

38 Obama, *Dreams*, p. 96.

39 Mendell, *Obama*, p. 61.

40 Mendell, *Obama*, p. 56.

41 Obama, *Dreams*, p. 100.

42 Obama, *Dreams*, p.100.

43 Janny Scott, "In Chicago, Obama Proved Pragmatic and Shrewd," *New York Times*, July 30, 2007.

44 Peter Baker, "On Sestak Matter, a 'Trust Us' Response from the White House," *New York Times*, May 24, 2010.

45 Editorial, "Romanoff job offer demands response from Obama," *Washington Post*, June 5, 2010.

46 Gwen Ifill, "Review of David Remnick's biography of Barack Obama, 'The Bridge,'" *Washington Post*, April 4, 2010.

47 Calvin Woodward, "Obama not above political manipulation after all," *Associated Press*, June 5, 2010.

48 Janny Scott, "Obama's Account of New York Years Often Differs from What Others Say," *New York Times*, October 30, 2007.

49 Quoted in Bob Secter and John McCormick, "Portrait of a Pragmatist," *Chicago Tribune*, March 30, 2007.

50 Obama quoted in Secter and McCormick, "Portrait of a Pragmatist."

51 Obama quoted in David Jackson and Ray Long, "Obama Knows His Way Around a Ballot: Some Say His Ability to Play Political Hardball Goes Back to His First Campaign," *Chicago Tribune*, April 3, 2007.

52 Robinson quoted in Liza Mundy, "A Series of Fortunate Events," *Washington Post*, 12 August, 2007.

53 Mundy, "A Series of Fortunate Events."

54 Jodi Kantor, "In Law School, Obama Found Political Voice," *New York Times*, January 28, 2007; see also Michael Levenson and Jonathan Saltzman, "At Harvard Law, a unifying voice," *Boston Globe*, January 28, 2007.

55 When attorney Judson Miner, who headed a Chicago civil rights focused firm, called Obama to offer him a job, the woman who answered the phone at the *Harvard Law Review* told him, "You can leave your name and take a number. You're No. 647." Quoted in Mike Robinson, "Obama Got Start in Civil Rights Practice," *Boston Globe*, February 20, 2007.

56 Robinson, "Obama Got Start in Civil Rights Practice."

57 Quoted in Peter Slevin, "Obama Forged Political Mettle In Illinois Capitol," *Washington Post*, February 9, 2007.

58 Rick Pearson and Ray Long, "Careful Steps, Looking Ahead," *Chicago Tribune*, 3 May, 2007; see also Janny Scott, "In Illinois, Obama Proved Pragmatic and Shrewd," *New York Times*, July 30, 2007.

59 Quoted in Scott, "In Illinois."

60 The quotes in this and the following three paragraphs are drawn from "Transcript: President Obama, Part 1," *CBS News 60 Minutes*, March 24, 2009. Available at: http://www.cbsnews.com/stories/2009/03/24/60minutes/main4890684.shtml?tag=mncol;lst;7 (accessed July 18, 2010).

61 "Transcript: President Obama, Part 2," *CBS News 60 Minutes*, March 24, 2009. Available at: http://www.cbsnews.com/stories/2009/03/24/60minutes/main4890687.shtml?tag=contentMain;contentBody (accessed July 18, 2010).

62 Sheryl Gay Stolberg, "White House Unbuttons Formal Dress Code," *New York Times*, January 28, 2009; see also Carrie Budoff Brown, "Obama returns night-owl presidency," *Politico*, January 15, 2009.

63 Mike Boehm, "Obamas Find a Way to Do Broadway at Home, Hosting Star-studded PBS Taping," *Los Angeles Times*, July 14, 2010.

64 Charles McNulty, "The Obamas Give their Regards to Broadway," *Los Angeles Times*, June 1, 2009.

65 David Jackson, "Obama: No Moratorium on Golf," *USA TODAY*, June 21, 2010.

66 Andrew Johnson, "President Obama Throws Out Ceremonial First Pitch in Washington," *MLB*, April 5, 2010.

67 "Toast Remarks by President Obama at Ceremonial Lunch with President Klaus of the Czech Republic and President Medvedev of Russia," The White House, April 8, 2010.

68 Neil King Jr. and Jonathan Weisman, "Detail Man: As a Manager, Obama Gets into the Weeds," *Wall Street Journal*, August 12, 2009. King and Weisman report what others close to the president say about his information gathering style, about which they caution. Still, the evidence, from a variety of sources, tends to support the view that the president likes to be informed about policy details and makes efforts toward that end.

69 Ben Smith, "Hazards of the Teleprompter," *Politico*, February 4, 2010.

70 Marie C. Kodama, "Obama Left Mark on HLS," *Harvard Crimson*, January 19, 2007.

71 Rauschenberger quoted in Jonathan Kaufman, "For Obama, Chicago Days Honed Tactics," *Wall Street Journal*, 21 April, 2008.

72 Walter Isaacson, *Einstein: His Life and Universe*, New York: Simon & Schuster, 2007.

73 Mendell says that Obama, "researched and wrote articles for the *Harvard Civil Rights– Civil Liberties Law Review*, but a search of that journal during the years that Obama attended Harvard failed to reveal them. See Mendell, *Obama*, p. 84.

74 Obama, *Dreams*, p. 171.

75 Obama quoted in Richard Wolffe, *Renegade: The Making of a President*, New York: Crown, 2009, p. 39.

76 Fred I. Greenstein, "Barack Obama: The Man and His Early Presidency," in Bruce Miroff, et al., ed. *Debating Democracy: A Reader in American Politics*, Florence, KY: Wadsworth, 2011.

77 Eli Saslow, "From Outsider To Politician," *Washington Post*, October 9, 2008.

78 Michael D. Shear, "White House Searching For a Way to Reconnect with Voters Over Economy," *Washington Post*, July 14, 2010.

79 Barack Obama, *The Audacity of Hope*, New York: Three Rivers Press, 2006, p. 21.

80 Joel Achenbach, "In a Heated Race, Obama's Cool Won the Day," *Washington Post*, November 6, 2008.

81 Greenstein, "Barack Obama" (emphasis in original).

82 "Review & Outlook: 'Feel the Rage,'" *Wall Street Journal*, June 9, 2010.

83 Q: Just a couple more quick ones on this. The President said when the top kill procedure failed over the weekend that the leak was as enraging as it is heartbreaking. Have you seen the President enraged about this?

MR. GIBBS: Throughout this process, absolutely.

Q: Do you think that that has come through to the American people?

MR. GIBBS: I think the American people are frustrated. I think the people of the Gulf are frustrated. I think the President is frustrated. I think the White House is frustrated. I don't see how anybody could look at what's happening in the Gulf and not be frustrated and heartbroken—absolutely. ...

Q: You said earlier that the President is enraged. Is he enraged at BP specifically?

MR. GIBBS: I think he's enraged at the time that it's taken, yes. I think he's been enraged over the course of this, as I've discussed, about the fact that when you're told something is fail-safe and it clearly isn't, that that's the cause for quite a bit of frustration. I think one of the reasons that—which is one of the reasons you heard him discuss the setting up of the oil commission in order to create a regulatory framework that ensures something like this doesn't happen again.

Q: Frustration and rage are very different emotions, though. I haven't—have we really seen rage from the President on this? I think most people would say no.

MR. GIBBS: I've seen rage from him, Chip. I have.

Q: Can you describe it? Does he yell and scream? What does he do? (Laughter.)

MR. GIBBS: He said—he has been in a whole bunch of different meetings—clenched jaw—even in the midst of these briefings, saying everything has to be done. I think this was an anecdote shared last week, to plug the damn hole.

(See "Press Briefing by Press Secretary Robert Gibbs," The White House, June 1, 2010. Available at: http://www.whitehouse.gov/the-press-office/ press-briefing-press-secretary-robert-gibbs-6110 (accessed July 14, 2010).)

84 Garrett M. Gaff, "The Legend of Barack Obama," *The Washingtonian*, November 1, 2006.
85 Ryan Lizza, "The Agitator," *New Republic*, 19 March, 2007.
86 Michael Powell, "A Deliberative Man in a Manic Game," *New York Times*, June 4, 2008.
87 Mendell, *Obama*, p. 70.
88 Ryan Lizza, "Making It: How Chicago Shaped Obama," *New Yorker*, July 21, 2008.
89 Secter and McCormick, "Obama: Part 3: Portrait of a Pragmatist."
90 David Jackson and Ray Long, "Showing His Bare Knuckles," *Chicago Tribune*, April 4, 2007; see also David Jackson and Ray Long, "Obama knows his way around a ballot: Some say his ability to play political hardball goes back to his first campaign," *Chicago Tribune*, April 3, 2007.
91 Quoted in Jackson and Ray Long, "Showing His Bare Knuckles."
92 "Review and Outlook, 'The Obama We Don't Know,'" *Wall Street Journal*, June 4, 2008.
93 Remnick, *The Bridge*, p. 283.
94 Evan Thomas, A *Long Time Coming; The Inspiring, Combative 2008 Campaign and the Historic Election of Barack Obama*, New York: Public Affairs Press, 2009, p. 139.
95 Remnick, *The Bridge*, pp. 392–93; see also Eli Saslow, "The 17 Minutes That Launched a Political Star," *Washington Post*, August 25, 2008.
96 Obama, *Dreams*, p. 106 (emphasis added).
97 Quoted in Mendell, *Obama*, p. 29.
98 David Maraniss, "Though Obama Had to Leave to Find Himself, It Is Hawaii That Made His Rise Possible," *Washington Post*, August 22, 2008.
99 Obama, *Dreams*, p. 67.
100 Obama, *Dreams*, p. 106.
101 James David Barber, *The Presidential Character: Predicting Performance in the White House*, Englewood Cliffs, N.J.: Prentice Hall, 1992, pp. 7–8.
102 "Transcript: Obama's Speech Against The Iraq War," NPR, January 20, 2009. Available at: http://www.npr.org/templates/story/story.php?storyId=99591469 (accessed June 26, 2010).
103 Anne E. Kornblut, "The Great Elaborator: Obama Gives 17-minute Answer to Health-care Query in N.C.," *Washington Post*, April 3, 2010.
104 Quoted in Powell, "Deliberative in a Manic Game."
105 Liza Mundy, "A Series of Fortunate Events," *Washington Post*, August 12, 2007.
106 Peter Slevin, "Obama Forged Political Mettle In Illinois Capitol," *Washington Post*, February 9, 2007.

107 Jodi Kantor, "In Law School, Obama found Political Voice," *New York Times*, January 28, 2007.

108 Kantor, "In Law School" (emphasis added).

109 Kantor, "In Law School."

110 Kantor, "In Law School."

111 Quoted in Fox Butterfield, "First Black Elected to Head Harvard's Law Review," *New York Times*, February 6, 1990.

112 Kantor, "In Law School."

113 Alec MacGillis, "Finding Political Strength in the Power of Words," *Washington Post*, February 26, 2008.

114 Bradford Berenson, a Washington lawyer and former associate counsel in the Bush administration, says of Obama, "this is a very gifted individual who has a way with words and an interest and ability in communication." Quoted in MacGillis, "Finding Political Strength in the Power of Words."

115 Kate Zernike, "The Charisma Mandate," *New York Times*, February 17, 2008.

116 Joe Klein, "Inspiration vs. Substance," *Time*, February 7, 2008; See also Sebastian Mallaby, "Obama's Missing Ideas," *Washington Post*, February 25, 2008 and Michael Gerson, "Words Aren't Cheap," *Washington Post*, February 29, 2008.

117 Peter Applebome, "Is Eloquence Overrated?" *New York Times*, January 13, 2008.

118 Stephen F. Hayes, "Obama and the Power of Words," *Wall Street Journal*, February 26, 2008.

119 Hayes, "Obama and the Power of Words."

120 Barack Obama, "Remarks of Senator Barack Obama: Final Primary Night," June 3,2008. Available at: http://www.barackobama.com/2008/06/03/remarks_of_senator_barack_obam_73.php (accessed June 26, 2010).

4 Obama's Presidential Leadership: Transformation and Redemption

1 Matt Taibbi, "The Low Post: Between Barack and a Hard Place," *Rolling Stone*, February 15, 2007.

2 Fred Hiatt, "Obama's Empathy Meets the Politics of Governing," *Washington Post*, March 1, 2010.

3 Rick Pearson and Ray Long, "Obama: I'm Running for President," *Chicago Tribune*, February 10, 2007.

4 Its importance to Obama is reflected in the number of times that he has used that quote in talking to friends and interviewers but also in his efforts to find out more about it. Journalists researching Obama's life learned that,

> Until recently, he thought it came from Lyndon B. Johnson who had his own unresolved issues with his father. At one point in the campaign, Obama asked an aide to call Robert A. Caro, the preeminent Johnson biographer, to check. Caro said no, the quote was not from Johnson. The biographer was reminded though of something Johnson's brother had told him. The most important thing to Johnson, the brother had told Caro, was "not to be like Daddy," whom LBJ had once idolized but who later lost the family ranch and became a laughingstock.
>
> (See Kevin Merida, "The Ghost of a Father," *Washington Post*, December 14, 2007)

5 NPR Interview: "Barack Obama Discusses His Background, Career and His Future Political Plans as He Prepares to Give Tonight's Keynote Address at

the Democratic National Convention," July 27, 2004. Available at: www.nacdl. org/sl_docs.nsf/freeform/Mandatory:306 (accessed October 21, 2010); see also David Mendell, *Obama: From Promise to Power*, New York: HarperCollins, 2007, p. 40; Barack Obama, *The Audacity of Hope*, New York: Three Rivers Press, 2006, p. 11.

6 Barack Obama, *Dreams from My Father*, New York: Three Rivers Press, 2004, p. 227 (emphasis added).

7 Bill Sammon, *Meet the Next President: What You Don't Know About the Candidates*, New York: Threshold, 2007, p. 35.

8 Evan Thomas, *A Long Time Coming: The Inspiring, Combative 2008 Campaign and the Historic Election of Barack Obama*, New York: Public Affairs Press, 2009, p. ix (emphasis added).

9 David Remnick, *The Bridge: The Life and Rise of Barack Obama*, New York: Knopf, 2010, p. 231.

10 Remnick, *The Bridge*, p. 231.

11 Remnick, *The Bridge*, p. 235.

12 Remnick, *The Bridge*, p. 235.

13 I use that phrase "in one telling" because elsewhere Obama writes of his family not having enough money for a car or to afford the international school that most expats attended: "as a boy of seven or eight, none of this concerned me very much. I remember these years as a joyous time full of adventure and mystery. … " See Obama, *Audacity*, p. 274.

14 Richard Wolffe, *Renegade: The Making of a President*, New York: Crown, 2009, p. 236 (emphasis added).

15 Obama quoted in Remnick, *The Bridge*, p. 92.

16 Obama quoted in Remnick, *The Bridge*, p. 92.

17 Obama, *Dreams*, p. 93.

18 Kirsten Scharnberg and Kim Barker, "The Not-so-simple Story of Barack Obama's Youth," *Chicago Tribune*, March 25, 2007.

19 Obama quoted in Remnick, *The Bridge*, p. 113.

20 Obama quoted in Remnick, *The Bridge*, p. 113 (emphasis added).

21 Obama, *Dreams*, p. 120 (emphasis added).

22 Obams, *Dreams*, p. 120 (emphasis added): see also Remnick, *The Bridge*, p. 113.

23 Obama, *Dreams*, p. 119 (emphasis added).

24 Obama, *Dreams*, p. 134.

25 Obama, *Dreams*, p. 135.

26 Obama, *Dreams*, p. 135 (emphasis added).

27 Obama, *Dreams*, p. 136.

28 Obama, *Dreams*, p. 136 (emphasis added).

29 Obama letter to Ann Dunham quoted in Remnick, *The Bridge*, p. 119.

30 "An authorized transcript of an Eye on Books author interview": "Barack Obama 'Dreams From My Father,'" Interview recorded 8/9/1995. Available at: http://www. eyeonbooks.com/obama_transcript.pdf (accessed June 30, 2010).

31 Remnick, *The Bridge*, p. 40.

32 Mendell, *Obama*, p. 374 (emphasis added).

33 Obama quoted in Bob Secter and John McCormick, "Portrait of a Pragmatist," *Chicago Tribune*, March 30, 2007; see also Obama, *Dreams*, p. 344.

34 David Mendell, *Obama*, p. 28.

35 Obama, *Dreams*, pp. 429–30.

36 Remnick, *The Bridge*, p. 238.

37 Remnick, *The Bridge*, pp. 236–37.

38 Obama, *Dreams*, p. 209.

39 Obama, *Dreams*, p. 220.

40 Obama, *Dreams*, p. 220 (emphasis added).

41 Obama, *Dreams*, p. 220.

42 "Senator Barack Obama's Announcement for President," Springfield, IL., February 10, 2007. Available at: http://www.barackobama.com/2007/02/10/remarks_of_senator_barack_obam_11.php (accessed July 14, 2010).

43 Quoted in Wolffe, *Renegade*, p. 67.

44 Toby Harnden, "Barack Obama vows to 'change the world,'" *Telegraph*, October 17, 2008.

45 President Barack Obama's Inaugural Address, January 21, 2009. Available at: http://www.whitehouse.gov/blog/inaugural-address/ (accessed June 28, 2010).

46 "Remarks by the President in Arnold, Missouri Town Hall," April 29, 2009. Available at: http://www.whitehouse.gov/the_press_office/Remarks-by-the-President-at-Arnold-Missouri-Town Hall/ (accessed March 22, 2010).

47 Obama quoted in Wolffe, *Renegade*, p.188.

48 Peter Baker, "For Obama, Steep Learning Curve as Chief in War," *New York Times*, August 28, 2010.

49 Obama quoted in Michael Scherer, "How Barack Obama Became Mr. Unpopular," *Time*, September 2, 2010 (emphasis added).

50 Ryan Lizza, "Above the Fray," *GQ*, September, 2007 (emphasis added).

51 Obama quoted in Robin Givhan, "Mussed for Success: Barack Obama's Smooth Wrinkles," *Washington Post*, August 11, 2006.

52 Transcript, "Meet the Press," *NBC*, October 22, 2008. Available at: http://www.msnbc.msn.com/id/15304689/# (accessed August 29, 2010).

53 "Remarks of President Barack Obama—As Prepared for Delivery Address to Joint Session of Congress," White House, February 24, 2009. Available at: http://www.whitehouse.gov/the_press_office/remarks-of-president-barack-obama-address-to-joint-session-of-congress/ (accessed July 12, 2010).

54 Jonathan Alter, *The Promise: President Obama, Year One*, New York: Simon and Schuster, 2010, p. 244 (emphasis added).

55 The quote is: "Reagan changed the trajectory of America in a way that Richard Nixon did not and in a way that Bill Clinton did not. He put us on a fundamentally different path because the country was ready for it." See Nedra Pickler, "Rivals Slam Obama over Reagan Praise," *Associated Press*, February 19, 2008.

56 Philip Rucker, "A Familiar Precedent For a President-Elect: Obama Inspired by, Compared to Lincoln," *Washington Post*, November 19, 2008.

57 Joe Klein, "Obama's Team of Rivals," *Time*, June 18, 2008.

58 Rick Pearson and Ray Long, "Obama's Kickoff is Steeped in Symbolism: Imagery of Lincoln is Backdrop for Launch," *Chicago Tribune*, February 10, 2007.

59 Mark Halperin, "President-Elect Obama to be Sworn in Using the Lincoln Bible," *Time*,December 23, 2008.

60 AFP, "Obama Strives for the Lincoln Touch," *ABC News*, January 19, 2009.

61 Tom Bevan, "A Self-Inflicted Expectations Gap," *RealClearPolitics*, November 25, 2009.

62 Christi Parsons, "Obama Hopes to Appoint a 'Team of Rivals': President-elect Looks to Follow Lincoln's Model for his Cabinet," *Chicago Tribune*, November 15, 2008.

63 Sasha Issenberg, "In Tribute to Lincoln, Obama Rides the Rails, *Boston Globe*, January 18, 2009.

64 Katharine Q. Seelye, "The Abraham Lincoln Analogy," *New York Times*, February 12, 2009.

65 Barack Obama, "What I See in Lincoln's Eyes," *Time*, January 26, 2005.

66 Allan C. Guelzo, *Abraham Lincoln: Redeemer President*, Grand Rapids Michigan and Cambridge, U.K.: William B. Eerdmans Publishing Company, 1999, pp. 439–63.

67 Interview with Allen C. Guelzo, author of *Abraham Lincoln: Redeemer President* (December 2000). http://www.eerdmans.com/Interviews/guelzointerview.htm (accessed March 5, 2011).

68 Barack Obama, "What I See in Lincoln's Eyes," *Time*, January 26, 2005.

69 Barack Obama, "Remarks on the Federal Budget," March 17, 2009. Available at: http://www.gpoaccess.gov/presdocs/2009/DCPD200900159.pdf (accessed July 5, 2010).

70 Paul Kane, "Congress, Obama Brace for Showdown as Government Shutdown Looms," *Washington Post*, February 20, 2011; see also "Press Conference by the President," The White House, February 15, 2011; and Fred Hiatt, "Could Obama Decide a Deficit Deal is in His Interest?" *Washington Post*, February 20, 2011.

71 "Remarks by the President on Comprehensive Immigration Reform," The White House, July 1, 2010.

72 "Remarks by President Barack Obama, Prague, Czech Republic," April 5, 2009. Available at: http://www.whitehouse.gov/the_press_office/Remarks-By-President-Barack-Obama-In-Prague-As-Delivered (accessed May 9, 2010).

73 Remarks by President Obama at Strasbourg Town Hall, April 3, 2009. Available at: http://www.whitehouse.gov/the_press_office/Remarks-by-President-Obama-at-Strasbourg-Town-Hall/ (accessed May 2, 2010).

74 Barack Obama, "Renewing American Leadership," *Foreign Affairs*, July/August 2007, p.11.

75 Obama, "Renewing American Leadership," p. 11.

76 "Remarks by President Obama to the Turkish Parliament," Turkish Grand National Assembly Complex Ankara, Turkey. April 6, 2009. Available at: www.whitehouse.gov/the_press_office/Remarks-By-President-Obama-To-The-Turkish-Parliament (accessed May 9, 2010).

77 "Remarks by the President on National Security," National Archives, May 21, 2009. Available at: http://www.whitehouse.gov/the_press_office/Remarks-by-the-President-On-National-Security-5-21-09/ (accessed May 9, 2010).

78 "Official Remarks of the United States President Barack Obama at the Opening Ceremony of the Fifth Summit of the Americas, Port of Spain, Trinidad & Tobago," April 17–19, 2009. Available at: http://www.summitamericas.org/V_Summit/remarks_usa_en.pdf (accessed May 9, 2010).

79 "Transcript: Obama's Interview with Al Arabiya," January 27, 2009. Available at: http://www.alarabiya.net/articles/2009/01/27/65087.html (accessed May 9, 2010).

80 "Transcript: Obama's Interview with Al Arabiya."

81 Evan Ramstad, "North Korea threatens Military Strikes," *Wall Street Journal*, May 27, 2009.

82 Choe Sang-Hun, "North Korea Claims to Conduct 2nd Nuclear Test," *New York Times*, May 25, 2009.

83 Choe Sang-Hun, "North Korea is Said to Test-Fire 3 More Missiles," *New York Times*, May 27, 2009.

84 Cf., Kasie Hunt, "Dem: Ariz. law like 'Nazi Germany,'" *Politico*, April 26, 2010; Kasie Hunt, "Dems: Ariz law like Jim Crow, apartheid," *Politico*, April 28, 2010.

85 Pew Research Center for the People & the Press, "Democrats Divided, But Support Key Provisions: Broad Approval for New Arizona Law," May 12, 2012, p. 1. Available at: http://people-press.org/reports/pdf/613.pdf (accessed May 25, 2010).

86 Quoted in David Jackson, "Obama: U.S. 'a nation of immigrants and a nation of laws,' Blasts Arizona Law," *USA TODAY*, April 23, 2010.

87 Roger Runningen, "Obama Seeks Immigration Overhaul, Slams Arizona Law," *Bloomberg News*, April 23, 2010.

88 Jacobs quoted in Mimi Hall, "On visit, Calderon, Obama assails Ariz. Law," *USA TODAY*, May 19, 2010.

89 "Remarks by President Obama and President Calderón of Mexico at Joint Press Availability," May 19, 2010. Available at: http://www.whitehouse.gov/the-press-office/ remarks-president-obama-and-president-calder-n-mexico-joint-press-availability (accessed May 25, 2010).

90 *C-SPAN*, "Mexican President Calderon Address to Joint session of Congress," May 20, 2010. Available at: http://www.c-spanvideo.org/program/293616–2 (accessed May 25, 2010). The president's remarks quoted here begin at 43:32 on the video.

91 "White House, Democrats Applaud Mexican President Slamming Arizona Law," *FOXNews.com*, May 20, 2010. Available at: http://www.foxnews.com/politics/2010/ 05/20/mexicos-calderon-takes-case-congress/ (accessed March 5, 2011).

92 Alexis de Tocqueville, *Democracy in America* (Harvey Mansfield and Delba Winthrop, trans., ed.), Chicago: University of Chicago Press, 2000.

93 James Q. Wilson, "American Exceptionalism," American Enterprise Institute on line, August 29, 2006. Available at: http://www.aei.org/docLib/200608291_wilson_ oti_2. pdf (accessed May 1, 2010).

94 Seymour Martin Lipset, *American Exceptionalism: A Double Edged Sword*, New York: Norton, 1997, p. 33.

95 Godfrey Hodgson, *The Myth of American Exceptionalism*, New Haven, Ct.: Yale University Press, 2009.

96 "Transcript: President Obama News Conference," Strasbourg, France, April 4, 2009. Available at: http://www.whitehouse.gov/the_press_office/News-Conference-By-President-Obama-4-04-2009 (accessed October 2010).

97 Barack Obama, "Remarks by the President in Address to the Nation on the Way Forward in Afghanistan and Pakistan," December 1, 2009. Available at: http:// www.whitehouse.gov/the-press-office/remarks-president-address-nation-way-forward-afghanistan-and-pakistan (accessed May 1, 2010).

98 Remnick, *The Bridge*, p. 23 (emphasis added).

99 Karen Tumulty and David Von Drehle, "Obama on His Veep Thinking," *Time*, August 20, 2008. Available at: http://www.time.com/time/printout/ 0,8816,1834309,00.html (accessed June 28, 2010).

100 Quoted in Alex Spillius, "Barack Obama Says US Must Lead by Example," *Telegraph*, June 2, 2009.

101 Barack Obama, "Responsibility for our Common Future: Address to the United Nations General Assembly," September 23, 2009. Available at: http://usun. state.gov/briefing/statements/2009/september/129519.htm (accessed June 28, 2010).

102 Richard H. Thaler and Cass R. Sunstein, *Nudge: Improving Decisions about Health, Wealth, and Happiness*, New Haven, Ct.: Yale University Press, 2008.

103 Thaler and Sunstein, *Nudge*, p. 14.

104 Michael Grunwald, "How Obama Is Using the Science of Change," *Time*, April 2, 2009.

105 Solomon Asch, "Effects of Group Pressure Upon Modification and Distortion of Judgments," (pp. 222–36) in Mary Henle, *Documents of Gestalt Psychology*, Berkeley and Los Angeles, Ca.: University of California Press, 1961.

106 "Executive Order: Federal Leadership on Reducing Text Messaging While Driving," October 1, 2009. Available at: http://www.whitehouse.gov/the_press_office/Executive-Order-Federal-Leadership-on-Reducing-Text-Messaging-while-Driving (accessed May 14, 2010).

107 Editorial, "Mr. Obama's Nuclear Policy," *New York Times*, April 7, 2010.

108 David McKeeby, "Obama, Russia's Medvedev Announce New Arms Control Plan First Official Meeting Sets Broad Agenda for U.S.-Russian Relations," *America.Gov*, April 1, 2009. Available at: http://www.america.gov/st/peacesec-english/ 2009/April/20090401132246idybeekcm0.7817499.html (accessed March 5, 2011).

109 "Transcript: President Obama News Conference," Strasbourg, France.

110 "Transcript: Obama's Summit of the Americas Press Conference," April 19, 2009. Available from: http://www.realclearpolitics.com/articles/2009/04/19/obama_summit_americas_press_conference_96076.html (accessed May 2, 2010).

111 Jonathan Weisman, "Obama Presses Nuclear Issue," *Wall Street Journal*, April 12, 2010.

112 Josh Rogin, "Obama: We're Still Working on Our Democracy," *Foreign Policy*, April 11, 2010.

113 "Transcript remarks by President Obama at Strasbourg Town Hall," April 3, 2009. Available at: http://www.whitehouse.gov/blog/09/04/03/A-Town-Hall-in-Strasbourg/ (accessed October 21, 2010).

114 "White House Budget Director Defends Spending Plan," *NPR*, February 15, 2011.

5 The Moral Thrust of Obama's Ambition: Fairness

1 Harold D. Lasswell, *Power and Personality*, New York: Norton, 1948.

2 Stanley A. Renshon, *High Hopes: The Clinton Presidency and the Politics of Ambition*, New York: NYU Press, 1996 (1998 paperback edition, with afterword, published by Routledge).

3 Barack Obama, *Dreams from My Father*, New York: Three Rivers Press, 2004, p. 49; see also David Mendell, *Obama: From Promise to Power*, New York: Harper Collins, 2007, p. 34.

4 Mendell, *Obama*, p. 6.

5 Quoted in Mendell, *Obama*, p. 202 (emphasis added).

6 Obama quoted in Jake Tapper, "Share the Wealth?" *ABC News*, October 14, 2008.

7 Obama quoted in Steven G. Calabresi, "Obama's 'Redistribution' Constitution, *Wall Street Journal*,October 28, 2008. The audiotape of the interview can be found at "Audio Tape: Obama Interview," Chicago Public Radio Station WBEZ-FM, Sept. 6, 2001. Available at: http://www.youtube.com/watch?v=iivL4c_3pck (accessed July 6, 2010). Later in that same interview he said,

> I think, one of the tragedies of the civil rights movement was, um, because the civil rights movement became so court focused I think there was a tendency to lose track of the political and community organizing and activities on the ground that are able to put together the actual coalition of powers through which you bring about redistributive change.

8 "Transcript: Democratic Debate in Philadelphia," *New York Times*, April 16, 2008. Available at: http://www.nytimes.com/2008/04/16/us/politics/16textdebate.html?_r=1&pagewanted=print (accessed June 28, 2010).

9 David Leonhardt, "In Health Care Bill, Obama Attacks Wealth Inequality," *New York Times*, March 23, 2010.

10 Mendell, *Obama*, p. 201

11 Remnick, *The Bridge: The Life and Rise of Barack Obama*, New York: Knopf, 2010, p. 13. As it turns out, however, both the president and Mr. Remnick are mistaken. The quote comes from the writings of the 19th-century abolitionist, Thomas Parker. See Mark S. Smith, "White House Defends King Quote on Oval Office Rug," *Associated Press*, September 10, 2010.

12 Quoted in Mendell, *Obama*, p. 201 (emphasis added).

13 Barack Obama, "Commencement Address at Knox College," June 4, 2005. Available at: http://www.americanrhetoric.com/speeches/barackobamaknoxcollege.htm (accessed May 9, 2010).

14 Obama, *Dreams*, p xi.
15 Christine Finn and Tony Allen-Mills, "Jungle Angel was Barack Obama's Mother," *Sunday Times*, November 8, 2009.
16 Quoted in Judith Kampfner, "The Untold Story of Obama's Mother," *Independent*, September 16, 2009.
17 Remnick, *The Bridge*, p. 53.
18 Barack Obama, "Preface to the 2004 Edition," *Dreams*, p. xii.
19 Obama, *Dreams*, p. 60.
20 Jonathan Alter, *The Promise: President Obama, Year One*, New York: Simon & Schuster, 2010, p. 143.
21 Alter, *The Promise*, p. 143.
22 Obama, *Dreams*, p. 275 (emphasis added).
23 Obama, *Dreams*, p. 54.
24 Obama, *Dreams*, p. 54.
25 Obama, *Dreams*, p. 75.
26 Obama, *Dreams*, p. 75.
27 Quoted in Amanda Ripley, "The Story of Barack Obama's Mother," *Time*, April 9, 2008.
28 Obama quoted in Mendel, *Obama*, p. 19.
29 Obama quoted in John Meacham, "Interview: I Had to Learn How to Fight," *Newsweek*, August 23, 2008 (emphasis added). Available at: http://www.newsweek.com/id/155175 (accessed July 6, 2010).
30 Kirsten Scharnberg and Kim Barker, "The Not-so-simple Story of Barack Obama's Youth," *Chicago Tribune*, March 25, 2007.
31 Obama, *Dreams*, p. xi.
32 Quoted in Amanda Ripley, "The Story of Barack Obama's Mother," *Time*, April 9, 2008.
33 Quoted in Ripley, "The Story of Barack Obama's Mother."
34 Quoted in Ripley," The Story of Barack Obama's Mother."
35 Obama, "Preface to the 2004 Edition," *Dreams*, p. xii.
36 Remnick, *The Bridge*, pp. 288–89.
37 Remnick, *The Bridge*, p. 294 (emphasis added).
38 Douglas Brinkley, "Review of 'The Bridge The Life and Rise of Barack Obama,'" by David Remnick, *Los Angeles Times*, March 28, 2010 (emphasis added).
39 Obama, *Dreams*, pp. 79, 81–84; see also Obama, *Audacity*, p. 30.
40 Obama, *Dreams*, p. 81 (emphasis in original).
41 Obama, *Dreams*, p. 81.
42 Obama, *Dreams*, p. 195 (emphasis added).
43 Obama, *Dreams*, p. 84 (emphasis added).
44 Obama, *Dreams*, p. 85.
45 Obama, *Dreams*, p. 91.
46 Obama, *Dreams*, p. 97.
47 Obama, *Dreams*, p. 97.
48 Obama, *Dreams*, p. 82.
49 Cf., Erik H. Erikson, *Childhood and Society*, New York: Norton, 1950; see also Erik H. Erikson, *Identity: Youth and Crisis*, New York: Norton, 1968.
50 Obama, *Dreams*, p. xiv.
51 Obama, *Dreams*, p. 101.
52 Obama, *Dreams*, p. 101–2 (emphasis added).
53 Obama, *Dreams*, p. 142.
54 Obama, *Dreams*, p. 199 (emphasis added).
55 Obama, *Dreams*, p. 401 (emphasis added)
56 Obama, *Dreams*, p. 406 (emphasis added).

57 Obama *Dreams*, p. 312 (emphasis added).
58 Obama, *Dreams*, p. 314 (emphasis added).
59 "News Conference by the President," July 23, 2009. Available at: http://www. whitehouse.gov/the_press_office/News-Conference-by-the-President-July-22-2009/ (accessed May 6, 2010).
60 Cf., Greg Ridgeway, "Analysis of Racial Disparities in the New York Police Department's Stop, Question, and Frisk Practices," Santa Monica, Ca.: Rand Corporation, 2007. Available at: http://www.rand.org/pubs/technical_reports/2007/ RAND_TR534.pdf (accessed May 6, 2010).
61 Quoted in Carol E. Lee, "POTUS's Outlook on Black America," *Politico*, December 21, 2009 (emphasis added).
62 Obama, *Dreams*, p. 80; see also Barack Obama, *The Audacity of Hope*, New York: Three Rivers Press, 2006, p. 233 and Remnick, *The Bridge*, pp. 79–80.
63 Obama's mother did have an issue with her insurance company about the extent of her coverage when she fell ill, but the issue was eventually resolved and, in any event, had nothing to do with the company dropping coverage.
64 "Transcript of Obama's speech," CNN, March 18, 2008. Available at: http://www.cnn. com/2008/POLITICS/03/18/obama.transcript/index.html (accessed July 12, 2010).
65 Obama, *Dreams*, p. 88.
66 "Obama interview with 610 WIP host Angelo Cataldi (Partial transcript)," March 20, 2008. Available at: http://www.philly.com/philly/blogs/phillygossip/Obama_ on_WIP_My_grandmothers_a_typical_white_person.htm (accessed July 12, 2010). The full radio interview can be found at: http://www.redlasso.com/Clip Player.aspx? id=8a521134-e10b-4bfb-8aec-690d61794d50 (accessed July 12, 2010).
67 Obama, *Audacity*, p 10.
68 "Remarks by President Obama to the Turkish Parliament," April 6, 2009. Available at: http://www.whitehouse.gov/the_press_office/Remarks-By-President-Obama-To-The-Turkish-Parliament/ (accessed July 12, 2010).
69 Obama, *Dreams*, p. 293.
70 Quoted in Manya A. Brachear, "Rev. Jeremiah A. Wright, Jr.: Pastor Inspires Obama's 'audacity,'"*Chicago Tribune*, January 21, 2007.
71 These and other quotes are found in Remnick, *The Bridge*, pp. 518–19.
72 Remnick, *The Bridge*, p. 533.
73 Jeff Poor, "Wolffe: President Missed Reverend's Rantings Because 'He Wasn't Much of a Churchgoer,'" Business & Media Institute, June 16, 2009. The transcript of Wolffe's remarks may be found at: http://www.cultureandmediainstitute.org/printer/ 2009/20090616113245.aspx (accessed May 28, 2010).
74 Remnick, *The Bridge*, p. 521.
75 Remnick, *The Bridge*, p. 521.
76 Obama, *Audacity*, p. 10.
77 "Saddleback Civil Forum on the Presidency: Interview with Senator Barack Obama (D-Il) and Senator John McCain (R-Az): Interviewer Rick Warren," August 16, 2008. Available at: http://www.clipsandcomment.com/2008/08/17/full-transcript-saddleback-presidential-forum-sen-barack-obama-john-mccain-moderated-by-rick-warren/ (accessed June 28, 2010).
78 Jake Tapper, "Stumbles," *Political Punch-ABC News*, August 8, 2008.
79 The complete segment can be found at: http://www.youtube.com/watch? v=d667NAI9HIM (accessed August 9, 2010).
80 Tapper, "Stumbles" (emphasis added).
81 "Remarks by the President to the United Nations General Assembly," September 23, 2009. Available at: http://www.whitehouse.gov/the_press_office/ remarks-by-the-president-to-the-united-nations-general-assembly (accessed May 3, 2010).

82 "Remarks by the President on Wall Street Reform in Quincy, Illinois," Oakley Lindsay Civic Center, Quincy, Illinois, April 28, 2010. Available at: http://www.whitehouse.gov/the-press-office/remarks-president-wall-street-reform-quincy-illinois (Accessed May 2, 2010).

83 Obama, *Audacity*, p. 193 (emphasis added).

84 Dennis Ross, "Greed on Wall Street: The Rise and Fall of Tyco's Dennis Kozlowski," *ABC News*, November 11, 2006.

85 Editorial, "An Obama 'Rescue' Plan That Doesn't," *Investor's Business Daily*, October 13, 2008.

86 Office of Management and Budget, *A New Era of Responsibility: Renewing America's Promise*, p. 5 (emphasis added). Available at: http://www.whitehouse.gov/omb/assets/fy2010_new_era/a_new_era_of_responsibility2.pdf (accessed September 16, 2010).

87 Jackie Calmes and Robert Pear, "To Pay for Health Care, Obama Looks to Tax the Affluent," *New York Times*, February 26, 2009.

88 Mark Halperin, "Politics Up to the Minute: Obama Interview on CNBC," February 15, 2010.

89 Office of Management and Budget, *A New Era of Responsibility*, p. 5.

90 "People at the commanding heights of the economy with incomes over $250,000 a year have been receiving trillions of dollars of tax cuts, while the middle class has been squeezed like never before." "Transcript: Austan Goolsbee on 'FNS'," *Fox News*, March 16, 2010. (Available at: http://www.foxnews.com/printer_friendly_story/0,3566,509314,00.html) (accessed September 16, 2010).

91 Lori Montgomery, "In $3.6 Trillion Budget, Obama Signals Broad Shift in Priorities," *Washington Post*, February 27, 2009.

92 Office of Management and Budget, *A New Era of Responsibility*, p. 1.

93 Alter, *The Promise*, p. 153.

94 Jarrett quoted in Alter, *The Promise*, p. 153.

95 Obama, *Dreams*, p. 78.

96 Obama, *Dreams*, p. 80.

97 Quoted in Remnick, *The Bridge*, p. 91.

98 Mendell, *Obama*, p. 45.

99 Brian Robb, "Julius Erving at the Finals," *ESPN*, June 12, 2010.

100 Bill Reynolds, *Cousy: His Life, Career, and the Birth of Big-Time Basketball*, New York, Simon & Schuster, 2005.

101 Obama quoted in Remnick, *The Bridge*, pp. 91–92.

102 Remnick, *The Bridge*, p. 91.

103 Obama, *Dreams*, p. 74.

104 See Remnick, *The Bridge*, pp. 91–92; Mendel, *Obama*, pp. 47–48.

105 See Mendell, *Obama*, p. 49.

106 Mendell, *Obama*, p. 61.

107 Remnick, *The Bridge*, p. 119.

108 Ryan Lizza, "Above the Fray," GQ,September, 2007.

109 Alter, *The Promise*, p. 428.

110 Obama quoted in Alter, *The Promise*, p. 429.

111 Obama quoted in Alter, *The Promise*, p. 415.

112 *Rasmussen Reports*, May 24, 2010. Available at: http://news.yahoo.com/s/rasmussen/healthcareupdate20100524 (accessed July 16, 2010).

113 Press Conference by the President After G20 Meetings in Seoul, Korea," The White House, November 12, 2010. http://www.whitehouse.gov/the-press-office/2010/11/12/press-conference-president-after-g20-meetings-seoul-korea (accessed May 13, 2011).

114 Chip Reid, "White House Push-Back on Asia Trip Failure Meme," *CBS News*, November 14, 2010. The complete press conference transcript can be found at "President Conference with President Obama and President Lee of the Republic of

Korea in Seoul," November 11, 2010. Available at: http://www.whitehouse.gov/the-press-office/2010/11/11/president-conference-with-president-obama-and-president-lee-republic-kor (accessed November 21, 2010).

6 The Question of Leadership Integrity

1 Stanley A. Renshon, *The Psychological Assessment of Presidential Candidates*, New York: New York University Press, 1996 (1998 paperback edition, with afterword, published by Routledge), pp. 38–40.

2 Harold D. Lasswell, *Power and Personality*. New York: Norton, 1948; see also Alexander L. George and Juliette L. George, *Woodrow Wilson and Colonel House: A Personality Study*, New York: Dover, 1956.

3 Robert J. Samuelson, "A Vote for McBama," *Washington Post*, June 11, 2008.

4 Douglas E. Schoen and Patrick H. Caddell, "One and Done: To Be a Great President, Obama Should Not Seek Reelection in 2012," *Washington Post*, November 14, 2010.

5 Byron York, "Should Obama Quit After One Term?" *The Examiner*, November 13, 2010.

6 "Remarks by the President to the United Nations General Assembly, September 23, 2009." Available at: http://www.whitehouse.gov/the-press-office/remarks-president-united-nations-general-assembly)(accessed July 10, 2010).

7 Jeffrey M. Jones, "Obama Job Approval Rating Down to 38% Among Independents," *Gallup*, July 7, 2010.

8 These figures can be found at: http://www.gallup.com/poll/124922/Presidential-Approval-Center.aspx (accessed August 19, 2010).

9 On The Plan, see David Mendell, *Obama: From Promise to Power*, New York: Harper Collins, 2007, pp. 305–9; David Remnick, *The Bridge: The Life and Rise of Barack Obama*, New York: Knopf, 2010, pp. 431–32; Richard Wolffe, *Renegade: The Making of a President*, New York: Crown, 2009, pp. 39–45; and John Heilemann and Mark Halperin, *Game Change: Obama and the Clintons, McCain and Palin, and the Race of a Lifetime*, New York: Harper, 2010, pp. 27–33.

10 Mendell, *Obama*, p. 305 (emphasis added).

11 Mendell, *Obama*, p. 306.

12 Mendell, *Obama*, p. 309 (emphasis added).

13 Quoted in David Remnick, "Testing the Waters," *New Yorker*, November 6, 2008.

14 Barack Obama, *The Audacity of Hope*, New York: Three Rivers Press, 2006, p. 131.

15 Obama, *Audacity*, p. 131.

16 Ross Douthat, "Let's Make a Deal," *New York Times*, February 15, 2010.

17 He said, "I continue to believe that a public option within the basket of insurance choices would help improve quality and bring down costs." *MSNBC News*, "Obama: Public option should be part of reform," September 9, 2009.

18 Ceci Connolly, "Key Feature of Obama Health Plan May Be Out," *Washington Post*, August 17, 2009; see also Ryan Grim, "Obama Health Care Plan Drops Public Option," *Huffington Post*, February 22, 2010.

19 Sam Youngman, "Obama: Public Option 'not the most important' Part of Healthcare Bill," *The Hill*, December 21, 2009.

20 Mark Murray and Domenico Montanaro, "Did Obama Campaign on Public Option?" *NBC-First Read*, December 23, 2009.

21 Quoted in Connolly, "Key Feature of Obama Health Plan May Be Out."

22 Editorial, "No Longer an Option," *Washington Post*, August 20, 2010.

23 "Transcript, John Harwood Interviews Barack Obama," *New York Times*, January 7, 2009. Available at: http://www.nytimes.com/2009/01/07/us/politics/07text-harwood.html?pagewanted=print (accessed July 10, 2010).

24 "Transcript, John Harwood Interviews Barack Obama."

25 Obama, *Audacity*, p. 24 (emphasis added).

26 Sheryl Gay Stolberg, "Obama Weighs Paring Goals for Health Care," *New York Times*, January 21, 2010.

27 Editorial, "The Obama Enigma: Where Would he Lead?"; On Obama's going back on his word regarding immigration see Evan Thomas, *A Long Time Coming: The Inspiring, Combative Campaign and the Historic Election of Barack Obama*, New York: Public Affairs Press, 2009, p. 99; also Heilemann and Halperin, *Game Change*, p. 325.

28 Thomas, *A Long Time Coming*, p. 97.

29 James Fallows, "Two Rhetorical Missteps by Team Obama," *The Atlantic*, April 22, 2008.

30 As one editorial put it, "He dared to mention the notion of 'merit pay' in an appearance before the teachers union." See Editorial, "The Obama Enigma. Where Would he Lead?" *Washington Post*, February 24, 2008.

31 "Obama: Issues: Education." Available at: http://www.barackobama.com/issues/education/#teachers (accessed July 5, 2010).

32 David Brooks, "Obama, Liberalism and the Power of Reform," *New York Times*, June 13, 2008.

33 Sheryl Gay Stolberg and Robert Pear, "Obama Open to Reining in Medical Suits," *New York Times*, June 15, 2009.

34 Ricardo Alonso-Zaldivar and Erica Werner, "Obama Gives Proponents Hope for Medical Malpractice Reform," *Insurance Journal*, September 14, 2009.

35 Jonathan D. Salant, "Trial Lawyers Sidestep Malpractice Curbs With Blitz in Congress," *Bloomberg News*, December 30, 2009.

36 N.C. Aizenman, "Grants to Aid Projects on Improving Patient Safety, Curbing Malpractice Suits," *Washington Post*, June 11, 2010; see also Jane Adamy, "U.S. to Begin Handing Out Grants to Reduce Medical Malpractice Suits," *Wall Street Journal*, June 11, 2010.

37 *Wall Street Journal*, "What Might Medical Malpractice Test Projects Look Like?" June 11, 2010.

38 Laura Landro, "Doctors Learn to Say 'I'm Sorry,'" *Wall Street Journal*, January 24, 2007.

39 The glimpse of the political debates that take place in the context of evaluating federal programs can be seen with Head Start, the government program to help early learning development. A recently completed major review of Head Start found:

> In sum, this report finds that providing access to Head Start has benefits for both 3-year-olds and 4-year-olds in the cognitive, health, and parenting domains, and for 3-year-olds in the social-emotional domain. **However the benefits of access to Head Start at age four are largely absent by 1st grade for the program population as a whole.** For 3-year-olds, there are few sustained benefits, although access to the program *may* lead to improved parent-child relationships through 1st grade, a *potentially* important finding for children's longer term development. Moreover, several subgroups of children in this study experience benefits of Head Start into 1st grade. It will be important in future research to examine whether the positive parent-child relationships for the 3-year-old cohort translate into improved outcomes as children get older, as well as whether the findings for subgroups of children persist over the longer term. To that end, the study children have been followed through 3rd grade. The 3rd grade report will examine the extent to which impacts of Head Start on initial school readiness are altered or maintained as children enter pre-adolescence. Further, that report will provide a greater focus on how children's later experiences in the school and community affect their outcomes at 1st and 3rd grades.

The study concludes with a list of large questions still unanswered:

> Finally, this study leaves many important questions about Head Start unanswered. These questions include, but are certainly not limited to, questions such as: Is there a benefit to having two years of Head Start rather than one year? What types of programs, centers, classrooms, and other experiences relate to more positive impacts for children and families? What accounts for the subgroup patterns observed in this report? Are there some later experiences that help to sustain impacts through the early elementary grades? Hopefully, researchers will take advantage of the data from this study, which will be made available through a data archive, to further the understanding of the role Head Start plays in the well-being of children and families.

U.S. Department of Health and Human Services, "Head Start Impact Study Final Report: Executive Summary," January 2010, pp. xvi–xvii (emphasis added). Available at: http://www.acf.hhs.gov/programs/opre/hs/impact_study/executive_summaryfinal.pdf (emphasis added) (accessed February 24, 2011).

40 Maureen Dowd, "Praying and Preying," *New York Times*, April 30, 2008.
41 Jimmy Carter won the presidency after Richard Nixon resigned in part by promising as a campaign theme "I will never lie to you. I will never make a misleading statement. I will never betray the confidence any of you has in me. ... " See Carter quoted in "Transcript: American Experience, Jimmy Carter Part II," PBS, July 25, 2010. Available at: http://www.pbs.org/wgbh/amex/carter/filmmore/pt.html (accessed August 5, 2010).
42 Carla Marinucci, "On S.F. Tour, Obama Takes on the Clintons," *San Francisco Chronicle*, January 18, 2008.
43 "Obama Acceptance Speech in Full," *Guardian*, November 5, 2008. Available at: http://www.guardian.co.uk/commentisfree/2008/nov/05/uselections2008-barack obama/print (accessed August 5, 2010).
44 Obama quoted in John Meacham, "A Highly Logical Approach," *Newsweek*, May 25, 2009.
45 Obama quoted in Dan Balz and Haynes Johnson, *The Battle for America 2008*, New York: Viking, 2010, p. 380.
46 Peter Baker, "Obama's Pledge to Reform Ethics Faces an Early Test," *New York Times*, February 3, 2009 (emphasis added).
47 Chris Frates, "Lobbyists: W.H. Hides Meetings Off-site," *Politico*, February 24, 2011.
48 Rich Miller, "Obama 'Agnostic' on Deficit Cuts, Won't Prejudge Tax Increases," *Bloomberg Business Week*, February 11, 2010.
49 Jay Heflin, "JCT: Healthcare Law to Sock Middle Class with a $3.9 Billion Tax Increase in 2019," *The Hill*, April 10, 2010.
50 Josh Gerstein, "Obama: Not Showing Talks a 'Mistake,'" *Politico*, January 25, 2010.
51 Paul Kane, "To Sway Nelson, a Hard Won Compromise on Abortion," *Washington Post*, December 20, 2009.
52 Cf. "I've got a question for all those folks: What are you going to do? (Applause.) What's your answer? (Applause.) What's your solution? (Applause.) And you know what? They don't have one. (Applause.) Their answer is to do nothing. Their answer is to do nothing." See "Remarks By the President at AFL-CIO Labor Day Picnic, Coney Island, Cincinnati, Ohio," September 7, 2009. Available at: http://www.whitehouse.gov/the_press_office/Remarks-by-the-President-at-AFL-CIO-Labor-Day-Picnic (accessed August 5, 2010); see also "The White House Blog: Word from the White House: House Republican Health Care 'Plan' Putting Families at Risk," November 4, 2009. Available at: http://www.whitehouse.gov/blog/2009/11/04/word-white-house-house-republican-health-care-plan-putting-families-risk (accessed August 5, 2010).
53 "Price says Obama and his aides have said Republicans have 'no ideas' on health care," *Politi-Fact.com*, January 29, 2010.

54 "President Obama Calls for Restoring Statutory Pay-As-You-Go Requirements," The White House June 9, 2009. Available at: http://www.whitehouse.gov/omb/news_060909_paygo/ (accessed August 5, 2010).

55 Jim Acosta, "Critics question 'pay-as-you-go' approach," *CNN*, Wednesday June 10, 2010.

56 Editorial, "The Obama Diet," *Washington Post*, June 12, 2009.

57 "President-elect Obama seventh press conference. Transcript," December 8, 208. Available at: http://blogs.suntimes.com/sweet/2008/12/presidentelect_obama_seventhp.html (accessed August 6, 2010).

58 Cf. "Remarks by The President In Discussion of the Deficit at Bipartisan Meeting on Health Care Reform, Blair House," The White House, February 25, 2010. Available at: http://www.whitehouse.gov/the-press-office/remarks-president-discussion-deficit bipartisan meeting health care reform (accessed August 6, 2010).

59 CBO, Director's Blog, "Health Costs and the Federal Budget," May 28, 2010. Available at: http://cboblog.cbo.gov/?p=1034 (accessed August 6, 2010).

60 Ben Smith, " Dems retreat on health care cost pitch," *Politico*, August 19, 2010.

61 "Remarks by the President on the Auto Industry," Grand Foyer April 30, 2009. Available at: http://www.whitehouse.gov/the_press_office/Remarks-by-the-President-on-the-Auto-Industry/ (accessed August 6, 2010).

62 Paul Kiel, "Gov't Official Suggests Much of Chrysler Loan Won't be Repaid," *ProPublica*, May 7, 2009.

63 "Remarks by the President at the Annual Conference of the American Medical Association," Hyatt Regency Chicago, Chicago, Illinois, June 15, 2009. Available at: http://www.whitehouse.gov/the_press_office/Remarks-by-the-President-to-the-Annual-Conference-of-the-American-Medical-Association/ (accessed August 6, 2010).

64 Ricardo Alonso-Zaldivar, "Health Overhaul to Force Changes in Employer Plans," *Associated Press*, June 11, 2010.

65 Ben Smith, "Despite Snubs, Dems Back Obama," *Politico*, March 21, 2009.

66 Mary Lu Carnevale, "Obama: Mortgage Plan 'Will Not Help Speculators,'" *Wall Street Journal*, February 18, 2009.

67 Renae Merle and Dina Elboghdady, "U.S. Launches Wide-Ranging Plan to Steady Housing Market," *Washington Post*, March 5, 2009.

68 "Remarks by the President at Iftar Dinner, State Dining Room," August 13, 2010. Available at: http://www.whitehouse.gov/the-press-office/2010/08/13/remarks-president-iftar-dinner (accessed August 14, 2010).

69 Peter Nicholas and Nicole Santa Cruz, "Obama Again Defends Right to Put Mosque Near Ground Zero," *Los Angeles Times*, August 15, 2010.

70 Ben Smith, "Obama Narrows Mosque Defense," *Politico*, August 14, 2010.

71 Scott Shane and Mark Lander, "Obama Clears way for Guantánamo Trials," *New York Times*, March 7, 2011.

72 White House, "Executive Order–Periodic Review of Individuals Detained at Guantánamo Bay Naval Station Pursuant to the Authorization for Use of Military Force," March 7, 2011. http://www.whitehouse.gov/the-press-office/2011/03/07/executive-order-periodic-review-individuals-detained-guant-namo-bay-nava (accessed March 12, 2011).

73 White House, "Statement by President Barack Obama: New Actions on Guantanamo Bay and Detainee Policy," March 7, 2011. http://www.whitehouse.gov/the-press-office/2011/03/07/new-actions-guantanamo-bay-and-detainee-policy (accessed March 12, 2011).

74 Peter Finn and Anne E. Kornblut, "Obama Creates Indefinite Detention System for Prisoners at Guantanamo Bay," *Washington Post*, March 8, 2011.

75 "Review and Outlook: 'Obama Ratifies Bush,'" *Wall Street Journal*, March 8, 2011.

76 White House, "Fact Sheet: New Actions on Guantánamo and Detainee Policy," March 7, 2011. http://www.whitehouse.gov/the-press-office/2011/03/07/fact-sheet-new-actions-guant-namo-and-detainee-policy (accessed March 12, 2011) (emphasis added).

77 "Article 75 of the First Additional Protocol to the Geneva Conventions," *Worldpress. org*. http://www.worldpress.org/specials/justice/Article_75.htm (accessed March 12, 2011).

78 The full "Protocol Additional to the Geneva Conventions of 12 August 1949, and relating to the Protection of Victims of International Armed Conflicts (Protocol I), 8 June 1977" may be found at International Committee of the Red Cross (ICRC): http://www.icrc.org/ihl.nsf/7c4d08d9b287a42141256739003e636b/f6c8b9fee14a77f dc125641e0052b079 (accessed March 12, 2011).

79 U.S. Department of the Army, "Army Field Manual, FM 2-22.3 (FM 34-52 Human Intelligence Collector Operations," Washington D.C., September 2006. http://www.army.mil/institution/armypublicaffairs/pdf/fm2-22-3.pdf (accessed March 12, 2011).

80 Obama quoted in Balz and Johnson, *The Battle for America*, p. 38.

81 "Obama's Question Time with Senate Dems: Video and Full Text," *Huffington Post*, March 10, 2009. Available at: http://www.huffingtonpost.com/2010/02/03/obamas-question-time-with_n_447409.html (accessed July 12, 2010).

82 Obama, *Audacity*, p. 24.

83 "Remarks of President Barack Obama—As Prepared for Delivery Address to Joint Session of Congress," The White House, February 24, 2009. Available at: http://www.whitehouse.gov/the_press_office/remarks-of-president-barack-obama-address-to-joint-session-of-congress/ (accessed July 12, 2010).

84 Jonathan Alter, *The Promise: President Obama, Year One*, New York: Simon and Schuster, 2010, p. 136.

85 All quotes are from David S. Broder, "Obama Rolls The Dice," *Washington Post*, February 26, 2009.

86 Alex Isenstadt, "Some Dems Walk Plank With 'Yes' Vote," *Politico*, March 21, 2010.

87 Obama, *Audacity*, p. 66.

88 Obama quote in Thomas, *A Long Time Coming*, p. 199 (emphasis added).

89 Lydia Saad, "Tea Partiers Are Fairly Mainstream in Their Demographics," *Gallup*, April 5, 2010.

90 Pew Research Center for the People & the Press, "Obama's Ratings Little Affected by Recent Turmoil," June 24, 2010, p. 7. Available at: http://people-press.org/reports/pdf/627.pdf (accessed July 12, 2010).

91 Gerald F. Seib, "In Crisis, Opportunity for Obama," *Wall Street Journal*, November 21, 2008.

92 Chris Frates and Ben White, "Obama's Policy Time Bombs," *Politico*, July 11, 2010.

93 All quotes drawn from, "Remarks by the President on the Economy at Carnegie Mellon University, Carnegie Mellon University, Pittsburgh, Pennsylvania, June 2, 2010." Available at: http://www.whitehouse.gov/the-press-office/remarks-president-economy-carnegie-mellon-university (accessed August 10, 2010).

94 "Remarks by the President on the Economy at Carnegie Mellon University."

95 Greg Sargent, "Book: Rahm 'Begged' Obama for Days not to Pursue Ambitious Health Reform," *Washington Post*, May 14, 2010.

96 Alter, *The Promise*, p. 79.

97 Alter, *The Promise*, p. 268.

98 "Interviews: Dan Pfeiffer, *Frontline*: Obama's Deal," *PBS*, March 20, 2010. Available at: http://www.pbs.org/wgbh/pages/frontline/obamasdeal/interviews/pfeiffer.html (accessed March 5, 2011).

99 David Brooks, "The Government War," *New York Times*, April 22, 2010.
100 Jake Tapper, "White House: Berwick Appointment 'Too Important' to Wait for a Hearing," *ABC News*, July 11, 2010.

7 Ambition's Confidence

1 Michael Powell, "A Deliberative Man in a Manic Game," *New York Times*, June 4, 2008.
2 Barack Obama, *The Audacity of Hope*, New York: Three Rivers Press, 2006, p. 10.
3 Jessica Curry, "Barack Obama: Under the Lights," *Chicago Life*, August 1, 2004.
4 Obama, *Audacity*, p. 253.
5 Obama, *Audacity*, p. 134,
6 Harold D. Lasswell, *Power and Personality*, New York: Norton, 1948; see also Alexander L. George and Juliette L. George, *Woodrow Wilson and Colonel House: A Personality Study*, New York: Dover, 1956.
7 Dan Balz and Haynes Johnson, *The Battle for America 2008*, New York: Viking, 2010, p.19 (emphasis added).
8 Obama quoted in Richard Wolffe, *Renegade: The Making of a President*, New York: Crown, 2009, p. 51.
9 See Stanley A. Renshon, *High Hopes: The Clinton Presidency and the Politics of Ambition*, New York: New York University Press, 1996 (1998 paperback edition, with afterword, published by Routledge).
10 Harold D. Lasswell, *Psychopathology and Politics,* Chicago, Ill.: University of Chicago Press, 1930, p.75.
11 David Mendell, *Obama: From Promise to Power*, New York: Harper Collins, 2007, p. 19.
12 Mendell, *Obama*, p. 257.
13 Mendell, *Obama*, p. 1.
14 Mendell, *Obama*, p. 154.
15 Jonathan Alter, *The Promise: President Obama, Year One*, New York: Simon and Schuster, 2010, p. 140.
16 Scott Wilson, "Bruised by Stimulus Battle, Obama Changed His Approach to Washington," *Washington Post*, April 29, 2009.
17 Faye Fiore and Mark Z. Baraba, "Ambition and Audacity: Obama begins leading America in a new direction," *Los Angeles Times*, April 19, 2009.
18 Elizabeth Drew, "The Thirty Days of Obama," *New York Review of Books*, March 26, 2009.
19 Obama quoted in Mendell, *Obama*, pp. 278–79.
20 "Obama Told Sen. Reid, 'I Have a Gift,'" *Associated Press*, April 22, 2009.
21 Obama quoted in David Remnick, *The Bridge: The Life and Rise of Barack Obama*, New York: Knopf, 2010, p. 573 (emphasis added).
22 Steve Kroft, "Obama on Economic Crisis, Transition," *CBS News,* November 16, 2008. Available at: http://www.cbsnews.com/stories/2008/11/16/60minutes/main4607893.shtml (accessed July 23, 2010).
23 Obama quoted in Alter, *The Promise*, pp. 4–5 (emphasis added).
24 Barack Obama, *Dreams from My Father*, New York: Three Rivers Press, 2004, p. 120.
25 Obama, *Dreams*, p. vii.
26 Alter, *The Promise*, p. 158.
27 Mendell, *Obama*, p. 100.
28 Obama, *Dreams*, p. 55.
29 Mendell, *Obama*, p. 30
30 Mendell, *Obama*, p. 10.
31 Obama quoted in Mendell, *Obama*, p. 24.
32 Mendell, *Obama*, p. 34 (emphasis added).

33 Mendell, *Obama*, p. 34.

34 Obama quoted in Alter, *The Promise*, p. 147.

35 Remnick, *The Bridge*, p. 426.

36 Obama quoted in Dan Balz and Haynes Johnson, "A Political Odyssey," *Washington Post*, August 2, 2009.

37 John Heilemann and Mark Halperin, *Game Change: Obama and the Clintons, McCain and Palin, and the Race of a Lifetime*, New York: Harper Collins, 2007, p. 247 (emphasis added).

38 Jodi Kantor, "An Old Hometown Mentor, Still at Obama's Side," *New York Times*, November 4, 2004.

39 This list draws on, but is not synonymous with, the list in Remnick, *The Bridge*, p. 132.

40 John Meacham, "Interview: I Had to Learn How to Fight," *Newsweek*, August 23, 2008 (emphasis added).

41 Kevin Merida, "The Ghost of a Father," *Washington Post*, December 14, 2007.

42 Gerald Kellman quoted in Merida, "The Ghost of a Father."

43 Remnick, *The Bridge*, p. 131.

44 Remnick, *The Bridge*, pp.131–32.

45 Edley quoted in Remnick, *The Bridge*, p. 217 (emphasis added).

46 Jones quoted in William Finnegan, "The Candidate," *New Yorker*, May, 31, 2004.

47 Ryan Lizza, "The Political Scene: Making It," *New Yorker*, May 6, 2010.

48 Quoted in Scott, "In Illinois, Obama Proved Pragmatic and Shrewd," *New York Times*, July 30, 2007.

49 Jo Becker and Christopher Drew, "Pragmatic Politics, Forged on the South Side," *New York Times*, May 11, 2008.

50 Becker and Drew, "Pragmatic Politics, Forged on the South Side"

51 Ryan Lizza, "Making it: How Chicago Shaped Obama," *New Yorker*, July 21, 2008.

52 Evan Thomas, "How He Did It," *Newsweek*, October 5, 2008. Available at: http://www.newsweek.com/2008/11/05/how-he-did-it.html# (accessed March 5, 2011).

53 Rick Zorn quoted in Remnick, *The Bridge*, pp. 261–62.

54 Mendell, *Obama*, p. 36.

55 Obama quoted in Balz and Johnson, "A Political Odyssey," *Washington Post*, August 2, 2009.

56 Michiko Katutani, "Presidential Horse Race, the 2008 Version," *New York Times*, August 11, 2009.

57 Milton Rokeach, *The Open and Closed Mind*, New York: Basic Books, 1960.

58 Karen Tumulty, "Obama: 'We Have a Daunting Task,'" *Time*, July 22, 2008 (emphasis added). Available at: http://www.time.com/time/printout/0,8816, 1825738,00. html (accessed July 31, 2010).

59 Alter, *The Promise*, p. 140.

60 John Podesta quoted in Alter, *The Promise*, p. 140.

61 Richard Wolffe, *Renegade: The Making of a President*, New York: Crown, 2009, p. 187.

62 Mendell, *Obama*, p. 1.

63 Remnick, *The Bridge*, p. 334.

64 Toni Preckwinkle quoted in Remnick, *The Bridge*, p. 330.

65 Thomas, *A Long Time Coming*, p. 6.

66 Alter, *The Promise*, p. 150.

67 Alter, *The Promise*, p. 231.

68 Quoted in Edward Luce and Daniel Dombey, "US Foreign Policy: Waiting on a Sun King," *Financial Times*, March 30, 2010.

69 Quoted in Mayhill Fowler, "Obama: No Need for Foreign Policy Help from V.P.," *Huffington Post*, April, 7 2008 (emphasis in original).

70 Balz and Johnson, *The Battle for America*, p. 28.

71 Obama quoted in Alter, *The Promise: President Obama, Year One*. New York: Simon & Schuster, 2010, p. 150.

72 Obama quoted in Lizza, "Battle Plans: How Obama Won," *New Yorker* (November 17, 2008).

73 Obama quoted in Alter, *The Promise*, p. 348.

74 Obama quoted in Alter, *The Promise*, p. 429.

75 Heilemann and Halperin, *Game Change*, p. 25.

76 "President Obama to Pastor Jones: 'Stunt' Endangers Troops—Full Transcript of Exclusive Interview," *ABC News*, September 9, 2010. Available at: http://blogs. abcnews.com/george/2010/09/president-obama-to-pastor-jones-stunt-endangers-troops-full-transcript-of-exclusive-interview.html (accessed September 11, 2010).

77 Wolffe, *Renegade*, p. 136.

78 Transcript, "Obama's Interview Aboard Air Force One," *New York Times*, March 8, 2009.

79 Mendell, *Obama*, p. 59.

80 Obama, *Dreams*, p. 123 (emphasis added).

81 Obama quoted in Mayhill Fowler, "Obama: No Surprise That Hard-Pressed Pennsylvanians Turn Bitter," *Huffington Post*, April 11, 2008.

82 Axelrod quoted in Mendell, *Obama*, p. 230.

83 Jeff Zeleny, "Going for That Presidential Look, but Trying Not to Overdo It," *New York Times*, July 27, 2008.

84 Mendell, *Obama*, p. 217–18.

85 Remnick, *The Bridge*, p. 426 (emphasis added).

86 David Ignatius, "Bumpy Road Ahead for a Traveler," *Washington Post*, November 2008.

87 Laureen Collins, "The Other Obama," *New Yorker*, March 10, 2008.

88 Quoted in Mendell, *Obama*, p. 278.

89 Mendell, *Obama*, p. 278.

90 Christi Parsons, Bruce Japsen, and Bob Secter, "Barack's Rock: Michelle Obama," *Chicago Tribune*, April 22, 2007.

91 Parsons, Japsen, and Secter, "Barack's Rock."

92 Parsons, Japsen, and Secter, "Barack's Rock."

93 Obama quoted in Mendell, *Obama*, p. 243 (emphasis added).

94 Obama quoted in Heilemann and Halperin, *Game Change*, p. 29.

95 Heilemann and Halperin, *Game Change*, p. 29

96 Obama, *Dreams*, p. 211.

97 Remnick, *The Bridge*, p. 139.

98 Sandra Sobieraj Westfall, "Michelle Obama: 'This is Who I Am,'" *People*, June 18, 2007.

99 Parsons, Japsen, and Secter, "Barack's Rock."

100 Lauren Collins, "The Other Obama," *New Yorker*, March 10, 2008.

101 Michelle Obama quoted in Manya Selsay, "Michelle Obama: Overcoming Fear," *Suite 101.com*. February 28, 2008. Available at: http://us-elections.suite101.com/article.cfm/the_vision_of_michelle_obama (accessed August 5, 2010).

102 Michelle Obama quoted in Leslie Bennetts, "First Lady in Waiting," *Vanity Fair*, December 27, 2007 (emphasis added).

103 Collins, "The Other Obama" (emphasis added).

104 Collins, "The Other Obama."

105 Jodi Kantor, "The Careful Rollout of a Warmer Michelle Obama," *New York Times*, August 26, 2008.

106 Heilemann and Halperin, *Game Change*, p. 349.

8 A Zen-like President's Emotional Undercurrents

1 Obama quoted in David Mendell, *Obama: From Promise to Power*, New York: Harper Collins, 2007, pp. 103–4.

2 Mike Robinson, "Obama Got Start in Civil Rights Practice," *Associated Press*, February 20, 2007.

3 Mendell, *Obama*, p. 307.

4 Barack Obama, *The Audacity of Hope*, New York: Three Rivers Press, 2006, p. 3.

5 Eli Saslow, "From Outsider To Politician," *Washington Post*, October 9, 2008.

6 Saslow, "From Outsider To Politician."

7 David Remnick, *The Bridge: The Life and Rise of Barack Obama*, New York: Knopf, 2010, p. 304.

8 Mendell, *Obama*, p. 126.

9 Remnick, *The Bridge*, p. 313.

10 Quoted in Mendell, *Obama*, p. 304.

11 Obama quoted in John Heilemann and Mark Halperin, *Game Change: Obama and the Clintons, McCain and Palin, and the Race of a Lifetime*, New York: Harper, 2010, p. 28.

12 Heilemann and Halperin, *Game Change*, p. 28.

13 David Axelrod quoted in Remnick, *The Bridge*, p. 444.

14 Remnick, *The Bridge*, p. 444.

15 Eli Saslow, "A Rising Political Star Adopts a Low-Key Strategy," *Washington Post*, October 17, 2008.

16 Davis quoted in Remnick, *The Bridge*, p. 220.

17 David Brooks, "Where's the Landslide?" *New York Times*, August 5, 2008.

18 Jodi Kantor, "Teaching Law, Testing Ideas, Obama Stood Slightly Apart," *New York Times*, July 30, 2008; see also Richard A. Epstein, "The Obama I (Don't) Know," *Forbes*, October 21, 2008.

19 Mikva quoted in Kantor, "Teaching Law."

20 Remnick, *The Bridge*, p. 111.

21 Obama, *Dreams from My Father*, New York: Three Rivers Press, 2004, p. 437.

22 Remnick, *The Bridge*, p. 217.

23 Mendell, *Obama*, pp. 288–89.

24 Jarrett quoted in Mendell, *Obama*, p. 257.

25 Mendell, *Obama*, p. 19.

26 Remnick, *The Bridge*, p. 138.

27 Mendell, *Obama*, pp. 291, 292.

28 Peter Baker, "Education of a President," *New York Times*, October 12, 2010.

29 "ABC's Gibson Interviews Barack Obama," *ABC News*, September 14, 2008. Available at: http://abcnews.go.com/print?id=5000184 (accessed July 23, 2010).

30 Larry King Live, "Interview with Barack Obama," *CNN*, June 3, 2010. Available at: http://transcripts.cnn.com/TRANSCRIPTS/1006/03/lkl.01.html (accessed July 23, 2010).

31 Hamil R. Harris, "At D.C. Church, Obama Invokes King and Calls for Keeping Faith," *Washington Post*, January 17, 2010. Available at: http://voices.washingtonpost.com/44/2010/01/obamas-sermon-remembering-mart.html (accessed July 23, 2010).

32 Sheryl Gay Stolberg, "He Breaks for Band Recitals," *New York Times*, February 12, 2010 (emphasis added).

33 Gwen Ifill, "Review of David Remnick's Biography of Barack Obama, 'The Bridge,'" *Washington Post*, April 4, 2010.

34 "Transcript: Diane Sawyer Interviews Obama," *ABC News*, January 25, 2010. Available at: http://abcnews.go.com/print?id=9659064 (accessed July 23, 2010).

35 Toby Harden, "Joe Biden Blurts Out That He Will Be Barack Obama's 2012 Running Mate," *The Telegraph*, October 14, 2010.

36 Byron York, "Has Obama Become Bored with Being President?" *The Examiner*, January 29, 2010.

37 Fred Hiatt, "Obama's Happiness Deficit," *Washington Post*, March 15, 2010.

38 David Ignatius, "A President Tripped Up By the Spontaneous," *Washington Post*, July 25, 2010.

39 Jarrett quoted in Remnick, *The Bridge*, p. 274 (emphasis added).

40 Jarrett quoted in Remnick, *The Bridge*, p. 274 (emphasis added).

41 Remnick, *The Bridge*, p. 463 (emphasis added).

42 Quoted in Richard Wolffe, *Renegade: The Making of a President*, New York: Crown, 2009, p. 202.

43 Quoted in Wolffe, *Renegade*, p. 202 (emphasis added).

44 David Maraniss, *First in His Class*, New York: Simon & Schuster, 1995, p. 383.

45 I analyze this trait and its implications for Clinton's presidency in Stanley A. Renshon, *High Hopes: The Clinton Presidency and the Politics of Ambition*, New York: New York University Press, 1996 (1998 paperback edition, with afterword, published by Routledge), pp. 57–59.

46 John Brummett, *Highwire: From the Back Roads to the Beltway—The Education of Bill Clinton*, New York: Hyperion, 1994, p. 146.

47 Meredith L. Oakley, *On the Make: The Rise of Bill Clinton*, Washington, D.C.: Regnery, 1994, p. 93.

48 Remnick, *The Bridge*, p. 217.

49 On Clinton's mother, her psychology and its effect on her son see Renshon, *High Hopes*, pp. 145–99.

50 Cf., Evan Thomas, *A Long Time Coming: The Inspiring, Combative 2008 Campaign and the Historic Election of Barack Obama*, New York: Public Affairs Press, 2009, p.141, 187, 192; Michael Powell, "A Deliberative Man in a Manic Game," *New York Times*, June 4, 2008.

51 Chrystia Freeland, "Calmer Obama Ushers New Age," *Financial Times*, April 10, 2009.

52 Mike Maddon, "Mr. Calm," *Salon*, April 30, 2009.

53 Jeff Greenwald, "Obama is Spock: It's Quite Logical," *Salon*, May 7, 2009; see also Maureen Dowd, "Spock at the Bridge," *New York Times*, March 1, 2009.

54 Kathleen Parker, "How Does America's First Family Behave at 30,000 Feet? Very Graciously, Our Columnist Discovers," *Daily Beast*, February 18, 2009.

55 David Brooks and Gail Collins, "A Good but Puzzling Speech," *New York Times*, December 2, 2009.

56 Monica Langley, "Michelle Obama Solidifies Her Role in the Election," *Wall Street Journal*, February 11, 2008.

57 Quoted in Thomas, *A Long Time Coming*, p. 9.

58 Obama quoted in Peter Baker, "Transition Holds Clues to How Obama Will Govern," *New York Times*, January 20, 2009.

59 "Barack Obama interview on Jan. 2, 2008," *Chicago Tribune*, January 2, 2008.

60 Obama, *Audacity*, p. 21.

61 Maya Soetoro-Ng quoted in Amanda Ripley, "The Story of Barack Obama's Mother," *Time*, April 9, 2008.

62 Ann Durham quoted in Remnick, *The Bridge*, p. 81.

63 Obama, *Dreams*, p. 51.

64 Remnick, *The Bridge*, p. 239.

65 Obama, *Dreams*, p. 63 (emphasis added). Obama writes that after he had been in Hawaii for a while his grandmother received a telegram and said to Obama, "your father's coming to see you. Next month, two weeks after your mother arrives. They'll both stay through New Year's." That wording suggests that Obama's mother remained in Indonesia through the summer and fall of Obama's return to Hawaii and left again for Indonesia after a brief interlude.

66 Obama, *Dreams*, p. 75; see also Janny Scott, "A Free-Spirited Wanderer Who Set Obama's Path," *New York Times*, March 14, 2008.

67 Obama, *Dreams*, p. 94.

68 Obama, *Dreams*, p.xii (emphasis added).

69 Obama. *Dreams*, p. 430.

70 Wolffe, *Renegade*, p. 147.

71 Obama quoted in Jon Meacham. "Interview: 'I had to Learn to Fight,'" *Newsweek*, August 23, 2008. Available at: http://www.newsweek.com/id/155175/output/print (accessed April 3, 2010)

72 Obama quoted in Mendell, *Obama*, p. 19.

73 Obama, *Dreams*, p. 430.

74 Michelle Obama quoted in Jonathan Alter, *The Promise: President Obama, Year One*, New York: Simon and Schuster, 2010, p. 142.

75 Obama, *Dreams*, p. 75.

76 Kirsten Scharnberg and Kim Barker, "The Not-so-simple Story of Barack Obama's Youth," *Chicago Tribune*, March 25, 2007.

77 Mendell, *Obama*, p. 59.

78 Obama quoted in Mendell, *Obama*, p. 59 (emphasis added).

79 Obama quoted in Remnick, *The Bridge*, p. 114 (emphasis added).

80 Obama quoted in Mendell, *Obama*, p. 53 (emphasis added).

81 Mendell, *Obama*, p. 61.

82 James T. Kloppenberg, *Reading Obama: Dreams, Hope, and the American Political Tradition*, Princeton, N.J.: Princeton University Press, 2010, p. xvii.

83 Martha Neil, "Abe Lincoln's Self-Study Route to Law Practice a Vanishing Option," *ABA Journal*, January 22, 2008.

84 It is not only Obama's public emotional style that reflects his interpersonal preferences; it can be seen as well in how he spends his vacation time. One analysis noted, "While other presidents have repeatedly visited the same place for a reprieve from Washington, they occasionally brought outsiders with them ... By contrast, Obama prefers his privacy and tends not to mix business with pleasure. The president typically keeps a low profile with few public appearances, and would rather unwind with an intimate circle – several family members, a tight-knit group of Chicago friends and a couple of childhood pals from Hawaii." See Carol E. Lee, "For Obama vacation, comfort is key," *Politico*, December 22, 2010.

85 Mendell, *Obama*, p. 30.

86 Obama quoted in Mendell, *Obama*, p. 31.

87 Obama quoted in Meacham, "Interview: 'I Had to Learn to Fight.'"

88 "Transcript: President Obama," *CBS News 60 Minutes*, September 11, 2009. Available at: http://www.cbsnews.com/stories/2009/09/13/60minutes/main5307481.shtml (accessed July 31, 2010).

89 CBO, Director's Blog, "Health Costs and the Federal Budget," May 28, 2010. Available at: http://cboblog.cbo.gov/?p=1034 (accessed August 6, 2010).

90 Obama, *Audacity*, p. 66.

91 Obama, *Audacity*, p. 66.

92 The quotes that follow in this and the following paragraph are drawn from Obama, *Audacity*, p. 67.

93 Alan Steinberg, "N.J. School Budget Elections: The New Christie Paradigm is Triumphant," *NewJerseynewsroom.com*, April 21, 2010. Available at: http://www.newjerseynewsroom.com/commentary/nj-school-budget-elections-the-new-christie- paradigm-is-triumphant (accessed March 5, 2011).

94 Obama, *Audacity*, p. 68 (emphasis added).

95 Cf., Thomas, *A Long Time Coming*, p.141, 187, 192; Powell, "Deliberative in a Manic Game."

96 Mayhill Fowler, "Obama: No Surprise That Hard Pressed Pennsylvanians Turn Bitter," *Huffington Post*, April 11, 2008.

97 Walter Russell Mead, "Honolulu, Harvard, and Hyde Park," *Foreign Affairs*, July/ August, 2010.
98 Obama quoted in Remnick, *The Bridge*, p. 361.
99 Obama, *Dreams*, pp. 94–95 (emphasis mine).
100 Obama, *Dreams*, p. 82.
101 Obama, *Dreams*, p. 86.
102 Obama, *Dreams*, p. 111.
103 Cf. Thomas, *A Long Time Coming*, p. 192.
104 Kantor, "Teaching Law, Testing Ideas, Obama Stood Slightly Apart."
105 Thomas, *A Long Time Coming*, p. 118.
106 Remnick, *The Bridge*, p. 433.
107 Eli Saslow, "From Outsider To Politician," *Washington Post*, October 9, 2008
108 Link quoted in Remnick, *The Bridge*, p. 300.
109 Saslow, "From Outsider To Politician."
110 Powell, "Deliberative in a Manic Game."
111 Remnick, *The Bridge*, p. 339.
112 Alter, *The Promise*, p. 150 (emphasis added).
113 Pal Eldredge quoted in Remnick, *The Bridge*, p. 78.
114 Bobby Rush quoted in Remnick, *The Bridge*, pp. 316–17.
115 Rush quoted in Remnick, *The Bridge*, p. 316 (emphasis added).
116 Robert Putnam quoted in Remnick, *The Bridge*, pp. 305–6.

9 Psychology in the White House: Leadership and Judgment

1 Michael D. Shear and Ceci Connolly, "Obama Assembles Powerful West Wing: Influential Advisers May Compete With Cabinet," *Washington Post*, January 8, 2009; see also Jonathan Martin, "West Wing on Steroids in Obama W.H.," *Politico*, January 25, 2009.
2 Athena Jones, "Obama: Change Comes from Me," *NBC-First Read*, November 26, 2008.
3 Gerald F. Seib, "Obama will be Hands-on Chief," *Wall Street Journal*, January 13, 2009.
4 Juliet Eilperin, "Senators Predict a Climate Bill Capping Emissions Only for Utilities," *Washington Post*, June 30, 2010.
5 Gordon Craig, "Angry Liberals: Why Didn't Obama Fight?" *Politico*, December 15, 2009.
6 Janet Adamy and Elizabeth Williamson, "As Congress Goes on Break, Health Lobbying Heats Up," *Wall Street Journal*, August 5, 2009.
7 Michael Barone, "Chaos on Capitol Hill: All Politics is Loco," *The Examiner*, July 12, 2009.
8 David Kirkpatrick, "Obama Is Taking an Active Role in Talks on Health Care Plan," *New York Times*, August 13, 2009.
9 Barack Obama, *The Audacity of Hope*, New York: Three Rivers Press, 2006, p. 51.
10 Obama, *Audacity*, p. 55.
11 Richard Wolffe, *Renegade: The Making of a President*, New York: Crown, 2009, p. 66.
12 Jonathan Alter, *The Promise: President Obama, Year One*, New York: Simon and Schuster, 2010, p. 265.
13 Avi Zenilman and Ben Smith, "Barack Obama's Counterpunching Style," *Politico*, April 14, 2008.
14 "Remarks of Illinois State Sen. Barack Obama Against Going to War with Iraq," October 2, 2002. Available at: http://www.barackobama.com/2002/10/02/remarks_of_ illinois_state_sen.phps (accessed March 16, 2009).

15 Jonathan Weisman, "Obama's Gloves Are Off—And May Need to Stay Off," *Washington Post*, April 23, 2008.

16 Hank De Zutter, "What Makes Obama Run?" *Chicago Reader*, December 8, 1995.

17 Robin Toner, "Obama's Test: Can a Liberal be a Unifier?" *New York Times*, March 25, 2008; see also Peter Baker, "Harsh Words for G.O.P.," *New York Times*, June 30, 2010.

18 Kevin Sack and Sheryl Gay Stolberg, "As Law Takes Effect, Obama Gives Insurers a Warning," *New York Times*, June, 21, 2010.

19 Robert J. Samuelson, "Obama's Energy Pipe Dreams," *Washington Post*, June 21, 2010.

20 Obama quoted in Faye Fiore and Mark Z. Baraba, "Ambition and Audacity: Obama begins leading America in a new direction," *Los Angeles Times*, April 19, 2009.

21 Elizabeth Williamson, "Obama Slams 'Fat Cat Bankers,'" *Wall Street Journal*, December 2009.

22 "Remarks by the President on the Economy at Carnegie Mellon University, Pittsburgh, Pennsylvania," The White House, June 2, 2010. Available at: http://www.whitehouse.gov/the-press-office/remarks-president-economy-carnegie-mellon-university (accessed August 5, 2010).

23 Mark Ambinder, "Straw Men," *The Atlantic,* February 16, 2009.

24 Jonathan Allen and Carol E. Lee, "Obama Strategy Gets Personal," *Politico*, April 27, 2010.

25 Patrick O'Connor, "Cantor, Obama Let Sparks Fly," *Politico*, April 27, 2009.

26 Jonathan Martin and Jonathan Allen, "Obama Takes on Talkers," *Politico*, April 3, 2010.

27 Marc Ambinder, "The White House Takes on Politico," *The Atlantic*, November 30, 2009.

28 Josh Gerstein, "Gibbs Rebukes CNBC's Santelli," *Politico*, February 20, 2009.

29 Anne E. Kornblut, "Obama Criticizes Hoekstra on Congressman's Home Turf," *Washington Post*, July 15, 2010.

30 "Remarks by President Barack Obama, Hradcany Square Prague, Czech Republic, April 5, 2009" (emphasis added). Available at: http://www.whitehouse.gov/the_press_office/Remarks-By-President-Barack-Obama-In-Prague-As-Delivered/ (accessed August 5, 2010).

31 "Transcript: Obama's Fifth News Conference," *New York Times*, July 22, 2009 (emphasis added). Available at: http://www.nytimes.com/2009/07/22/us/politics/22obama.transcript.html?pagewanted=print (accessed August 5, 2010).

32 "Text: News Conference in Guadalajara," *New York Times*, April 11, 2009. Available at: http://www.nytimes.com/2009/08/11/world/americas/11prexy.text.html?pagewanted=print (accessed August 5, 2010).

33 Obama quoted in Ashley Southall, "Obama Vows to Push Immigration Reform," *New York Times*, October 25, 2010 (emphasis added).

34 Steve Holland, "Obama Seeks to Blunt Republican Attack Over Comment," *Reuters*, November 1, 2010 (emphasis added).

35 Kimberley A. Strassel, "Bonfire of the Populists,' *Wall Street Journal*, January 28, 2010. The quotes are all taken from "Remarks by the President in State of the Union Address," U.S. Capitol, January 27, 2010. Available at: http://www.whitehouse.gov/the-press-office/remarks-president-state-union-address (accessed August 5, 2010).

36 David Brooks and Gail Collins, "Obama, the Attack Dog," *New York Times*, October 13, 2010.

37 Peter Baker, "Obama Ratchets Up Tone Against G.O.P.," *New York Times*, October 10, 2010 (emphasis added).

38 Baker, "Obama Ratchets Up Tone Against G.O.P."

39 Alan Silverleib, "Gloves Come Off after Obama Rips Supreme Court Ruling," *CNN*, January 28, 2010; see also Robert Barnes, "Reactions Split on Obama's Remark, Alito's Response at State of the Union," *Washington Post*, January 29, 2010.

40 Linda Greenhouse, "Justice Alito's Reaction," *New York Times*, January 27, 2010.

41 Jay Reeves, "Roberts: Scene at State of Union 'very troubling,'"*Associated Press*, March 9, 2010.

42 Sam Stein, "Gibbs Fires Back at Chief Justice Roberts Over Obama Criticism," *Huffington Post*, March 9, 2010.

43 "Remarks by the President on the Economy in Parma, Ohio," The White House, September 8, 2010. Available at: http://www.whitehouse.gov/the-press-office/2010/09/08/remarks-president-economy-parma-ohio (accessed September 11, 2010).

44 "Transcript: President Barack Obama, Part 2," *CBS News 60 Minutes*, November 4, 2010 (emphasis added). Available at: http://www.cbsnews.com/stories/2010/11/07/60minutes/main7032277.shtml?source=related_story&tag=related (accessed November 13, 2010).

45 "Obama's Sermon Remembering Martin Luther King Jr.," *Washington Post*, January 17, 2010 (emphasis added). Available at: http://voices.washingtonpost.com/44/2010/01/obamas-sermon-remembering-mart.html (accessed July 10, 2010).

46 "In Obama's Words: Obama, with Vice President Joe Biden, Hold Town Hall on High Speed Rail in Tampa, Fla.," *Washington Post*, January 29, 2010 (emphasis added). Available at: http://projects.washingtonpost.com/obama-speeches/speech/170 accessed July 10, 2010).

47 Joe Klein, "Q&A: Obama on His First Year in Office," *Time*, January, 21, 2010 (emphasis added). Available at: http://www.time.com/time/printout/0,8816,1955072,00.html (accessed July 10, 2010)

48 "Remarks by President Obama and King Abdullah of Jordan in Joint Press-Availability," April 21, 2009 (emphasis added). Available at: http://www.whitehouse.gov/the_press_office/Remarks-by-President-Obama-and-King-Abdullah-of-Jordan-in-joint-press-availability/ (accessed July 10, 2010)

49 Obama quoted in Richard Wolffe, "'Hungry for Change': Obama's Afterglow," *Newsweek*, January 4, 2008 (emphasis added). Available at: http://www.newsweek.com/2008/01/04/hungry-for-change.html (accessed July 31, 2010).

50 Obama quoted in Jake Tapper, "Obama: 'Better Judgment' on Foreign Policy," *ABC News*, July 25, 2007.

51 Quoted in Mark Memmott and Jill Lawrence, "Obama Launches Tour to Highlight 'Judgment, Experience' on Iraq," *USA TODAY*, October 1, 2007.

52 "Remarks of Illinois State Sen. Barack Obama Against Going to War with Iraq."

53 Kenneth Pollack, *The Threatening Storm: The Case for Invading Iraq*, New York: Random House, 2002.

54 Obama quoted in Andrew Malcolm, "Top of the Ticket," *Los Angeles Times*, July 16, 2008.

55 Shailagh Murray, "Obama Bill Sets Date For Troop Withdrawal. Candidate Goes Further Than Rivals," *Washington Post*, January 31, 2007.

56 Bill Schneider "Clinton, Obama War Funding Votes Draw Criticism," *CNN*, May 26, 2007; see also James W. Pindell and Rick Klein, "Obama Defends Votes in Favor of Iraq Funding," *Boston Globe*, March 22, 2007.

57 A number of Obama's statements on the surge may be found in Peter Wehner, "Obama in Iraq's Quicksand," *Commentary*, 2010. Available at: http://www.commentarymagazine.com/printarticle.cfm/obama-in-iraq-s-quicksand-11869 (accessed August 1, 2010).

58 Obama quoted in Wehner, "Obama in Iraq" (emphasis added).

59 "Transcript: The Democratic Debate in New Hampshire," *New York Times*, January 5, 2008. Available at: http://www.nytimes.com/2008/01/05/us/politics/05text-

ddebate.html?_r=4&oref=slogin&adxnnlx=1217243316-S8%20BYIFAXHCH%20D6m
2qwOkQ&pagewanted=print (accessed July 31, 2010).

60 Barack Obama, "My Plan for Iraq," *New York Times*, July 14, 2008.

61 David Stout, "Obama to Urge Afghans 'Into the Fight,'" *New York Times*, December 2, 2009.

62 Obama quoted in Alter, *The Promise*, p. 377.

63 Katie Couric, "Obama: Surge Doesn't Meet Long-Term Goals," *CBS News*, July 22, 2008 (emphasis added). Available at: http://www.cbsnews.com/stories/2008/07/22/eveningnews/main4283623.shtml (accessed July 31, 2010).

64 Obama quoted in Ann Gearan, "US Officials Say War Goals Modest in Afghanistan," *Associated Press*, August 1, 2010.

65 Peter Baker, "Obama Speech Begins Effort to Highlight Iraq Drawdown," *New York Times*, August 2, 2010.

66 Secretary of Defense Gates quoted in John J. Kurzel, "Gates: Decisions on Afghanistan Most Important of His Presidency," *Armed Forces Press Services*, October 6, 2009. Available at: http://www.centcom.mil/en/news/gates-upcoming-decisions-on-afghanistan-most-important-of-presidency.html (accessed July 31, 2010).

67 Bob Woodward, "McChrystal: More Forces or 'Mission Failure,'" *Washington Post*, September 21, 2009.

68 Greg Jaffe, Scott Wilson, and Karen DeYoung, "U.S. Envoy Resists Increases in Troops," *Washington Post*, November 12, 2009.

69 Robert Gibbs, "Press Briefing," October 14, 2009. Available at: http://www.whitehouse.gov/the-press-office/briefing-white-house-press-secretary-robert-gibbs-101409 (accessed March 5, 2011); see also Robert Gibbs, "Press Gaggle Aboard Air Force One," November 12, 2009. Available at: http://www.whitehouse.gov/the-press-office/gaggle-press-secretary-gibbs-aboard-air-force-one-en-route-anchorage-alaska (accessed March 5, 2011).

70 Anne E. Kornblut, Scott Wilson, and Karen DeYoung, "Obama pressed for a faster surge," *Washington Post*, December 6, 2009; Peter Baker, "How Obama Came to Plan for 'Surge' in Afghanistan," *New York Times*, December 6, 2009; and Christi Parsons and Julian E. Barnes, "Obama homed in on an Afghanistan pullout date," *Los Angeles Times*, December 4, 2009. For an inquiry into the usefulness of these stories from both a news and White House perspective see Ben Smith, "Tic Toc," *Politico*, December 6, 2009.

71 Cf., "State of the Union with John King: Interview with General Jim Jones," *CNN*, October 4, 2009.

72 Cf., Barack Obama, "Remarks by the President in Address to the Nation on the Way Forward in Afghanistan and Pakistan," The White House, December 1, 2009; Barack Obama, "Remarks by the President at the Veterans of Foreign Wars Convention," The White House, April 17, 2009; and Barack Obama, "Remarks by the President on a New Strategy for Afghanistan and Pakistan," The White House, March 27, 2009.

73 Marc Ambinder, "Lunch With The President: The Politics of Obama's War Plan," *The Atlantic*, December 1, 2009; and Doyle McManus, "Obama's Afghanistan Strategy Counts on Time as an Ally," *Los Angeles Times*, December 1, 2009.

74 A top White House official said of the process, "We take the competing views and collapse them toward the middle." Quoted in David Ignatius, "Careful to a Fault on Afghanistan," *Washington Post*, October 15, 2009.

75 Michele Norris, "Obama Seeks Middle Ground on Afghanistan," *NPR*, October 8, 2009.

76 Alter, *The Promise*, p. 384.

77 Obama quoted in Ann Gearan, "US Officials Say War Goals Modest in Afghanistan," *Associated Press*, August 1, 2010.

78 David Stout, "Obama to Urge Afghans 'Into the Fight,'" *New York Times*, December 2, 2009.

79 Barnes quoted in Peter Baker, "Education of a President," *New York Times*, October 12, 2010.

80 William Galston, "The Future of President Obama's Agenda," *Sunday Times*, April 19, 2009.

81 David Mendell, *Obama: From Promise to Power*, New York: Harper Collins, 2007, p. 128.

82 Obama quoted in Mendell, *Obama*, p. 141 (emphasis added).

83 Charles Savage, "Closing Guantánamo Fades as a Priority," *New York Times*, June 25, 2010.

84 Glenn Thrush, "Obama's Mosque Moment Frustrates Dems," *Politico*, August 21, 2010 (emphasis added).

85 John Harwood, "Running on Risk, Then Sticking With It," *New York Times*, March 2, 2009.

86 David Plouffe quoted in Harwood, "Running on Risk, Then Sticking With It."

87 Mike Allen and Jim VandeHei, "Obama's Big Bang Could Go Bust," *Politico*, August 29, 2009.

88 These risks are drawn from, but are not exactly the same as, those listed in the Editorial, "Health Reform is a Risk Worth Taking," *Washington Post*, March 19, 2010.

89 Chris Frates and Ben White, "Obama's Policy Time Bombs," *Politico*, July 11, 2010.

90 David S. Broder, "Obama Rolls The Dice," *Washington Post*, February 26, 2009 (emphasis added).

91 Andrew Jacobs, "China Warns U.S. to Stay Out of Islands Dispute," *New York Times*, July 26, 2010.

92 Frates and White, "Obama's Policy Time Bombs."

93 David Brooks, "The Pragmatic Leviathan," *New York Times*, January 19, 2010 (emphasis added).

94 NBC News/Wall Street Journal Survey, Study #10651, August, 2010. Available at: http://online.wsj.com/public/resources/documents/wsjnbcpoll-08122010.pdf (accessed August 18, 2010).

95 Douglas Schoen, "Why He Turns Voters off," *Daily Beast*, August 18, 2010.

96 Sheryl Gay Stolberg, "Obama Pushes Agenda, Despite Political Risks," *New York Times*, July 15, 2010.

97 "President Obama to Pastor Jones: 'Stunt' Endangers Troops—Full Transcript of Exclusive Interview," *ABC News*, September 9, 2010.

98 Gerald F. Seib, "Why Political Sage Sees GOP Romp in November," *Wall Street Journal*, August 20, 2010.

99 Charles Cook, "Obama Gives Democrats Another Headache," *National Journal*, August 18, 2010.

100 Margaret Carlson, "Smart President Fails Test at Ground Zero," *Bloomberg*, August 18, 2010.

10 Transformation's Collapse and the Redemption of the Obama Presidency

1 Peter Baker, "In Republican Victories, Tide Turns Sharply," *New York Times*, November 2, 2010.

2 John F. Harris, "Change Has Come ... or Has It?" *Politico*, November 4, 2010.

3 Jeremy P. Jacobs, "Devastation: GOP Picks up 680 State Leg. Seats," *National Journal*, November 4, 2010. In the 1994 GOP wave, Republicans picked up 472 seats. The previous record was in the post-Watergate election of 1974, when Democrats picked up 628 seats. The GOP gained majorities in at least fourteen state house chambers.

Republicans now have unified control—meaning both chambers—of twenty-six state legislatures.

4 James Ceaser, "The 2010 Verdict," *RealClearPolitics*, November 10, 2010.
5 Tim Story, "GOP Gains in Legislatures are Historic," National Conference of State Legislatures, November 4, 2010. Available at: http://ncsl.typepad.com/the_thicket/2010/11/by-tim-storey-updated-at-thursday-nov-4-1115am-mdt-republicans-have-added-over-675-seats-to-their-ranks-in-this-elec.html (accessed October 10, 2010).
6 Howard Kurtz, "A Democratic Bloodbath," *Daily Beast*, November 3, 2010; Ben Smith and Jonathan Martin, "Republicans Tear Up Obama's Map," *Politico*, November 3, 2010.
7 Heidi Przybyla, "Republicans Predict Obama Rebuff in Election; Democrats Foresee Surprise," *Bloomberg News*, October 31, 2010.
8 Shane D'Aprile, "Midterm Blowout: 50 or More Democratic Seats Set to Fall in Tuesday's Election," *The Hill*, October 26, 2010.
9 Thomas Sowell, "A Crossroads Election," *Townhall*, October 29, 2010.
10 Ron Brownstein, "Converging Fronts Create Perfect Storm for Republicans in Midterms," *National Journal*, November 3, 2010.
11 Karl Rove, "Signs of the Democratic Apocalypse," *Wall Street Journal*, October 28, 2010.
12 Jeremy P. Jacobs, "New Polls Suggest Sizable GOP Landslide," *The Hill*, October 26, 2010.
13 Michael Barone, "Voters Reject Obama's Big-Government Ambitions," *San Francisco Examiner*, November 4, 2010.
14 Baker, "In Republican Victories, Tide Turns Sharply."
15 Smith and Martin, "Republicans Tear Up Obama's Map."
16 Richard Cohen, "A No-confidence Vote in Obama," *Washington Post*, November 2, 2010; see also Ronald Brownstein, "Past as Prologue," *National Journal*, November 4, 2010;
17 Gail Russell Chaddock, "On Historic Night, Republicans Sweep House Democrats From Power," *Christian Science Monitor*, November 3, 2010.
18 Senate Republican leader Mitch McConnell quoted in Gerald Seib, "McConnell Softens Tone on Working with Obama," *Wall Street Journal*, November 5, 2010.
19 William Galston, "It's the Ideology Stupid," *New Republic*, November 4, 2010.
20 Gregor Peter Schmitz, "Obama's Election Debacle," *Der Spiegel*, November 3, 2010.
21 The White House, "Press Conference by the President," November 3, 2010. Available at: http://www.whitehouse.gov/the-press-office/2010/11/03/press-conference-president (accessed November 17, 2010).
22 CNN/Opinion Research Poll conducted November 11–14, 2010, pp.9–10, Questions 5, 6. Available at: http://i2.cdn.turner.com/cnn/2010/images/11/15/rel16a.pdf (accessed November 14, 2010).
23 Charles Krauthammer, "A Return to the Norm," *Washington Post*, November 5, 2010
24 E.J. Dionne Jr., "And Now for the Next Battle," *Washington Post*, November 3, 2010.
25 Editorial, "Sorting Out the Election," *New York Times*, November 3, 2010.
26 Jeff Zeleny, "G.O.P. Captures House, but Not Senate," *New York Times*, November 2, 2010.
27 Jeanne Cummings, "Dems' 2010 Crisis has Roots in 2009," *Politico*, October 26, 2010.
28 Karen Tumulty, "Once Again, the Electorate Demanded a New Start," *Washington Post*, November 3, 2010.
29 Scott Rasmussen, "A Vote Against Dems, Not for the GOP," *Wall Street Journal*, November 1, 2010.
30 Jay Cost, "Back to the Bush Coalition," *Weekly Standard*, November 15, 2010, Vol. 16, No. 09.

31 Dan Balz, "Election Results are Open to (Careful) Interpretation,"*Washington Post*, November 4, 2010.

32 William A. Galston, "President Barack Obama's First Two Years: Policy Accomplishments, Political Difficulties," *New Republic*, November 6, 2010.

33 Jackie Calmes and Megan Thee-Brenan, "Independents Fueled G.O.P Gains," *New York Times*, November 2, 2010.

34 Baker, "In Republican Victories, Tide Turns Sharply."

35 John Harwood, "Serving Big Initiatives in Bite-Size Portions," *New York Times*, July 26, 2010.

36 Peter Baker, "In Losing the Midterms, There May Be Winning," *New York Times*, October 23, 2010.

37 Baker, "In Losing the Midterms, There May Be Winning."

38 Ben Smith, "On Call, Officials Stress Public Options in Health Care Shift," *Politico*, February 28, 2011.

39 Richard Cohen, "Obama Borrows GOP Lingo on Tax Reform," *Politico*, December 10, 2010.

40 John Bresnahan and Jake Sherman, "W.H. launches charm offensive with new GOP chairs," *Politico*, December 13, 2010.

41 Karl Rove, "Why Obama Chose Bill Daley," *Wall Street Journal*, January 13, 2011.

42 Lisa Rein, "More Civil Servants are Now Subject to Two-Year Pay Freeze," *Washington Post*, December 28, 2010.

43 Executive Order, "Improving Regulation and Regulatory Review," White House, January 18, 2011.

44 Barack Obama, "Toward a 21st-Century Regulatory System," *Wall Street Journal*, January 18, 2011.

45 Eric Lipton, "With Obama, Regulations are Back in Fashion," *New York Times*, May 12, 2010.

46 Jackie Calmes, "Obama Asks for Review of Rules Stifling Jobs," *New York Times*, January 18, 2011.

47 Executive Order, "Improving Regulation and Regulatory Review," White House, January 18, 2011, p. 1 (emphasis added).

48 Lori Montgomery, Shailagh Murray, and William Branigin, "Obama signs bill to extend Bush-era tax cuts for two more years," *Washington Post*, December 17, 2010.

49 David M. Herszehorn, "Congress Sends $801 Billion Tax Cut Bill to Obama," *New York Times*, December 16, 2010.

50 Scott Wilson, "The President Extends an Olive Branch to GOP," Washington Post, December 7, 2010.

51 "I understand the desire for a fight. I'm sympathetic to that. I'm as opposed to the high-end tax cuts today as I've been for years. In the long run, we simply can't afford them. And when they expire in two years, I will fight to end them." See "Press Conference by the President," The White House, December 7, 2010. http://www. whitehouse.gov/the-press-office/2010/12/07/press-conference-president (accessed March 11, 2011).

52 A video of the news conference is available at http://www.youtube.com/watch? v=JNz321HpTko (assessed March 11, 2011).

53 Michael D. Shear, "The Surprise Trip to the Briefing Room," *New York Times*, December 10, 2010. See http://www.whitehouse.gov/the-press-office/2010/12/10/remarks-president-obama-and-former-president-clinton (accessed March 11, 2011).

54 Dan Balz, "Lights, Camera, Clinton," *Washington Post*, December 11, 2010.

55 Roger Runningen and Brian Faler, "Obama's $3.7 Trillion Budget Sets Fight in Congress," *Bloomberg News*, February 14, 2011.

56 Ibid.

57 Sam Dillon and Tamar Lewin, "Obama's Budget Proposes a Significant Increase for Schools," *New York Times*, February 14, 2011.
58 John M. Broder, "Few Significant Changes in Energy-Area Spending," *New York Times*, February 14, 2011.
59 Jackie Calmes, "Budget Seeks Deep Cuts in Domestic Spending," *New York Times*, February 12, 2011 (emphasis added).
60 "The Obama budget's assumptions include a substantial increase in rates. It predicts that the interest rate on 10-year Treasury notes will climb from 3 percent this year to 3.6 percent next year. It forecasts rates of 5 percent by 2015 and 5.3 percent at the end of the decade." See Steven Mufson, "Obama Budget Plan Shows Interest Owed on National Debt Quadrupling in Next Decade," *Washington Post*, February 17, 2011. Also, "From 2013 to 2016, the administration estimates the economy will grow at an average rate of nearly 3.9 percent per year, while the Congressional Budget Office projects a growth rate of just 3.4 percent. That could make an enormous difference in the amount of revenue generated and, consequently, the size of deficits." See Editorial, "President Obama's Budget Kicks the Hard Choices Further Down the Road," *Washington Post*, February 15, 2011.
61 Mufson, "Obama Budget."
62 John Merlne, "How Deep are Those Spending Cuts?" *AOL News*, February 14, 2011.
63 Jake Tapper, "President Obama's Budget and the Pending Budget Fight," *ABC News*, February 14, 2011.
64 John T. Bennett, "Obama: I'm not moving to center," *The Hill*, February 6, 2001; see also "Transcript of President Obama's Super Bowl Interview with Bill O'Reilly." *Politics Daily*. http://www.politicsdaily.com/2011/02/06/transcript-of-president-obamas-pre-super-bowl-interview-with-bi/ (accessed March 11, 2011).
65 See Thomas E. Cronin, *The State of the Presidency*, Boston: Little Brown, 1975, p. 238.
66 Mark Lander and Helene Cooper, "Obama Seeks a Course of Pragmatism," *New York Times*, March 10, 2011.
67 Obama quoted in Dan Balz and Haynes Johnson, *The Battle for America 2008*, New York: Viking, 2010, p. 377.
68 "Transcript: President Barack Obama, Part 1, Nov. 4, 2010," *CBS News 60 Minutes*, November 7, 2010.
69 The quotes that follow, unless otherwise noted, are taken from Peter Baker, "Education of a President," *New York Times*, October 12, 2010.
70 Baker, "Education of a President."
71 David Brooks, "The Next Two Years," *New York Times*, October 28, 2010.
72 Mike Rosenberg, "State High-speed Train Rides to Be Costlier, Ridership Lower than Promised to Voters," *San Mateo County Times*, December 14, 2009.
73 Jim Hoagland, "Insecurities Beneath China's Prosperous Exterior," *Washington Post*, November 14, 2010.
74 These figures are derived from Robert J. Samuelson, "Obama's Stunted Stimulus," *Washington Post*, February 23, 2009.
75 Obama quoted in Baker, "Education of a President."
76 Jake Tapper, "An Interview with President Obama," *ABC News*, July 7, 2009.
77 Mark Silva, "Obama: 150,000 Road Jobs: 'Shovel Ready,'" *Chicago Tribune*, March 3, 2009.
78 Manuel Roig-Franzia, "The Obama Buzzword That Hit Pay Dirt," *Washington Post*, January 8, 2009.
79 Silva, "Obama: 150,000 Road Jobs."
80 Mike Allen and Eamon Javers, "Obama: Stimulus saved 1 million jobs," *Politico*, October 30, 2009.
81 *Associated Press*, "30,000 Stimulus Jobs Figure is Way Off the Mark," November 29, 2009.

82 Jared A. Favole, "Obama Advisers Say Stimulus Saved or Created Three Million Jobs," *Wall Street Journal*, July 14, 2010.

83 Executive Office of the President Council of Economic Advisers, "The Economic Impact of the American Recovery and Reinvestment Act of 2009," Fourth Quarter Report, July 14, 2010. Available at: http://www.whitehouse.gov/files/documents/cea_4th_arra_report.pdf (accessed November 14, 2010).

84 Executive Office of the President Council of Economic Advisers, "The Economic Impact of the American Recovery and Reinvestment Act of 2009," p. 7.

85 Lori Montgomery, "CBO Says Stimulus May Have Added 3.3 Million Jobs," *Washington Post*, August 24, 2010.

86 Doug Elmendorf, Director, Congressional Budget Office, speech at the National Association for Business Economics' annual economic policy conference, March 8, 2010. Available at: http://www.cspan.org/Watch/Media/2010/03/08/HP/A/30436/CBO+Director+Elmendorf+on+Stimulus+Law+and+the+Economy.aspx (accessed November 14, 2010).

87 Sheryl Gay Stolberg, "Obama Pushes Jobs Plan, and Assails GOP for Criticism," *New York Times*, September 6, 2010; see also The White House, "President Obama to Announce Plan to Renew and Expand America's Roads, Railways and Runways," September 6, 2010. Available at: http://www.whitehouse.gov/the-press-office/2010/09/06/president-obama-announce-plan-renew-and-expand-america-s-roads-railways- (accessed November 17, 2010).

88 "Transcript: President Barack Obama, Part 2, Nov. 4, 2010," *CBS News 60 Minutes*, November 7, 2010.

89 Carol E. Lee, "Obama: 'Campaigning is Different than Governing,'" *Politico*, November 14, 2010.

90 "Transcript: President Barack Obama, Part 2."

91 "Remarks by the President in a Discussion on Women and the Economy in Seattle, Washington, Foss Residence, Seattle, Washington," October 21, 2010 (emphasis added). Available at: http://www.whitehouse.gov/the-press-office/2010/10/21/remarks-president-a-discussion-women-and-economy-seattle (accessed November 14, 2010).

92 Ron Fournier and Ronald Brownstein, "Obama to Republicans: Let's Build Consensus,' *National Journal*, October 27, 2010 (emphasis added).

93 Baker, "Education of a President."

94 Baker, "Education of a President."

95 The White House, "Press Conference by the President." The other Q&As are:

> Q: Are you willing to concede at all that what happened last night was not just an expression of frustration about the economy, but a fundamental rejection of your agenda?
>
> THE PRESIDENT: I think that there is no doubt that people's number-one concern is the economy. And what they were expressing great frustration about is the fact that we haven't made enough progress on the economy. We've stabilized the economy. We've got job growth in the private sectors. But people all across America aren't feeling that progress.
>
> Q: Would you still resist the notion that voters rejected the policy choices you made?
>
> THE PRESIDENT: Well, Savannah, I think that what I think is absolutely true is voters are not satisfied with the outcomes. If right now we had 5 percent unemployment instead of 9.6 percent unemployment, then people would have more confidence in those policy choices. The fact is, is that for most folks, proof of whether they work or not is has the economy gotten back to where it needs to be. And it hasn't.

96 The White House, "Press Conference by the President"(emphasis added).
97 Tapper, "Interview with the President."
98 Baker, "Education of a President."
99 The White House, "Press Conference by the President."
100 Baker, "Education of a President."
101 Obama quoted in David Kerley and Cait Taylor, "President Obama and the Lame Duck Congress," *ABC News*, November 14, 2010.
102 Obama quoted in Carol E. Lee, "Obama: 'Fear and Frustration' Drive Voters," *Politico*, October 16, 2010 (emphasis added). The complete remarks may be found at "Remarks by the President at DSCC Fundraiser," De La Torre Residence, Boston, Massachusetts, October 16, 2010. Available at: http://www.whitehouse.gov/the-press-office/2010/10/16/remarks-president-dscc-fundraiser (accessed November 14, 2010).
103 Karen Tumulty and Dan Balz, "Assessing Midterm Losses, Democrats Ask Whether Obama's White House Fully Grasped Voters' Fears," *Washington Post*, November 7, 2010.
104 Joel Achenbach, "In a Heated Race, Obama's Cool Won the Day," *Washington Post*, November 6, 2008.
105 The White House, "Press Conference by the President" (emphasis added).
106 Baker, "Education of a President"(emphasis added).
107 Jeff Zeleny, "President's Political Protector Is Ever Close at Hand," *New York Times*, March 9, 2009.
108 http://www.gpoaccess.gov/presdocs/browse.html (accessed March 5, 2011).
109 Elizabeth Williamson, "Trivial Pursuit: One Man's Quest to Catalog Presidential Minutiae," *Wall Street Journal*, March 31, 2010.
110 Mark Knoller, "Obama's First Year: By the Numbers," *CBS News*, January 20, 2010.
111 Julie Mason, "Obama Pushes the Limits of Media Exposure," *Washington Examiner*, June 25, 2009.
112 Jarrett quoted in David Remnick, *The Bridge: The Life and Rise of President Barack Obama*, New York: Knopf, 2010, p. 274 (emphasis added).
113 Biden quoted in Lisa DePaulo, "$#!% Joe Biden Says," *GQ*, December, 2010 (emphasis in original).
114 Matthew Mosk, "Tom Donilon's Revolving Door,' *ABC News*, October 10, 2010.
115 Chip Reid, "White House Push-Back on Asia Trip Failure Meme," *CBS News* (November 14, 2010) (emphasis added).
116 "Joint Statement Between President George W. Bush and Prime Minister Manmohan Singh," The White House George W. Bush, July 18, 2005. Available at: http://georgewbush-whitehouse.archives.gov/news/releases/2005/07/print/20050718-6.html (accessed March 11, 2010).
117 The numbers that follow are drawn from the *Washington Post-ABC News Poll*, August 30–September 2, 2010. Available at: http://www.washingtonpost.com/wp-srv/politics/polls/postpoll_09072010.html (accessed November 19, 2010).
118 Aamer Madhani, "Does He Feel Your Pain?" *National Journal*, October 29, 2010.
119 Obama quoted in Baker, "Education of a President;" see also David Jackson, "Obama Echoes Reagan: 'Stay On Course,'" *USA TODAY-The Oval*, October 1, 2010.
120 Baker, "Education of a President."
121 Baker, "Education of a President"(emphasis added).
122 "Remarks by the President and the First Lady in Town Hall with Students in Mumbai, India, St. Xavier College Mumbai, India," November 7, 2010. Available at: http://www.whitehouse.gov/the-press-office/2010/11/07/remarks-president-and-first-lady-town-hall-with-students-mumbai-india (accessed November 11, 2010).
123 Baker, "Education of a President" (emphasis added).
124 Mike Allen, "Obama Plans Truce with Chamber," *Politico*, November 20, 2010.

125 Fournier and Brownstein, "Obama to Republicans"(emphasis added).
126 Baker, "Education of a President."
127 Baker, "Education of a President."
128 The White House, "Press Conference by the President."
129 Barack Obama, *The Audacity of Hope*, New York: Three Rivers Press, 2006, p. 105.
130 Obama, *Audacity*, p. 107.
131 "If right now we had 5 percent unemployment instead of 9.6 percent unemployment, then people would have more confidence in those policy choices." See The White House, "Press Conference by the President."

Appendix A: Analyzing Barack Obama

1 Stanley A. Renshon, *High Hopes: The Clinton Presidency and the Politics of Ambition*, New York: New York University Press, 1996 (1998 paperback edition, with afterword, published by Routledge).
2 Stanley A. Renshon, *In his Father's Shadow: The Transformations of George W. Bush*. New York: Palgrave/Macmillan, 2004.
3 Stanley A. Renshon, *The Psychological Assessment of Presidential Candidates*, New York: New York University Press, 1996 (1998 paperback edition, with afterword, published by Routledge).
4 Renshon, *Assessment*, chapters 2 and 12.
5 Renshon, *Assessment*, appendix 1.
6 Renshon, *Assessment*, chapter 5.
7 Renshon, *Assessment*, chapter 6.
8 Renshon, *Assessment*, chapter 9.
9 Renshon, *Assessment*, chapters 10 and 11.
10 Stanley A. Renshon, "After the Fall: The Clinton Presidency in Psychological Perspective," *Political Science Quarterly*, 115:1 (Spring 2000), pp. 41–65.
11 Renshon, *High Hopes*, Appendix I.
12 Stanley A. Renshon, "The Comparative Psychoanalytic Study of Political Leaders: John McCain and the Limits of Trait Psychology" in Ofer Feldman and Linda O. Valenty (eds.), *Profiling Political Leaders and the Analysis of Political Leadership: Methods and Cross-Cultural Applications*, Westport, C.T.: Greenwood, 2001, pp. 233–53.
13 Stanley A. Renshon, "Analyzing the Psychology and Performance of Presidential Candidates at a Distance: Bob Dole and the 1996 Presidential Campaign," *Journal of Leadership Studies* (Special Issue on Political Leadership) 9: 3 (1998), pp. 253–81.
14 Stanley A. Renshon, "Psychoanalyzing Presidents without a Couch: Lessons from the William J. Clinton and George W. Bush Presidencies," Center for Political Leadership: Working Papers. Cambridge, Ma.: The John F. Kennedy School of Government, 2004. Available at: http://content.ksg.harvard.edu/leadership/images/stories/ksg/PDF/Publications/renshonworkingpaper.pdf?phpMyAdmin=LTiBtEu99qkd5KYdIryaR2-3Jp7 (accessed August 16, 2009).
15 Stanley A. Renshon, "Assessing the Character and Performance of Presidential Candidates: Some Observations on Theory and Method," in Jerrold M. Post, M.D. (ed.), *The Psychological Assessment of Political Leaders: Theories, Methods, and Applications*, Ann Arbor, Mich.: University of Michigan Press, 2003.
16 Stanley A. Renshon, "Psychological Reflections on Barack Obama and John McCain: Assessing the Contours of a New Administration," *Political Science Quarterly* 123:3 (Fall 2008), pp. 391–433.
17 Renshon, *Assessment*, chapters 7 and 8.
18 Quoted in Michael Powell, "A Deliberative Man in a Manic Game," *New York Times*, June 4, 2008. During a campaign interview with the *Chicago Tribune* Obama

said, "I am much more likely I think at the end of this process to view myself as a vehicle, this campaign as a vehicle by which the American people can express their hopes and their dreams and their aspirations." See the *Chicago Tribune* interview with Sen. Barack Obama on January 2, 2008. Available at: www.chicagotribune.com/news/politics/chi-080102-obama-interview,0,6853972.story (accessed August 23, 2009).

19 Lisa Wangsness, "Health Plan's Effect on Costs May Be Slight," *Boston Globe*, October 12, 2009. In that same article Henry J. Aaron, a health economist at the Brookings Institution who has spent his career studying health costs, is quoted as saying "When exactly the [cost] curve gets bent and how far it bends eventually is something no responsible person can give a hard answer to today."

20 Dale Andrade, "Three Lessons from Vietnam," *Washington Post*, December 29, 2009; Melvin R. Laird, "Iraq: Learning the Lesson of Vietnam," *Foreign Affairs*, November/December, 2005; John Kerry, "Testing Afghanistan Assumptions," *Wall Street Journal*, September 27, 2009; Lewis Sorley, *A Better War: The Unexamined Victories and Final Tragedy of America's Last Years in Vietnam*, New York: Harcourt, 1999; Lewis Sorley, "The Real Afghan Lessons From Vietnam," *Wall Street Journal*, October 11, 2009; Gordon Goldstein, *Lessons in Disaster: McGeorge Bundy and the Path to War in Vietnam*, New York: Times Books, 2008; and Max Boot, "The Incurable Vietnam Syndrome," *Weekly Standard*, 15: 5, October 19, 2009.

21 Amity Shales, *The Forgotten Man: A New History of the Great Depression*, New York: Harper Collins, 2007.

22 These details are drawn from Robert Draper, "The Prez & I," *GQ*, January 2009. Available at: http://www.gq.com/news-politics/newsmakers/200812/george-w-bush-robert-draper-interview-president (accessed July 23, 2010). The book that came out of those interviews was Robert Draper, *Dead Certain: The Presidency of George W. Bush*, New York: Free Press, 2007.

23 Obama quoted in Evan Thomas, *A Long Time Coming: The Inspiring, Combative 2008 Campaign and the Historic Election of Barack Obama*, New York: Public Affairs Press, 2009, p. 210 (emphasis added).

24 Obama quoted in John Meacham, "Interview: I Had to Learn to Fight," *Newsweek*, August 23, 2008 (emphasis added). Available at: http://www.newsweek.com/id/155175 (accessed August 9, 2010).

25 "Q & A: *New York Times* Reporter Michael Powell," *Columbia Journalism Review*, August 13, 2010 (emphasis added). Available at: http://www.cjr.org/behind_the_news/q_a_new_york_times_reporter_mi.php?page=all&print=true (accessed August 14, 2010).

26 Sigmund Freud, "A Note on the Unconscious in Psycho-analysis," *S.E.* 12, pp. 205–12.

27 Cf. R.E. Nisbett and T.D. Wilson, "Telling More than We Know; Verbal Reports on Mental Process," *Psychological Review*, 84: 3 (March 1977), pp. 231–69; T.D. Wilson, *Strangers to Ourselves*, Cambridge, MA: Harvard University Press, 2002.

28 Robert Jervis, "Understanding Beliefs," *Political Psychology*, 27:5 (October 2006), p. 645 (emphasis added).

29 Robert Gibbs, "Press Briefing," October 14, 2009. Available at: http://www.whitehouse.gov/the-press-office/briefing-white-house-press-secretary-robert-gibbs-101409 (accessed March 6, 2011, see also Robert Gibbs, "Press Gaggle Aboard Air Force One," November 12, 2009. Available at: http://www.whitehouse.gov/the-press-office/gaggle-press-secretary-robert-gibbs-aboard-air-force-one-en-route-anchorage-alaska (accessed March 6, 2011). Columnist David Ignatius was also briefed about the process and reported a number of details regarding it in his October 15, 2009 column. See David Ignatius, "Careful to a Fault on Afghanistan," *Washington Post*, October 15, 2009.

30 "Transcript of CNBC's Barack Obama Interview," *CNBC*, January 7, 2009. Available at: http://www.msnbc.msn.com/id/28546772/ns/business-cnbc_tv/ (accessed July 23, 2010).

31 *C-SPAN* Interview Transcript, "President Barack H. Obama," May 22, 2009. Available at: http://www.c-span.org/pdf/obamainterview.pdf (accessed July 23, 2010).

32 Pew Research Center for the People & the Press, "Partisan Gap in Obama Job Approval Widest in Modern Era," April 2, 2009.

33 Eric Schmitt and Eric Lipton, "U.S. Charges Suspect, Eyeing Link to Qaeda in Yemen," *New York Times*, December 27, 2009.

34 Scott Wilson, "Cheney Criticizes Obama on National Security Policy, and Biden Fires Back," *Washington Post*, February 15, 2010, A01.

35 Dana Priest, "U.S. Military Teams, Intelligence Deeply Involved in Aiding Yemen on Strikes," *Washington Post*, January 27, 2010, A01.

36 Declan McCullah, "Feds Push for Tracking Cell Phones," *Cnet News*, February 11, 2010.

37 David Remnick, "Testing the Waters," *New Yorker*, October 30, 2006.

38 Jessica Curry, "Barack Obama: Under the Lights," *Chicago Life*, August 1, 2004.

39 Barack Obama, "Preface to the 2004 Edition," *Dreams from My Father*, New York: Three Rivers Press, 2004, p. xii.

40 Obama quoted in David Mendell, *Obama: From Promise to Power*, New York: Harper Collins, 2007, p. 19.

41 Obama quoted in Meacham, "Interview: I had to Learn to Fight" (emphasis added).

42 Obama, *Dreams*.

43 Michiko Kakutani, "Obama's Foursquare Politics: With a Dab of Dijon," *New York Times*, October 17, 2006.

44 Robert McCrum, "A Candidate's Tale," *Guardian*, August 26, 2007.

45 Oona King, "Oona King on Barack Obama's Dreams from My Father," *The Times*, September 15, 2007.

46 David Remnick, *The Bridge: The Life and Rise of Barack Obama*, New York: Knopf, 2010.

47 David Maraniss, "Though Obama Had to Leave to Find Himself, It is Hawaii that Made His Rise Possible," *Washington Post*, August 22, 2008.

48 Kirsten Scharnberg and Kim Barker, "The Not-so-simple Story of Barack Obama's Youth," *Chicago Tribune*, March 25, 2007.

49 Obama, *Dreams*, p. 36.

50 Scharnberg and Barker, "The Not-so-simple Story of Barack Obama's Youth."

51 Obama, *Dreams*, pp. 51–52.

52 Scharnberg and Barker, "The Not-so-simple Story of Barack Obama's Youth"; see also Remnick, *The Bridge*, p. 238.

53 Maraniss, "Though Obama Had to Leave to Find Himself."

54 Scharnberg and Barker, "The Not-so-simple Story of Barack Obama's Youth."

55 Obama, *Dreams*, p. xvi.

56 Obama, *Dreams*, pp. xvi-xvii.

57 Barack Obama, *The Audacity of Hope*, New York: Three Rivers Press, 2006, p. 338.

58 *USA TODAY*, "The Oval, Tracking the Obama Presidency," September 15, 2007. Available at: http://content.usatoday.com/communities/theoval/index (accessed July 23, 2010); *New York Times*, "Caucus: The Politics and Government Blog of the Times: Barack Obama." Available at: http://thecaucus.blogs.nytimes.com/tag/barack-obama/ (accessed July 23, 2010).

59 *Politico*, "44: A living Diary of the Obama Presidency." Available at: http://www.politico.com/politico44/ (accessed July 23, 2010); Lynn Sweet Blog, *Chicago Sun-Times*. Available at: http://blogs.suntimes.com/sweet/ (accessed July 23, 2010).

60 *Time*, "The Page/Politics up to the Minute." Available at: http://thepage.time.com/ (accessed July 23, 2010).
61 *ABC News*, "The Note." Available at: http://blogs.abcnews.com/thenote/ (accessed July 23, 2010); *MSNBC*, "First Read." Available at: http://firstread.msnbc.msn.com/ (accessed July 23, 2010).
62 *The Atlantic*, "Politics edited by Mark Ambinder." Available at: http://politics.theatlantic.com/ (accessed July 23, 2010); *The Washington Note*. Available at: http://www.thewashingtonnote.com/ (accessed July 23, 2010).
63 *Powerline*. Available at: http://www.powerlineblog.com/ (accessed July 23, 2010); *Commentary Magazine*. "Contentions." Available at: http://www.commentarymagazine.com/blogs/index.php/category/contentions (accessed July 23, 2010).
64 Thomas, *A Long Time Coming*.
65 Available at: http://www.youtube.com/watch?v=Zr4VZ8xCzOg (accessed July 23, 2010).
66 Richard Wolffe, *Renegade: The Making of a President*, New York: Crown, 2009.
67 Wolffe, *Renegade*, p. 329.
68 Theodore White, *The Making of the President: 1960*, New York: Atheneum, 1961.
69 Wolffe, *Renegade*, p. 330.
70 Ben Smith, "A Sheep in Wolffe's Clothing," *Politico*, June 3, 2009.
71 Obama quoted in Wolffe, *Renegade*, p. 303.

Obama and his Family: An Annotated Timeline

1 David Maraniss, "Though Obama Had to Leave to Find Himself, It Is Hawaii That Made His Rise Possible," *Washington Post*, August 22, 2008. Maraniss writes,

> the story goes, he opted for Harvard because of the world-class academic credentials a Crimson degree would bring. But there is an unresolved part of the story: Did Ann try to follow him to Cambridge? Her friends from Mercer Island were left with that impression. Susan Botkin, Maxine Box and John W. Hunt all remember Ann showing up in Seattle late that summer with little Barry, as her son was called.
>
> "She was on her way from her mother's house to Boston to be with her husband," Botkin recalled. "[She said] he had transferred to grad school and she was going to join him. And I was intrigued with who she was and what she was doing. Stanley was an intense person ... but I remember that afternoon, sitting in my mother's living room, drinking iced tea and eating sugar cookies. She had her baby and was talking about her husband, and what life held in store for her. She seemed so confident and self-assured and relaxed. She was leaving the next day to fly on to Boston."
>
> But as Botkin and others later remembered it, something happened in Cambridge, and Stanley Ann returned to Seattle. They saw her a few more times, and they thought she even tried to enroll in classes at the University of Washington, before she packed up and returned to Hawaii.

2 There is some small ambiguity, as to whether Obama, Sr., who was accepted into an economics doctoral program at Harvard, ever received his PhD. Obama recounts in *Dreams from My Father* that his father won a scholarship "to pursue a PhD at Harvard." See Barack Obama, *Dreams from My Father*, New York: Three Rivers Press, 2004, p. 10. Obama also recalls his quandary about how to address the letters that he wrote to his father—"Dear Father. Dear Dad. Dear Dr. Obama." See Obama, *Dreams*, p. 114.

However, an author's note in a journal article published in Kenya in 1965 lists him as "currently in Nairobi working for his doctorate"; see "the authors" followed by Barak [sic] H. Obama, "Problems Facing Our Socialism, *East African Journal*, July 1965. http://www.politico.com/pdf/PPM41_080411_bhobama_article_1965.pdf. (accessed March 10, 2011). Some of this ambiguity may stem from the fact that, "He often introduced himself as 'Dr. Obama,' though there is no record of him completing a doctorate." See Edmund Sanders, "So Alike and Yet So Different," *Los Angeles Times*, July 17, 2008.

3 Andrew Higgins, "Catholic School in Indonesia Seeks Recognition for Its Role in Obama's Life," *Washington Post*, April 9, 2010.

4 Obama, *Dreams*, p. 60; see also David Remnick, *The Bridge: The Life and Rise of Barack Obama*. New York: Knopf, 2010, p. 70.

5 Obama, *Dreams*, p. 75.

6 There is some ambiguity about when, exactly, Obama's mother returned to Hawaii for the three-year sojourn before going back to Indonesia for three years to do field work for her doctoral degree. Obama writes that after he had been in Hawaii for a while his grandmother received a telegram and said to Obama, "your father's coming to see you. Next month, *two weeks after your mother arrives. They'll both stay through New Year's*" (emphasis added). That wording suggests that Obama's mother remained in Indonesia through the summer and fall of Obama's return to Hawaii at age 10 and left again for Indonesia after a brief interlude. See Obama, *Dreams*, p. 63 (emphasis added). In his book *The Audacity of Hope*, Obama writes that he was sent to live in Hawaii in 1971 and "a year later, she and my sister would join me." See Obama, *The Audacity of Hope*, New York: Three Rivers Press, 2006, p. 275.

Janny Scott writes that "by 1974, Ms. Soetoro was back in Honolulu, a graduate student and raising Barack and Maya, nine years younger." That would have made Barack Obama thirteen years old at the time and sixteen when his mother left for Indonesia again to do her fieldwork. See Janny Scott, "A Free-Spirited Wanderer Who Set Obama's Path," *New York Times*, March 14, 2008.

However, Amanda Ripley in a *Time* profile writes that, "After three years of living with her children in a small apartment in Honolulu, subsisting on student grants, Ann decided to go back to Indonesia to do fieldwork for her Ph.D. Obama, *then about 14*, told her he would stay behind." See Amanda Ripley, "The Story of Barack Obama's Mother," *Time*, April 9, 2008 (emphasis added). Obama was fourteen in 1975, and if his mother returned to Indonesia after having spent three years in Hawaii that would make the date for her return to Hawaii 1972, when her son was eleven. However, Scharnberg and Barker write in their biographical story, "In the spring of 1979, Obama's mother and Maya, Barack's younger half sister by almost nine years, flew to Hawaii for his high school graduation." See Kirsten Scharnberg and Kim Barker, "The Not-so-simple Story of Barack Obama's Youth," *Chicago Tribune*, March 25, 2007.

This would seem to be consistent with David Remnick's observation that, "During Barry's last three years at Punahou, Ann worked in Jakarta doing the fieldwork for her doctorial dissertation in Anthropology." See Remnick, *The Bridge*, p. 83.

7 Here again there is some ambiguity about Obama's mother's presence. Maraniss writes that, "His senior year, his mother was back home from Indonesia and concerned that her son had not sent in his college applications." See Maraniss. "Though Obama Had to Leave to Find Himself."

8 There is some disagreement about whether Obama graduated with honors. An article on Obama's Columbia years quotes a university spokesman as confirming, "that Mr. Obama spent two years at Columbia College and graduated in 1983 with a major in political science. He did not receive honors, Mr. Connolly said, though

specific information on his grades is sealed." See Ross Goldberg, "Obama's Years at Columbia are a Mystery," *New York Sun*, September 2, 2008.

9 Obama, *Dreams*, pp. 212–21.

10 There is some discrepancy regarding dates here; the *Washington Post*'s Kevin Merida writes, "It would take Barry years—and a 1987 sojourn to Kenya—to unravel the mystery of his father. ... " However one of his biographers, David Remnick, writes that the trip to Kenya was "made in the summer of 1988." See Kevin Merida, "The Ghost of a Father," *Washington Post*, December 14, 2007, and Remnick, *The Bridge*, p. 245.

11 Remnick, *The Bridge*, p. 92.

12 Ryan Lizza, "The Agitator," *New Republic*, March 19, 2007.

13 Dan Balz and Hayes Johnson, *The Battle for America 2008*, New York: Viking, 2010, p. 28; See also Jonathan Alter, *The Promise: President Obama, Year One*, New York: Simon & Schuster, 2010, p. 147.

14 Balz and Johnson, *The Battle for America*, p. 29.

15 Balz and Johnson, *The Battle for America*, p. 32.

BIBLIOGRAPHY

ABC News. "The Note." http://blogs.abcnews.com/thenote/ (accessed July 23, 2010).
———. "Obama Strives for the Lincoln Touch." (January 19, 2009).
———."Transcript: Diane Sawyer Interviews Obama." (January 25, 2010). Available at: http://abcnews.go.com/print?id=9659064 (accessed July 23, 2010).
———."President Obama to Pastor Jones: 'Stunt' Endangers Troops—Full Transcript of Exclusive Interview." (September 9, 2010).
Achenbach, Joel. "In a Heated Race, Obama's Cool Won the Day." *Washington Post* (November 6, 2008).
Acosta, Jim. "Critics Question 'Pay-as-you-go' Approach." *CNN* (Wednesday June 10, 2010).
Adamy, Jane. "U.S. to Begin Handing Out Grants to Reduce Medical Malpractice Suits." *Wall Street Journal* (June 11, 2010).
——— and Elizabeth Williamson. "As Congress Goes on Break, Health Lobbying Heats Up." *Wall Street Journal* (August 5, 2009).
Al Arabiya. "Transcript: Obama's Interview with Al Arabiya." (January 27, 2009) http://www.alarabiya.net/articles/2009/01/27/65087.html (accessed May 9, 2010).
Allen, Jonathan and Carol E. Lee. "Obama Strategy Gets Personal." *Politico* (April 27, 2010).
Allen, Mike. "Obama Plans Truce with Chamber." *Politico* (November 20, 2010).
——— and Eamon Javers. "Obama: Stimulus Saved 1 Million Jobs," *Politico*, October 30, 2009.
——— and Jim VandeHei. "Obama's Big Bang Could Go Bust." *Politico* (August 29, 2009).
Alonso-Zaldivar, Ricardo. "Health Overhaul to Force Changes in Employer Plans." *Associated Press* (June 11, 2010).
——— and Erica Werner. "Obama Gives Proponents Hope for Medical Malpractice Reform." *Insurance Journal* (September 14, 2009).
Alter, Jonathan. "Obama's Vulnerability." *Newsweek* (April 16, 2008).
———. *The Promise: President Obama, Year One*. New York: Simon & Schuster, 2010.
Ambinder, Mark. "Straw Men." *The Atlantic* (February 16, 2009).
———. "The White House Takes on Politico." *The Atlantic* (November 30, 2009).
———. "Lunch With The President: The Politics of Obama's War Plan." *The Atlantic* (December 1, 2009).
American Society of Magazine Editors. http://www.magazine.org/asme/2009-best-magazine-cover-winners-finalists.aspx (accessed March 10, 2011).

Anderson, Jeffrey H. "Comprehensive Failure." *Weekly Standard* (February 22, 2010).

Andrade, Dale. "Three Lessons from Vietnam." *Washington Post* (December 29, 2009).

Applebome, Peter. "Is Eloquence Overrated?" *New York Times* (January 13, 2008).

Asch, Solomon. "Effects of Group Pressure Upon Modification and Distortion of Judgments." In *Documents of Gestalt Psychology*, ed. Mary Henle, 222–36. Berkeley and Los Angeles, Ca.: University of California Press, 1961.

Associated Press. "Obama Told Sen. Reid, 'I Have a Gift.'" (April 22, 2009).

——. "30,000 Stimulus Jobs Figure is Way Off the Mark." (November 29, 2009).

Atlantic. "Politics edited by Mark Ambinder." http://politics.theatlantic.com/ (accessed July 23, 2010).

Avila, Oscar. "Obama's Census Choice: Simply African-American." *Chicago Tribune* (April 2, 2010).

Avlon, John. "Irrational Obama Exuberance." *Daily Beast* (November 26, 2008).

Aizenman, N.C. "Grants to Aid Projects on Improving Patient Safety, Curbing Malpractice Suits." *Washington Post* (June 11, 2010).

Bai, Matt. "Debt-Busting Issue May Force Obama Off Fence." *New York Times* (November 30 2010).

Baker, Peter. "Transition Holds Clues to How Obama Will Govern." *New York Times* (January 20, 2009).

——. "Obama's Pledge to Reform Ethics Faces an Early Test." *New York Times* (February 3, 2009).

——. "The Limits of Rahmism." *New York Times Magazine* (March 14, 2009).

——. "A Presidential Pitfall: Speaking One's Mind." *New York Times* (July 27, 2009).

——. "No Walk in the Park: For Obama One Year Later, It's the Slog of Governance." *New York Times* (November 4, 2009).

——. "How Obama Came to Plan for 'Surge' in Afghanistan." *New York Times* (December 6, 2009);

——. "The Pragmatic Leviathan." *New York Times* (January 19, 2010).

——. "On Sestak Matter, a 'Trust Us' Response from the White House." *New York Times* (May 24, 2010).

——. "Harsh Words for G.O.P." *New York Times* (June 30, 2010).

——. "Obama Speech Begins Effort to Highlight Iraq Drawdown." *New York Times* (August 2, 2010).

——. "For Obama, Steep Learning Curve as Chief in War." *New York Times* (August 28, 2010).

——. "Obama Ratchets Up Tone Against G.O.P." *New York Times* (October 10, 2010).

——. "Education of a President." *New York Times* (October 12, 2010).

——. "In Losing the Midterms, There May Be Winning." *New York Times* (October 23, 2010).

——. "In Republican Victories, Tide Turns Sharply." *New York Times* (November 2, 2010).

Balz, Dan. "Election Results are Open to (Careful) Interpretation." *Washington Post* (November 4, 2010).

—— and Jon Cohen. "Confidence in Obama Reaches New Low, Washington Post-ABC News Poll Finds," *Washington Post* (July 13, 2010).

—— and Haynes Johnson. "A Political Odyssey." *Washington Post* (August 2, 2009).

——. *The Battle for America 2008.* New York: Viking, 2010.

Barber, James David. *The Presidential Character: Predicting Performance in the White House.* Englewood Cliffs, N.J.: Prentice Hall, 1992.

Barnes, Robert. "Reactions split on Obama's remark, Alito's response at State of the Union." *Washington Post* (January 29, 2010).

—— and Michael D. Shear. "McCain Gets an Earful on 'The View.'" *Washington Post* (September 12, 2008).

Barone, Michael. "Chaos on Capitol Hill: All Politics is Loco." *The Examiner* (July 12, 2009).

—— "Voters Reject Obama's Big-Government Ambitions." *San Francisco Examiner* (November 4, 2010).

Becker, Jo and Christopher Drew. "Pragmatic Politics, Forged on the South Side." *New York Times* (May 11, 2008).

Bennetts, Leslie. "First Lady in Waiting." *Vanity Fair* (December 27, 2007).

Benoit, W. L. "Framing Through Temporal Metaphor: The 'Bridges' of Bob Dole and Bill Clinton in Their 1996 Acceptance Addresses." *Communication Studies* (Spring 2001), pp. 70–84.

Bevan, Tom. "A Self-Inflicted Expectations Gap." *RealClearPolitics* (November 25, 2009).

Boehm, Mike. "Obamas Find a Way to Do Broadway at Home, Hosting Star-studded PBS taping," *Los Angeles Times* (July 14, 2010).

Boot, Max. "The Incurable Vietnam Syndrome." *Weekly Standard* 15, no. 5 (October 19, 2009).

Brachear, Manya A. "Rev. Jeremiah A. Wright, Jr.: Pastor Inspires Obama's 'Audacity.'" *Chicago Tribune* (January 21, 2007).

Brands, H.W. "What Obama Can Learn from FDR and Reagan." *NPR* (November 20, 2008).

Brinkley, Douglas. "'The Bridge: The Life and Rise of Barack Obama' by David Remnick." Review. *Los Angeles Times* (March 28, 2010).

Broder, David S. "Getting to Know Obama." *Washington Post* (June 22, 2008).

——. "Obama Rolls The Dice." *Washington Post* (February 26, 2009).

——. "Will the Real President Stand Up?" *Washington Post* (October 4, 2009).

——. "The Obama Effect—Are You With Him or Against Him?" *Washington Post* (May 23, 2010).

Brooks, David. "Obama, Liberalism and the Power of Reform." *New York Times* (June 13, 2008).

——. "The Two Obamas." *New York Times* (June 20, 2008).

——. "Where's the Landslide?" *New York Times* (August 5, 2008).

——. "The Obama Slide." *New York Times* (September 1, 2009).

——. "Getting Obama Right." *New York Times* (March 12, 2010).

——. "The Government War." *New York Times* (April 22, 2010).

——. "The Next Two Years." *New York Times* (October 28, 2010).

——and Gail Collins, "A Good but Puzzling Speech.' *New York Times* (December 2, 2009).

——. "Obama, the Attack Dog." *New York Times* (October 13, 2010).

Brown, Carrie Budoff. "Barack Obama's Flip Side Revealed." *Politico* (April 14, 2008).

——. "Obama Returns Night-owl Presidency." *Politico* (January 15, 2009).

Brown, Carrie Budoff, and Nia-Malika Henderson. "Paparazzo Snaps Shirtless Obama." *Politico* (December 23, 2008).

Brown, Carrie Budoff and Patrick O'Connor. "New Plan, Same Old Problems." *Politico* (February 22, 2010).

Brownstein, Ronald. "An Eternal Optimist—but Not a Sap." *National Journal* (February 14, 2009).

——. "Converging Fronts Create Perfect Storm for Republicans in Midterms." *National Journal* (November 3, 2010).

——. "Past as Prologue." *National Journal* (November 4, 2010).

Brummett, John. *Highwire: From the Back Roads to the Beltway—The Education of Bill Clinton.* New York: Hyperion, 1994.

Butterfield, Fox. "First Black Elected to Head Harvard's Law Review," *New York Times* (6 February 1990).

Calabresi, Steven G. "Obama's 'Redistribution' Constitution. *Wall Street Journal* (October 28, 2008).

Calmes, Jackie and Robert Pear, "To Pay for Health Care, Obama Looks to Tax the Affluent." *New York Times* (February 26, 2009).

—— and Megan Thee-Brenan, "Independents Fueled G.O.P Gains." *New York Times* (November 2, 2010).

Carlson, Margaret. "Smart President Fails Test at Ground Zero." *Bloomberg* (August 18, 2010).

Carnevale, Mary Lu. "Obama: Mortgage Plan 'Will Not Help Speculators.'" *Wall Street Journal* (February18, 2009).

CBO, Director's Blog, "Health Costs and the Federal Budget." (May 28, 2010). Available at: http://cboblog.cbo.gov/?p=1034 (accessed August 6, 2010).

CBS News 60 Minutes. "Transcript: President Obama, Part 1." (March 24, 2009). Available at: http://www.cbsnews.com/stories/2009/03/24/60minutes/main4890684.shtml?tag= mncol;l st;7 (accessed July 18, 2010).

——."Transcript: President Barack Obama, Part 2." (November 4, 2010). Available at: http://www.cbsnews.com/stories/2010/11/07/60minutes/main7032277.shtml?source= related_story&tag=related (accessed November 13, 2010).

——. "Transcript: President Obama." (September 11, 2009). Available at:http://www. cbsnews.com/stories/2009/09/13/60minutes/main5307481.shtml (accessed July 31, 2010).

——. "Mexican President Calderon Address to Joint Session of Congress." (May 20, 2010).

Ceaser, James. "The 2010 Verdict." *RealClearPolitics* (November 10, 2010).

Center for Media and Public Affairs. "Media Boast Obama, Bash His Policies." (April 27, 2009).

——. "Obama Media Coverage Sours." (September 14, 2009).

——. "Obama's Media Image: Compared to What?" (January 25, 2010). http://www. cmpa.com/media_room_press_1_25_10.html (accessed July 6, 2010).

Chaddock, Gail Russell. "On Historic Night, Republicans Sweep House Democrats from Power." *Christian Science Monitor* (November 3, 2010).

Charlie Rose. "Historians on Obama" (November 7, 2008). http://www.charlierose.com/ view/interview/9389 (accessed August 8, 2010).

Chicago Tribune. "Barack Obama Interview on Jan. 2, 2008." (January 2, 2008).

Cillizza, Chris. "White House Cheat Sheet: Obama Beloved, Policies Be-Liked." *Washington Post* (April 30, 2009).

Cliff, Eleanor. "Halfhearted Soul-Searching at the White House." *Newsweek* (November 21, 2010).

Clinton, William J. "State of the Union Address." (January 23, 1996).

CNBC. "Transcript of CNBC's Barack Obama Interview." (January 7, 2009), http:// www.msnbc.msn.com/id/28546772/ns/business-cnbc_tv/ (accessed July 23, 2010).

CNN. "State of the Union with John King: Interview with General Jim Jones" (October 4, 2009).

CNN/Opinion Research Poll. (February 17, 2010).

——. (November 11–14, 2010). Available at: http://i2.cdn.turner.com/cnn/2010/images/ 11/15/rel16a.pdf (accessed November 14, 2010).

Cohen, Ed. "Get Bold, Barack." *New York Times* (November 1, 2010).

Cohen, Jon and Dan Balz, "U.S. Outlook Is Worst Since '92, Poll Finds." *Washington Post* (May 13, 2008).

Cohen, Richard. "Obama's Identity Crisis." *Washington Post* (October 20, 2009).

——. "President Obama's Enigmatic Intellectualism." *Washington Post* (June 22, 2010), A19.

——. "Who is Barack Obama?" *Washington Post* (July 20, 2010), A21.

——. "A No-confidence Vote in Obama." *Washington Post* (November 2, 2010).

Collins, Laureen. "The Other Obama." *New Yorker* (March 10, 2008).

Columbia Journalism Review. "Q & A: *New York Times* Reporter Michael Powell" (August 13, 2010). http://www.cjr.org/behind_the_news/q_a_new_york_times_reporter_mi. php?page=all& p rint = true (accessed August 14, 2010).

Commentary Magazine. "Contentions." http://www.commentarymagazine.com/blogs/index.php/category/contentions.

Connolly, Ceci. "Key Feature of Obama Health Plan May Be Out." *Washington Post* (August 17, 2009).

Cook, Charles. "Obama Gives Democrats Another Headache." *National Journal* (August 18, 2010).

Cooper, Helene. "For Obama, Talk About Economy Goes Into Late Night." *New York Times* (March 20, 2009).

Cost, Jay. "The Celebrity-in-Chief." *RealClearPolitics* (February 3, 2009).

———. "Back to the Bush Coalition." *Weekly Standard* (November 15, 2010), Vol. 16, No. 09.

Couric, Katie "Obama: Surge Doesn't Meet Long-Term Goals." *CBS News* (July 22, 2008). http://www.cbsnews.com/stories/2008/07/22/eveningnews/main4283623.shtml (accessed July 31, 2010).

Craig, Gordon, "Angry Liberals: Why didn't Obama Fight?" *Politico* (December 15, 2009).

C-SPAN Interview Transcript. "President Barack H. Obama." (May 22, 2009), http://www.c-span.org/pdf/obamainterview.pdf (accessed July 6, 2010).

Cummings, Jeanne. "Dems' 2010 Crisis has Roots in 2009." *Politico* (October 26, 2010).

Curry, Jessica. "Barack Obama: Under the Lights." *Chicago Life* (August 1, 2004).

Dallek, Robert. "Obama's Historic Health Care Victory." *Wall Street Journal*, December 29, 2009.

D'Aprile, Shane. "Midterm Blowout: 50 or More Democratic Seats Set to Fall in Tuesday's Election." *The Hill* (October 26, 2010).

Davis, Teddy. "Obama Dubs Himself a 'Pragmatic Progressive.'" *ABC News* (January 8, 2009).

———. Sunlen Miller, and Gregory Wallace. "Obama Kisses Millions Goodbye." *ABC News* (June 18, 2008).

de Moraes, Lisa. "John Walsh to Interview President Obama on Fox's 'America's Most Wanted.'" *Washington Post* (March 4, 2010).

DePaulo, Lisa. "$#!% Joe Biden Says." *GQ* (December, 2010).

de Tocqueville, Alexis. *Democracy in America.* Chicago, Il.: University of Chicago Press, 2000.

De Zutter, Hank. "What Makes Obama Run?" *Chicago Reader* (December 8, 1995).

Der Spiegel. "Niall Ferguson on Obama and the Global Crisis." (November 11, 2008). http://www.spiegel.de/international/world/0,1518,druck-589735,00.html (accessed July 6, 2010).

Derschowitz, Jessica. "'The View:' Obama Not Invited to Chelsea Clinton's Wedding." *CBS* (July 29, 2010).

Dionne Jr., E.J. "Audacity Without Ideology." *Washington Post* (January 15, 2009) A19.

———. "What is Obamaism? President Must Do Better in Explaining His Policies." *Washington Post* (July 19, 2010).

———. "And Now for the Next Battle." *Washington Post* (November 3, 2010).

Dombey, Daniel and Edward Luce, "Obama Camp Signals Robust Approach on Iran," *Financial Times* (July 1, 2008).

Douthat, Ross. "The Obama Way." *New York Times* (December 26, 2009).

———. "Let's Make a Deal." *New York Times* (February 15, 2010).

Dowd, Maureen. "Praying and Preying." *New York Times* (April 30, 2008).

———. "Spock at the Bridge." *New York Times* (March 1, 2009).

Draper, Robert. *Dead Certain: The Presidency of George W. Bush.* New York: Free Press, 2007.

Drew, Elizabeth. "The Thirty Days of Barack Obama." *New York Review of Books* (March 26, 2009).

———. "The Prez & I." *GQ* (January 2009).

Dwyer, Paula. "How the Political Gridlock in Washington Might End." *Bloomberg-Business Week* (February 24, 2010).

Easton, Nina. "Obama: NAFTA Not so Bad After All." *Fortune* (June 18, 2008).

Edwards, George C., III. *On Deaf Ears: The Limits of the Bully Pulpit*. New Haven, Ct.: Yale University Press, 2003.

Eilperin, Juliet. "Senators Predict a Climate Bill Capping Emissions Only for Utilities." *Washington Post* (June 30, 2010).

Elmendorf, Douglas W. "An Analysis of Health Insurance Premiums under the Patient Protection and Affordable Care Act." *Congressional Budget Office: Director's Blog* (November 30, 2009).

———. Speech at the National Association for Business Economics' annual economic policy conference, March 8, 2010. Available at: http://www.cspan.org/Watch/Media/2010/03/08/HP/A/30436/CBO+Director+Elmendorf+on+Stimulus+Law+and+the+Economy.aspx (accessed November 14, 2010).

Erikson, Erik H. *Childhood and Society*. New York: Norton, 1950.

———. *Identity: Youth and Crisis*. New York: Norton, 1968.

Executive Office of the President Council of Economic Advisers. "The Economic Impact of the American Recovery and Reinvestment Act of 2009." Fourth Quarter Report (July 14, 2010). Available at: http://www.whitehouse.gov/files/documents/cea_4th_arra_report.pdf (accessed November 14, 2010).

Fallows, James. "Two Rhetorical Missteps by Team Obama." *The Atlantic* (April 22, 2008).

Favole, Jared A. "Obama Advisers Say Stimulus Saved or Created Three Million Jobs." *Wall Street Journal* (July 14, 2010).

Fineman, Howard. "Channeling the Gipper." *Newsweek* (November 30, 2009).

Finn, Christine and Tony Allen-Mills. "Jungle Angel was Barack Obama's Mother." *Sunday Times* (November 8, 2009).

Finn, Peter and Anne E. Kornblut. "Obama Creates Indefinite Detention System for Prisoners at Guantanamo Bay." *Washington Post* (March 8, 2011).

Finnegan, William. "The Candidate." *New Yorker* (May, 31, 2004).

Fiore, Faye and Mark Z. Baraba. "Ambition and Audacity: Obama Begins Leading America in a New Direction." *Los Angeles Times*, April 19, 2009.

Fiorina, Morris P. and Samuel J. Adams. "Political Polarization in the American Public." *Annual Review of Political Science* 11 (2008): 563–88.

Foster, Richard S. "Estimated Financial Effects of the 'Patient Protection and Affordable Care Act,' as Amended." *Center for Medicare and Medicaid Services* (April 22, 2010), http://graphics8.nytimes.com/packages/pdf/health/oactmemo1.pdf (accessed July 6, 2010).

Fournier, Ron. "Essay: Obama's Transcendence Is Beyond Race." *Associated Press* (November 5, 2008).

——— and Ronald Brownstein. "Obama to Republicans: Let's Build Consensus." *National Journal* (October 27, 2010).

Fowler, Mayhill. "Obama: No Need for Foreign Policy Help from V.P." *Huffington Post* (April 7, 2008).

———. "Obama: No Surprise That Hard Pressed Pennsylvanians Turn Bitter." *Huffington Post* (April 11, 2008).

Fox News. "Transcript: Austan Goolsbee on 'FNS.'" March 16, 2010. Available at: http://www.foxnews.com/printer_friendly_story/0,3566,509314,00.html) (accessed September 16, 2010).

———. "White House, Democrats Applaud Mexican President Slamming Arizona Law." (May 20, 2010).

Frates, Chris and Ben White. "Obama's Policy Time Bombs." *Politico* (July 11, 2010).

——— "Lobbyists: W.H. Hides Meetings Off-site." *Politico* (February 24, 2011).

Freeland, Chrystia. "Calmer Obama Ushers New Age." *Financial Times* (April 10, 2009).

Freud, Sigmund. "A Note on the Unconscious in Psycho-analysis." *S. E.* 12, pp. 205–12.

Friel, Brian, Richard E. Cohen, and Kirk Victor, "Obama: Most Liberal Senator in 2007." *National Journal* (January 31, 2008).

Fund, John. "Obama the Great?" *Wall Street Journal* (July 3, 2010).
———. "The Carter-Obama Comparisons Grow." *Wall Street Journal* (September 22, 2010).
Gaff, Garrett M. "The Legend of Barack Obama." *The Washingtonian* (November 1, 2006).
Galston, William A. "The Future of President Obama's Agenda." *Sunday Times* (April 19, 2009).
———. "It's the Ideology Stupid." *New Republic* (November 4, 2010).
———. "President Barack Obama's First Two Years: Policy Accomplishments, Political Difficulties." *New Republic* (November 6, 2010).
Gearan, Ann. "US Officials Say War Goals Modest in Afghanistan." *Associated Press* (August 1, 2010).
George, Alexander L. and Juliette L. George. *Woodrow Wilson and Colonel House: A Personality Study*. New York: Dover, 1956.
Gerson, Michael. "Words Aren't Cheap," *Washington Post* (February 29, 2008).
Gerstein, Josh. "Gibbs Rebukes CNBC's Santelli." *Politico* (February 20, 2009).
———. "Obama: Not Showing Talks a 'Mistake.'" *Politico* (January 25, 2010).
———. "Obama, Gibbs Split over Perfect Game." *Politico* (June 6, 2010).
Givhan, Robin. "Mussed for Success: Barack Obama's Smooth Wrinkles." *Washington Post* (August 11, 2006).
Goldberg, Jeffrey. "Is Obama God?" *The Atlantic* (June 8, 2009).
Goldberg, Ross. "Obama's Years at Columbia are a Mystery." *New York Sun* (September 2, 2008).
Goldstein, Gordon. *Lessons in Disaster: McGeorge Bundy and the Path to War in Vietnam*. New York: Times Books, 2008.
Greenberg, David. "Playing the Tolerance Card: How Obama is like JFK." *Slate* (April 20, 2007).
Greenhouse, Linda. "Justice Alito's Reaction." *New York Times* (January 27, 2010).
Greenstein, Fred I. The *Hidden-Hand Presidency: Eisenhower as Leader*. New York: Basic Books, 1982.
———. "Barack Obama: The Man and His Early Presidency." In Bruce Miroff, Raymond Seidelman, and Todd Swanstrom, ed. *Debating Democracy: A Reader in American Politics*, Florence, KY: Wadsworth, 2011.
Greenwald, Jeff. "Obama is Spock: It's Quite Logical." *Salon* (May 7, 2009).
Grim, Ryan. "Obama Health Care Plan Drops Public Option." *Huffington Post* (February 22, 2010).
Grunwald, Michael. "How Obama Is Using the Science of Change." *Time* (April 2, 2009).
Guardian. "Obama acceptance speech in full." (November 5, 2008). Available at: http://www.guardian.co.uk/commentisfree/2008/nov/05/uselections2008-barackobama/ print (accessed August 5, 2010).
Guelzo, Allan C. *Abraham Lincoln: Redeemer President*. Grand Rapids, Michigan and Cambridge, U.K.: William B. Eerdmans Publishing Company, 1999.
Hall, Mimi. "On visit, Calderon, Obama assails Ariz. Law." *USA TODAY* (May 19, 2010).
Halperin, Mark. "President-Elect Obama to be Sworn in Using the Lincoln Bible." *Time* (December 23, 2008).
———. "Politics Up to the Minute: Obama Interview on CNBC." (February 15, 2010).
Harnden, Toby. "Barack Obama is JFK Heir, Says Kennedy Aide," *Telegraph* (October 12, 2007).
———. "Barack Obama Vows to 'Change the World.'" *Telegraph* (October 17, 2008).
———. "Joe Biden Blurts Out That He Will Be Barack Obama's 2012 Running Mate." *Telegraph* (October 14, 2010).
Harris, Hamil R. "At D.C. Church, Obama Invokes King and Calls for Keeping Faith." *Washington Post* (January 17, 2010). Available at: http://voices.washingtonpost.com/44/2010/01/obamas-sermon-remembering-mart.html (accessed July 23, 2010).

Harris, John F. "Change Has Come ... or Has It?" *Politico* (November 4, 2010).
——— and James Hohmann. "Dems Urge Obama to Take a Stand." *Politico* (August 23, 2010).
——— and Jim VandeHei. "Why Obama Loses by Winning." *Politico* (July 15, 2010).
Hart, Jeffrey. "Obama is the New Reagan." *Daily Beast* (November 4, 2008).
Hartocollis, Anemona. "New York Offers Costly Lesson on Insurance." *New York Times* (April 17, 2010).
Harwood, John. "Running on Risk, Then Sticking With It." *New York Times* (March 2, 2009).
———. "Serving Big Initiatives in Bite-Size Portions." *New York Times* (July 26, 2010).
Hayes, Stephen F. "Obama and the Power of Words." *Wall Street Journal* (February 26, 2008).
Healy, Gene. *The Cult of the Presidency: America's Dangerous Devotion to Executive Power.* Washington, D.C.: CATO Institute, 2008.
Heflin, Jay. "JCT: Healthcare Law to Sock Middle Class with a $3.9 Billion Tax Increase in 2019." *The Hill* (April 10, 2010).
Heilemann, John and Mark Halperin. *Game Change: Obama and the Clintons, McCain and Palin, and the Race of a Lifetime.* New York: Harper Perennial, 2010.
Hiatt, Fred. "Obama's Empathy Meets the Politics of Governing." *Washington Post* (March 1, 2010).
———. "Obama's Happiness Deficit." *Washington Post* (March 15, 2010).
———. "Could Obama Decide a Deficit Deal is in His Interest?" *Washington Post* (February 20, 2011).
Higgins, Andrew. "Catholic School in Indonesia Seeks Recognition for Its Role in Obama's Life." *Washington Post* (April 9, 2010).
Hoagland, Jim. "Insecurities Beneath China's Prosperous Exterior." *Washington Post* (November 14, 2010).
Hodgson, Godfrey. *The Myth of American Exceptionalism.* New Haven, Ct: Yale University Press, 2009.
Holland, Steve."Obama Seeks to Blunt Republican Attack Over Comment." *Reuters* (November 1, 2010).
Holtz-Eakin, Douglas. "The Real Arithmetic of the Health Care Reform." *New York Times* (March 21, 2010).
Hook, Janet. "Democrats in Congress Fail the Sales Pitch." *Los Angeles Times* (June 2, 2010).
Huffington Post, "Obama's Question Time with Senate Dems: Video and Full Text." March 10, 2009. Available at:http://www.huffingtonpost.com/2010/02/03/obamas-question-time- with_n_447409.html (accessed July 12, 2010).
———. "Obama Talks LeBron James Free Agency During Marv Albert TNT Interview." (May 23, 2010).
Humes, Michael. "President Obama Fills Out Men's & Women's Brackets in Exclusive ESPN Interview." *ESPN* (March 16, 2010).
Hunt, Kasie. "Dem: Ariz. Law Like 'Nazi Germany.'" *Politico* (April 26, 2010).
———. "Dems: Ariz Law Like Jim Crow, Apartheid." *Politico* (April 28, 2010).
Ifill, Gwen. "Review of David Remnick's Biography of Barack Obama, 'The Bridge.'" *Washington Post* (April 4, 2010).
Ignatius, David. "Bumpy Road Ahead for a Traveler." *Washington Post* (November 2008).
———. "Careful to a Fault on Afghanistan." *Washington Post* (October 15, 2009).
———. "A President Tripped Up by the Spontaneous." *Washington Post* (July 25, 2010).
International Committee of the Red Cross (ICRC). "Protocol Additional to the Geneva Conventions of 12 August 1949, and relating to the Protection of Victims of International Armed Conflicts (Protocol I), 8 June 1977." Available at: http://www.icrc.org/ihl.nsf/7c4d08d9b287a42141256739003e636b/f6c8b9fee14a77fdc125641e0052b079 (accessed March 12, 2011).

Investor's Business Daily. "An Obama 'Rescue' Plan That Doesn't." Editorial (October 13, 2008).

Isaacson, Walter. *Einstein: His Life and Universe.* New York: Simon & Schuster, 2007.

Isenstadt, Alex. "Some Dems Walk Plank with 'Yes' Vote." *Politico* (March 21, 2010).

Issenberg, Sasha. "In Tribute to Lincoln, Obama Rides the Rails." *Boston Globe* (January 18, 2009).

Jackson, David. "Obama: U.S. 'A Nation of Immigrants and a Nation of Laws,' Blasts Arizona Law." *USA TODAY,* April 23, 2010.

——. "Obama: No Moratorium on Golf." *USA TODAY* (June 21, 2010).

——. "Obama Echoes Reagan: 'Stay On Course.'" *USA TODAY-The Oval* (October 1, 2010).

—— and Ray Long, "Obama Knows His Way Around a Ballot: Some Say His Ability to Play Political Hardball Goes Back to His First Campaign." *Chicago Tribune* (April 3, 2007).

——. "Showing His Bare Knuckles." *Chicago Tribune* (April 4, 2007).

Jacobs, Andrew. "China Warns U.S. to Stay Out of Islands Dispute." *New York Times* (July 26, 2010).

Jacobs, Jeremy P. "New Polls Suggest Sizable GOP Landslide." *The Hill* (October 26, 2010).

——. "Devastation: GOP Picks up 680 State Leg. Seats." *National Journal* (November 4, 2010).

Jaffe, Greg, Scott Wilson, and Karen DeYoung. "U.S. Envoy Resists Increases in Troops." *Washington Post* (November 12, 2009).

Javers, Eamon and Zachary Abrahamson. "Obama's Words Downplay Wars." *Politico* (August 13, 2009).

Jensen, Tom. "Obama's December Standing." *Public Policy Polling* (December 9, 2009).

Jervis, Robert. "Understanding Beliefs." *Political Psychology* 27, no. 5 (October 2006).

Joffe, Joseph "Who is this Guy?" *The American Interest* (January-February 2010).

Johnson, Andrew. "President Obama Throws Out Ceremonial First Pitch in Washington." *MLB* (April 5, 2010).

Johnson, Bridget. "Obama: Critics 'Talk About Me Like a Dog.'" *The Hill* (September 6, 2010).

Johnson, Sasha and Candy Crowley. "Winfrey Tells Iowa Crowd: Barack Obama is 'the One,'" *CNN* (December 8, 2007).

Jones, Athena. "Obama: Change Comes from Me." *NBC-First Read* (November 26, 2008).

Jones, Jeffrey M. "Party Affiliation Gap in U.S. Narrowest Since 2005: Democratic Advantage Shrinks as More Independents Lean to the Republican Party." *Gallup* (April 23, 2010). http://www.gallup.com/poll/127499/party-affiliation-gap-u.s.-narrowest-2005.aspx?version=print (accessed April 25, 2010).

——. "Obama Job Approval Rating Down to 38% Among Independents." *Gallup* (July 7, 2010).

——. "Obama's Approval Ratings More Polarized in Year 2 Than Year 1." *Gallup* (February 4, 2011).

Jones, Tim. "Barack Obama: Mother Not Just a Girl from Kansas." *Chicago Tribune* (March 27, 2007).

Kahneman, Daniel and Amos Tversky. "Prospect Theory: An Analysis of Decision Under Risk," *Econometrica* 47, no. 2 (1979): 263–92.

Kakutani, Michiko. "Obama's Foursquare Politics: With a Dab of Dijon," *New York Times* (October 17, 2006).

——. "Presidential Horse Race, the 2008 Version." *New York Times* (August 11, 2009).

——. "Books of the Times; Seeking Identity, Shaping a Nation's." *New York Times* (April 5, 2010).

——. "Penetrating the Process of Obama's Decisions," *New York Times* (May 12, 2010).

Kampfner, Judith. "The Untold Story of Obama's Mother." *Independent* (September 16, 2009).

Kane, Paul. "To Sway Nelson, a Hard Won Compromise on Abortion." *Washington Post* (December 20, 2009).

———. "Congress, Obama Brace for Showdown as Government Shutdown Looms." *Washington Post* (February 20, 2011).

Kantor, Jodi. "An Old Hometown Mentor, Still at Obama's Side." *New York Times* (November 4, 2004).

———. "In Law School, Obama Found Political Voice." *New York Times* (January 28, 2007).

———. "Teaching Law, Testing Ideas, Obama Stood Slightly Apart." *New York Times* (July 30, 2008).

———. "The Careful Rollout of a Warmer Michelle Obama." *New York Times* (August 26, 2008).

Karl, Jonathan. "Obama's Evolving Position on Iran." *ABC News* (June 4, 2008).

Kaufman, Jonathan. "For Obama, Chicago Days Honed Tactics." *Wall Street Journal* (April 21, 2008).

Kaylan, Kaylan. "Obama: More Like Nixon Than Carter." *Daily Beast* (September 25, 2010).

Kerley, David and Cait Taylor. "President Obama and the Lame Duck Congress." *ABC News* (November 14, 2010).

Kerry, John. "Testing Afghanistan Assumptions." *Wall Street Journal* (September 27, 2009).

Kiel, Paul. "Gov't Official Suggests Much of Chrysler Loan Won't be Repaid." *ProPublica* (May 7, 2009).

Kiely, Kathy. "Obama Urges Expansion of His Agenda." *USA TODAY* (June 2, 2010).

Kirsch, Richard. "What Obama Can Learn from Reagan." *Huffington Post* (December 10, 2010).

Kirkpatrick, David. "Obama Is Taking an Active Role in Talks on Health Care Plan." *New York Times* (August 13, 2009).

King, Neil, Jr. and Jonathan Weisman, "Detail Man: As a Manager, Obama Gets into the Weeds." *Wall Street Journal* (August 12, 2009).

King, Oona. "Oona King on Barack Obama's Dreams from My Father." *The Times* (September 15, 2007).

Klein, Joe. "Inspiration vs. Substance," *Time* (February 7, 2008).

———. "Obama's Team of Rivals." *Time,* (June 18, 2008).

———. "National Security Team of Rivals." *Time* (November 21, 2008).

———. "Q&A: Obama on His First Year in Office." *Time* (January 21, 2010). Available at: http://www.time.com/time/printout/0,8816,1955072,00.html (accessed July 10, 2010).

———. "Where Obama Goes From Here." *Time* (November 4, 2010).

Kloppenberg, James T. *Reading Obama: Dreams, Hope, and the American Political Tradition.* Princeton, N.J.: Princeton University Press, 2010.

Knoller, Mark. "Obama's First Year: By the Numbers." *CBS News* (January 20, 2010).

Kodama, Marie C. "Obama Left Mark on HLS." *Harvard Crimson* (January 19, 2007).

Kohut, Andrew. "Americans Are More Skeptical of Washington Than Ever." *Wall Street Journal* (April 19, 2010).

Kornblut, Anne E. "Obama Holds Traditional News Conference to Talk Bipartisanship," *Washington Post* (February 10, 2010).

———. "Obama's 17-minute, 2,500-word Response to Woman's Claim of Being 'Over-taxed.'" *Washington Post* (April 2, 2010).

———. "The Great Elaborator: Obama Gives 17-minute Answer to Health-care Query in N.C." *Washington Post* (April 3, 2010).

———. "Obama Criticizes Hoekstra on Congressman's Home Turf." *Washington Post* (July 15, 2010).

———, Scott Wilson, and Karen DeYoung. "Obama Pressed for a Faster Surge." *Washington Post* (December 6, 2009).

Korneich, Laureen. "Obama: New Dog Could be 'Mutt Like Me.'" *CNN News* (November 7, 2008).

Krauthammer, Charles. "Obama's Inaugural Surprise." *Washington Post* (January 23, 2009).

———. "A Return to the Norm." *Washington Post* (November 5, 2010).

Kravitz, Derek and Keith B. Richburg, "Obama Quits Longtime Church Over Inflammatory Comments." *Washington Post* (June 1, 2008).

Kristoff, Nicholas D. "Franklin Delano Obama." *New York Times* (March 1, 2009).

Kroft, Steve. "Obama on Economic Crisis, Transition." *CBS News* (November 16, 2008). http://www.cbsnews.com/stories/2008/11/16/60minutes/main4607893.shtml (accessed July 23, 2010).

Krugman, Paul. "What Didn't Happen," *New York Times* (January 18, 2010).

Kurzel, John J. "Gates: Decisions on Afghanistan Most Important of His Presidency." *Armed Forces Press Services* (October 6, 2009). Available at: http://www.centcom.mil/en/news/gates-upcoming-decisions-on-afghanistan-most-important-of-presidency.html (accessed July 31, 2010).

Kurtz, Howard. "Pretzel Logic." *Washington Post* (June 27, 2008).

———. "A Giddy Sense of Boosterism." *Washington Post* (November 17, 2008).

———. "Missing the Mark in Massachusetts: Honeymoon is History," *Washington Post* (January 25, 2010).

———. "A Democratic Bloodbath." *Daily Beast* (November 3, 2010).

Laird, Melvin R. "Iraq: Learning the Lesson of Vietnam." *Foreign Affairs*, (November/December, 2005).

Lakoff, George. *Don't Think of an Elephant! Know Your Values and Frame the Debate.* Vermont: Chelsea Green Publication, 2004.

Landro, Laura. "Doctors Learn to Say 'I'm Sorry.'" *Wall Street Journal* (January 24, 2007).

Lang, Derrik J. "Obama Appears on George Lopez's Late Night Talk Show." *Huffington Post* (July 29, 2009).

Langley, Monica. "Michelle Obama Solidifies Her Role in the Election." *Wall Street Journal,* (February 11, 2008).

Larry King Live. "Interview with Barack Obama." *CNN,* (June 3, 2010). Available at: http://transcripts.cnn.com/TRANSCRIPTS/1006/03/lkl.01.html (accessed July 23, 2010).

Lasswell, Harold D. *Psychopathology and Politics*, Chicago, Ill.: University of Chicago Press, 1930.

———. *Power and Personality.* New York: Norton, 1948.

Lau, Richard R., David O. Sears, and Richard Centers. "The 'Positivity Bias' in Evaluations of Public Figures: Evidence Against Instrumental Artifacts." *American Journal of Public Opinion* 43 (1979): 347–58.

Lawrence, Jill. "Poll: Americans Have High Hopes for Obama." *USA TODAY* (November 12, 2008).

Lee, Carol E. "POTUS's Outlook on Black America." *Politico* (December 21, 2009).

———. "Obama: 'Fear and Frustration' Drive Voters." *Politico* (October 16, 2010).

———. "Obama: 'Campaigning is Different than Governing.'" *Politico* (November 14, 2010).

Lee, Don and Jim Puzzanghera. "Obama Critics Say his Economic Vision is Hazy." *Los Angeles Times* (January 25, 2010).

Leonhardt, David. "In Health Care Bill, Obama Attacks Wealth Inequality." *New York Times* (March 23, 2010).

Levenson, Michael and Jonathan Saltzman, "At Harvard Law, a Unifying Voice," *Boston Globe* (January 28, 2007).

Lewis Sorley, *A Better War: The Unexamined Victories and Final Tragedy of America's Last Years in Vietnam.* New York: Harcourt, 1999.

Lexington. "The Obama Cult: If Barack Obama Disappoints His Supporters, They Will Have Only Themselves to Blame." *The Economist* (July 23, 2009).

Libit, Daniel, and Jeffey Ressner. "Obama's Paparazzi Presidency." *Politico* (January 1, 2009).

Lipset, Seymour Martin. *American Exceptionalism: A Double Edged Sword.* New York, NY: Norton, 1997.

Lizza, Ryan. "The Agitator." *New Republic* (March 19, 2007).

——. "Above the Fray." *GQ* (September 2007).

——. "Making It: How Chicago Shaped Obama." *New Yorker* (July 21, 2008).

——. "Battle Plans: How Obama Won." *New Yorker* (November 17, 2008).

——. "The Political Scene: Making It." *New Yorker* (May 6, 2010).

Loumena, Dan. "President Obama a Hit as a TV Broadcaster." *Los Angeles Times* (January 30, 2010).

Luce, Edward and Daniel Dombey. "US Foreign Policy: Waiting on a Sun King." *Financial Times* (March 30, 2010).

Luo, Michael and Jeff Zeleny. "Obama, in Shift, Says He'll Reject Public Financing." *New York Times* (June 20, 2008).

Lynn Sweet Blog. *Chicago Sun-Times*, http://blogs.suntimes.com/sweet/ (accessed July 23, 2010).

MacFarquhar, Larissa. "The Conciliator." *New Yorker* (May 7, 2007).

MacGillis, Alec. "Finding Political Strength in the Power of Words." *Washington Post* (26 February 2008).

——. "In Obama's New Message, Some Foes See Old Liberalism." *Washington Post* (March 26, 2008), A01.

Maddon, Mike. "Mr. Calm." *Salon* (April 30, 2009).

Madhani, Aamer. "Does He Feel Your Pain?" *National Journal* (October 29, 2010).

Malcolm, Andrew. "Top of the Ticket." *Los Angeles Times* (April 2, 2010).

——. "New poll to Obama: It's the Economy, Stupid." *Los Angeles Times* (July 13, 2010).

Mallaby, Sebastian. "Obama's Missing Ideas." *Washington Post* (February 25, 2008).

Maraniss, David. *First in His Class.* New York: Simon & Schuster, 1995.

——. "Though Obama Had to Leave to Find Himself, It Is Hawaii That Made His Rise Possible." *Washington Post* (August 22, 2008)

Marcus, Ruth. "Patriot Games." *Washington Post* (June 25, 2008).

——. "President Obama Is Making Nobody Happy." *Washington Post* (April 3, 2010).

Marin, Carol. "President's Connection to Voters Broken." *Chicago Sun-Times* (November 17, 2010).

Marinucci, Carla. "On S.F. Tour, Obama Takes On the Clintons." *San Francisco Chronicle* (January 18, 2008).

Marist College Poll, "Turning Tides … Half View Obama as Not Meeting Expectations." June 30, 2010.

Martin, Jonathan. "West Wing on Steroids in Obama W.H." *Politico* (January 25, 2009).

—— and Jonathan Allen. "Obama Takes on Talkers." *Politico* (April 3, 2010).

—— and Carol E. Lee, "Obama to GOP: 'I won.'"*Politico* (January 23, 2009).

Mason, Julie. "Obama Pushes the Limits of Media Exposure." *Washington Examiner* (June 25, 2009).

McCullah, Declan. "Feds Push for Tracking Cell Phones." *CNet News* (February 11, 2010).

McKeeby, David. "Obama, Russia's Medvedev Announce New Arms Control Plan First Official Meeting Sets Broad Agenda for U.S.–Russian Relations." *America.Gov* (April 1, 2009).

McManus, Doyle. "Obama's Afghanistan Strategy Counts on Time as an Ally." *Los Angeles Times* (December 1, 2009).

McNulty, Charles. "The Obamas Give their Regards to Broadway," *Los Angeles Times* (June 1, 2009).

McCrum, Robert. "A Candidate's Tale." *Guardian* (August 26, 2007).

Meacham, Jon. "Interview: I Had to Learn to Fight." *Newsweek* (August 23, 2008).
———. "A Highly Logical Approach." *Newsweek* (May 25, 2009).
———. "What He's Learned: A Conversation with Barack Obama, *Newsweek* (May 25, 2009), http://www.newsweek.com/id/197891/page/1.
Mead, Walter Russell. "Liberal Internationalism: The Twilight of a Dream." *American Interest* (April 1, 2010).
———. "Honolulu, Harvard, and Hyde Park." *Foreign Affairs* (July/August, 2010).
Meckler, Laura. "On 'Tonight Show,' Obama Urges Steadiness in Face of Crisis." *Wall Street Journal* (March 19, 2009).
Memmott, Mark and Jill Lawrence. "Obama Launches Tour to Highlight 'Judgment, Experience' on Iraq." *USA TODAY* (October 1, 2007).
Mendell, David. *Obama: From Promise to Power*. New York: Harper Collins, 2007.
Merida, Kevin. "The Ghost of a Father." *Washington Post* (December 14, 2007).
Merle, Renae and Dina Elboghdady. "U.S. Launches Wide-Ranging Plan to Steady Housing Market." *Washington Post* (March 5, 2009).
Miller, Rich. "Obama 'Agnostic' on Deficit Cuts, Won't Prejudge Tax Increases." *Bloomberg Business Week* (February 11, 2010).
Miroff, Bruce, Raymond Seidelman, and Todd Swanstrom. *Debating Democracy: A Reader in American Politics*. Florence, KY: Wadsworth, 2011.
Montgomery, Lori. "In $3.6 Trillion Budget, Obama Signals Broad Shift in Priorities." *Washington Post* (February 27, 2009).
———. "CBO Says Stimulus May Have Added 3.3 Million Jobs." *Washington Post* (August 24, 2010).
Moore, Frazier. "Obama to Appear on ABC's 'The View' on Thursday." *Associated Press* (July 26, 2010).
Morgan, David. "President Vows to Press Ahead on Big Challenges." *Reuters* (March 30, 2010).
Mosk, Matthew. "Tom Donilon's Revolving Door." *ABC News* (October 10, 2010).
MSNBC. "First Read." http://firstread.msnbc.msn.com/ (accessed July 23, 2010).
MSNBC News. "Obama: Public Option Should Be Part of Reform." (September 9, 2009).
Mundy, Liza. "A Series of Fortunate Events." *Washington Post* (12 August 12, 2007).
Murray, Mark and Domenico Montanaro. "Did Obama Campaign on Public Option?" *NBC-First Read* (December 23, 2009).
Murray, Shailagh. "Obama Bill Sets Date For Troop Withdrawal. Candidate Goes Further Than Rivals," *Washington Post* (January 31, 2007).
———. "Obama to Accept Nomination at Broncos' Stadium," *Washington Post* (July 8, 2008).
——— and Paul Kane. "Obama Meets with Republicans to Bridge Partisan Divide." *Washington Post* (February 10, 2010), A01.
Nagourney, Adam. "Obama Elected President as Racial Barriers Fall." *New York Times* (November 5, 2008).
NBC News/Wall Street Journal Survey (November 2007). Available at: http://msnbcmedia.msn.com/i/msnbc/sections/news/071107_NBC-WSJ_Full.pdf (accessed March 5, 2011).
———. (December 2007). Available at: http://online.wsj.com/public/resources/documents/wsjnbcpoll20071219.pdf (accessed March 5, 2011).
———. Study #10651 (August, 2010). Available at: http://online.wsj.com/public/resources/documents/wsjnbcpoll-08122010.pdf (accessed August 18, 2010).
Neil, Martha. "Abe Lincoln's Self-Study Route to Law Practice a Vanishing Option." *ABA Journal* (January 22, 2008).
Newport, Frank. "Bush Job Approval at 28%, Lowest of His Administration." *Gallup* (April 11, 2008).
New York Times. "Transcript: The Democratic Debate in New Hampshire." (January 5, 2008). Available at: http://www.nytimes.com/2008/01/05/us/politics/05text-ddebate.html?_r=4&oref=slogin&adxnnlx=1217243316-S8%20BYIFAXHCH%20D6m2qwOkQ&pagewanted=print (accessed July 31, 2010).

——. "Transcript: Democratic Debate in Philadelphia" (April 16, 2008). Available at: http://www.nytimes.com/2008/04/16/us/politics/16textdebate.html?_r=1&pagewanted=print (accessed June 28, 2010).

——."Transcript: John Harwood Interviews Barack Obama" (January 7, 2009). Available at: http://www.nytimes.com/2009/01/07/us/politics/07text-harwood.html?pagewanted=print (accessed July 10, 2010).

——."Obama's Interview Aboard Air Force One." Transcript (March 8, 2009).

——."Text: News Conference in Guadalajara." (April 11, 2009). Available at: http://www.nytimes.com/2009/08/11/world/americas/11prexy.text.html?pagewanted=print (accessed August 5, 2010).

——."Transcript: Obama's Fifth News Conference" (July 22, 2009) (emphasis added). Available at: http://www.nytimes.com/2009/07/22/us/politics/22obama.transcript.html?pagewanted=print (accessed August 5, 2010).

——. "Mr. Obama's Nuclear Policy." Editorial (April 7, 2010).

——. "Caucus: The Politics and Government Blog of the Times: Barack Obama." http://thecaucus.blogs.nytimes.com/tag/barack-obama/ (accessed July 23, 2010).

——. "Sorting Out the Election." Editorial (November 3, 2010).

Nicholas, Peter and Janet Hook. "Obama the Velcro President." *Los Angeles Times* (July 30, 2010).

——. and Nicole Santa Cruz. "Obama Again Defends Right to Put Mosque Near Ground Zero." *Los Angeles Times* (August 15, 2010).

Nisbett, R. E. and T. D. Wilson. "Telling More than We Know; Verbal Reports on Mental Process." *Psychological Review* 84, no. 3 (March 1977): 231–69.

Noonan, Peggy. "Look at the Time." *Wall Street Journal* (January 30, 2009).

——. "We Just Don't Understand." *Wall Street Journal* (August 27, 2010).

Norris, Michele. "Obama Seeks Middle Ground on Afghanistan." *NPR* (October 8, 2009).

NPR. "NPR Interview: Barack Obama Discusses His Background, Career and His Future Political Plans asHe Prepares to Give Tonight's Keynote Address at the Democratic National Convention" (July 27, 2004). www.nacdl.org/sl_docs.nsf/freeform/Mandatory:306 (accessed October 21, 2010).

——. "All Things Considered: Iran Requires Direct Diplomacy." (October 13, 2007). http://www.npr.org/templates/story/story.php?storyId=15251928 (accessed March 5, 2011).

——. "White House Budget Director Defends Spending Plan." (February 15, 2011).

Oakley, Meredith L. *On the Make: The Rise of Bill Clinton.* Washington, DC: Regnery, 1994.

Obama, Barak [sic], Sr. "Problems Facing Our Socialism," *East African Journal*, July 1965. http://www.politico.com/pdf/PPM41_080411_bhobama_article_1965.pdf (accessed March 10, 2011).

Obama, Barack. "Remarks of Illinois State Sen. Barack Obama Against Going to War with Iraq" (October 2, 2002). http://www.barackobama.com/2002/10/02/remarks_of_illinois_state_sen.phps

——. *Dreams from My Father.* New York: Three Rivers Press, 2004.

——. "What I See in Lincoln's Eyes." *Time* (January 26, 2005).

——. "Commencement Address at Knox College." June 4, 2005. http://www.american-rhetoric.com/speeches/barackobamaknoxcollege.htm (accessed May 9, 2010).

——. *The Audacity of Hope.* New York: Three Rivers Press, 2006.

——. "Senator Barack Obama's Announcement for President." Springfield, IL (February 10, 2007).

——. "Renewing American Leadership." *Foreign Affairs* (July/August 2007). http://www.americanrhetoric.com/speeches/barackobamaknoxcollege.htm (accessed May 9, 2010).

——."Obama Interview with 610 WIP Host Angelo Cataldi (Partial Ttranscript)" (March 20, 2008). Available at: http://www.philly.com/philly/blogs/phillygossip/Obama_on_WIP_My_grandmothers_a_typical_white_person.htm (accessed July 12, 2010). The full radio interview can be found at: http://www.redlasso.com/ClipPlayer.aspx? id=8a521134-e10b-4bfb-8aec-690d61794d50 (accessed July 12, 2010).

——. "My Plan for Iraq." *New York Times* (July 14, 2008).

——. "Remarks on the Federal Budget" (March 17, 2009). Available at: http://www. gpoaccess.gov/presdocs/2009/DCPD200900159.pdf (accessed July 5, 2010).

——. "Transcript: Obama's Summit of the Americas Press Conference." *RealClearPolitics* (April 19, 2009). http://www.realclearpolitics.com/articles/2009/04/19/obama_ summit_americas_press_conference_96076.html (accessed May 2, 2010).

——. "Responsibility for our Common Future: Address to the United Nations General Assembly." *United States Mission to the United Nations* (September 23, 2009). http://usun. state.gov/briefing/statements/2009/september/129519.htm (accessed June 28, 2010).

O'Boyle, John. "The Professor and the Prosecutor." *Newsweek* (November 29, 2010).

O'Connor, Patrick "Cantor, Obama Let Sparks Fly " *Politico* (April 27, 2009)

Office of Management and Budget. *A New Era of Responsibility: Renewing America's Promise.* Washington, D.C.: U.S. Government Printing Office, 2009. http://www.whitehouse.gov/ omb/assets/fy2010_new_era/a_new_era_of_responsibility2.pdf (accessed May 4, 2010).

"Official Remarks of the United States President Barack Obama at the Opening Ceremony of the Fifth Summit of the Americas, Port of Spain, Trinidad & Tobago" (April 17–19, 2009). http://www.summitamericas.org/V_Summit/remarks_usa_en.pdf (accessed May 9, 2010).

Packer, George. "Obamaism." *New Yorker* (April 13, 2009).

Paige, Susan. "1-year Poll Shows Changed View on Obama," *USA Today* (November 28, 2009).

Parker, Kathleen. "How Does America's First Family Behave at 30,000 Feet? Very Graciously, Our Columnist Discovers." *Daily Beast* (February 18, 2009).

Parsons, Christi. "Obama Hopes to Appoint a 'Team of Rivals': President-elect Looks to Follow Lincoln's Model for His Cabinet." *Chicago Tribune* (November 15, 2008).

—— and Julian E. Barnes. "Obama Homed In on an Afghanistan Pullout Date." *Los Angeles Times* (December 4, 2009).

——, Bruce Japsen, and Bob Secter, "Barack's Rock: Michelle Obama." *Chicago Tribune* (April 22, 2007).

PBS. "Transcript: Lincoln, Roosevelt Presidencies Offer Lessons for Obama." *PBS News Hour,* (November 27, 2008). Available at: http://www.pbs.org/newshour/bb/white_ house/july-dec08/historians_11-27.html (accessed February 19, 2011).

——. "Interviews: Dan Pfeiffer, Obama's Deal." *Frontline* (March 20, 2010). http://www. pbs.org/wgbh/pages/frontline/obamasdeal/interviews/pfeiffer.html.

——. "Transcript: American Experience, Jimmy Carter Part II." (July 25, 2010). Available at: http://www.pbs.org/wgbh/amex/carter/filmmore/pt.html (accessed August 5, 2010).

Pear, Robert. "Health Care Costs Increase is Projected for New Law." *New York Times* (April 23, 2010).

Pearson, Rick and Ray Long, "Obama: I'm Running for President." *Chicago Tribune* (February 10, 2007).

——. "Obama's Kickoff is Steeped in Symbolism: Imagery of Lincoln is Backdrop for Launch." *Chicago Tribune,* February 10, 2007.

——. "Careful Steps, Looking Ahead." *Chicago Tribune* (3 May 2007).

Pew Research Center for the People & the Press. "Trends in Political Values and Core Attitudes: 1987–2007" (March 22, 2007). http://people-press.org/reports/pdf/312.pdf (accessed July 6, 2010).

——. "Partisan Gap in Obama Job Approval Widest in Modern Era" (April 2, 2009).

——. "Obama at 100 Days: Strong Job Approval, Even Higher Personal Ratings Better Ratings for Foreign Policy than Domestic Issues." (April 23, 2009).

——. "Obama's Approval Ratings Slide: By the Numbers." (September 4, 2009).

——. "Distrust, Discontent, Anger and Partisan Rancor: The People and Their Government." (April 18, 2010).

——. "Democrats Divided, But Support Key Provisions: Broad Approval for New Arizona Law" (May 12, 2010).

——. "Obama's Ratings Little Affected by Recent Turmoil." (June 24, 2010).

Pickler, Nedra. "Rivals Slam Obama Over Reagan Praise." *Associated Press* (February 19, 2008).

Pindell, James W. and Rick Klein. "Obama Defends Votes in Favor of Iraq Funding." *Boston Globe* (March 22, 2007).

Politico. "44: A Living Diary of the Obama Presidency." http://www.politico.com/politico44/ (accessed July 23, 2010).

Politi-Fact.com. "Price Says Obama and His Aides Have Said Republicans Have 'No Ideas' on Health Care." (January 29, 2010).

Pollack, Kenneth. *The Threatening Storm: The Case for Invading Iraq.* New York: Random House, 2002.

Poor, Jeff. "Wolffe: President Missed Reverend's Rantings Because 'He Wasn't Much of a Churchgoer,'" *Business & Media Institute* (June 16, 2009).

Powell, Michael. "A Deliberative Man in a Manic Game." *New York Times* (June 4, 2008).

——. "Man in the News: Calm in the Swirl of History." *New York Times* (June 4, 2008).

——. "For Obama, a Pragmatist's Shift Toward the Center." *New York Times* (June 27, 2008).

Powerline. http://www.powerlineblog.com/ (accessed July 23, 2010).

Priest, Dana. "U.S. Military Teams, Intelligence Deeply Involved in Aiding Yemen on Strikes." *Washington Post* (January 27, 2010), A01.

Przybyla, Heidi. "Republicans Predict Obama Rebuff in Election; Democrats Foresee Surprise." *Bloomberg News* (October 31, 2010).

Ramstad, Evan. "North Korea Threatens Military Strikes." *Wall Street Journal* (May 27, 2009).

Rasmussen, "More Voters than Ever See Obama as Partisan Democrat." (March 29, 2010).

Rasmussen Reports. "Toplines: Minnesota Governor" (May 24, 2010). Available at http://news.yahoo.com/s/rasmussen/healthcareupdate20100524 (accessed July 16, 2010).

Rasmussen, Scott. "A Vote Against Dems, Not for the GOP." *Wall Street Journal* (November 1, 2010).

Reeves, Jay. "Roberts: Scene at State of Union 'Very Troubling.'" *Associated Press* (March 9, 2010).

Reid, Chip. "White House Push-Back on Asia Trip Failure Meme." *CBS News* (November 14, 2010).

Remnick, David. "Testing the Waters." *New Yorker* (November 6, 2006).

——. *The Bridge: The Life and Rise of Barack Obama.* New York: Knopf, 2010.

Renshon, Stanley A. *High Hopes: The Clinton Presidency and the Politics of Ambition.* New York: New York University Press, 1996 (1998 paperback edition, with afterword, published by Routledge).

——. *The Psychological Assessment of Presidential Candidates.* New York: New York University Press, 1996 (1998 paperback edition, with afterword, published by Routledge).

——. "Analyzing the Psychology and Performance of Presidential Candidates at a Distance: Bob Dole and the 1996 Presidential Campaign." *The Journal of Leadership Studies* 9, no. 3 (1998 Special Issue on Political Leadership): 253–81.

——. "After the Fall: The Clinton Presidency in Psychological Perspective." *Political Science Quarterly,* 115, no. 1 (Spring 2000): 41–65.

——. "The Comparative Psychoanalytic Study of Political Leaders: John McCain and the Limits of Trait Psychology." In *Profiling Political Leaders and the Analysis of Political Leadership: Methods and Cross-Cultural Applications,* ed. Ofer Feldman and Linda O. Valenty: 233–53. Westport, Ct.: Greenwood, 2001.

——. "Assessing the Character and Performance of Presidential Candidates: Some Observations on Theory and Method." In *The Psychological Assessment of Political Leaders:*

Theories, Methods, and Applications, ed. Jerrold M. Post. Ann Arbor, Mi: University of Michigan Press, 2003.

——. *In His Father's Shadow: The Transformations of George W. Bush.* New York: Palgrave/ Macmillan, 2004.

——. "Psychoanalyzing Presidents Without a Couch: Lessons from the William J. Clinton and George W. Bush Presidencies." Center for Political Leadership, working papers, Cambridge, Ma.: The John F. Kennedy School of Government, 2004. Available at: http://content.ksg.harvard.edu/leadership/images/stories/ksg/PDF/Publications/renshon workingpaper.pdf?phpMyAdmin=LTiBtEu99qkd5KYdIryaR2–3Jp7 (accessed August 16, 2009).

——. "The Political Mind: Obama Denounces Flag-pin Patriotism." *Politico* (10 October 2007).

——. "Psychological Reflections on Barack Obama and John McCain: Assessing the Contours of a New Administration." *Political Science Quarterly* 123, no. 3 (Fall 2008): 391–433.

Reynolds, Bill. *Cousy: His Life, Career, and the Birth of Big-Time Basketball.* New York: Simon & Schuster, 2005.

Rich, Frank. "The Up or Down Vote on Obama's Presidency." *New York Times* (March 7, 2010).

Ridgeway, Greg. *Analysis of Racial Disparities in the New York Police Department's Stop, Question, and Frisk Practices.* Santa Monica, Ca.: Rand Corporation, 2007. http://www. rand.org/pubs/technical_reports/2007/RAND_TR534.pdf (accessed May 6, 2010).

Ripley, Amanda. "The Story of Barack Obama's Mother." *Time* (April 9, 2008).

Robb, Brian. "Julius Erving at the Finals." *ESPN* (June 12, 2010).

Robinson, Mike. "Obama Got Start in Civil Rights Practice." *Associated Press* (February 20, 2007).

Rogin, Josh. "Obama: We're Still Working on Our Democracy." *Foreign Policy* (April 11, 2010).

Roig-Franzia, Manuel. "The Obama Buzzword That Hit Pay Dirt." *Washington Post* (January 8, 2009).

Rokeach, Milton. *The Open and Closed Mind.* New York: Basic Books, 1960.

Rose, Richard. *The Post Modern President: George Bush Meets the World.* 2nd ed. New York: Chatham House, 2000.

Rosenberg, Mike. "State High-speed Train Rides to Be Costlier, Ridership Lower than Promised to Voters." *San Mateo County Times* (December 14, 2009).

Ross, Dennis. "Greed on Wall Street: The Rise and Fall of Tyco's Dennis Kozlowski." *ABC News* (November 11, 2006).

Rove, Karl. "It's All About Obama." *Wall Street Journal* (June 26, 2008).

——. "Signs of the Democratic Apocalypse." *Wall Street Journal* (October 28, 2010).

Rucker, Philip. "A Familiar Precedent For a President-Elect: Obama Inspired by, Compared to Lincoln." *Washington Post* (November 19, 2008).

Runningen, Roger. "Obama Seeks Immigration Overhaul, Slams Arizona Law." *Bloomberg News* (April 23, 2010).

Rutterberg, Jim. "The Tonight Show With … President Obama?" *New York Times* (June 3, 2009).

Saad, Lydia. "Disapproval of Bush Spans the Issues." *Gallup* (February 20, 2008).

——. "In U.S., Majority Now Say Obama's Policies 'Mostly Liberal.'" *Gallup* (November 4, 2009).

——. "Tea Partiers Are Fairly Mainstream in Their Demographics." *Gallup* (April 5, 2010).

——. "Americans Unsure About 'Progressive' Political Label." *Gallup* (July 10, 2010). Available at: http://www.gallup.com/poll/141218/americans-unsure-progressive-political-label.aspx?version=print (accessed July 23, 2010).

Sack, Kevin. "Massachusetts: Insurers Sue." *New York Times* (April 5, 2010).

—— and Sheryl Gay Stolberg. "As Law Takes Effect, Obama Gives Insurers a Warning." *New York Times* (June, 21, 2010).

"Saddleback Civil Forum on the Presidency: Interview with Senator Barack Obama (D-Il) and Senator John McCain (R-AZ): Interviewer Rick Warren" (August 16, 2008). (http://www.clipsandcomment.com/2008/08/17/full-transcript-saddleback-presidential-forum-sen-barack-obama-john-mccain-moderated-by-rick-warren/) (accessed June 28, 2010).

Salant, Jonathan D. "Trial Lawyers Sidestep Malpractice Curbs With Blitz in Congress. *Bloomberg News* (December 30, 2009).

Sammon, Bill. *Meet the Next President: What You Don't Know About the Candidates.* New York: Threshold, 2007.

Samuelson, Robert J. "A Vote for McBama." *Washington Post* (June 11, 2008).

——. "Obama's Stunted Stimulus." *Washington Post* (February 23, 2009).

——. "The Obama Infatuation." *Washington Post* (June 1, 2009).

——. "Obama's Energy Pipe Dreams." *Washington Post* (June 21, 2010).

Sanders, Edmund. "So Alike and Yet So Different." *Los Angeles Times* (July 17, 2008).

Sang-Hun, Choe. "North Korea Claims to Conduct 2nd Nuclear Test." *New York Times* (May 25, 2009).

——. "North Korea is Said to Test-Fire 3 More Missiles." *New York Times* (May 27, 2009).

Sargent, Greg. "Book: Rahm 'Begged' Obama for Days Not to Pursue Ambitious Health Reform." *Washington Post* (May 14, 2010).

Saslow, Eli. "The 17 Minutes That Launched a Political Star." *Washington Post* (August 25, 2008).

——. "From Outsider to Politician." *Washington Post* (October 9, 2008).

——. "A Rising Political Star Adopts a Low-Key Strategy." *Washington Post* (October 17, 2008).

Savage, Charles. "Closing Guantánamo Fades as a Priority." *New York Times* (June 25, 2010).

Scharnberg, Kirsten and Kim Barker. "The Not-so-simple Story of Barack Obama's Youth," *Chicago Tribune* (March 25, 2007).

Scherer, Michael. "How Barack Obama Became Mr. Unpopular." *Time* (September 2, 2010).

Schmitt, Eric and Eric Lipton, "U.S. Charges Suspect, Eyeing Link to Qaeda in Yemen." *New York Times* (December 27, 2009).

Schmitz, Gregor Peter. "Obama's Election Debacle." *Der Spiegel* (November 3, 2010).

Schneider, Bill. "Clinton, Obama War Funding Votes Draw Criticism." *CNN* (May 26, 2007).

Schoen, Douglas E. "Voters to Democrats: Jobs, Jobs, Jobs." *Wall Street Journal* (February 18, 2010).

——. "Why He Turns Voters Off." *Daily Beast* (August 18, 2010).

—— and Patrick H. Caddell, "One and Done: To Be a Great President, Obama Should Not Seek Reelection in 2012." *Washington Post* (November 14, 2010).

Scott, Janny. "In Illinois, Obama Proved Pragmatic and Shrewd." *New York Times* (July 30, 2007).

——. "Obama's Account of New York Years Often Differs from What Others Say." *New York Times*, October 30, 2007.

——. "A Free Spirited Wanderer Who Set Obama's Path." *New York Times* (March 14, 2008).

Secter, Bob and John McCormick. "Portrait of a Pragmatist." *Chicago Tribune* (30 March 2007).

Seelye, Katharine Q. "The Abraham Lincoln Analogy." *New York Times* (February 12, 2009).

Seib, Gerald F. "In Crisis, Opportunity for Obama." *Wall Street Journal* (November 21, 2008).

——. "Obama will be Hands-on Chief." *Wall Street Journal* (January 13, 2009).

——. "An Engaged, Yet Elusive President." *Wall Street Journal* (April 29, 2009).

——. "Why Political Sage Sees GOP Romp in November." *Wall Street Journal* (August 20, 2010).

——. "McConnell Softens Tone on Working with Obama." *Wall Street Journal* November 5, 2010.

Selsay, Manya. "Michelle Obama: Overcoming Fear." *Suite 101.com* (February 28, 2008).

Shales, Amity. *The Forgotten Man: A New History of the Great Depression.* New York: Harper-Collins, 2007.

Shane, Scott and Mark Lander. "Obama Clears Way for Guantánamo Trials." *New York Times* (March 7, 2011).

Shear, Michael D. "White House Searching For a Way to Reconnect with Voters Over Economy." *Washington Post* (July 14, 2010).

——. "Obama to Appear on the 'Daily Show.'" *New York Times* (October 27, 2010).

—— and Ceci Connolly. "Obama Assembles Powerful West Wing: Influential Advisers May Compete With Cabinet." *Washington Post* (January 8, 2009).

Sidoti, Liz. "McCain Backs Gun Decision, Obama Straddles Issue." *Associated Press* (June 26, 2008).

Silva, Mark. "Obama: 150,000 Road Jobs: 'Shovel Ready.'" *Chicago Tribune* (March 3, 2009).

Silverleib, Alan. "Gloves Come Off after Obama Rips Supreme Court Ruling." *CNN* (January 28, 2010).

Simon, Roger. "It's All Obama, All the Time." *Politico* (April 16, 2009).

Slevin, Peter. "Obama Forged Political Mettle in Illinois Capitol." *Washington Post* (February 9, 2007).

Smith, Ben. "Despite snubs, Dems back Obama." *Politico* (March 21, 2009).

——. "A Sheep in Wolffe's Clothing." *Politico* (June 3, 2009).

——. "Tic Toc." *Politico* (December 6, 2009).

——. "Hazards of the Teleprompter." *Politico* (February 4, 2010).

——. "Obama Narrows Mosque Defense." *Politico* (August 14, 2010).

——. "Dems Retreat on Health Care Cost Pitch." *Politico* (August 19, 2010).

—— and Jonathan Martin. "Republicans Tear Up Obama's Map." *Politico* (November 3, 2010).

Smith, Mark S. "White House Defends King Quote on Oval Office Rug." *Associated Press* (September 10, 2010).

Sobieraj Westfall, Sandra. "Michell Obama: 'This is Who I Am.'"*People* (June 18, 2007).

Sorley, Lewis. *A Better War: The Unexamined Victories and Final Tragedy of America's Last Years in Vietnam.* New York: Harcourt, 1999.

——. "The Real Afghan Lessons From Vietnam." *Wall Street Journal* (October 11, 2009).

Southall, Ashley. "Obama Vows to Push Immigration Reform." *New York Times* (October 25, 2010).

Sowell, Thomas. "A Crossroads Election." *Townhall* (October 29, 2010).

Spillius, Alex. "Barack Obama Says US Must Lead by Example." *The Telegraph* (June 2, 2009).

State of the Union With John King. "Interview with General Jim Jones." *CNN* (October 4, 2009).

Stein, Sam. "Gibbs Fires Back at Chief Justice Roberts Over Obama Criticism." *Huffington Post* (March 9, 2010).

Steinberg, Alan. "N.J. School Budget Elections: The New Christie Paradigm is Trium-phant." *NewJerseynewsroom.com* (April 21, 2010).

Stevenson, Richard W. "The Muddled Selling of the President." *New York Times* (January 29, 2010).

Stolberg, Sheryl Gay. "White House Unbuttons Formal Dress Code." *New York Times* (January 28, 2009).

——. "Obama Weighs Paring Goals for Health Care." *New York Times* (January 21, 2010).

——. "He Breaks for Band Recitals." *New York Times* (February 12, 2010).

——. "Obama Pushes Agenda, Despite Political Risks." *New York Times* (July 15, 2010).

——. "Obama Pushes Jobs Plan, and Assails GOP for Criticism." *New York Times* (September 6, 2010).

——. "Obama's Playbook After Nov. 2." *New York Times* (October 24, 2010).

—— and Robert Pear. "Obama Open to Reining in Medical Suits." *New York Times*. (June 15, 2009).

Story, Tim. "GOP Gains in Legislatures are Historic." National Conference of State Legislatures, November 4, 2010. Available at: http://ncsl.typepad.com/the_thicket/2010/11/by-tim-storey-updated-at-thursday-nov-4-1115am-mdt-republicans-have-added-over-675-seats-to-their-ranks-in-this-elec.html (accessed October 10, 2010).

Stout, David. "Obama to Urge Afghans 'Into the Fight.'" *New York Times* (December 2, 2009).

Strassel, Kimberley A. "Bonfire of the Populists." *Wall Street Journal* (January 28, 2010).

Taibbi, Matt. "The Low Post: Between Barack and a Hard Place." *Rolling Stone* (February 15, 2007).

Taplin, Jon. "Obama's Victory Strategy." *TPM* (February 12, 2010).

Tapper, Jake. "Obama: 'Better Judgment' on Foreign Policy." *ABC News* (July 25, 2007).

——. "Obama Proposes 'Team of Rivals' Cabinet." *ABC News* (May 22, 2008).

——. "Stumbles." *Political Punch-ABC News* (August 8, 2008).

——. "Share the Wealth?" *ABC News* (October 14, 2008).

——. "An Interview with President Obama." *ABC News* (July 7, 2009).

——. "White House: Berwick Appointment 'Too Important' to Wait for a Hearing." *ABC News* (July 11, 2010).

Thaler, Richard, and Cass Sunstein. *Nudge: Improving Decisions about Health, Wealth, and Happiness*. New Haven, Ct.: Yale University Press, 2008.

Thernstrom, Abigail. "Obama's Census Identity." *Wall Street Journal* (April 16, 2010).

Thiessen, Marc A. "Democrats and the 'Evil Eye.'" *Washington Post* (August 23, 2010).

Thomas, Evan. "How He Did It." *Newsweek* (October 5, 2008). Available at: http://www.newsweek.com/2008/11/05/how-he-did-it.html# (accessed March 5, 2011).

——. *A Long Time Coming: The Inspiring, Combative 2008 Campaign and the Historic Election of Barack Obama*. New York: Public Affairs Press, 2009.

Thrush, Glenn. "Obama's Mosque Moment Frustrates Dems." *Politico* (August 21, 2010).

Time. "The Page/Politics up to the Minute." http://thepage.time.com/ (accessed July 23, 2010).

Toner, Robin. "Obama's Test: Can a Liberal Be a Unifier?" *New York Times* (March 25, 2008).

Topeka Capital-Journal. "Planning Under Way for Obama Holiday." November 9, 2009.

Touré, "And Next: Mt. Rushmore?" *Daily Beast* (November 11, 2008).

Travers, Karen. "Overachiever-in-Chief: Is There an Issue the President Won't Weigh in On?" *ABC News* (July 28, 2009).

Tumulty, Karen. "Obama: 'We Have a Daunting Task.'" *Time* (July 22, 2008). Available at: http://www.time.com/time/printout/0,8816,1825738,00.html (accessed July 31, 2010).

——. "Once Again, the Electorate Demanded a New Start." *Washington Post* (November 3, 2010).

—— and Dan Balz, "Assessing Midterm Losses, Democrats Ask Whether Obama's White House Fully Grasped Voters' Fears." *Washington Post* (November 7, 2010).

—— and David Von Drehle. "Obama on His Veep Thinking." *Time* (August 20, 2008). http://www.time.com/time/printout/0,8816,1834309,00.html (accessed June 28, 2010).

Tversky, Amos and Daniel Kahneman, "The Framing of Decisions and the Psychology of Choice." *Science* 211, no. 4481 (1981).

USA TODAY. "The Oval, Tracking the Obama Presidency." (September 15, 2007). Available at: http://content.usatoday.com/communities/theoval/index (accessed July 23, 2010).

U.S. Department of the Army. "Army Field Manual, FM 2-22.3 (FM 34-52 Human Intelligence Collector Operations." Washington D.C. (September 2006). http://www.army.mil/institution/armypublicaffairs/pdf/fm2-22-3.pdf (accessed March 12, 2011).

U.S. Department of Health and Human Services. "Head Start Impact Study Final Report: Executive Summary." (January 2010). Available at: http://www.acf.hhs.gov/programs/opre/hs/impact_study/executive_summaryfinal.pdf (accessed February 24, 2011).

Vargas, Jose Antonio. "Obama Defends Compromise on New FISA Bill." *Washington Post* (July 4, 2008).

Vennochi, Joan. "The Audacity of Ego." *Boston Globe* (July 20 2008).

Vogel, Kenneth P. "Obama: Change Agent Goes Conventional." *Politico* (June 27, 2008).

Wallace-Wells, Ben. "Destiny's Child." *Rolling Stone* (February 22, 2007).

Wallsten, Peter and Faye Fiore. "Getting to Know the Obamas, on their Terms." *Los Angeles Times* (April 30, 2009).

—— and Eliza Grey. "Confidence Waning in Obama, U.S Outlook." *Wall Street Journal* (June 23, 2010).

Wall Street Journal. "Review and Outlook: 'The Obama We Don't Know'" (June 4, 2008).

——. "Review & Outlook: 'Feel the Rage.'" (June 9, 2010).

——. "Review and Outlook: 'Obama Ratifies Bush.'" (March 8, 2011).

Wangsness, Lisa. "Health Plan's Effect on Costs May Be Slight." *Boston Globe* (October 12, 2009).

Warner, Judith. "Sometimes a President Is Just a President." *New York Times* (February 5, 2009).

——. "A Hot Time in Washington." *New York Times* (May 14, 2009).

Washington Note, The. Available at: http://www.thewashingtonnote.com/ (accessed July 23, 2010).

Washington Post. "The Obama Enigma: Where Would he Lead?" Editorial (February 24, 2008).

——. "Barack Obama for President." Editorial (October 17, 2008).

——. "The Obama Diet." Editorial (June 12, 2009).

——. "Obama's Sermon Remembering Martin Luther King Jr." (January 17, 2010). Available at: http://voices.washingtonpost.com/44/2010/01/obamas-sermon-remembering-mart.html (accessed July 10, 2010).

——."In Obama's Words: Obama, with Vice President Joe Biden, Hold Town Hall on High Speed Rail in Tampa, Fla.," (January 29, 2010). Available at: http://projects.washingtonpost.com/obama-speeches/speech/170 accessed July 10, 2010).

——."Health Reform Is a Risk Worth Taking." Editorial (March 19, 2010).

——. "Romanoff Job Offer Demands Response from Obama." Editorial (June 5, 2010).

——. "No Longer an Option." Editorial (August 20, 2010).

Washington Post-ABC News Poll (August 30–September 2, 2010). Available at: http://www.washingtonpost.com/wp-srv/politics/polls/postpoll_09072010.html (accessed November 19, 2010).

Wayne, Stephen. "Barack Obama: Character and Temperament for the Presidency." Paper prepared for delivery at the annual meeting of the American Political Science Association, Boston Massachusetts, August 28–31, 2008.

Wehner, Peter. "Obama in Iraq's Quicksand." *Commentary* (2010). Available at: http://www.commentarymagazine.com/printarticle.cfm/obama-in-iraq-s-quicksand-11869 (accessed August 1, 2010).

Weisman, Jonathan. "Obama's Gloves Are Off—And May Need to Stay Off." *Washington Post* (23 April 2008).

——. "In Campaign, One Man's Pragmatism Is Another's Flip-Flopping." *Washington Post* (June 28, 2008).

——."Obama May Consider Slowing Iraq Withdrawal." *Washington Post* (July 4, 2008).

——. "Obama Presses Nuclear Issue." *Wall Street Journal* (April 12, 2010).

——. "What Might Medical Malpractice Test Projects Look Like?" (June 11, 2010).

Wells, Ben Wallace. "Destiny's Child." *Rolling Stone* (February 22, 2007).

Wenner, Jann S. "Obama in Command: The Rolling Stone Interview." *Rolling Stone* (October 15, 2010).

West, Darrell M. "Is Obama the New Reagan?" *Brookings Institution* (July 8, 2008).

White, Theodore. *The Making of the President: 1960.* New York: Atheneum, 1961.

White House Archives. "Joint Statement Between President George W. Bush and Prime Minister Manmohan Singh" (July 18, 2005). Available at: http://georgewbush-whitehouse. archives.gov/news/releases/2005/07/print/20050718-6.html (accessed March 11, 2011).

White House Blog. "Word from the White House: House Republican Health Care 'Plan' PuttingFamilies at Risk." (November 4, 2009).

White House Press Office. "Remarks of President Barack Obama—As Prepared for Delivery Address to Joint Session of Congress." (February 24, 2009). Available at: http://www.whitehouse.gov/the_press_office/remarks-of-president-barack-obama-address-to-joint-session-of-congress/ (accessed July 12, 2010).

——. "Remarks by the President on a New Strategy for Afghanistan and Pakistan" (March 27, 2009). Available at: http://www.whitehouse.gov/the_press_office/Remarks-by-the-President-on-a-New-Strategy-for-Afghanistan-and-Pakistan/ (accessed March 5, 2011).

——. "Remarks by President Obama at Strasbourg Town Hall" (April 3, 2009). http://www.whitehouse.gov/the_press_office/Remarks-by-President-Obama-at-Strasbourg-Town-Hall/ (accessed May 2, 2010).

——. "Transcript: President Obama News Conference, Strasbourg, France" (April 4, 2009). http://www.whitehouse.gov/the_press_office/News-Conference-By-President-Obama-4-04-2009/ (accessed October 2009).

——. "Remarks by President Barack Obama, Prague, Czech Republic" (April 5, 2009). http://www.whitehouse.gov/the_press_office/Remarks-By-President-Barack-Obama-In-Prague-As-Delivered/ (accessed May 9, 2010).

——. "Remarks by President Obama to the Turkish Parliament" (April 6, 2009). http://www.whitehouse.gov/the_press_office/Remarks-By-President-Obama-To-The-Turk-ish-Parliament/ (accessed May 9, 2010).

——. "Remarks by the President at the Veterans of Foreign Wars Convention" (April 17, 2009). Available at: http://www.whitehouse.gov/the_press_office/Remarks-by-the-President-at-the-Veterans-of-Foreign-Wars-convention/ (accessed March 5, 2011).

——. "Remarks by President Obama and King Abdullah of Jordan in Joint Press-Availability" (April 21, 2009). http://www.whitehouse.gov/the_press_office/Remarks-by-President-Obama-and-King-Abdullah-of-Jordan-in-joint-press-availability/ (accessed July 10, 2010).

——."Remarks by the President on the Auto Industry," Grand Foyer (April 30, 2009). Available at: http://www.whitehouse.gov/the_press_office/Remarks-by-the-President-on-the-Auto-Industry/ (accessed August 6, 2010).

——. "Remarks by the President on National Security" (May 21, 2009). http://www.whitehouse.gov/the_press_office/Remarks-by-the-President-On-National-Security-5-21-09/ (accessed May 9, 2010).

——. "President Obama Calls for Restoring Statutory Pay-As-You-Go Requirements" (June 9, 2009). Available at: http://www.whitehouse.gov/the_press_office/President-Obama-Calls-for-Restoring-Statutory-Pay-As-You-Go-Requirements/ (accessed March 5, 2011).

——. "News Conference by the President" (July 23, 2009). http://www.whitehouse.gov/the_press_office/News-Conference-by-the-President-July-22-2009/ (accessed May 6, 2010).

——. "Remarks by the President at AFL-CIO Labor Day Picnic, Coney Island, Cincinnati, Ohio" (September 7, 2009). Available at: http://www.whitehouse.gov/

the_press_office/Remarks-by-the-President-at-AFL-CIO-Labor-Day-Picnic/ (accessed March 5, 2011).

——. "Remarks by the President to the United Nations General Assembly" (September 23, 2009). http://www.whitehouse.gov/the_press_office/remarks-by-the-president-to-the-united-nations-general-assembly/ (accessed May 3, 2010).

——."Executive Order: Federal Leadership on Reducing Text Messaging While Driving." (October 1, 2009). Available at: http://www.whitehouse.gov/the_press_office/Executive-Order-Federal-Leadership-on-Reducing-Text-Messaging-while-Driving (accessed May 14, 2010).

——."Press Briefing by Press Secretary Robert Gibbs" (October 14, 2009). Available at: http://www.whitehouse.gov/the-press-office/briefing-white-house-press-secretary-robert-gibbs-101409 (accessed March 5, 2011).

. "Press Gaggle by Press Secretary Robert Gibbs, Aboard Air Force One" (November 12, 2009). Available at: http://www.whitehouse.gov/the-press-office/gaggle-press-secretary-robert-gibbs-aboard-air-force-one-en-route-anchorage-alaska (accessed March 5, 2011).

——. "Remarks by the President in Address to the Nation on the Way Forward in Afghanistan and Pakistan" (December 1, 2009). Available at http://www.whitehouse.gov/the-press-office/remarks-president-address-nation-way-forward-afghanistan-and-pakistan (accessed May 1, 2010).

——. "Remarks by the President in State of the Union Address" (January 27, 2010). Available at: http://www.whitehouse.gov/the-press-office/remarks-president-state-union-address (accessed March 5, 2011).

——. "Remarks by the President before Meeting with Bipartisan Leaders of the House and Senate" (February 9, 2010). Available at: http://www.whitehouse.gov/the-press-office/remarks-president-meeting-with-bipartisan-leaders-house-and-senate (accessed March 5, 2011).

——. "Toast Remarks by President Obama at Ceremonial Lunch with President Klaus of the Czech Republic and President Medvedev of Russia" (April 8, 2010). Available at: http://www.whitehouse.gov/the-press-office/toast-remarks-president-obama-ceremonial-lunch-with-president-klaus-czech-republic- (accessed March 5, 2011).

——. "Remarks by the President on Wall Street Reform in Quincy, Illinois" (April 28, 2010). http://www.whitehouse.gov/the-press-office/remarks-president-wall-street-reform-quincy-illinois (accessed May 2, 2010).

——. "Remarks by President Obama and President Calderón of Mexico at Joint Press Availability" (May 19, 2010). Available at: http://www.whitehouse.gov/the-press-office/remarks-president-obama-and-president-calder-n-mexico-joint-press-availability (accessed March 5, 2011).

——. "Press Briefing by Press Secretary Robert Gibbs" (June 1, 2010). Available at: http://www.whitehouse.gov/the-press-office/press-briefing-press-secretary-robert-gibbs-6110 (accessed March 5, 2011).

——. "Remarks by the President on the Economy at Carnegie Mellon University" (June 2, 2010). Available at: http://www.whitehouse.gov/the-press-office/remarks-president-economy-carnegie-mellon-university (accessed July 12, 2010).

——. "Remarks by the President on Comprehensive Immigration Reform" (July 1, 2010). Available at: http://www.whitehouse.gov/the-press-office/remarks-president-comprehensive-immigration-reform (accessed March 5, 2011).

——. "Remarks by the President at Iftar Dinner, State Dining Room" (August 13, 2010). Available at: http://www.whitehouse.gov/the-press-office/2010/08/13/remarks-president-iftar-dinner (accessed March 5, 2011).

——. "President Obama to Announce Plan to Renew and Expand America's Roads, Railways and Runways" (September 6, 2010). Available at: http://www.whitehouse.gov/the-press-office/2010/09/06/president-obama-announce-plan-renew-and-expand-america-s-roads-railways- (accessed November 17, 2010).

———. "Remarks by the President on the Economy in Parma, Ohio" (September 8, 2010). Available at: http://www.whitehouse.gov/the-press-office/2010/09/08/remarks-president-economy-parma-ohio (accessed September 11, 2010).

———. "Remarks by the President at DSCC Fundraiser." De La Torre Residence, Boston, Massachusetts (October 16, 2010). Available at: http://www.whitehouse.gov/the-press-office/2010/10/16/remarks-president-dscc-fundraiser (accessed November 14, 2010).

———. "Remarks by the President in a Discussion on Women and the Economy in Seattle, Washington, Foss Residence, Seattle, Washington" (October 21, 2010). Available at: http://www.whitehouse.gov/the-press-office/2010/10/21/remarks-president-a-discussion-women-and-economy-seattle (accessed November 14, 2010).

———. "Press Conference by the President" (November 3, 2010). Available at: http://www.whitehouse.gov/the-press-office/2010/11/03/press-conference-president (accessed November 17, 2010).

———. "Remarks by the President and the First Lady in Town Hall with Students in Mumbai, India, St. Xavier College Mumbai, India" (November 7, 2010). Available at: http://www.whitehouse.gov/the-press-office/2010/11/07/remarks-president-and-first-lady-town-hall-with-students-mumbai-india (accessed November 11, 2010).

———. "Press Conference by the President" (February 15, 2011).

———."Executive Order—Periodic Review of Individuals Detained at Guantánamo Bay Naval Station Pursuant to the Authorization for Use of Military Force" (March 7, 2011). Available at: http://www.whitehouse.gov/the-press-office/2011/03/07/executive-order-periodic-review-individuals-detained-guant-namo-bay-nava (accessed March 12, 2011).

———. "Fact Sheet: New Actions on Guantánamo and Detainee Policy" (March 7, 2011). http://www.whitehouse.gov/the-press-office/2011/03/07/fact-sheet-new-actions-guant-namo-and-detainee-policy (accessed March 12, 2011).

———. "Statement by President Barack Obama: New Actions on Guantanamo Bay and Detainee Policy" (March 7, 2011). Available at: http://www.whitehouse.gov/the-press-office/2011/03/07/new-actions-guantanamo-bay-and-detainee-policy (accessed March 12, 2011).

Wickenden, Dorothy. "Talk of the Town—What's The Big Idea?" *New Yorker* (June 30, 2008).

Williamson, Elizabeth and Sam Schechner. "Obama Reinforces Policy Messages on Letterman's 'Late Night.'" *Wall Street Journal* (September 22, 2009).

———. "Obama slams 'Fat Cat Bankers.'" *Wall Street Journal* (December 2009).

———. "Trivial Pursuit: One Man's Quest to Catalog Presidential Minutiae." *Wall Street Journal* (March 31, 2010).

Wilson, James Q. "American Exceptionalism." *American Enterprise Institute on line* (August 29, 2006). http://www.aei.org/docLib/200608291_wilson_oti_2.pdf (accessed May 1, 2010).

Wilson, Scott. "Bruised by Stimulus Battle, Obama Changed His Approach to Washington." *Washington Post* (April 29, 2009).

———. "The Change Agenda At a Crossroads: From Health Care to Wars to Public Anxiety, Obama's Strength as a Leader Is Tested." *Washington Post* (September 6, 2009).

———. "Cheney Criticizes Obama on National Security Policy, and Biden Fires Back." *Washington Post* (February 15, 2010), A01.

Wilson, T. D. *Strangers to Ourselves.* Cambridge, MA.: Harvard University Press, 2002.

Winston, Diane. "Obama is the New Reagan." *Politics and Society* (June 27, 2008).

Wolffe, Richard. "'Hungry for Change': Obama's Afterglow." *Newsweek* (January 4, 2008) http://www.newsweek.com/2008/01/04/hungry-for-change.html (accessed July 31, 2010).

———. *Renegade: The Making of a President.* New York: Crown, 2009.

Woodward, Bob. "McChrystal: More forces or 'Mission Failure.'" *Washington Post* (September 21, 2009).

Woodward, Calvin. "Obama Not Above Political Manipulation After All." *Associated Press* (June 5, 2010).

Worldpress.org. "Article 75 of the First Additional Protocol to the Geneva Conventions." Available at: http://www.worldpress.org/specials/justice/Article_75.htm (accessed March 12, 2011).

Wright, Robin. " 'Progressive Realism:' In Search of a Foreign Policy." *New York Times* (July 18, 2006).

York, Byron. "Has Obama become bored with Being President?" *The Examiner* (January 29, 2010).

———. "Should Obama Quit After One Term?" *The Examiner* (November 13, 2010).

Youngman, Sam. "Obama: Public Option 'Not the Most Important' Part of Healthcare Bill." *The Hill* (December 21, 2009).

———. "President Obama calls African-Americans a 'Mongrel People.'" *The Hill* (July 29, 2010).

———. "Obama Boasts of Most 'Progressive' Political Triumphs in Decades." *The Hill* (August 17, 2010).

Zaldivar, Ricardo Alonso and Erica Werner. "Obama Gives Proponents Hope for Medical Malpractice Reform." *Insurance Journal* (September 14, 2009).

Zeleny, Jeff. "Going for That Presidential Look, but Trying Not to Overdo It." *New York Times* (July 27, 2008).

———. "President's Political Protector Is Ever Close at Hand." *New York Times* (March 9, 2009).

———. "G.O.P. Captures House, but Not Senate." *New York Times* (November 2, 2010).

Zelizer, Julian E. "What Obama Can Learn from Clinton, Reagan." *CNN* (January 24, 2011).

Zenilman, Avi and Ben Smith. "Barack Obama's Counterpunching Style." *Politico* (April 14, 2008).

Zernike, Kate. "The Charisma Mandate." *New York Times* (February 17, 2008).

NAME INDEX

SUBJECT INDEX